The Ancient Roman City

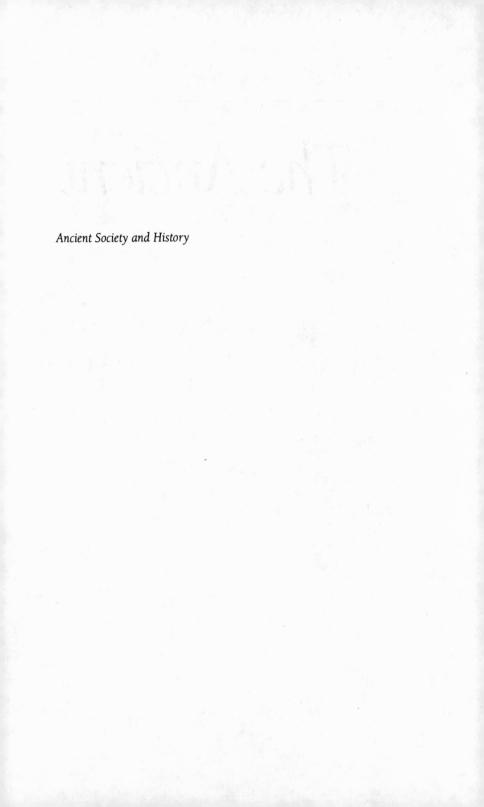

Ancient Society and History

The Ancient

JOHN E. STAMBAUGH

Roman City

The Johns Hopkins University Press
Baltimore and London

This book has been brought to publication with the generous assistance of the Graham Foundation for Advanced Studies in the Fine Arts.

Originally published, hardcover and paperback, 1988
Second printing, 1989

The Johns Hopkins University Press
701 West 40th Street
Baltimore, Maryland 21211
The Johns Hopkins Press Ltd., London

The paper used in this publication meets the minimum requirements of American National Standard for Information Sciences—Permanence of Paper for Printed Library Materials, ANSI Z39.48-1984. ∞

Library of Congress Cataloging-in-Publication Data
Stambaugh, John E.
   The ancient Roman city / John E. Stambaugh.
      p.   cm. — (Ancient society and history)
   Bibliography: p.
   Includes index.
   ISBN 0-8018-3574-7 (alk. paper)
   ISBN 0-8018-3692-1 (pbk. : alk. paper)
   1. Cities and towns, Ancient—Rome.   2. City and town life—Rome.
   3. Rome—Social conditions.   I. Title.   II. Series.
HT114.S7   1988
307.7'64'0937—dc 19   87-26861
                                                                      CIP

For Dan

Contents

Contents

Contents

List of Figures

Figures 1–9 and 11–29 were drawn by Elizabeth H. Riorden. Figure 10 is reproduced from G. Lugli, *Roma antica: Il centro monumentale* (Rome, 1946), by permission of Bardi Editore.

Preface

Most of us become interested in the ancient world because we love its classical literature or admire its great works of sculpture or architecture. This book is about the physical and social environment in which that literature, sculpture, and architecture were produced. It presents the urban history of ancient Rome as a combination of topography, politics, social institutions, and religion. This is hardly an unprecedented approach, but it has not yet been presented in a concise survey of the city of Rome throughout antiquity, testing the hypothesis that as art and literature provide evidence for the environment, the environment makes the art and literature comprehensible in new ways.

Certain themes constantly impose themselves on the materials: the characteristic Roman approach to space (subduing, enclosing, regularizing, imposing human technology); the predeliction for putting up imposing façades; and the habit of the upper classes of using buildings and games to affirm their position at the top of the social hierarchy.

Another theme is the way in which individuals perceived the physical and social frame of the city in which they lived. This is the territory of the sociology of knowledge, with its vocabulary of *perceptual world, matrix,* and *cognitive map,* and the traditional classicist approaches it gingerly. Yet it is the classicist, as ancient historian, literary critic, and archaeologist, who has access to the material for a guidebook into the living past of one of the most emphatically urban cities the world has ever known.

The five chapters of Part One survey Rome's topography and social history chronologically, from the eighth century B.C. to the third century A.D. Part Two then analyzes specific topics that illustrate how the city worked, how it influenced the lives and perceptions of its inhabitants, and how the architectural and topographical environments reflected and shaped their political, administrative, commercial, domestic, religious, and social activities. Finally, in Part Three, a series of shorter chapters surveys the extension of Roman urbanism out through the growing empire, with specific examples from Cosa, Pompeii, and Ostia in Italy, from Arelate in Gaul, and form Thamugadi in Africa.

This book was originally conceived as a text for the Intercollegiate Center for Classical Studies in Rome, and it is intended as an introductory guidebook to the artifacts of Rome and their context, for the newcomer to ancient Rome, for the person who has visited or become familiar with some of its richness (literature, for example) and is interested in learning more about other aspects of the ancient city, as well as for the one who already has some acquaintance with the Eternal City in its modern manifestation.

A guidebook to such a vast subject can indicate only major landmarks and areas of debate and inquiry, and point the way to further information. To encourage readers to look further, especially to primary documentary texts and archaeological publications for more detail, I have tried to make the book as "user friendly" as possible. Throughout the text ancient sources are cited in a form that should make it easy to look up the passage; where possible, titles of ancient works are those of the Loeb Classical Library.

For the most part, I have avoided the jargon of modern sociology or semiotics. Because of my own training, I have been less scrupulous about the jargon of classical studies. When a technical Latin term has been more precise than an English paraphrase, I have used it. The important Latin terms are listed in the index, and at their first appearance in the book, they are italicized and defined.

In general, place names are used in a form which allows easy reference to standard works, where the reader can find both a synopsis of what is known about a site or monument and the necessary bibliography. Monuments in Rome are normally given in their Latin form as cited in S. B. Platner and T. Ashby, *A Topographical Dictionary of Ancient Rome* (Oxford, 1929), and in E. Nash, *Pictorial Dictionary of Ancient Rome* (London, 1968), so that the student can conveniently find more detail in those indispensable mines of information. Names of monuments for which no standard Latin terms exist (such as the House of Livia) and names of churches are given in English. Similarly, I use English names for buildings at Cosa, Pompeii, and Ostia; their conventional Italian names are cross-referenced in the index. A few exceptions seem justified by universal usage and the awkwardness of English equivalents: the Cassette-tipo at Ostia, for example, and the names of all streets and squares. When a deity is referred to in connection with a temple, the deity's name is given in its Latin form, to conform to the practice of the Plater/Ashby and Nash dictionaries. Thus, for instance, the standard English form "Jupiter" is usually used, except in reference to a temple in Rome, when the form "Iuppiter" is used.

The general and detailed plans of Rome (Figs. 3, 4, 7–10, and 29) and the site plans of Cosa (Fig. 24), Pompeii (Fig. 25), Ostia (Fig. 26), Arelate (Fig. 27), and Thamugadi (Fig. 28) also may be useful to visitors. The sequence of identifying numbers at Pompeii and Ostia indicates a possible tour through these sites, and the book's index can help visitors locate the discussions of each specific monument. Buildings at Pompeii and Ostia are identified by their address (I.ii.4 means region I, block ii, doorway 4), as cited in the standard guidebooks, in L. Richardson, Jr., *Pompeii: An Architectural History* (Baltimore, 1988), and in R. Meiggs, *Roman Ostia* (Oxford, 1960, 1973).

Because of the synthetic nature of this work, I owe many debts to many people: John Arthur Hanson and my other colleagues at the Intercollegiate Center for Classical Studies—Peter Burian, Deborah Stott, Harry Evans, and Mary T. Boatwright—for helping me see Rome in new ways; Wayne A. Meeks for helping me define the enterprise; Carol Relihan and Priscilla Cohen for senior theses that offered inspiration and information; Jean D'Amato and Bernard Goldman for prodding me toward a more narrative approach; Paula Carew, Meredith Hoppin, Maureen Dietze, Peter Dorcey, Ronald Malmstrom, and E. J. Johnson for many specific suggestions; Donna Chenail for typing, retyping, and offering encouragement; John Stillwell and Stephen Theodore for resourceful editorial help; Eric Halpern and Penny Moudrianakis of the Johns Hopkins University Press for devoted professionalism that extended cheerful encouragement, keen-eyed advice, and unlimited patience; and Williams College for several leaves and research grants. I offer very special thanks to the Graham Foundation for Advanced Studies in the Fine Arts for a generous grant toward the costs of illustrations, and to Elizabeth H. Riorden, whose scholarship, sense of the past, and drafting skill have produced the original drawings throughout the text.

The Ancient Roman City

Introduction:
The Study of Roman Cities

Walk through the streets of Rome today, and you find the past made present at nearly every corner. Ancient buildings like the Pantheon stand virtually intact, proclaiming the durability of the Eternal City. Ruins from antiquity, as imposing as the Colosseum or as unobtrusive as a column built into a medieval façade, are ubiquitous and picturesque. Bits and pieces are ingeniously reused, like the three temples recycled into the Church of San Nicola in the Forum Holitorium or the miscellaneous fragments exuberantly collected into the Casa dei Crescenzi down the street. Whole buildings are converted to practical modern uses: the Temple of Hadrian into the stockmarket, the Tabularium into the city hall. Sites display a dogged continuity of habitation and utilization, as at San Clemente, where the medieval church with its Baroque ceiling sits on top of an early Christian church that sits on top of an ancient warehouse and a temple of Mithras inserted into an earlier house. Whole quarters of the city find new uses, such as the Stadium of Domitian, which was transformed by Renaissance and Baroque ingenuity into the Piazza Navona. Other elements of the ancient city—for instance, the obelisks—have been removed, reshuffled, reerected as evocations of the past and as steadying landmarks in the Renaissance street network.

The continuity of fabric, form, and function makes us curious about the shape of the ancient city, as well as the lives that were led, the events that were seen, the excitement that was felt, in it. To satisfy that curiosity, we could study the Roman city topographically, as a place with certain buildings at certain sites. Or we could study it historically, as a "diachronic" entity developing through time, with new buildings constructed, old ones demolished. Or typologically, concentrating on the characteristics of each kind of artifact found in the city, whether temple, aqueduct, house, mosaic, or pot. Or demographically, considering the social homogeneity and diversity of the population. Or institutionally, viewing the city as a politicoeconomic system. Or semiotically, analyzing the image of the city and the content of the message it conveyed.[1]

In this book, we use all these approaches, selectively, as the topics invite one or another, as we suggest answers to questions like these: What was life really like in the ancient Roman city? How did it look, feel, sound, smell? The cities we know firsthand are full of people interacting in various ways, their lives full of both social interaction and quiet, frustrated isolation. How different, how similar, were the lives of people in Rome, Pompeii, or Ostia? Why did people found cities where they did? How did they adapt the landscape and their buildings to each other? How did the cities grow and alter through time to meet changing needs? What types of buildings served the people, and what were their special characteristics? Who were the people who made up the city, both as individuals and as groups? How did society organize its administrative machinery, and who earned and spent the city's financial resources? How did the physical city express the needs and aspirations of its people, and how did it form their attitudes and the ways they expressed themselves in poetry, oratory, architecture, sculpture, interior decoration, and graffiti?

This is not a short book, but it is too short for more than a bare sketch of answers to questions like these. Some parts of the sketch are well limned, and here we can be content to report the accepted consensus. Other parts are disputed, and the sketch becomes vague to reflect the ambiguity of evidence and the blurred outlines of scholars' disagreements. Still other parts deal with almost totally uncharted territory.

As sources for our inquiry, we make use of two different kinds of evidence: material and written. The material artifacts are the archaeological finds, both those uncovered in recent excavations and those that have been known for centuries. The interpretation of this archaeological evidence is the result of long, often argumentative, sometimes still unfinished study by excavators, art historians, and topographers.[2] We also refer to written records: ancient lists of temples, texts of laws affecting urban life, inventories of buildings and monuments in the various regions of the city at different times, inscriptions recording dedications of buildings or deaths of individuals. A uniquely helpful document is the *Forma Urbis,* or "Marble Plan," a fragmentary but detailed map of the city as it was at the end of the second century A.D.[3]

By comparing ancient city life with modern, we begin to understand more profoundly what makes a city special, and what makes one city different from another. In the case of Rome, we gain a new perspective on a spectacular city that was the social and physical environment in which characters familiar from ancient political and literary history lived: Horatius defending the bridge, Cato and Cicero speaking in the Senate House, Horace and Juvenal observing the follies of urban man and woman. It was also the stage on which millions of ordinary people lived their ordinary lives in the midst of a grandeur that became more intense every year. Trying to understand their perceptions of the urban world in all its complexity is very good exercise for the creative, disciplined historical imagination.

As a conceptual guide in organizing this information, we start from the pious play on words the Pope uses, in virtue of his dual role as Bishop of Rome and head of the Roman Catholic church, when he pronounces his solemn blessing *urbi et orbi,* "to the city and the world." Rome the religious world city is heir to Rome the political world city: it was *caput mundi,* "head of the world." In addition, the space of the city was conceived as a model of the world, and was so defined in foundation rituals. And so it will be useful to notice, in Part One of the book, the ways in which Rome was both a world unto itself and head and center of the world it came to rule. Part Two continues this theme, but also draws on another aspect of the concept "world," the perceived world of home, family and casual contacts, physical landmarks, and social events. Part Three extends the approach to a few other cities in Italy and beyond, in order to depict the wider dimensions of Roman urbanism in the world outside Rome itself.

THE GROWTH
OF ROME

One

Earliest Rome

Proverbs about Rome—"When there, do as the Romans do"; "It has seven hills"; "All roads lead there"; "It wasn't built in a day"—show how it has come to represent the whole range of urban experience: a particular population with peculiar customs; a varied, exhilarating, and exhausting topography; a focus for the energies of an extensive hinterland; a historical fabric of buildings and space. As the Eternal City, it shelters the aspirations of generations; as the Great Harlot (Revelation 17–19), it signifies the corruptibility of all human achievement.

The rise and fall of Rome and its empire has inspired meditations on permanence and grandeur, on mutability and decay. In surveying ancient Rome as a functioning city, we begin in Part One by tracing the building of the city from the eighth century B.C. to the third century A.D., concentrating on intersecting patterns of tradition and innovation.

The Beginnings

Rome started as a little Italian hill town of shepherds and farmers. One way of explaining how it grew to be the capital of a vast empire is to emphasize its location. Because it lay at a focal point, the city enjoyed special advantages. These were both commercial and strategic, and they facilitated its rise to dominance over its neighbors. To the north across the Tiber were the Etruscans; to the east the Sabines and, beyond them, the Volscians, Hernicians, and Aequians; to the south the Latins; and, beyond them, the Greeks. Modern scholars tend to analyze the site in terms of its commercial advantages: because of the island in the Tiber, this is the only convenient place for crossing the river close to its mouth, and overland traffic from the south or east to the Etruscans would cross the river here. A perpendicular trade axis ran along the south bank of the river, leading from the mouth of the Tiber to the inland tribes; this route is still called the Via Salaria, "Salt Road," and sea salt would naturally have been an item of early trade, since the upland herdsmen needed it for their sheep and cattle, and to preserve meat and hides.

Ancient discussions, however, place much greater emphasis on strategic questions. In a famous passage, Cicero (*De Republica* 2.5–11) expressed the belief that Rome's inland location, accessible but not too accessible, gave the city a peculiar defensive advantage. It defended the Romans against the military threat of invasion and also against the moral threat to traditional ways of doing things. Such an attitude is a classic statement of the insular mentality that many Romans kept all through the time the city was becoming a cosmopolitan world capital and it appears constantly as a tension between openness to outsiders and their influence and a self-satisfied devotion to the *mos maiorum,* the "way our ancestors did things."

This ambivalence is evident in the diverse legends about the city's beginnings. According to one, there were Greeks living on the site in the Bronze Age when Aeneas arrived from Troy in the aftermath of the Trojan War, some time around the twelfth century B.C. According to another, Rome was founded on April 21, 753 B.C., by Romulus, with help and some obstruction from his twin, Remus.

On the one hand, the Aeneas legend connects Rome with the heroic world of Greek mythology. It allowed Rome to claim the same kind of noble pedigree claimed by all the other important cities in the Hellenistic world of the third and second centuries B.C.[1]

The tradition about Romulus and Remus, on the other hand, immediately suggests Roman virtues and values. Two twins descended from Mars, the primal god of the Latin race, were cast adrift on the Tiber, washed up by a typical central Italian flood onto the marshy land at the foot of the Palatine Hill, grew up as farmers and herdsmen, and eventually founded the city. The founding occurred under the auspices of the gods, but was marred by the twins' mutual rivalry, which ended in Romulus's murder of his brother. According to the tradition, the first settlement, on the Palatine, was founded with the same ceremonies that were used whenever a colony was founded: a pit was dug, called *mundus*, "world," and first-fruits were buried in it; then a pair of cattle—a bull and a cow—were yoked to a plow; with plow and team the founder made a furrow all around the city. This marked the line of the *pomerium*, a sacred boundary that reinforced the physical walls of the settlement by means of the gods' protection. Romulus, we read, borrowed some rites from nearby Latin towns, others from Greeks and Etruscans.[2] It was also said that he invited people from all over Italy, even fugitives, to settle. The famous story of the "Rape of the Sabine Women" (Livy 1.9) may reflect, dimly, an expanding ethnic base of early Roman society.

The ancient sources that tell us about Romulus are authors from the second century B.C. to the second century A.D. who looked back at Rome's founding with a vivid historical sense of place. This topographical sense focused on the Palatine, on which they imagined Greek refugees living before Aeneas's arrival (Vergil, *Aeneid* 8.91–369), and on which they believed Romulus erected his fortified settlement. These writers could feed their imaginations on a couple of archaeological monuments and a set of old customs which preserved a sense of earliest Rome.

One such archaeological monument was the Casa Romuli (Hut of Romulus) at the western corner of the Palatine overlooking the Circus Maximus and the site in the Forum Boarium where, according to the tradition, Romulus and Remus were washed up by the Tiber flood. It is described in the first century B.C. as a venerable artifact of sticks and reeds, "preserved as a shrine by officials, who add nothing to make it more impressive; if however storm or age

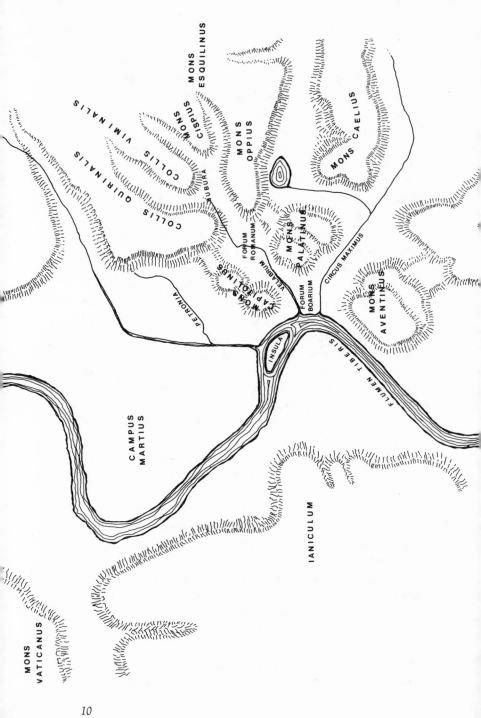

MONS ESQUILINUS

MONS CISPIUS

COLLIS VIMINALIS

MONS OPPIUS

MONS CAELIUS

COLLIS QUIRINALIS

SUBURA

FORUM ROMANUM

MONS PALATINUS

PETRONIA

MONS CAPITOLINUS

VELABRUM

CIRCUS MAXIMUS

FORUM BOARIUM

MONS AVENTINUS

INSULA

FLUMEN TIBERIS

CAMPUS MARTIUS

IANICULUM

MONS VATICANUS

10

does do any damage, they repair it and restore it as close to its original state as they can" (Dionysius of Halicarnassus, *Roman Antiquities* 1.79.11).

Other reminders of Rome's founding were the squared-off outcropping known as Roma Quadrata, on the brow of the hill overlooking the Circus Maximus, which was thought to be the spot from which Romulus took the auspices on the day of Rome's founding (Festus pp. 310–312L), and a cave known as the Lupercal, at the base of the hill, venerated as the den of the she-wolf who nursed the infants Romulus and Remus.[3]

When we turn to the archaeological evidence for earliest Rome, we find that much of this tradition has some historical basis. At the western corner of the Palatine, just where Dionysius describes the Casa Romuli, the foundations of a village of huts have been excavated (Pl. 1). In the lowest strata of the excavations, which would be contemporary with the first huts, the archaeologists found hearths with pottery of a type found throughout central Italy in the eighth century B.C., a date which reminds us that 753 is the traditional date of Romulus's founding of the city. In addition to these hut villages on the Palatine, archaeologists have discovered other evidence for the settlement of Rome in the second half of the eighth century. Graves, for instance, contained bronze implements and pottery resembling that of the contemporary cultures of the Alban hills to the south. Some graves, including those of children, show a greater profusion of luxury artifacts, which may be evidence for the emergence of family groups of relatively greater wealth and status.[4] Located on the Esquiline and also at the Sepulcretum, in the low-lying ground that was to become the Forum Romanum, the graves are of two types: the *fossa* ("ditch") graves, in which the deceased were buried in coffins made of oak tree trunks; and the *pozzo* ("pit") graves, in which the ashes of the deceased, after cremation, were placed in urns that sometimes had a shape imitating that of the huts in the villages. These archaeological finds imply a series of small villages on the hilltops in the eighth century, villages that were presumably inhabited by shepherds and farmers.

Fig. 1 (opposite). The Site of Rome: Hills and Streams

In addition to the graves, small deposits of offerings indicate the presence of religious shrines. These are important because they may indicate the growth of communal civic consciousness: families no longer were exclusively preoccupied with the rites of their own ancestors and immediate concerns, but willing to join with their neighbors in common religious celebrations. One such votive deposit dating from the eighth century was found on the Quirinal. Another was in the Forum Boarium,[5] a spot convenient to all the villages, at their most natural access to the river; it is also a spot dominated by the Palatine village, and near the place where the she-wolf was said to have found Romulus and Remus. Greek-style pottery found here was apparently made in Rome by Greek craftsmen; this seems to imply a market with extensive trade contacts with the outside world. Thus the archaeological record supplements the literary tradition, suggesting that the Palatine village had neighbors on some of the other hills, a cemetery outside its sacred boundary, and a market of some sort near the river.

Rome of the Kings

Our view of the two and a half centuries following the time of Romulus is occluded by the lack of historical records. (They do not begin until the dedication of the great Temple of Iuppiter Optimus Maximus on the Capitoline in 509 B.C.) The view was not much clearer to the Roman historians of the later republic, who constructed a series of tales to account for Rome's transition from the small hut village on the Palatine to the city of the late sixth century.[6] The tradition envisioned seven kings, whose reigns were calibrated to span the period from 753 to 509 B.C.: Romulus (753–710), Numa Pompilius (710–670), Tullus Hostilius (670–625), Ancus Marcius (625–600), Tarquinius Priscus ("the Elder," 600–570), Servius Tullius (570–530), Tarquinius Superbus ("the Proud," 530–509).

Details of the city's growth vary in different ancient accounts, but there were two distinct stages. The first four kings inaugurated Rome's political, religious, and military customs, and extended the boundary of the city to include the Palatine, Capitoline, Aventine, and some of the continuous highland between the Caelian and the Quirinal.[7] The second stage began when Tarquinius arrived from Tarquinia, an Etruscan city, and established a dynasty that included Servius Tullius (whose name is Latin, not Etruscan, and implies that he was of slave stock) and Tarquinius Superbus. According to tradition, the three kings of the second stage developed the Circus Maximus and the Forum, extended the city to take in Quirinal, Esquiline, and Caelian, protected it with a defensive rampart, reorganized the city into four "regions," began the monumental temple of Jupiter on the Capitoline, and dug a ditch (the Cloaca Maxima) to drain the valley through the Forum (Fig. 2).

Two documents of religious history contribute something to our understanding of Rome's early growth. One is the record of the Septimontium, a festival celebrated throughout the republic by the *montani,* the inhabitants of the hilltops of the Palatine, Caelian, and Esquiline. The other lists the Argeorum Sacraria, small shrines in various parts of the city visited in ceremonial processions in March and May: they are located on the Caelian, Esquiline, Quirinal, and Palatine. Both of these rituals seem to reflect a time shortly after the unification of the city, traditionally ascribed to the Etruscan kings, but before the inclusion of the Capitoline and the Aventine.[8]

Here again archaeology clarifies our understanding of the city's growth while supporting the main outlines of the historical tradition. Recent work of excavation and analysis recognizes two main periods corresponding roughly to the two groups of traditional kings. The earlier period is similar to that in other central Italian settlements. No more graves have been found in the Forum, which probably means that the area was used by the living as early as the eighth century, but graves found on the Esquiline contained bronze implements and pottery that show some modest prosperity. In one grave, dating from the late eighth century, remains of a chariot and bronze armor may imply some sort of emerging aristocracy. Pottery, imported from Greece and also made locally, shows continuing activity in the Forum Boarium, on the Quirinal, and on the Viminal. During this period Rome's standard of living seems to have been slightly less advanced than that of some of its neighbors, for on the other side of the Tiber an aristocratic class was forming a new civilization in the Etruscan cities, which were becoming more urbanized, literate, and sophisticated under the influence of Greek and Phoenician trade. South of the Tiber, fantastically rich treasures from Praeneste, Decima, and Satricum document an aristocratic, urbanized society of the Etruscan type during the seventh century. In Rome itself we should probably visualize a group of separate hilltop villages, each with its own wood-and-earth defensive wall. Although the Roman tombs of the period are not as rich as some found elsewhere, a few of them are elaborate enough to show that some residents were better off than others. As the population grew, the houses spread beyond the old village limits, to the area of the Forum. This must have brought the people closer together, and encouraged cooperative activity: common defensive action against threatening neighbors, a market in the Forum Boarium, perhaps a ferry service across the river, some agreement on the use of farm and grazing land beyond the village limits. A list of trade guilds in Plutarch's *Life of Numa* (17.2) may well be an authentic reflection of the organization of labor in Rome in the sixth century B.C.: flute players, goldsmiths, carpenters, dyers, shoemakers, tanners, coppersmiths, and potters. The scale of life did not require construction workers or even blacksmiths, and activities like baking and laundry were done at home without the need for specialists.[9]

The first archaeological confirmation of a unified "urban" consciousness is the drainage and paving of the Forum Romanum area, which is surely evidence of some degree of civic unity.[10] Archaeologists disagree about the dating of the first paving of the Forum: some put it as early as 650 B.C.; others contend it was as late as 575 B.C.[11] But it clearly marked the start of a new phase in the early urban history of Rome, one that corresponds to the reigns of the three "Etruscan" kings and emphasizes the construction of public works. The first real city wall was constructed on the Esquiline, the city's most vulnerable boundary. Real temple buildings—in the Forum Boarium and on the Capitoline, the Esquiline, and the Aventine—were constructed of brick, like Etruscan temples, and decorated with terra-cotta revetments molded and brightly painted in their characteristic orientalizing style (cf. Pl. 14). Other finds reinforce our impression that Rome in the sixth century, even though it retained its Latin language, looked like an Etruscan city. Etruscan pottery appears in great abundance, most commonly in the style of the dark gray, glossy, molded pottery known as *bucchero*. An inscription in the Etruscan language was found in the Forum Boarium, and the street connecting the Forum Boarium and the Forum Romanum was the Vicus Tuscus ("Etruscan Street") in the valley of the Velabrum (a name that seems to have an Etruscan derivation). In the surrounding countryside the Romans were undertaking a systematic drainage system, evidence of both a unified cooperative effort and technological skill of the sort we encounter in Etruscan cities. All this helps us imagine a city of hills and valleys surrounded by a unifying wall and by an organized system of fields. It had a common civic center with public buildings and shrines. And it had colorful temples of the most modern style commemorating public cults. Most spectacular was the immense temple on the Capitoline: its three shrines to accommodate Jupiter, Juno, and Minerva were a clear reflection of Etruscan temples with three cellas; its scale shows that its planners intended to build the largest temple of any Etruscan city.

Two

Expansion under the Republic

When a group of patricians under the leadership of Marcus Junius Brutus expelled the royal house of the Tarquins, they established an oligarchical republic which in its first three and a half centuries experienced a period of consolidation and expansion which was reflected in the the city's physical development. Initially the city's cultural world was informed by its contact with the Etruscans and the Greeks in southern Italy. Then there was withdrawal, a preoccupation with internal social problems. During the third and second centuries B.C., however, Rome's horizons expanded as it became the most important military and political force in the Mediterranean world.

The Fifth Century B.C.

When later historians wrote about Rome's transition from a typical Etruscan city to an independent Latin republic, they relied on a tradition about Tarquin's attempts to recapture Rome, and about wars with the Latins to the south and the Etruscans of Veii to the northeast. That tradition presented the internal history of the republic in its first century as a struggle between noble "patricians" and common "plebeians," and a gradual accommodation of the claims and prerogatives of these two orders. It also recorded the dates of temple dedications. which help us visualize the first stages in republican Rome's development. These began with the Temple of Iuppiter Optimus Maximus on the Capitoline; its Etruscan-style façade and tremendous bulk loomed over the Forum Romanum and the city for 400 years, a reminder of the ambitious urbanism of the Etruscan kings, but also a reminder of the founding of the republic, whose magistrates had dedicated it to the protection of the new order. Contacts with the Greek world and Greek artistic traditions continued. Several temples were dedicated to Greek gods like Castor and Pollux, Mercury, and Apollo.[1] Rome's growing influence over the neighboring towns of the Latin League was commemorated in the Temple of Diana on the Aventine and in the Temple of Castor in the Forum Romanum. The increasing power of the plebeians, and the growing wealth of certain individual plebeians, is attested by the Temple of Mercurius, a god of merchants, and the Temple of Ceres Liber Liberaque, agricultural deities whose shrine on the Aventine was always considered a special interest of the plebeian order. The temples also illustrate the physical growth of the city, from the Forum Romanum through the valley of the Circus Maximus up onto the brow of the Aventine Hill, which was always known as a residence of foreigners and plebeians.

A series of laws passed around the middle of the fifth century B.C. illustrates the same social and topographical realities. One law provided for the settling of plebeians on the Aventine: plots of land were distributed, and houses (some of several stories) were constructed (Dionysius of Halicarnassus, *Roman Antiquities* 10.31– 32). Another source is what remains of a major codification of law around 450 B.C., the Twelve Tables: these laws depict a society with merchants and traders, with regular market days, and with a stratified social order institutionalized in the relationship between patron and client.[2] Several laws restricted the display of wealth at funerals involving cremation pyres. These may reflect a concern about fire and may be evidence that some parts of the city were crowded. More likely, they were an attempt to tone down the open flaunting of wealth and privilege by the patricians, and to discourage the kind of elaborate funerals that were associated with the Etruscan aristocracy.

From archaeological excavations we know that the Etruscan architectural style continued through much of the fifth century B.C. In addition, imported Greek pottery was found regularly in graves dating up until the middle of the century, after which there was a sudden decline in Greek imports.[3] This may mean that between 450 and 400 the Romans withdrew from the Hellenizing atmosphere of the rest of Italy, becoming instead preoccupied with consolidating their city-state on their own terms.[4] Indigenous religious traditions were affirmed in 428, when a law was passed that banned any new foreign cults (Livy 4.30.9–11). For two primeval deities—Saturnus, with his roots on the Capitoline, and Dius Fidius on the Quirinal—new temples were built.

At the southeastern end of the Forum, on the site of the old royal palace, the new republic adapted the old forms of family life and the kings' religious duties. The royal fireplace was now set aside as a public hearth tended by six Vestal Virgins, who assumed in a public way the private duties of the king's daughters. They lived in the Atrium Vestae. The Regia ("king's house") was rebuilt as a repository for sacred implements, and the Domus Publica nearby housed the "King of Sacrifices," who performed on behalf of the state the sacred rites that had been the king's responsibility. Later in the century, around 435, a Villa Publica was constructed in the Campus Martius, for the use of military commanders.[5] These buildings— including an *atrium* and a *domus,* both terms for aristocratic town houses, and a suburban *villa*—reflect in their terminology how the royal family life of the past was continued by the farmer-soldier-citizens of the republican present, and how public life and buildings were modeled on this aristocratic life-style.[6]

If Greek or Etruscan tourists had visited Rome in the fifth century B.C., it would probably have struck them as rather rustic and provincial. They would have noticed individuals of different social classes: patricians and a few merchant plebeians with large houses near the Forum, and clumps of smaller huts and houses for the poorer citizens, separated by open fields. The general impression of our imaginary visitors would probably have been that the city was an unprepossessing place, a collection of villages with a small-town mentality, as conveyed in a vignette describing the townsfolk gathered around the Lacus Iuturnae, the Spring of Juturna, in the Forum Romanum in 496, waiting for news of the battle against the Latins at Lake Regillus:

> Late in the afternoon, when the battle was over, two tall, handsome young men appeared, they say, in the Forum Romanum. They wore military uniforms, their faces had the look of battle, and their horses were lathered with sweat. Both of them watered their horses and washed them at the fountain next to the Temple of Vesta, which makes a small, deep pool. A crowd gathered around them, asking if they brought any news from the battlefield. They described how it had gone, and said that the Romans had won. (Dionysius of Halicarnassus, *Roman Antiquities* 6.13.1–2)

The Fourth Century B.C.

Against a background of continuing warfare with Etruscans, Aequians, Volscians, Latins, and Samnites, Rome in the fourth century B.C. expanded its political influence abroad and attained a settlement of the patrician-plebeian rivalries at home. The points of punctuation are the defeat of Veii in 396; the destruction of Rome itself in 390 by a marauding band of Gauls; the Sextio-Licinian laws of 367, which opened the highest of the political magistracies to those plebeians who were rich enough to hold them; a treaty with the Latins in 338, which recognized Roman supremacy in central Italy; and a series of wars with the Samnites (343–341, 326–321, 315–304), mountaineers whom the Romans liked to view as enemies of the settled orderliness of urban civilization. These events brought an increase in prestige, which strengthened the Romans' urban confidence and produced a sense of "specialness" as they reached out to adapt and incorporate outside influences into a Roman urban synthesis.

The building activity of Marcus Furius Camillus, the general responsible for the defeat of Veii and the repulse of the Gauls, sets the tone for the fourth century. Under his sponsorship the shrines of Fortuna and Mater Matuta in the Forum Boarium were monumentalized with two temples in Etruscan style set side by side. The protective goddess of Veii, Juno Regina, was solemnly called forth from her Etruscan home to take up residence in a new temple on the

Aventine Hill. To celebrate the peaceful settlement of differences between patricians and plebeians, Camillus built in the Forum Romanum the Temple of Concordia, the first of a series of shrines to abstract divinities of Greek type. The enthusiasm for new cults became so intense that a commission was established (in 367—the *quindecimviri sacris faciundis*) to supervise the maintenance of the official cults.

The Gallic invasion of Rome in 390 B.C. destroyed most of the houses and a large number of the shrines, except on the fortified Capitoline.[7] This would have been a wonderful opportunity to call in Etruscan or Greek city planners and build a new city of the most modern fourth-century type, but the opportunity was lost. The invasion had taught the Romans that their city was vulnerable, and they decided to concentrate on a practical measure that was also profoundly symbolic: a city wall that enclosed in its circuit of 11 kilometers (6.5 miles) the Aventine, Capitoline, Palatine, Quirinal, Viminal, Esquiline and Caelian hills, as well as the valleys between them (Fig. 2). The wall included more territory than the ritual boundary of the pomerium. It excluded public areas like the Campus Martius and the Trans-Tiber region, which would be built up in future years. But for the next six and a half centuries, this wall defined the city of Rome proper: the *urbs,* covering over 400 hectares (1,000 acres), an area larger than any other city in Italy.

Within the city's walls, new temples, large and small, were scattered throughout all parts of the city, still made of the traditional mud brick and terra-cotta.[8] Outside the walls, Rome's growing dominance over its neighbors was symbolized by the temples that were built along the roads leading south and across the river.[9]

The trends of growth and development in the fourth century B.C. reached a climax in the career of Appius Claudius Caecus, who as censor in 312 addressed the needs of the city and its population. He built Rome's first aqueduct, the Aqua Appia, which fed water into a fountain near the Forum Boarium. This seems to mean that the quays along the river had grown so crowded that an artificial water supply was needed. Appius was also responsible for paving the Via Appia, the highway that ran south and assured communication with Campania and the territory troubled by the wars with the

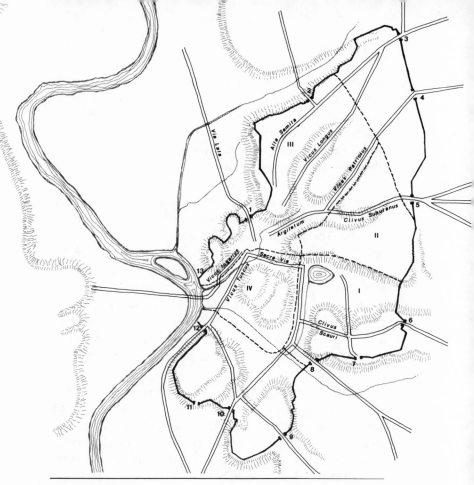

Fig. 2. Rome: The Republican City, showing the four regions ascribed to Servius Tullius as well as the walls in the fourth century B.C. *Regions:* **I** Suburana (Sucusana), **II** Esquilina, **III** Collina, **IV** Palatina. *Gates:* **1** Porta Fontinalis, **2** Porta Quirinalis, **3** Porta Collina, **4** Porta Viminalis, **5** Porta Esquilina, **6** Porta Caelimontana, **7** Porta Querquetulana, **8** Porta Capena, **9** Porta Naevia, **10** Porta R000 Rasdusculana, **11** Porta Lavernalis, **12** Porta Trigemina, **13** Porta Flumentana.

Samnites. In revising the roster of the Senate, Appius and the other censor are said to have included new members whose origins were in the lower classes, including the sons of manumitted slaves. They also revised the membership of the tribal voting units in an effort to improve the voting power of the city residents at the expense of the Roman citizens who lived in the rural hinterland. Although this controversial measure was rescinded in 304 B.C., it shows that tensions existed between various levels of the population, primarily between the nobility of patricians and wealthy plebeian ex-consuls on the one hand, and an upwardly mobile group that included even the sons of freedmen on the other. The source of the latter's wealth was apparently trade, for Livy refers to them (9.46.14) as "the whole forum crowd" (*omnem forensem turbam*).

The many facets of urbanistic activity in the second half of the fourth century B.C. make it logical to suppose that Rome's military, physical, and commercial growth produced problems that needed solutions. The immense area included within the city's walls implies the expectation of a large population. Colonies were sent out to patrol newly acquired territory, and that implies that there was some surplus population, without property and without many resources, for whom the grant of land and pioneer status in the colonies was a real attraction. The development of the Forum Boarium and of the riverside docks suggests that a resident urban population worked at industry, transport, and trade, while commerce produced new opportunities for employment, which attracted more outsiders to Rome and also widened the gap between rich and poor. And at about the same time in the later fourth century the Forum Romanum became more exclusively the preserve of politicians and—evidence of commercial and political involvements on an international scale—moneychangers. Older tenants of the Forum shops such as grocers, butchers, and fishmongers moved out to their own market, probably in the Argiletum.

When visitors walked through the streets of Rome on a market day at the end of the fourth century B.C., they found a more cosmopolitan city than their predecessors had a hundred years earlier. New temples were there, scattered thinly over the expanse of the city, and the new wall expressed a more conscious urban identity. There were more people in the streets, and there was more activity at the port and in the specialized markets of the Argiletum. Yet there was still an inescapable small-town look to the place. The houses built so quickly after the Gallic invasion of 390 had the crowded, meandering look (and also, one suspects, the charm) of Italian hill towns from the Iron Age to the present. In comparison with a city like Capua in Campania, with which Rome began an intermittent alliance in 343 and which boasted wide-open, sensibly planned spaces, the appearance of Rome was hopelessly provincial. Cicero, years later, had to lament that the contrast was still true: "Rome is perched on hills and propped in valleys, its tenements hanging aloft, its roads terrible, its alleys narrow!" (*Contra Rullum: De Lege Agraria* 2.96).

The Third Century B.C.

During the hundred years from 300 to 200 B.C., Rome's outlook expanded tremendously. The continuing wars with the Samnites brought the Romans into closer involvement with the Greek cities of Italy and Sicily. A new self-confidence was accompanied by an urban style which, inspired by the string of hard-won military victories, was more monumental than before but still cautious and conservative.

The difficult wars of the third century brought their share of serious setbacks. All of them, however, ended with the confirmation of Roman power: first in Italy, then in Sicily, Sardinia, and Spain. The year 295 B.C. was particularly difficult, with the Romans facing a coalition of Samnites, Gauls, and Etruscans. A plebeian leader, Decius Mus, won the decisive military victory at Sentium in 295 which made the Romans the supreme power in Italy. Shortly thereafter Rome was involved in a war with Tarentum, a Greek city at the southern end of the Italian peninsula. This was Rome's first real contact with a completely Hellenic city, and involved the dashing figure of Pyrrhus, a dynast from northern Greece who kept Roman generals busy until 272 B.C., when Tarentum made its peace with Rome. Dominance in Italy led to an interest in Sicily, its shores full of Greek cities, and in 264 a war broke out with the Carthaginians for control of the island: this is known as the First Punic War, and through imagination and determination the Romans overcame naval inexperience and tremendous losses to acquire Sicily as a province in 241, followed by Sardinia and Corsica in 238. The acquisition of all these Greek cities brought an unmistakable Greek influence on Roman taste.

Carthaginian and Roman clashes in Spain led to the Second
Punic War. The Romans had planned to fight this war in Africa and
Spain, but were taken by complete surprise when the Carthaginian
general Hannibal cut across southern Gaul and through the Alps to
invade Italy in the spring of 218 B.C. This action brought the war
into Italy, and it stayed there until 204. Hannibal never actually
attacked the city of Rome—the fourth-century fortifications were
too formidable—but the war came home to the Romans in a profound way, and it took a terrible toll on the city. The small farms
owned by average Roman citizens throughout central Italy were
abandoned as Hannibal's army made its raids, and the rural population took refuge in the cities, most particularly in Rome. The war
also, in the way of wars, brought prosperity, at least to some of
Rome's inhabitants. For those with enterprise and some capital,
there was money in manufacturing weapons, importing grain by
sea (from Sicily, mostly), and buying or selling slaves, of which the
constant fighting produced a nearly inexhaustible supply. At the
same time, the city as a whole was enriched: new ethnic groups
(both slave and free), new cults, and extensive new building activity all helped make the city a more crowded, diverse, and interesting place. The two most characteristic phenomena of third-
century urbanism in Rome were the tremendous impact of Greek
cultural patterns and the dominant role of the military-political
nobility.

Hellenic influence was not new in Rome, as we have seen; but
the pervasive force of its impression on Roman ways of doing
things became clearer than ever during the third century. New
temples honored Greek gods.[10] Statues were carried back from the
cities of Sicily to embellish Roman temples and public places, and
paintings inspired by Greek originals celebrated the exploits of Roman armies.[11]

When a general was victorious, the Senate often recognized him
as a *triumphator,* honoring him with a triumphal procession. Often,
in response, the general dedicated a temple; this not only expressed
his thanks to a protecting deity but also beautified the city and put
before the public his own name and the name of his family. Such
triumphal urban art is attested in the dedication of temples to Iup-

piter Victor, Victoria, and Bellona,[12] and in the development of the ritual of the triumphal celebration.[13]

The responsibilities and rewards of public service were spread widely throughout the ruling class, and the physical result for Rome was a great profusion of triumphal monuments: temples, statues, paintings, and tombs. The nobles, through their membership in the Senate, incarnated the political life of the Roman republic, and the pattern of their family life was so pervasive that even buildings constructed for specific public purposes were modeled on their mansions, their atria. The most famous was the Atrium Vestae, but during the third century B.C. we also hear of the Atrium Publicum, an archive building; the Atrium Libertatis, the censors' headquarters; the Atrium Maenium and the Atrium Titium, which combined official functions with some kind of enclosed shopping center; the Atrium Sutorium, which housed the shoemakers; and the Atria Licinia, an auction hall.[14]

The temples built by these triumphant nobles tell us more than their desire to thank the gods and to make a name for themselves. They also tell us that Rome was being beautified in all its parts.[15]

On the high ground inside the city wall on the Esquiline, the population grew quickly, and in 272 B.C. money from the Pyrrhic War was used to build an aqueduct, the Anio Vetus, to supply the hilltop.

Along the Tiber River, the markets took on a new dignity, appropriate to their role as a major entrance to the city. During the First Punic War the Forum Holitorium received a Temple of Ianus (god of entrances) and a Temple of Spes (goddess of hope). In the Forum Boarium old temples were refurbished and a new one, probably to Portunus (god of the commercial port), was built.[16] The Forum Boarium was apparently still used as a cattle market, and multistoried tenements leaned against the corner of the Capitoline or Aventine (Livy 21.62.2–4). When a fire swept through in 213 (or 210?) the whole area was rebuilt.

Upstream, in the lower Campus Martius, Gaius Flaminius Nepos—who had made a name for himself as a general and as a champion of the plebeians—constructed a new major monument, the Circus Flaminius, in 220 B.C. It immediately acquired symbolic importance as a rallying place for the plebeians, and it retained a down-to-earth architectural simplicity throughout the republic.[17]

The spread of Roman preeminence over all of Italy, Sicily, and Sardinia had inevitable consequences for the quality of urban life in third-century Rome. Citizens became more aware of conflicts within the social structure: between city and country, between the institutions of a city-state and the responsibilities of empire, and between native traditions and foreign innovations.

One such conflict was perceived between those who lived in the city and those who lived on their farms. By now Roman citizens held farms in all corners of Italy; many of these farms were too far away to permit their owners to come to Rome to exercise their rights as citizens. By now, too, the urban population was larger, denser, and more aware of its special needs and power. One attempt to deal with the conflict of interests concerned the *nundinae* (market days) held every eighth day, when the farmers from the surrounding countryside brought their products into the city, law cases were heard, and the popular assembly met to pass legislation in a kind of town meeting. The Lex Hortensia, passed probably in 287 B.C., moved the assembly meetings to days other than market days. The assembly's intention may have been to make its meetings more serious, less distracted by the bustle of market-day fairs, but one result was that fewer farmers came to town to vote in the assembly meetings, and the urban population thus acquired a more powerful voice in city affairs.

As the century went on, the balance shifted even further in favor of the city's inhabitants. In the First Punic War, the burdens of military service were fairly equally distributed. The extensive naval warfare created work for the unlanded poor in the city, who rowed the ships; the actual fighting, however, was done by the farmers, since only landowners served in the legions. In the Second Punic War this class of free landholders throughout Italy was clearly hardest hit. They contributed the soldiers who were cut down by Hannibal at Cannae and Lake Trasimene; they had to leave their farms to be pillaged by Hannibal's soldiers; they had to send their families to the relative safety of the cities. When the war was over, most of them were too uprooted, too disheartened, or too urbanized to return to their farms, and so they tended to settle with their families in the cities, especially Rome. From Rome's Latin allies, discharged soldiers whose hometowns had been destroyed in the war also migrated to the city to claim their traditional prerogative of Roman citizenship.

Tension also developed because existing Roman institutions, originally devised for the administration of a simple agrarian city-state, challenged the realities of governing a continental empire. Take, for example, a problem that arose during the war with Pyrrhus. Rome's traditional way of declaring war required that a group of priests, the *fetiales,* walk to the enemy's borders and perform certain ceremonies. But when you are fighting a Greek from across the sea, how do you do this? Ever resourceful, and ever faithful to the letter of the law, the Romans had one of their captives buy a small plot of Roman ground, which thereafter served as "enemy territory" for the purposes of this ritual.[18]

The relationship between native Roman traditions and imported ones also was problematic. In the 290s a large number of temples were built in honor of Greek gods, but for the next several decades new temples were dedicated mostly to traditional Italic deities like Quirinus, Summanus, Consus, Tellus, Pales, Ianus, and Portunus. The museum displays that were brought into the city—for example, the 200 statues from Volsinii in 264—were Italic and Etruscan. With the conclusion of the Pyrrhic War, however, Greeks came to Rome in greater numbers than ever, and the cultural tide turned decisively in their favor. The long involvement in Greek territory in Sicily during the First Punic War exposed a whole generation of Roman soldiers to Greek civilization, and these soldiers in time provided an interested audience for the Roman plays that were based on Greek originals and set in Greek lands, such as those produced, starting in 241, by Livius Andronicus (a hostage from Tarentum) and Gnaeus Naevius. Spoils and slaves brought from Syracuse and Tarentum during the Second Punic War, along with wider contacts for trade, brought new wealth and new standards of taste to the Romans.

Even Rome's sense of her own past was sharpened. The emphasis on military victory and the triumphal monuments of the noble aristocracy found literary expression in self-conscious historical records that were in turn influenced by the Greeks. The poet Naevius and the annalist Fabius Pictor reconstructed earlier Roman history in terms of Hellenistic traditions, while at the same time emphasizing the heroic contributions of Rome's great families. The result was a home-grown mythology of farmer-soldiers conquering the wilderness.

As the Second Punic War came to an end in 204 B.C., the city of Rome was demographically more complex than it had ever been, and the population was on the verge of acquiring a new sophistication. The physical fabric of the city was permeated with new buildings, still mostly in the traditional Italo-Etruscan style. Our typical visitors would see a more cosmopolitan city than their predecessors had, but Rome still had an unshakably provincial look in comparison with the fine Hellenistic cities of Campania, Sicily, and the East. Livy puts a negative assessment of the city into the mouths of Greek military men in Macedonia at the beginning of the second century B.C. Coming from a Roman pen, this assessment betrays an acute awareness of cultural deprivation as well as embarrassment over the humble beginnings of Roman urbanism: "Some made fun of the Romans' traditions and customs, others of their accomplishments, others of individual members of the aristocracy, others of the appearance of the city itself, not yet beautiful in either public or private domains" (Livy 40.5.7).

The Second Century, 200–146 B.C.

A larger, more diverse population, a more luxurious standard of living, and a greatly expanded political role—all these factors inevitably had an impact on the physical shape of Rome. The Pyrrhic and Punic wars of the third century had expanded the Romans' sense of their world, and in the first half of the second century, this cosmopolitanism found form and expression as the wealth of the whole Mediterranean streamed into the city in triumphal processions, revenues from Spanish mines, and provincial tax payments. The blossom of Hellenic culture came to full flower as Rome conducted a series of wars and diplomatic negotiations in the

Greek East—Macedonia, Achaea, the Aegean, Asia Minor, Syria, even Egypt—which resulted in complete political domination by Rome by the year 146 B.C. As the Romans attempted to make their city a worthy world capital in the first half of the second century, they introduced a series of urbanistic "firsts"—the first triumphal arches in 196, the first porticoes in 193, the first basilica in 184, the first stone bridge in 179, the first paved streets in 174, and the first marble temple in 146. Just as history and sculpture, in search of their proper forms, found Greek models to imitate and adapt, so too the architectural innovations of Rome drew inspiration from the Greek East.

To some extent the Romans had been prepared for Greek influence by the increased contacts of the third century, but the sheer volume of wealth, slaves, and art which was carried through the streets of Rome in triumphal processions must have been overwhelming. As triumph followed triumph year after year, lavish displays of spoils tended to become routine, and a triumphant general who wanted to make his accomplishments memorable had to stage ever more imaginative parades. Even a simple *ovatio* (one step below a triumph) in 196 conveyed great quantities of gold and silver (Livy 33.27.1–4), and successive generals like Titus Quinctius Flamininus in 194 (Livy 34.52.3–12), Gnaeus Manlius Volso in 187 (Livy 39.6.7–9), and Lucius Aemilius Paullus in 167 (Diodorus 31.8.10–13; Plutarch, *Aemilius Paullus* 32–34) carefully accentuated what was new and luxurious. Their contributions to the city, like those of earlier generals, were mostly temples vowed to gods in the heat of battle and conspicuously located to serve as a perpetual reminder of each general's great deeds on behalf of the republic. Whereas in the third century the responsibilities of leadership had been well distributed throughout the senatorial aristocracy, and all the votive temples tended to be built on a similar fairly modest scale and with conservative decoration, the generals of the second century found themselves competing to make both their triumphal processions and their triumphal monuments ever more conspicuous exhibits in the museum that Rome had become.[19]

The permanent physical effects of this "prestige urbanism" were most visible in the lower Campus Martius. A third large temple, known as Temple D, was added at the Area Sacra del Largo Argentina.[20] Elsewhere, the Temple of Fortuna Equestris (known from literature, not archaeology) was dedicated in 173 B.C., radiant with marble roof tiles pillaged from a temple in Croton, a Greek city in southern Italy. Near the Circus Flaminius small temples were built to Pietas, Apollo, and Diana. Larger temples celebrated important victories in Greece: Hercules Musarum, Iuno Regina, and Iuppiter Stator (Rome's first temple made of marble) lined up along the edge of the Circus (see Fig. 4),[21] and by the middle of the century they were embellished with porticoes of Greek columns.[22]

Just downstream, in the Forum Holitorium, a temporary wooden theater was built (Livy 40.51.3), and a new Temple of Iuno Sospita was squeezed between the two third-century temples (Fig. 3). The censors of 179 built a portico along the river "behind the Temple of Spes" which created a monumental approach to the Circus Flaminius (Livy 40.51).

Farther south, inside the city walls, the ground area of the Forum Boarium was raised and repaved, and the Temple of Portunus was reconstructed. It faced the road that led from the Forum Romanum through the Velabrum and the Forum Boarium to a new stone bridge (the Pons Aemilius), built across the Tiber in 179 to supplement the wooden Pons Sublicius just downstream.[23] On the other side of the square, two small arches gave monumental entrances to the twin temples of Fortuna and Mater Matuta.[24]

The southern end of the Forum Boarium was bounded by the city wall as it descended from the Aventine to the river. Access to the riverbank that lay below the Aventine was through the Porta Trigemina, and here the most important docks in the city were located. During and after the Second Punic War, of course, the volume of sea- and river-borne traffic increased tremendously, and to accommodate it the aediles of 193 planned a portico and emporium (Livy 35.10.12). The censors of 179 continued work on the harbor works, including the construction of an immense covered bazaar, the Porticus Aemilia, in which a series of concrete barrel vaults rested on widely spaced piers and permitted merchants, teamsters, and stevedores to circulate freely (Livy 40.51.6). The

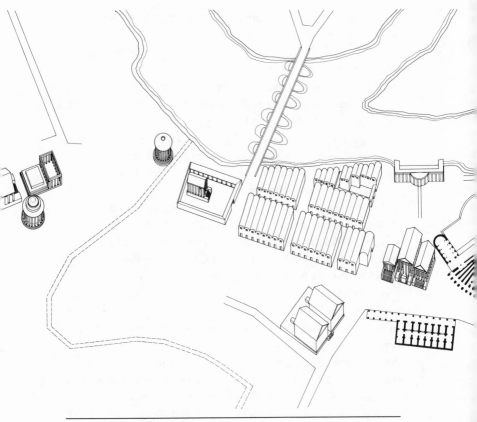

Fig. 3. Rome: Forum Boarium, second/first century B.C. *Far left:* Temple of Hercules Invictus (rectangular), Temple of Hercules Victor (round), Herculis Invicti Ara Maxima, colonnaded shrine (Statio Annonae?). *Center left:* Round Temple of the Forum Boarium, rectangular Temple of the Forum Boarium (Temple of Portunus?). *Center right, top:* Tiber and Pons Aemilius. *Center right, middle:* Horrea (provisional reconstruction). *Center right, bottom:* Temple of Fortuna, Temple of Mater Matuta (Area Sacra di S. Omobono). *Far right, top:* Tiber and Insula Tiberina. *Far right, middle:* Porticus post Spei; Temples of the Forum Holitorium (Spes, Iuno Sospita, Ianus); Theatrum Marcelli (plan). *Far right, bottom:* Porticus of late republic (plan).

censors of 174 continued the project, and paved the emporium with stone (Livy 41.27.8).

All this work served to create a proper entry to Rome from the outside world. Now, from the river, the first impression was of a porticoed façade, with the hills of the city rising behind it.

Along the major roads, too, the entrances to the city were embellished (cf. Fig. 2). Just outside the Porta Capena, where the Via Appia entered the city from southern Italy, a new Temple of Honos et Virtus displayed spoils brought back from the capture of Syracuse. On the other side of town, where the Via Flaminia from northern Italy passed through the Porta Fontinalis, the aediles of 193 monumentalized the approach to the city with a portico extending from the gate to the Altar of Mars in the Campus Martius (Livy 35.10.12). On the Quirinal, an elaborate porticoed Temple of Venus Erucina just outside the Porta Collina embellished the approach to the city from the Via Salaria or the Via Nomentana.

A parallel architectural development, the tendency to arrange temples in rows facing a common sacred area, also bespeaks a desire to create a good impression. It was a result of the grouping of large numbers of temples at important central spots, and we see it at the Largo Argentina, at the northern edge of the Circus Flaminius (Fig. 4), and at the Forum Holitorium. The temples produced a continuous façade, a backdrop, similar to the porticoes that were springing up all over Rome between 200 and 146 B.C. (Fig. 3).[25]

As we have seen, Rome had been borrowing Greek forms, either directly or through the Etruscans, for centuries. In these years between the Second Punic War and the destruction of Carthage and Corinth in 146 B.C., however, Greek decorative motifs, Greek intellectual ideas, and Greek political maneuverings all coincided with the responsibilities of governing a much larger empire and the claims to prestige of the powerful noble families. The result was a great deal of tension as the Romans tried to work out their sense of themselves in relation to the peoples with whom they had become so deeply involved, and in relation to the proper architectural stage-setting in which to lead their social and political lives.[26]

The impact of Greek influence was not limited, of course, to architecture. It was felt in the life-style of the whole city, of the poor as well as the rich. The poor suffered from the changes that came in the wake of the Hannibalic War: the influx of slaves brought new competition for work, and food was often scarce.[27] Not much wealth trickled down from the top, but job opportunities were created by the ships arriving at the docks, the constant construction projects, and the increased population to be served. The rich—those who could afford the luxury goods that were now available as never before—enjoyed amenities of all sorts. Our sources mention fads for furniture, textiles, cosmetics, and slaves (especially flute girls and cooks) (Livy 39.6.7–9). Greek literature invaded the city on many levels, most publicly in the plays of Plautus, whose adaptations of Greek comedy appealed to the well-traveled Romans who had fought in Sicily and Greece and also to the stay-at-homes who appreciated the rough-and-tumble slapstick. The plays of Terence, produced in the 160s, were more faithful to the spirit of their Greek originals and appealed to more refined tastes, such as those cultivated in the salon of Scipio Africanus the Younger, whose members included some of the brightest literary artists of Rome as well as the Greek historian Polybius. Greek ideas also found a response in the lower classes, which were attracted to the cult of Bacchus. This cult gained adherents throughout southern Italy and even in Rome in the first part of the century. Its upper-class counterpart was the enthusiasm with which Greek philosophers were welcomed in Rome: in 159 B.C., Crates the Stoic created a great sensation, and in 155, representatives of the three major philosophical schools in Athens came to Rome and were welcomed eagerly (Aulus Gellius 6.14.8–10).

But while the Scipios and those of similar taste were drinking in all the Greek culture they could, others viewed the whole proceeding with revulsion and considerable alarm. Cato the Censor is their best-known representative. In his public pronouncements he declined to accept the need for a veneer of Greek culture on the sturdy stock of Roman Italy. He inveighed against the moral degeneration represented by virtuous Roman matrons painting themselves with imported cosmetics,[28] he sneered at Greekling literary activity, and the sort of suspicions he voiced lay behind the decisive move to restrict the Bacchic cult in 186, on grounds that it was deleterious to public morals, and behind the senatorial edicts that expelled two Greek Epicurean philosophers in 173 and any remaining philosophers and rhetoricians in 161.

Cato has come to stand for the old traditional Roman ways of doing things, yet his career is a good illustration of the urban social conditions of the first half of the second century B.C. In his public image, he was a staunch defender of the idea of the Roman citizen-farmer, a loyal family man who educated his own son, a compiler of the history of Rome. Yet he was originally from Tusculum, not Rome; he came to Rome and entered public life during the latter years of the Second Punic War, and gained renown through adherence to traditional client-patron bonds. He was a man of the city, upwardly mobile, whose censorship was devoted to practical measures for improving city life (Livy 39.44). Even his work on agriculture was aimed not at the traditional Italian peasant but at the moderately prosperous urban dwellers, who had made money during the war and used it to buy up suburban farms from peasants who had abandoned them. Near the end of his career, he even overcame senatorial scruples in order to make money, like many an urban businessman, in commercial trade (Plutarch, *Cato Major* 21).

Cato is thus representative, in a way, of the mass of the urban population of Rome in the aftermath of the Hannibalic War. In spite of efforts during the war to send the peasants back to their farms (Livy 28.11.8–9), in spite of efforts in 187 and 177 to send the Italians who had come into Rome back to their hometowns (Livy 39.3.4–6; 41.8.6), the population had grown out of control. Vast numbers of people now considered themselves at home inside the city walls. Even those with farms in the neighborhood of Rome usually lived in their town houses, while the farms were tended by slaves.[29] The new pressures on urban space finally eliminated any open farmland within the walls, and in this period, both in Rome and in Pompeii, those who could afford it opened up small enclosed gardens at the rear of their houses.

The crowded city was also more and more obviously a cosmopolitan city. As the final visitors in our series approached Rome in 146 B.C., whether by river or by road, they were welcomed to the city by an appropriately imposing façade. The narrow winding streets with the old modest buildings inherited from the days of the early republic were now punctuated with occasional set pieces of "found art," proclaiming the power of Rome and the cultural glory of the lands it had been busy conquering. The city's streets were now thronged with people from every corner of the Mediterranean, and tenements reached several stories into the sky, making the forums and temple precincts welcome areas of refreshment and respite. Rome had come a long way from the simple Italian hill town of the fifth century B.C. As noted in a passage from Plautus that was probably written early in the second century B.C., the Romans were becoming deeply involved in the Greek homeland. Plautus's catalogue of urban landmarks with exotic Hellenic names redolent of Eastern luxury was supposed to be a description of Thebes in Greece. But just as the Greek terms jostle through the passage next to good Latin terms, so the Hellenic urban features must have been becoming familiar to the residents of Rome who saw Plautus's play *Amphitryon:* "I've crawled through all the streets [*plateae*], gymnasia, and perfume shops [*myropolia*], at the bazaar [*emporium*] and in the market, in the wrestling-hall [*palaestra*] and in the forum, in the doctors' and barbers' shops, and all the sacred temples. My expedition has worn me out!" (1011–1014).

Three

The Late Republic, 146–44 B.C.

The destruction of Corinth and Carthage in 146 B.C. inaugurated a new era in Rome's imperial expansion. It was time to adjust perceptions to reality, to consolidate and organize. The major battles had been won, for now, and in the second half of the second century there was hardly any temple-building to commemorate triumphs. Instead, the city's needs were practical: for a better supply of water and food, and for a relaxing of the tensions between aristocrats and proletarians, between Romans and Italians. Out of these needs arose a series of powerful individuals—Sulla, Pompey, Caesar—who dominated the political scene completely. An important part of the dominance of each was his urban building program; all three built on a scale without precedent since the Tarquins' temple on the Capitoline, on a scale made possible by bold technical inventiveness that matched the security of the empire the Romans found themselves ruling.

One of the first needs to be addressed was the water supply. In 144 B.C. a new aqueduct, the Aqua Marcia, was started by the praetor Quintus Marcius Rex.[1] The spoils of Corinth and Carthage paid for it, and the skill gained in building roads and bridges provided the engineering sophistication. It was a much bigger project than Rome's two earlier aqueducts, bringing water twice the distance, through underground channel and on stone arches, to the Viminal, then to the Caelian, Aventine, Palatine, and Capitoline (Fig. 11). The branch to the Capitoline was controversial because Marcius's opponents found a text in the *Sibylline Books* that forbade water on that sacred hill of Saturn and Jupiter. It was one more example of the tension between traditionalist sentiment and the forces of change, and as so often was the case, the need to accommodate the city to the needs of its modern condition prevailed. At about the same time, the same engineers closed in the sewer of the Cloaca Maxima with vaults of tufa. In 125 B.C. the Aqua Tepula was added to supplement the Marcia, thereby documenting for us an increased demand for water, the result of more people, more public fountains, and a heightened standard of living.

Not all the city's residents shared this improved standard of living, however. Many Roman citizens, including veterans of the wars, had lost their farms and crowded into Rome. This problem was confronted by the Gracchi—Tiberius Sempronius Gracchus, tribune in 133, and his brother Gaius, tribune in 123 and 122. In an eloquent speech, Tiberius described how "the wild beasts roam through Italy and each one has his den, his lair, his refuge; but the men who fight and die on behalf of Italy . . . wander about, homeless and houseless, with their wives and children. . . . Lacking a family altar or burial plot, they fight and die so that others can enjoy wealth and luxury" (Plutarch, *Tiberius Gracchus* 9.5). Many of these homeless Romans (and, in the same way, citizens of other Italian municipalities who had served as auxiliary troops in Rome's wars) must have wound up in the city. The program of the Gracchi offered relief to the urban proletariat, by introducing the redistribution of state-owned land to these poor citizens. Gaius also proposed a system of grain distribution to the citizens at a subsidized price, and he built roads to transport the grain to Rome and granaries to store it in once it got there.

But an improved system of water and grain did not solve all the problems. Indeed, it compounded them as even more people, both poor Romans from the country and footloose Italians, found city life more comfortable. The demand may have stimulated a building boom, especially in tenement housing.[2] Gaius Marius overturned tradition in the last decade of the second century when he recruited landless city dwellers for his armies,[3] offering them a chance to see the world and be settled on farms after the wars. What actually happened, however, was that many of them returned to Rome, feeling a new sense of power, along with non-Roman Italians who had fought in the auxiliary troops. In 95 an attempt was made to send such Italians back to their hometowns. When the Senate refused to acknowledge the contributions of the Italian allies to Rome's prosperity, the "Social War" broke out, a revolt that lasted from 93 to 89 B.C., eventually being resolved by the grant of citizenship and equal status to the Latins. This encouraged even more Italians to converge on Rome.

A recurring problem for the urban population was the warfare that was waged by members of the senatorial order. Single individuals with large armies of veterans battled throughout Italy, including the streets of Rome, in a bloody civil war. This began with the assassination of Tiberius Gracchus, and flared up again in the 80s between the forces of Marius, who gained power through the successes of his proletarian army, and the forces of Lucius Cornelius Sulla, who as dictator from 81 to 79 B.C. had thousands of opponents murdered. Sulla also introduced a new constitution, which placed power firmly in the hands of the Senate. The power struggle continued in the following generation, dominated by Gnaeus Pompeius Magnus, "Pompey the Great," who for most of his career was considered a champion of the established senatorial order, and by Gaius Julius Caesar, whose spectacular rise involved an armed march on Rome and a disregard for many of the niceties of republican forms.

The growth of empire had other repercussions in the population and appearance of Rome, for it created vast new opportunities for making money—importing grain and luxury goods, slave trading, real estate speculation, and tax contracting. A whole new class of businessmen, *negotiatores,* came into being to take advantage of these opportunities. They were symptomatic of the immense wealth and luxury that flowed into Rome in the century following the destruction of Corinth and Carthage. They were trend setters who accelerated the fashion for Greek luxury goods (Cicero, *Orator* 232), spending money on interior decoration (Pliny, *Natural*

History 36.48–50), portrait sculpture, and even privately constructed temples, in thanksgiving not for military victories but for
personal safety or for making a killing in business enterprises
(Macrobius, *Saturnalia* 3.6.11).

Architecture responded to the impact of Greek culture. At least
one temple was a pure Greek import, the round temple that still
stands in the Forum Boarium (Fig. 3). Its architect rejected Italic
frontality: Greek marble formed the temple's cella and surrounding
colonnade of graceful Corinthian columns, which could be approached from all sides.[4] Two temples in the Forum Romanum,
however, rejected Greek forms altogether. Concordia, rebuilt in 121
to celebrate the Senate's victory over Gaius Gracchus, and Castor,
rebuilt in 117 by Lucius Caecilius Metellus, were traditional in
plans and building materials (Fig. 8). Other architects combined
the two traditions in various ways. At the Largo Argentina, for instance, a Greek peristyle was added to the Italic cella of Temple A
(Fig. 4). Next to it, Temple B was built. Its circle of Corinthian columns was Greek, but a flight of steps in line with those of the adjacent temples imposed a strong Italic axis. The Roman architect who
designed Marius's Temple of Honos et Virtus in 101 took another
approach: Vitruvius (3.2.5; 7.praef.17) tells us that he used a traditional plan and materials, but decorated it in graceful accordance
with Greek aesthetic principles.[5]

Sulla

The bloody but effective ascendancy of Lucius Cornelius Sulla in
the late 80s and early 70s B.C. emphatically reaffirmed the political
dominance of the Senate and brought a new, peculiarly Roman architectural synthesis to the city. During the republic, we have seen
that a common type of urban architecture was the public building
erected by a senatorial general to celebrate a triumph and put his
and his family's name before the people. This tradition continued
under Sulla and his associate Quintus Lutatius Catulus, but on a
much grander scale and with a much more pervasive ideological
content. Sulla's building reflected his role as a great man (at the
time, the One Great Man in Roman politics), his global experience

of traveling on campaign in the Greek East, and his achievement of total victory over his rivals.

Most notable were two buildings on the Capitoline (Pl. 9), a new Temple of Iuppiter Optimus Maximus erected after a fire in 83 B.C., and a new record office, the Tabularium, in the saddle where Romulus's asylum had been. Viewed from the Forum Romanum or the hills to the east, the Tabularium with the columns, pediment, and gilded roof of the Temple of Iuppiter towering above it presented a spectacular façade to the Forum Romanum. It represented a new "aesthetic of size" in the repertory of Roman architecture, a lesson Sulla learned in the Greek East, where he had seen the immense hillside temple complexes at Cos and Lindus. The biggest temple he encountered was the still unfinished Temple of Zeus Olympius in Athens. After he conquered Athens (which had supported Mithridates against the Romans) he carried off that temple's marble columns and installed them in the new temple on the Capitoline. The temple retained its Etruscan plan and podium, but the Greek columns, so much richer and taller than the wooden Tuscan columns they replaced, made the temple loftier and much more imposing.[6] It announced to the world that the culture and material resources of Greece would henceforth, thanks to the military successes of Sulla, advertise and support the grandeur of Rome.[7]

In the Tabularium the blend of Italic and Greek themes on the façade also suggested the mastery of Rome over Greece. At the bottom there was simple ashlar masonry of local tufa. Above, two stories of tall, vaulted arcades looked out on the Forum Romanum. They were perhaps inspired by the arches of the Aqua Marcia, and in a masterpiece of architectural innovation each arch was framed by a pair of engaged Greek half-columns—sturdy Tuscan-Doric on the lower story, light Ionic on the upper. This eloquent synthesis of Greek and Roman elements would serve as a trademark on the façades of public buildings in Rome and its empire for centuries to come.[8]

In the Forum Romanum below, the ground level was raised nearly a meter, and a showy pavement of marble was laid down. Shrines in the middle of the Forum were rearranged, and the borders of the space were regularized. Along the northern side, the

Curia was rebuilt. Years later, Cicero would venture a critical comment on its architecture—it was too tall, he said, and ill proportioned (*De Finibus* 5.2).[9] Its location bespoke Sulla's restoration of rights and powers to the traditional aristocracy, for it stood next to the Temple of Concordia (another monument to a senatorial political victory) and dominated the Forum and the Comitium, where the popular assembly met.

This grand display at the northern end of the Forum Romanum and on the adjacent slope of the Capitoline was more than a museum exhibit. Its scale suggests that it was intended to be a museum in itself. The Sullan constructions did not yet show an attempt to reshape the entire city, but they reshaped the city's monumental center so successfully that they constituted a major step in that direction.

Pompey

When Gnaeus Pompeius Magnus returned to Rome in 61 B.C., he celebrated his victories and political settlement of the eastern provinces with a magnificent triumph. In the tradition of triumphant generals, he also inaugurated a building project, which in size and glamour rivaled that of Sulla. The project, completed in 55 B.C., consisted of a permanent stone theater—Rome's first—and a large enclosed public garden—also Rome's first—located in the lower Campus Martius just beyond (to the west of) the four temples of the Largo Argentina (Fig. 4). Pompey was a complicated man whose policies vacillated greatly during his career. He could be decisive and innovative as a general, but tended to be timid and malleable in his political actions, often veiling his opinions in a murky rhetoric and amiable expression that made it hard to divine his real thoughts.

The Theatrum Pompei shows some of this same ambiguity.[10] It followed Sulla in its magnificent scale and adventuresome combination of Roman and Greek features, but it also revealed a timid respect for traditional scruples. No one had ever before been permitted to build a permanent theater in Rome; it was considered a decadent luxury. To meet the scruple, a Temple of Venus Victrix was built at the center of the top row of seats; the vast seating space thus served as a glorified staircase to the temple, in the manner of earlier Italian temples with semicircular theatrical areas in front (Plutarch, *Pompey* 42.4, 52.4; Aulus Gellius 10.1.7). The shape of the *cavea,* or seating area, was inspired by the Dionysiac theaters of Greece, but Greek theaters were placed on hillsides to utilize the natural slope. There was no such natural slope on the Campus Martius, so Pompey used good Roman concrete and the technology of the arch, which had produced the Porticus Aemilia and the Tabularium: an artificial hill of concrete vaulted passageways was erected to support the semicircular rows of seats. Today nothing remains of the exterior, but it was probably decorated with the arch and column motif introduced in the Tabularium.

Between the theater and the temples of the Largo Argentina lay the vast enclosed green space known as the Porticus Pompei, "Pompey's Porch." It contained trees, fountains, meeting rooms, and statues (Propertius 2.32.11–16)—the features of a public park in a Hellenistic city.

The complex of theater and portico added a new monumental focus to the Campus Martius. It introduced the Hellenistic topiary garden (the likes of which the rich had been enjoying in their homes for the past century) to the Roman public. It also put Pompey's name and accomplishments before the public, both literally in the dedicatory inscription and symbolically in its synthesis of Greek structures and Roman materials. Pompey had imposed a rational administrative plan on the Greek lands of the Near East, and here on the Campus Martius he presented to the city of Rome a Greek theater and a garden that was tamed, framed, and domesticated by Roman know-how to the needs of a particular site and the leisure of the Roman people. The complex was also significant in the subsequent history of Roman public architecture, for it introduced a strong emphasis on regular enclosed spaces, confining large expanses of ostensibly open country within vaulted walls and Greek colonnades. This trend can be seen in contemporary interior decoration as well: the "Second Style" of wall painting enclosed a Hellenistic landscape within an architectural frame.

Caesar

Pompey's rival, sometime collaborator, and eventual conqueror was Gaius Julius Caesar, whose achievements and ambitions have become the stuff of poetry. His career combined astute politics with brilliant military skill and the willingness to be revolutionary, whether by crossing the Rubicon with his army in defiance of the Senate and tradition, or by boldly revising the calendar, or—for the first time in Rome's history—by developing a master plan for the city.

In the 50s, when Caesar was in Gaul, he kept his name before the Roman public through dispatches to the home front concerning the "Gallic Wars," and also by means of a building program designed to monumentalize a new part of the Campus Martius and Forum Romanum along the end of the Via Flaminia by which a traveler from northern Italy or Gaul would enter the heart of Rome. The lower Campus Martius, from the river to the Via Flaminia, had filled up with monuments, as we have seen, and also with the less prepossessing shanties of the poor (Varro, *On Agriculture* 3.2.6). But north of the Largo Argentina and the Theater of Pompey the area was still a fairly open space for exercise and military drills; its only major structure was the Ovile, "Sheepfold," a simple enclosure where the citizens voted. Caesar planned to emphasize his devotion to the people by rebuilding the enclosure—thenceforth to be known as the Saepta Iulia—with marble colonnades a full mile long. In addition, he was already buying up property below the Capitoline, just outside the Forum Romanum, on which to construct a new unroofed but enclosed area that would extend the usable space of the Forum in the complex known as the Forum Iulium. His agent in Rome was none other than the orator Cicero, who described the plans in a letter written in July 54 B.C. (*Letters to Atticus* 4.16.8).

In the next decade, as Caesar became more and more surely the single most important person in the republic, his plans for the capital city of its empire became even more ambitious. In 45 B.C. we hear of a plan to divert the course of the Tiber westward in order to double the size of the Campus Martius (Cicero, *Letters to Atticus*

13.33a).[11] At the lower end of the Campus Martius, next to the Forum Holitorium, Caesar planned to build a theater to rival that of Pompey (Dio Cassius, *Roman History* 43.49). He also planned a great temple of Mars, and Rome's first public library (Suetonius, *Julius Caesar* 44).

The most significant element in his plans was the Forum Iulium (Fig. 10). This complex overwhelmed Sulla's organization of the west end of the Forum Romanum and marked the first appearance in Rome of an important kind of architectural complex: the Temple of Venus Genetrix (Pl. 12A) was placed at the rear of a sacred area bordered on three sides by colonnades, with shops, and arcades (Appian, *Civil Wars* 2.102). In one sense this was a perfectly typical late republican temple precinct, but in another it was an important innovation. Venus, after all, was supposed to be the progenitress of the *gens Iulia,* and hence the divine ancestor of Julius Caesar. The whole complex was in effect a temple to the Julian family, and the architectural shape may even derive, iconographically, from shrines in the Hellenistic world dedicated to the worship of kings and queens.[12]

Adjacent to this Forum Iulium, a new Senate House, the Curia Iulia, was built. Sulla's Curia had burned in the civil disturbances of 52 B.C., and the new forum encroached on its location. Caesar's Curia was no longer a focal point; instead, it was tucked away as an appendage to the Forum Iulium, a remarkably blunt reflection of the political realities in 45 B.C. (Fig. 9). The Rostra, where speakers stood to address the people, also were moved. Now no longer subordinated to the Curia, they were placed on the central axis of the Forum Romanum.

A final project was the Basilica Iulia along the southern side of the Forum Romanum. It faced the Forum with the arch and column motif borrowed from the Tabularium, and joined with the Forum Iulium in proclaiming the prestige of the man whose name it bore.

Beyond the physical shape of the city, Julius Caesar also revised the laws pertaining to its administration. He did not live to complete this legislation, but after his death it was collated by Mark Antony and passed by the Senate. With Caesar, we have reached a new stage in the conception of urban planning in Rome: the old practice of juxtaposing monuments of increasing grandeur like random bits of a collage has given way to a sense of the city as a unity.[13] Sulla may have been moving toward this idea; Caesar surely was. Neither lived long enough to realize any such plans, however. That was the job of Caesar's heir.

The City in Republican Literature

In the building programs of Sulla, Pompey, and Caesar we have witnessed different attempts to develop a new urban aesthetic synthesis setting the standards for classical Roman architecture. Four representative writers of the first century B.C. were engaged in similar attempts to develop forms and content that would set the standards for classical Roman literature. In their subject matter, too, these writers reflect individual but compatible perspectives on the city Rome had become.

Marcus Tullius Cicero, an active participant in and interested observer of the late republic, left so many writings that a rich and complicated picture emerges of the city he knew. Cicero was a politician from the country town of Arpinum who came to Rome and rose to the consulship, an orator who articulated a vision of social and political cooperation and set a standard for Latin rhetoric adapted from the Greek, a writer who exercised a formative influence on the vocabulary and grammar of the Latin language, a philosophical journalist who interpreted Greek philosophy to Roman readers, and a correspondent whose letters give us a vivacious account of everyday life in the city. That city, to Cicero, was a city still under construction, where it was important to live in the right neighborhood and be seen with the right people. His city was all animation, a stage for the high drama of politics and the heartbreaking spectacle of gang warfare. He was a country boy, and he shared the conventional Roman fondness for the country. Whenever possible he retired to one or another of his many rustic villas, but was always eager to get back to the political action in the city Romulus had founded under the heady breath of divine inspiration (*De Republica* 2.10). He could criticize Pompey for staging games that were too elaborate (*Letters to His Friends* 7.1), and he could complain about the smelly, lousy dregs of the urban mob (*Letters to Atticus* 1.16.11; *Letters to Quintus* 2.4.5), but he could also cooperate enthusiastically with Caesar's plans for the Forum Iulium (*Letters to Atticus* 4.16.8) and complain bitterly whenever he was forced, by exile or government duty abroad, to be absent from the only city that mattered.[14]

Marcus Terentius Varro was, like Cicero, from an Italian country town (Reate, in the Sabine hills), an intellectual, and a political conservative. Of the 620 books he wrote, we have only 6 *On the Latin Language,* 3 *On Agriculture,* and a handful of much shorter fragments. He preferred the old ways, the traditional values that he associated with Pompey. When Caesar defeated the Pompeians, he twice pardoned Varro and eventually put him to work at the ideal job for an academic, that of chief librarian. Varro was the complete antiquarian, and this colored his view of the city of Rome. He loved to report the old ways of doing things, and he contrasted them explicitly or implicitly with contemporary society, which he painted in horrific colors. Contemporary Romans had sold their birthright for a mess of circuses and theaters, and the streets were so unsafe that a minor official running an errand for a magistrate was casually killed in broad daylight by a mugger (Varro, *On Agriculture* 1.2.2, 1.69). The traditions of country life were safer, more noble than city life, and ineluctably rooted in Roman institutions and vocabulary. Varro thus took up Cato's refrain about the moral superiority of the old Roman rural life, which would become commonplace in the literature of the Augustan Age.[15]

Gaius Valerius Catullus, from a well-off provincial family of Sirmio, in Cisalpine Gaul, exhibited considerably more gusto for the life of Rome. His experience with the political life that so excited Cicero and dismayed Varro was, as far as we know, limited to a tour of duty in Bithynia. This was not a very happy experience, and Catullus's occasional references to the world of politics are offhand and vaguely contemptuous, made in the vocabulary and style of the pasquinade or street-corner graffito (49, 52, 57). For the most part his poems express a highly personal view, but when we do see the world around him, it tends to be an urban world, full of both poverty (13, 23) and luxury (64.43–52). Catullus takes us into the *dolce vita* of literary figures vibrating with creative excitement and judgmental criticism; of aristocratic ladies more liberated than any of their ancestors; and of a bevy of women and men bringing a decidedly demimondaine ambiance to the squares and back alleys of the city (10, 37, 55, 56, 58).[16]

We do not have much independent information about Titus Lucretius Carus, but there are enough sketches in the epic sweep of his *De Rerum Natura* to reveal a widely focused perception of the life of Rome. Lucretius was well acquainted with the luxurious mansions of the rich (2.24–28; 4.304–307, 400–403), and also with the workshops of carpenters and goldsmiths (2.196–200; 4.296–299, 513–519). The landmarks were the theaters and the Circus, and his city was a crowded place, full of color and of colorful people (2.618–623; 4.75–80, 528–532).[17]

Four

The Augustan City

Gaius Octavius, as Caesar's adopted son and heir, took the name Gaius Julius Caesar Octavianus (Octavian) and joined with Marcus Antonius (Mark Antony) and Marcus Aemilius Lepidus to become the *triumviri rei publicae constituendae,* "commission of three to manage the republic," in 43 B.C. This title, bestowed by the Senate, gave some legal status to the three, who purged Rome of their personal and political enemies in proscriptions even more vicious than those of Marius and Sulla, and who then waged war on the republican senators who had assassinated Caesar. After the republicans were defeated at Philippi in 42 B.C., and Lepidus lapsed into insignificance, Octavian and Antony confronted each other. Antony received the eastern half of the empire, and under the influence of local custom and his involvement with Cleopatra of Egypt, his rule had the mark of Hellenistic royalty. Octavian administered the western half of the empire, including Italy, and when he eventually defeated Antony and Cleopatra at Actium in 31 B.C., he became the undisputed ruler of the Roman world. He is known to history as "Augustus," the title he received from the Senate in 27 B.C. Until his death, in A.D. 14, he guided the empire and the city from the chaos of 100 years of civil war to peace and order.[1]

Goals and Methods

Peace and order were the watchwords of the new regime. Peace was restored at home as Octavian's forces gradually subdued the opposition within the empire. Peace was still to be won on the borders of the empire, threatened especially by Parthians on the east and Germans on the north. Order would be difficult to impose after the turmoil of the past century. In the 20s Octavian/Augustus needed to root out political opposition, or threaten it into silence, or cajole it into cooperation. He needed to devise an effective administration both for the provinces of the empire and for its capital city, and to reconcile all segments of the state to the new political realities. Toward the goals of political stability, military efficiency, and moral reliability, Augustus mobilized a formidable public-relations machine. The message was a vision of Rome's past, a myth to reassure all about the transcendent greatness of Rome, and an image of Augustus himself as bringer of peace and prosperity. The means were Hellenic form to express Italic content, republican form to express autocratic content.[2]

Rome itself, as head and center of the empire, had a special role to play. Archaeological renovations like the Casa Romuli, refurbished public buildings like the Regia and Basilica Aemilia, and an elaborate sculptural and epigraphic program advertised the continuity of republican urban tradition under Augustus. The city had to look the part of an imperial capital, and set a standard of urban beauty consonant with its political importance, proclaiming the greatness and beneficence of the *princeps,* the "first man" of the state.

Three famous sayings of Augustus help us understand his approach to implementing these goals. The first, "Make haste slowly" (Suetonius, *Augustus* 25.4), reveals a sense of urgency to do what has to be done, but to do so in a careful manner informed by a deliberate seriousness of purpose. More subtly, "Make haste slowly" reminds us that Augustus had plenty of time not only to develop a coordinated plan that would put his distinctive mark on the city of Rome but also to carry out that plan.[3] As political opposition was eliminated between 43 and 20 B.C., Augustus became more secure in his position. Unlike his republican predecessors, he did not have to use his building program to score short-term propaganda gains.

In the first ten years after Caesar's assassination, building policy proceeded by fits and starts as Octavian and the other triumvirs felt their way. They completed Caesar's most practical projects—the Forum Iulium, the Basilica Iulia, and the Saepta Iulia—and dropped others—the deviation of the Tiber and the large theater for which Caesar had torn down the temple of Pietas—either out of respect for republican opposition or because the projects were too expensive. Temples in honor of Caesar and in thanksgiving for his murderers' punishment were vowed and begun: the deified Iulius in the Forum Romanum and the Mars Ultor (Avenger) next to the Forum Iulium. Throughout the 30s, partisans of Antony and partisans of Octavian used construction in Rome in time-honored ways: to establish the legitimacy of their claims to power and prestige, and to win the loyalty of the citizens.

Once Antony was isolated in the east and eventually defeated at Actium, there was time to proceed more systematically, and to show discreet respect for the traditions of the republic, with the confidence that everything would eventually redound to the glory of the princeps. This policy became clear around 33 B.C., when Agrippa was aedile and attended to the water supply. Then Octavian began in his own name to donate to the city memorials of his triumphs in the civil wars: the Forum Augustum, the Porticus Octaviae, the Temple of Apollo Palatinus, and the Arcus Augusti. In 29 B.C., with Antony dead and Lepidus out of the way, Octavian dedicated three projects that all the triumvirs had begun in the Forum Romanum (Fig. 9): the Temple of the Deified Iulius (next to Octavian's own triumphal arch) and the Curia and Chalcidicum (next to the Forum Iulium). The next year, he restored eighty-two temples that had fallen into disrepair. This demonstrated his piety to the gods and his loyalty to the republic, and it is a good indication of the scope of his program at this stage. Octavian was involved all over town, attending to the neglected business of the republic before beginning any ambitious new projects.

Once the principate was firmly established, Augustus was more systematic in using his buildings to support the official line that the republic was being restored. In the Forum Romanum, where earlier a triumphal arch had commemorated his personal victory over Antony, a new, triple-spanned one was erected, containing a list of all those who had served as consuls and those who had won triumphs on behalf of the state. The Forum Augustum took on richer symbolism than the mere punishment of Caesar's murderers. The paradox of "making haste slowly" demonstrates the way Augustus accepted and exploited the tensions he inherited—those between tradition and innovation, between the claims of the past and the need to accommodate the present and anticipate the future.

Another famous saying, "I found the city made of brick and left it made of marble" (Suetonius, *Augustus* 28.3), crystallizes the program to make Rome look the part of world capital, exploiting a new supply of bright white marble from the quarries at Luna (Carrara), near Pisa, and colored marbles from Africa. Some buildings that were supposed to be particularly impressive—for example, the Temple of Apollo Palatinus, the Temple of Iuppiter Tonans, and the Ara Pacis—had walls of solid marble, but generally marble was used for decoration (pavements, veneers, columns, friezes, and inscriptions).[4] The actual fabric of the buildings was still for the most part local stone (tufa and travertine) and concrete, to which marble revetment gave an aura of Greek respectability. This façade also covered a multitude of city-planning sins, sins of omission at any rate. Throughout the city one could find, just around the corner from the Augustan monuments of public grandeur, vacant lots and ramshackle tenements signifying private squalor.[5]

The Augustan fascination with façades and their value for public relations is expressed even more clearly in the words supposedly spoken by Augustus on his death bed: "How does it look? Have I performed the comic opera of life properly?" (Suetonius, *Augustus* 99.1). These words highlight the need to keep up appearances, to make everything—from details of architecture to the public personality of the emperor—look right. Julius Caesar also had been aware of the importance of appearances—his wife, after all, had to be above suspicion. Yet the façade Caesar presented was revolutionary, boldly innovative. Augustus and his policy demanded a different public face. While insuring order through a stable administration and an autocratic dynastic succession, he based his authority in the institutions of the republic and presented to the people the image of the wise, tolerant, moral leader who was dutiful to the gods of the state and to the old-time virtues. He appeared as the *paterfamilias* of a devoted, loyal family, and he aimed to win the adherence of the whole mass of society. To the Senate, he returned most of the prerogatives that had been threatened during the confusion of the civil wars: the Senate retained the old *cursus honorum* and other status symbols, and kept control over the more tranquil provinces. To the order of wealthy businessmen known as the equestrians he restored many privileges, and added new responsibilities in the army and the administrative bureaucracy. The political role of the common people also was preserved, for they continued to vote in the elections, and Augustus voted along with them.

Augustus utilized the traditional social institution of patronage as well, but did so on a new scale. During the late republic the momentum of the patron-client relationship had changed dramatically, with only a handful of very powerful patrons controlling vast groups of political clients. Now Augustus became in effect the sole patron of the whole empire. He was patron of the senatorial order because he had the power of censorship in determining the membership of the Senate, and he was patron of the individual senators, whom he helped with political support and gifts. He was also the patron of individual equestrians, of the rich freedmen who were appointed to the priestly colleges of the Augustales, and of the common people as well, for his tribunician power put him in the legal position of being the one who looked after the people's interests. He distributed money to the urban population, sponsored games, and settled his soldiers in colonies—three tried and true republican methods of building a following of clients.

The ideology of the restored republic and the autocratic dominance of Augustus were reconciled by portraying him as the restorer of the old ways, as princeps, and as the bringer of peace.[6] The means that conveyed the message had all been used by republican politicans at one time or another. What was new was the thorough-

ness of the Augustan campaign. Poetry, history, and theatrical exhibitions addressed the intelligentsia. Religious celebrations, triumphal processions, gladiatorial shows, and circus races reached
the masses. Coins proclaimed the Augustan peace and the restored
republic. Sculpture and architecture were permanent reminders to
the urban populace—in Rome and most cities throughout the empire—of the Augustan synthesis of old and new.

Contradiction and Synthesis in Augustan Urbanism

The moral dimension of Augustus's campaign to conjure up a restored republic was symbolized by his cultivation of traditional religious rites, many of which had long since lapsed, and his legislation to encourage more stable marriages and larger families among
Roman citizens, particularly the aristocracy. Much attention was
paid to encouraging respect for the *mos maiorum,* "the way our ancestors did things." The architectural counterpart was the respect
shown to old shrines, and the combination of Italic and Greek elements. A Roman-Greek tension had been noticeable in past centuries, but in Augustan Rome it reached a resolution, a classical
formulation, in architecture and sculpture as well as in literature.

The "Greek" and "Italic" strands were spun into a single thread, a
classic Roman synthesis, with a heavy emphasis on appearance,
form, and façade. The Greek inspiration was adopted and naturalized, as surely as Greece and the Hellenistic world had become
fully integrated parts of the Roman world, and as surely as Evander,
a refugee from Greek myth, was turned into a naturalized Italian in
Vergil's *Aeneid.*

The Mausoleum of Augustus (Pl. 8) illustrates the point. Modern
scholarship has been unable to state clearly whether it is derived
from Etruscan family tombs at Cerveteri or from Hellenistic royal
tombs; it suggests both, of course, affirming not only the pure Italic
nature of the Augustan policy but also the saving permanence of
the Julian dynasty.[7]

Ever since the founding of Rome, the Greeks had been the intellectual and artistic *maiores* ("ancestors") of the Romans. Thus, to
use Greek columns and moldings was simply to respect the tradi-

tional *mos maiorum*. Whereas Sulla, Pompey, and Caesar had favored Hellenistic fashions, the sort of thing that was being done in the contemporary Greek world, the Augustan architects and sculptors favored the "Neo-Attic" style, derived from the high classical art of Athens in the fifth century B.C.[8]

Three examples demonstrate how the synthesis of Greek and Italic elements produced a complex expression of Augustan policy—political, moral, and artistic. The three illustrative monuments are those singled out by Suetonius (*Augustus* 29) as the outstanding architectural works of the reign: the Forum Augustum, with its Temple of Mars; the Temple of Apollo Palatinus; and the Temple of Iuppiter Tonans.

The Forum Augustum was central to the building program, both in its location and in its bulk (Fig. 10; Pl. 3). Vowed during the battle of Philippi in 42 B.C. and begun five years later to celebrate the victory over Caesar's assassins, the Forum was dedicated in 2 B.C., by which time it had assumed a complex symbolic content that transcended the military gains of Octavian's youth. Its scale and design, and the military victory it commemorated, were all very bold, as was the amount of space it occupied, mostly on Octavian's own land. Yet in counterpoint to this boldness, we hear that Augustus modified the plan of his forum somewhat in order to respect the wishes of the owners of abutting property (Suetonius, *Augustus* 56.2), a typical gesture of deferential discretion.

The basic shape of the Forum Augustum imitated that of the adjacent Forum Iulium: an enclosed Italic piazza dominated by a temple, with the temple placed axially on a tall podium at one end, yet with the whole influenced vaguely by intimations of Hellenistic ruler cult. Where Caesar had used concrete vaulting in the Forum Iulium, the Augustan architects preferred a Greek post-and-lintel colonnade crowned with an order of classicizing caryatids. One architectural innovation was the pair of hemicycles set behind the colonnades (perhaps derived from Greek exedrae, and certainly suggesting a paternalistic, embracing gesture), a motif later adapted by Trajan in his forum and eventually by Bernini in the great piazza in front of Saint Peter's in the Vatican.

Within the architectural frame, the sculptural scheme expressed—and reconciled—the contradictions between republican façade and dynastic realities. The Forum's temple was dedicated to Mars, the most authentically Roman of all the gods, patron of agriculture and war, father of Romulus and Remus. As Mars Ultor, however, he was the avenger of the murderers of Julius Caesar, Augustus's adopted father. In Greek myth Mars was also the mate of Aphrodite/Venus, the mother of Aeneas, the divine ancestor of the Julian *gens*. In niches along the hemicycles and colonnades on each side of the Forum stood 108 statues: along the left as one faced the temple were the *triumphatores,* the heroes of Rome's past, each with an inscription recording his exploits on behalf of the republic. On the other side was a parallel collection of the men of the Julian gens, starting with Aeneas himself (Suetonius, *Augustus* 31.5). Both series culminated in a large statue of the princeps, standing in the center of the Forum, receiving visitors.[9]

The Forum was very large, but the immense temple (one of the few temples in the city at the time large enough to have, like the Parthenon in Athens, eight columns across the front), the tall flanking colonnades, and the high fire wall must have created a paradoxical sense of intimacy in the enclosed space. It was perhaps like the atrium of a great private house, in which the *paterfamilias* received his clients. Here, in the presence of images of his ancestors, Augustus (who received the title *pater patriae,* "father of the fatherland," in the same year the Forum Augustum was dedicated) received foreign princes and administered the oath of obedience; here the Senate deliberated about war, governors were sent out to their provinces, military trophies were displayed, the priestly confraternities celebrated festivals, and young Romans assumed the toga of manhood. Like any tasteful atrium of a prosperous family of the time, it was decorated not only with the images of ancestors but also with reminders of military and political successes and with art objects imported from the Greek East.[10] The Forum Augustum functioned as the official reception room of city and empire, integrating the traditions of the Julian family with those of the republic.

Whereas the Forum Augustum reconciled the republic with the principate, the temple of Apollo Palatinus (Fig. 5) helps us appreciate Augustus's synthesis of the heritage of Italy with that of Greece.

Like the temple of Mars Ultor, this temple was vowed during the wars against the republicans between 38 and 36 B.C., but only after the victory at Actium in 31 B.C. did it become a major project. Apollo had a shrine at Actium, and in presiding over the defeat of Antony in those Greek waters he had established a special relationship with Octavian. That special relationship was emphasized by the location of the temple, next door to the princeps' house, and by its chronological primacy, for in 28 B.C. it was the first new temple dedicated by Octavian in his own name. Apollo was a patron of the arts, and the precinct had two libraries, one Greek and one Latin. In contrast to the Forum Augustum, which was decorated with statues of warriors, these libraries were decorated with busts of poets and orators, and with museum pieces of classical Greek art. If the Forum Augustum functioned as the atrium of the Augustan state, the precinct of Apollo suggested the more homey atmosphere of an interior peristyle, where friends were entertained amid more personal treasures. As in so many Roman houses of the period, and as in so much of Augustan propaganda, the treasures were borrowed from the Greeks but were put to thoroughly Roman use.[11]

The third example, the temple of Iuppiter Tonans on the Capitoline (Pl. 9), illustrates another contradiction, the tendency of the Augustan order to supplant and obscure the very traditions it was ostensibly preserving. The temple was a personal monument, vowed in 26 B.C. during a campaign in Spain, to thank Jupiter for saving Augustus from a lightning bolt. Dedicated in 22 B.C., it was a small monument, but it must have been a jewel: its walls were of solid marble, its statues by classical Greek sculptors. It was so graceful that it detracted from the larger-scale beauty of the great temple of Iuppiter Capitolinus, and Suetonius (*Augustus* 91) reports a dream of Augustus in which Jupiter complained that the new temple was stealing his worshipers. In response, and to proclaim his deference, Augustus installed a set of bells on the little temple, to show that his Iuppiter Tonans was nothing more than the *ianitor,* the doorkeeper, of the great temple on top of the hill. In this instance the tension was resolved through a trivial gesture of compromise, but that gesture reflects realistically both the profound spirit of accommodation that animated the Augustan restoration and the style of many of its methods, superficial but effective.[12]

The Augustan Building Program

If we were to follow a contemporary observer like Strabo, Horace, or Ovid through the streets and squares of Rome, we would see a distinctively Augustan stamp on the façade of the city. With all the marble and travertine the city looked whiter, and perhaps— thanks to the urban legislation of Caesar and Augustus and to a more efficient bureaucracy—it even looked cleaner. Access to the city was easier and more impressive. The roads had been improved, and at the two main entrances to the city, altars had been erected as reminders of Augustus's authority and the gods' grace.[13] On the Esquiline, the Porticus Liviae and the Macellum Liviae provided open, colonnaded spaces for lounging and shopping. Augustus's friend Maecenas had bought up a large plot of ground on the Esquiline just outside the walls (formerly a pauper's cemetery), and had turned it into a public park.[14] New buildings were being constructed and old ones refurbished throughout the city, but the major building projects of the regime were concentrated in the monumental center: in the Campus Martius, the Forum Romanum, and the Palatine.

The Campus Martius had changed more than any other region (Pl. 8, foreground). When visitors approached the city from the north, they encountered, on the right, the crematorium (*ustrinum*) and, beyond it along the river, the Mausoleum of Augustus, surrounded by gardens and cypress trees. Farther along the road, again on the right, a visitor could pause at the Ara Pacis Augustae, its sculptural scheme celebrating the blessings of peace brought to Italy by Augustus. Beyond it to the west, the Horologium Augusti was oriented to the Ara Pacis; the pointer of this immense sundial was an obelisk brought by the princeps from Egypt, conquered Cleopatra's realm.[15] Farther on to the south, a complex of new buildings was coordinated by Agrippa in a great burst of activity (Dio Cassius, *Roman History* 53.27.1–3). Along the east lay the

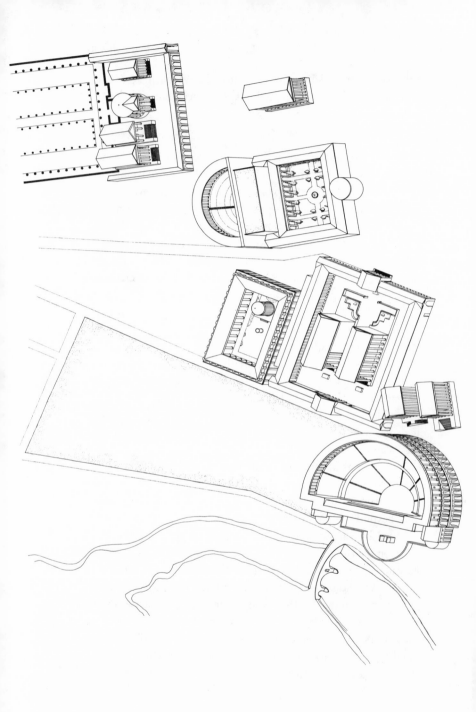

long marble enclosure, begun by Julius Caesar, of the Saepta. West of it, toward the northern end of the complex, Agrippa built the Pantheon, shrine to all the gods. The exact plan of its first stage is not well known, but nineteenth-century excavations suggested that it was a paved, round, unroofed space with an open colonnade. At the northern end, under the porch of Hadrian's Pantheon, there may have been a rectangular shrine, or entrance porch, on an axis that extended northward to the Mausoleum Augusti. To the south of the Pantheon extended a large public park with a lake (the Stagnum Agrippae), and the Thermae Agrippianae, Rome's first monumental public baths. Other facilities for relaxation were the Porticus Argonautarum, the rebuilt Theatrum Pompei, and the new wooden Amphitheatrum Statilii Tauri.[16]

The monumental zone at the lower end of the Campus Martius was the site of much activity, mostly in the name of persons outside the immediate circle of the princeps. Gaius Sosius completely rebuilt the Temple of Apollo in marble; Lucius Marcius Philippus rebuilt the Temple of Hercules Musarum and surrounded it with the Porticus Philippi; next to it Augustus replaced the Porticus Metelli with the new Porticus Octaviae in honor of his sister.[17] In addition to the repairs made to the Theatrum Pompei, the small Theatrum Balbi was dedicated in 13 B.C., and finally, after a decent interval, Caesar's plans for a large theater at the Forum Holitorium were revived, resulting in the Theatrum Marcelli.

The Forum Romanum had undergone considerable rearrangement at the western end because of Caesar's plans (Fig. 9). Augustus completed the Curia and the Forum Iulium, and enlarged the Basilica Iulia. New Rostra imposed a significant axial focus on the Forum, a reflection of contemporary taste and the relentless Augustan desire for orderliness. The rebuilt Temple of Saturnus

Fig. 4 (opposite). Rome: Southern Campus Martius, first century B.C. *Lower left:* Pons Fabricius, Theatrum Marcelli, Circus Flaminius (empty space beyond Theatrum Marcelli, to the west). *Center, bottom to top:* Temple of Bellona (?); Temple of Apollo; Temples of Iuppiter Stator and Iuno Regina, enclosed by Porticus Octaviae; Temple of Hercules Musarum, enclosed by Porticus Philippi; *Center right:* Crypta Balbi, Theatrum Balbi. *Far right, bottom to top:* Temple on the Via delle Botteghe Oscure (Temple of Bellona?); Area Sacra del Largo Argentina (*left to right* — Temples D, C, B, A); Porticus Pompei (plan).

and Temple of Concordia gave the northern end of the Forum the final monumental shape it was to retain for two centuries.[18] At the opposite end Augustus composed a monumental façade around the Temple of the Deified Iulius, celebrating three generations of the family of Augustus.

The Palatine, already an exclusive residential area, gained new prestige as Augustus's birthplace. After Caesar's assassination in 44 B.C., he (now Octavian) bought a house at the southwestern corner of the hill, near the site of the legendary Casa Romuli and near the temple of the Magna Mater, a goddess brought to Rome in 204 B.C. from Phrygia, the land of Troy and thus the home of Aeneas. By upper-class standards the house was modest (Suetonius, *Augustus* 72.1–2). It and an adjoining house known as the House of Livia have been excavated, and confirm the picture of a comfortable but unpretentious dwelling.[19] The luxurious temple of Apollo, just to the south, provided dramatic contrast to the studied residential simplicity of Augustus's house.

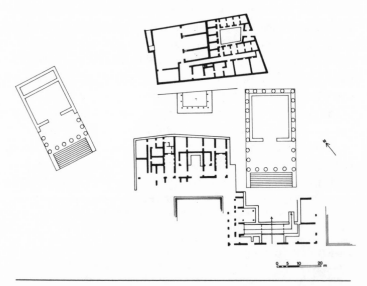

Fig. 5. Rome: House of Augustus and House of Livia. *Left:* Temple of Magna Mater. *Center top:* House of Livia. *Center bottom:* House of Augustus. *Right:* Temple of Apollo Palatinus.

The City in Augustan Literature

e writers of the period have given us eyewitness accounts of the
ıstan city, its monuments, and the people in its houses and
.[20] In one way or another, all these writers expressed a
ꞓristically Augustan view of the city in which they lived.
ꞓsented Rome within the timelessness of mythology—
was identified with Aeneas, his deeds were compared to
Ꞁorace, *Odes* 3.5.1–4). Even the events of everyday life
meless quality as contemporary writers compared their
ꞁith the liaisons of the great gods and heroes. An indig-
ꞁ mythology also was forged, wherein the Romans
ꞁestiny to organize and rule the world while holding
virtues that made Rome great. In their more "offi-
ꞁ writers of the period tended to look for origins, to
ꞓfit from the old ways of doing things.

...ꞁɛm with the physical restoration of archaic monuments
like the Casa Romuli on the Palatine and the Lacus Curtius, Lacus
Iugurthae, and Lapis Niger in the Forum Romanum, we find Livy,
Vergil, and Ovid (among others) digging up and dusting off curious
rites and ceremonies, interpreting them to their contemporary
world. They had a peculiarly Augustan sense of the past, one in
which all previous history, Greek as well as Italian, culminated in
the golden age ushered in by the princeps. This teleological view
was expressed not only in the statues and labels of great republicans in the Forum Augustum and in the list of consuls and triumphs on the Arcus Augusti, but also in the panoramic sweep of
Livy's history and in the parade of heroes on Aeneas's shield. The
writers of the day articulated the gratitude of the citizens for the
Augustan peace, but as individuals they reacted individually to the
party line of Augustan rectitude. Some shrank from the frenetic
pace of city life; others embraced it with gusto. As each of them
tried to cope with the demands of the regime on their talents, they
confronted a personal conflict between duty to Augustus's ideals
and freedom to follow their own inclinations.

Quintus Horatius Flaccus gives us the most complete picture, as
observer and participant in the official life of Augustus's city. Start-

ing as the son of a freedman in Venusia, Horace was brought by his father to Rome for an education. Eventually he was introduced to Maecenas, a close influential friend of Augustus's, under whose patronage Horace entered the very highest levels of Roman society. This upward mobility gave him a stake in the official values of the regime, and although he modestly declined to write verse on the epic scale, he proclaimed the virtues of a simple life-style and the glories of Augustus in peace and war. To do this he consciously used Greek material and meters, adapting them to the peculiar spirit of the Latin language in a manner closely parallel to the synthesis achieved by Augustus's architects. The city that Horace describes is a big, busy, crowded place, filled with annoying social obligations and material distractions:[21] adulterers (*Satires* 1.2); lechers, collectors of silver and bronze, salesmen, book shops, poets declaiming in Forum and baths (*Satires* 1.4); snobs and confidence men (*Satires* 1.6); witches (*Satires* 1.8); boring social climbers and unreliable acquaintances (Satires 1.9), tedious gourmets (*Satires* 2.4); inconvenient invitations to dinner (*Satires* 2.7.29–35; 2.8); and disastrous floods (*Odes* 1.2.13–20). Whenever possible, he resists all these vain blandishments in favor of an economical stroll for window-shopping in one of the porticoes (*Satires* 1.4.133–134), the Circus, or the Forum, or a simple meal at home (*Satires* 1.6.111–117), or a quiet reading of his poems to a few friends (*Satires* 1.4.73–74). His desire for simplicity was compatible with the goals of Augustan propaganda, and the villa that Maecenas gave him in the Sabine hills became the symbol of escape from the distractions of the city (*Satires* 1.6; *Epistles* 1.14). That, and his repeated refusals to write epic, show us an individual's attempt to interpret the urban world in a personal way, and eventually to escape to the morally tranquil life of the farm.

Publius Vergilius Maro came from a propertied family, part of the local aristocracy at Mantua in Cisalpine Gaul. His family's land had been confiscated to pay the veterans of the triumvirs in 41 B.C., and his earliest poems, the *Eclogues,* represent a rejection of the urban values and turmoil that led to the Civil Wars: the poems portray an innocent pastoral society, subject to buffeting by foreign forces but hopeful that a new golden age might dawn (*Eclogues* 4).

In the *Georgics,* published in 30 B.C., Vergil celebrated the virtuous life of the Italian countryside. Although this picture is less rosy than that in the *Eclogues,* Vergil's praise of the country suited a population that was decorating its town houses in the cities of Italy with "Second Style" paintings and reliefs of bucolic landscapes. His praise of rustic virtue was in keeping with the Augustan program, with its settlement of veterans in colonies and its encouragement of a traditional morality. Vergil's mature meditation on the Augustan achievement produced the *Aeneid,* in which a hero drawn from Greek mythology is, like Augustus himself, faced with similar problems and founding a new nation out of the ruins of a devastated city. Although the whole action of the epic leads to Rome, the physical site of Rome appears only briefly, in an episode in which the hero is guided around the Roman hills and valleys by Evander, as the poet points out how much things have changed, mixing pride in the urban accomplishments of his own age with nostalgia for the good old days of rustic simplicity (*Aeneid* 8.101–369). In several passages, the heroes of the republic pass in review as an honor guard for the culminating hero of Roman history, Augustus (*Aeneid* 6.756–846; 8.626–728). In terms of its political/historical perspective, the *Aeneid* is the literary counterpart of the Forum Augustum,[22] though it is richer than the architectural monument in its nuanced humanity, its sense of irony about the blood that was shed to realize the Augustan peace. In that humanity and irony, we perceive Vergil's gentle assertion of his own individuality within the tremendous political, physical, and propaganda structure erected by Augustus, Agrippa, and Maecenas.

Albius Tibullus, of a wealthy family with roots in the Latin hills near Praeneste, was a friend of Vergil's. Like him, he was devoted to the Italian countryside and the homely rituals of the farmer's life. But while Vergil turned to the epic genre, Tibullus resolutely used elegiac poetry to celebrate the very personal world of his loves. His poetry barely mentions the city. Its only landmarks are the thresholds of his girlfriends' houses (1.2.93–96; 1.5.69–74; 2.1.74; 2.4.31–32; 2.6.12–14, 44–50) and the temples of foreign gods (1.3.24–32; 1.6.45–50), which keep his girls from him and from the rites of the native agricultural religion. Its only features are fires

(2.4.40–42), curious crowds (1.2.93–96), and an occasional triumphal procession (1.7). When he celebrates the triumph of Messalla, his patron, he saves most of his enthusiasm for Messalla's rebuilding of the Via Latina (1.7.57–62), which let the farmer get
back to the farm after a brief visit to the city.[23]

Shortly after the victory of Octavian at Actium, Titus Livius began to write his monumental survey of Roman history. For more
than forty years, which coincided with the entire principate of Augustus, he worked to research and interpret the whole sweep of
history *Ab Urbe Condita,* "from the founding of the city." Livy cap-
tures the whole panorama of Rome, from Romulus to Augustus,
seen through the lens of the contemporary city. An archaeological
sense of place as keen as Vergil's relates legendary events of the past
to urban concerns of Livy's own day.[24] Were many foreigners coming in to Rome? Livy assures his audience that that is a long tradition, starting with Evander's arrival from Greece (1.1), continuing
with Romulus's invitation to fugitives (1.8) and the Sabines (1.9–
14), on to the absorption of conquered peoples (1.33) and the arrival of Etruscans as kings (1.35). Had there been talk that Antony
might move the seat of government from Egypt? Livy puts an eloquent speech into Camillus's mouth, arguing why Romans are
rooted on the good hills of Rome (5.51).

Sextus Propertius, an equestrian from Umbria, knew firsthand
the horrors of the Civil Wars. His father died early, and the family's
land was lost in the confiscations of 41 B.C. He devoted himself to
poetry, which reflects a conflict between personal freedom and the
Augustan moral program. A few poems gently mock the more ag-
gressive campaigns of Augustus (3.4), but others fervently celebrate the blessings of peace (3.9, 11), and some are devoted to the
construction and reconstruction projects of the Augustan building
program (2.31; 4.1, 2). He freely accepts the official task of adapting
Greek forms to celebrate Italian customs (3.1), and he contributes
to the evolving Roman mythology (4.2, 4, 9, 10). His poems' mythological allusions bring the great heroes of legend into the streets of
Rome (2.32, 34; 3.11). He knows the luxury of the houses of the
rich (1.14; 2.6.33–36; 3.2.11–16), but his own house on the Esquiline is simple, although it does have a garden (4.8). In his poems

we see him strolling about the Porticus Pompei, watching gladiatorial shows in the Forum, attending the theater, peeking in litters
as they pass (2.16.33–34; 2.22.3–4), and spending time at the
Temple of Apollo Palatinus (2.31; 4.6). He speaks of the city as a
little town, where everyone knows and gossips about his business
(1.12.2; 2.5.1–2; 2.20.21–22; 2.24; 2.26.21–22; 2.32.21–28).
Even nature is seen from the perspective of the town: the people he
describes lying by the Tiber and drinking imported wine watch the
boats passing on the river and raise their eyes to the woods beyond
on the hilltops (1.14), the same woods he goes to visit when he
needs solace from an unhappy love affair (1.18). Since he is a poet
of love, the most interesting activity in the city takes place at night,
and yet he is aware of the dangers of the nocturnal streets (3.16.5–
6); in one poem (2.29), the ever-present danger of being mugged
turns into a pretty conceit as a threatening gang of young men on a
street corner turns out to be a group of Cupids come to accompany
the lover home. The poet moves in interesting social circles: he
knows the upper levels, represented by Maecenas himself (2.1;
3.9), but he also introduces us to his slave Lygdamus (3.6), a
Babylonian astrologer (4.1a), two party girls (Teia from the Capitoline and Phyllis from the Aventine—4.8), and the love of his life,
Cynthia.[25]

Publius Ovidius Naso was born twenty years later than the
abovementioned poets. For his generation the Civil Wars were
something his parents talked about. He could take the Augustan
peace for granted. His first work, the *Amores,* was published when
he was twenty-three, in 20 B.C., when the bulk of the other poets'
work had already appeared. With youthful exuberance he mocks
the serious tone of his older contemporaries and embraces the life
of the city. Unlike Propertius, his assignations take place at noon
(1.5), though he is not afraid of the night (1.6.5–12). He takes us to
racy dinner parties (1.4), into a prostitute's boudoir (1.8.63), to
work at dawn with the soldier, farmer, schoolboy, lawyer, and
housewife (1.13.23–26), and to the horse races at the Circus Maximus (3.2).

Even after Augustus promulgated his legislation of moral reform
aimed at family stability and an increased birth rate, Ovid con-

tinued to celebrate the pleasures of urban childless bachelorhood in the *Art of Love,* published around 1 B.C. In this parody of earnest didactic poetry he revels in the cultivated sophistication of the city. The variety and color of the city scene are present in his list of landmarks—porticoes, especially the Porticus Pompei; temples, especially that of Apollo Palatinus; all three theaters; the Circus (1.67–170, 491–497; 3.385–396)—which take on value because they are convenient places to meet girls. Like Augustus, Ovid knows the importance of a good façade; his goal, however, is to help a girl look her best when looking for a man (3.255–348, 499–522). Because of his very visual quality, Ovid reminds us how colorful the city was (3.169–192), and how both in their public spaces and in their homes the residents of Augustan Rome were surrounded by statues and paintings showing scenes from nature and scenes from mythology (1.525–564; 2.21–96, 125–142; 3.687–746).

In the *Fasti,* Ovid made some effort to support the policy of the princeps, describing the rituals of the Roman year and the traditions behind them. Pontiffs, magistrates, and senators ascend the Capitoline to sacrifice on New Year's Day (1.70–88), the common people go out to picnic and drink on the feast day of Anna Perenna (3.523–542), and neglected temples receive their traditional rites (6.213–218). The *Fasti,* and parts of the *Metamorphoses,* show that Ovid was trying to conciliate Augustus.

But his earlier poetry, still embarrassingly popular with the reading public, flew too obviously in the face of the official program of moral reform. In A.D. 8 Ovid was sent into exile at Tomis, on the western shore of the Black Sea. In a poem written from exile (*Tristia* 1.3.27–90) he recalls his last night in Rome, the first quiet one we have met in Augustan literature. He focuses on the silhouette of the Capitoline and its temples, on the grieving friends and family gods at home, and on the silent presence of the princeps over on the Palatine. When daylight comes and he must go, he leaves without even noticing all the pleasures of the everyday scene in which his earlier poetry had exhibited so much delight. Ovid is a vivid, sad example of the power of Augustus and of his belief in the capacity of "the media" to influence the public's perception of his program, negatively as well as positively.

Five

Rome under the Emperors

The length and thoroughness of the Augustan principate imposed a new look on Rome, while retaining some of the sense of individual initiative that had characterized the republic. Augustus's successors in the Julio-Claudian dynasty continued to meet the urbanistic needs of Rome as each of them perceived those needs, sometimes in individualistic and quirky ways.

The Julio-Claudians

The urban projects of Augustus's immediate successors reflect their individual characteristics: parsimonious under Tiberius, wildly haphazard under Caligula, conscientious and practical with an antiquarian tone under Claudius, imaginative and trendy under Nero.

Tiberius (A.D. 14–37) had a reputation for fiscal restraint and left the state treasury full when he died. His policies show some respect for republican traditions on the one hand, and, on the other, an assumption of the responsibilities of dynastic autocracy. He completed several works that had been started during Augustus's lifetime.

In his predecessor's honor he constructed the Temple of the Deified Augustus. No remains have been identified with any certainty, but literary references (Suetonius, *Gaius Caligula* 22.4) indicate that the temple stood in the Velabrum, just south of the Basilica Iulia. This would mean that it was now impossible to enter the Forum Romanum from any direction without passing a major monument of the family of Caesar and Augustus. The new order had completely surrounded the old. A triumphal arch near the Temple of Saturnus celebrated a diplomatic victory in A.D. 16, and the Temple of Concordia next to it was rebuilt (Pl. 12B; Fig. 9).

In a significant innovation, Tiberius established the Castra Praetoria. This camp for the elite corps of the Praetorian Guard was located, with a nod at traditional sensibilities, outside the pomerium on the Via Tiburtina, but never before had soldiers been stationed permanently within the built-up part of the city; from this time the praetorians exercised considerable power in the political life of city and empire. The camp itself was strictly rectangular, with a gate at the center of each of its four walls, in accordance with the traditional rules for laying out Roman military encampments. Its circuit walls are the first large-scale example in Rome of brick-faced concrete, which during the next century became the normal building material of the imperial city.

Finally, Tiberius began the construction of a proper imperial palace, the Domus Tiberiana, at the northern corner of the Palatine, looking down into the Forum. Its ruins lie under the Farnese Gardens and have not been extensively excavated, but the fact of its construction shows that Tiberius realized it was no longer possible to imitate Augustus's conspicuously simple house. If nothing else, the expanding imperial bureaucracy needed office space.

Gaius, usually known as Caligula (A.D. 37–41), displayed none of Augustus's and Tiberius's respect for the appearance of republican institutions. He undermined the traditional aristocracy (or what was left of it) through intimidation and execution. The monumental expression of this tendency was his expansion of the Domus Tiberiana (Suetonius, *Gaius Caligula* 22.2): substructures extended the palace out into the Forum Romanum, and the Temple of Castor and Pollux was somehow incorporated as a vestibule; a kind of viaduct was then built over the Temple of the Deified Augustus to give direct access from the palace to the Temple of Iuppiter Optimus

Maximus on the Capitoline. He built or expropriated other residences, mostly villas on the fringes of Rome, including one at the base of the Vatican Hill, where he built the Circus Gai for private entertainments.[1] He built several temples to himself, one on the Capitoline and one on the Palatine. In contrast to the very cautious attitude of Augustus and Tiberius to Eastern religions, under Caligula the temple of Isis was begun in the Campus Martius, outside the pomerium but in the middle of such venerable buildings as the Saepta Iulia and the Thermae Agrippianae. Not all the building activity of Caligula's reign was empty display: the bureaucracy responsible for the water supply of Rome initiated a pair of new aqueducts to bring water to the outer parts of the Esquiline Hill.

The administration of Claudius (A.D. 41–54) was marked less by new buildings than by a conscientious regard for the smooth functioning of the city. Claudius completed the two aqueducts begun by Caligula, the Aqua Claudia and the Aqua Anio Novus, and repaired the Aqua Virgo (*CIL* 6.1252; Fig. 11). To improve the administration of the aqueduct system, Claudius instituted the office of *procurator aquarum,* and filled it with an imperial freedman; this was a significant step in the creation of an imperial bureaucracy staffed by former slaves of the emperor. In a parallel development, administration of the grain system was put into the hands of an equestrian *praefectus annonae,* and the Porticus Minucia Frumentaria was constructed in the Campus Martius to serve as the office and distribution center for the annona.[2]

Claudius's most ambitious building scheme, in Ostia, provided Rome with a harbor appropriate to its needs. From the new harbor at Ostia increased traffic came up the Tiber. Various surveys and engineering works were undertaken to keep the river channel open and to control floods (*CIL* 6.31545 and 14.85).

Claudius's scholarly antiquarian taste was reflected in the fabric of the city. The Aqua Claudia was built of large blocks of stone worked with a rough "rusticated" finish that manneristically suggested old construction; the rustic appeal is most apparent at the Porta Maggiore, where the aqueducts crossed the Via Labicana and Via Praenestina (Pl. 11). Furthermore, to mark his military victories in Britain, Claudius in A.D. 50 imitated Sulla and Augustus by enlarging the pomerium of the city in a quaint ceremony going back to the days of Romulus (*CIL* 6.1231; Tacitus, *Annals* 12.23–24).

At Claudius's death Nero became emperor (A.D. 54–68). A showman, Nero was interested in the most modern styles in literature, music, painting, and architecture. His early building activity included a wooden amphitheater for gladiatorial contests (Pliny, *Natural History* 19.24), and the Thermae Neronianae, which continued the series of monumental public baths begun by Agrippa in the Campus Martius. He also completed the Circus Gai et Neronis and added a bridge, the Pons Neronianus, for easy access across the Tiber.[3] On the Caelian, he built the Macellum Magnum, a large marketplace with two-storied colonnades. During the first part of his reign most of Nero's architectural ingenuity focused on a new imperial residence, the Domus Transitoria, which reached from the old palace of Tiberius on the Palatine across the Velia to the Esquiline. In this grandiose architectural project the architects created baroque effects of light and shade, and proclaimed the power and taste of the emperor to all the world.[4]

In A.D. 64 a great fire started at the Circus Maximus and spread through the crowded wood-frame buildings, destroying nearly all the monumental center of the city, including the new palace (Tacitus, *Annals* 15.38–43). In the aftermath of the disaster, Nero instituted a building code intended to make the city more resistant to fire and more orderly and modern. According to Tacitus, streets were widened, fire-resistant stone was required for certain parts of buildings, and a limit was set on the height of buildings. Branches of the old aqueducts brought water to the Caelian, Aventine, Palatine, and Trans-Tiber regions, thereby assuring that water would be available to the public, for fighting fires and for drinking.

The showpiece of the Neronian plan was at the eastern end of the Forum Romanum, and stretched on and on to the slopes of the Esquiline and Caelian. This was the Domus Aurea, (Golden House), which attracted the attention of contemporary Romans because of its rich materials and its prodigal use of open space in the middle of the crowded city. The valley between the Quirinal and the Palatine, where the Sacra Via climbed up from the Forum Romanum over the Velia, had been completely cleared by the fire.

Nero's architects covered the space with a new Sacra Via, which embodied the principles of the new building code: it was a straight avenue extending east from the Temple of Vesta and a new Atrium Vestae, and was bordered by colonnades and shops laid out according to a regular and rational plan. At the eastern end the new Sacra Via led through an entrance pylon into another colonnaded square, where an immense statue of Nero as the sun god, the *Colossus,* was placed. To the east lay a country villa in the middle of the city, with a lake, fields, vineyards, pastures, groves, zoos, and rustic villages artfully arranged like the vignettes in a manneristic garden. The Domus Aurea itself was a row of residential and reception rooms built into the slope of the Esquiline Hill.[5] Its walls were covered with paintings in the "Third Style," a combination of mythological and nature scenes with frames of fanciful painted columns intertwined with motifs borrowed from Egypt.[6] The rooms of the Domus Aurea can be visited today; interred beneath the Thermae Traiani, they create a spooky, evocative ambiance, covered as they are with paintings that inspired Renaissance visitors to create "grotesque" designs in imitation of these dank grottoes. A visitor to the Domus Aurea in Nero's day, however, would have been impressed by the light and the color—by the gold and ivory paneling, the mother-of-pearl inlays, the vistas through the wide windows. Even people who had never set foot inside the place knew of the circular dining room with its revolving ceiling (Suetonius, *Nero* 31), and the exhibits of natural wonders like the amazingly hard stone preserved in a chapel.

The fire of A.D. 64 served as a catalyst for extensive urban renewal in the crowded center of Rome. Rebuilt streets were wider and more open, sunny and airy. New insulae stood straighter and on firmer foundations. For the first time, Rome began to look like a city whose development was in some way being ordered and controlled.

The Flavians

The year A.D. 69 was one of uncertainty and chaos following Nero's death. In different parts of the empire military legions proclaimed

their generals as emperor, and Galba, Otho, and Vitellius all had a
few months on the throne in Rome. Out of the chaos Titus Flavius
Vespasianus emerged victorious. He had made his reputation as
leader of the Roman forces against the Jewish revolts in Palestine,
and his son Titus continued the campaign, destroyed the Temple in
Jerusalem, and returned to celebrate a joint triumph with Vespasian in A.D. 70. The three emperors of the Flavian dynasty presented very different public personalities: Vespasian was a blunt,
thrifty man of the people; Titus was a competent, generous
charmer; and his brother, Domitian, was an ambitious, extravagant, jealous purveyor of regal splendor. But in the twenty-seven
years of their reign, they imposed a characteristic look on Rome.

Vespasian (A.D. 69–79) resembled Augustus in coming to
power at the end of a bitter civil war, and in facing the need to
restore public confidence and establish his own claim to supreme
authority. Like Augustus, he used buildings to establish the place
of his dynasty in the life of the city.

First he repaired the Temple of Iuppiter Optimus Maximus on
the Capitoline, which had been destroyed in the fighting (Suetonius, *Vespasian* 8.5). Then he inaugurated a construction program
that both alluded to the building program of Augustus and also
reversed the urban priorities of Nero. Where Nero had built a private pleasure preserve in the very center of the city, Vespasian constructed buildings for the benefit of all the city's residents. The
Temple of Pax in the Forum Pacis celebrated the return of peace
under Vespasian, just as the Ara Pacis had celebrated the return of
peace under Augustus, and its location, facing across the Argiletum
toward the Forum Augustum (Fig. 10), emphasized the connection
with the first princeps. Libraries and lecture halls faced a large tree-
lined park, which considerably expanded the open green space in
the most crowded part of the city.[7] The Forum Pacis was easily accessible, and was used as a museum for spoils brought back by
Titus from the sack of Jerusalem as well as for works of art taken
from Nero's Domus Aurea and put on display for the public to
enjoy.

A similar quiet, secluded, but centrally located green space in the
center of town was arranged around the Temple of the Deified

Claudius, on an immense terrace at the end of the Caelian. In this temple the Flavians expressed their piety toward a predecessor who, like them, had attended to the city's needs with quiet efficiency.

At the very spot where Nero had put his private lake, Vespasian began a permanent stone amphitheater, the Amphitheatrum Flavium (Pl. 10, 12D). The colossal statue of Nero as the sun god was allowed to remain next to it, and lent its name to the amphitheater, thenceforth known as the Colosseum.[8] The Colosseum's immense bulk and its impressive exterior with three superimposed orders of columned arcades showed more clearly than anything else the Flavian determination to put urban space to work for the urban populace (Suetonius, *Vespasian* 9.1; Martial, *On the Spectacles* 2).

After Vespasian died, his son Titus (A.D. 79–81) continued his policies. On the edge of the Esquiline facing the Colosseum, public baths, the Thermae Titi, converted still more of Nero's Domus Aurea to public use (Pl. 10). Titus also began a Temple to the Deified Vespasianus at the western end of the Forum, filling in an empty space behind the Temple of Saturnus. A major fire in A.D. 80 destroyed the new Temple of Iuppiter Optimus Maximus on the Capitoline, and Titus began still another reconstruction before his death in A.D. 81 (Pl. 9).

Domitian (A.D. 81–96) completed these projects and started a building campaign of his own that encompassed the whole city.[9] The latter included shrines in honor of his father and brother: the Temple of the Gens Flavia on the site of the family home on the Quirinal, and the Porticus Divorum in the monumental zone of the Campus Martius. In the relatively narrow space between the Forum Augustum and the Temple of Pax, Domitian constructed the Forum Transitorium with its Temple of Minerva to create an appropriate monumental entrance into the Forum Romanum for pedestrian traffic moving down through the Argiletum from the Subura (Fig. 10). In the Campus Martius he restored the Temple of Isis and built the Temple of Minerva Chalcidica. Farther west, beyond the Baths of Nero, the Stadium Domitiani, which has left its imprint in the Piazza Navona, was built for foot races in the Greek fashion. A two-storied version of the columned arcade, made of travertine, covered its exterior. Just to the south was the Odeum, a Greek-style hall for concerts. It probably had an exterior like the Stadium's, which joined both buildings visually to the Theatrum Pompei to the south.

Greek architectural forms like these suited Domitian's view of his position as emperor, colored as it was with the tints of Hellenistic kingship. He spent money lavishly, wore the purple robe of a triumphator even to meetings of the Senate, and liked to be saluted with the title *Dominus et Deus,* "Lord and God." To provide the proper setting for this role, Domitian reconstructed the Domus Tiberiana, which had been damaged in the fire of A.D. 80, and then, on the southern half of the Palatine, he built a magnificent new palace, which is known in reference books as the Domus Augustiana (Pl. 4). The new palace towered over the Circus Maximus on one side. On the other side, where visitors approached from the Forum Romanum and the Velia, its façade had the pediment and columns of a very large temple, which suggested the divine presence of the emperor within. The public wing contained a basilica, a reception hall, and a shrine to the Lares, all of which had walls and vaulted ceilings dazzling with marbles. Beyond lay a courtyard with an elaborate pond in the center and a state dining hall paved in marble. Both courtyard and dining hall were flanked by fountains and pools. To the southeast, private quarters were arranged in several stories around a courtyard. Throughout, apsidal rooms, long vistas, pools, and splashing fountains created baroque effects as light and dark, round and square, convex and concave, interacted. Such swelling, swirling forms, characteristic of Flavian taste, occur in elaborate coloristic effects, projecting columns and cornices, and contrived vistas in the grandiose halls and complicated fountains of the palace; in the details of architectural carving in public buildings; and on a more modest scale in the wall paintings of private homes—the "Fourth Style" known from the houses of Pompeii.

The imperial residence on the Palatine was the crown jewel of Flavian construction, but the dynasty built all over the city. The buildings of Vespasian and Titus were conspicuously devoted to public needs, and those of Domitian were devoted to the glorification of the Flavian family and to the refined pleasures of Greek types of entertainment. The columns and arcades of the Flavian buildings blended into the older buildings standing near them—the Theatrum Pompei next to the Odeum and the Stadium Domitiani, the Circus Maximus below the Domus Augustiana, the Tabularium at the far end of the valley from the Colosseum—but their scale tended to impress the spectator with the power and resources of the dynasty and the imperial office.

The High Empire

Domitian was assassinated in A.D. 96, and the senatorial aristocracy, which had often been the victim of his absolutist tendencies, chose as emperor one of their own, Marcus Cocceius Nerva (A.D. 96–98). In his short reign Nerva reestablished the aristocracy's prestige, but had little opportunity to contribute to Rome's physical development. He did, however, complete Domitian's Forum Transitorium, which he dedicated as the Forum Nervae.

Trajan (A.D. 98–117), however, exercised a firm but benevolent leadership of the army, the provinces, and the city. Throughout the empire, he expanded the limits of Roman rule with conquests in Mesopotamia and Dacia, kept close control over details of provincial administration, founded new colonies and modernized old ones, and gave new impetus to the port of Rome, which amounted to a total renovation of the city of Ostia (Pl. 22). Within Rome, the control of a coordinated, versatile intelligence clearly appears in the three major projects of Trajan and his architect, Apollodorus of Damascus. The Forum, Market, and Baths of Trajan reshaped large parts of the monumental center of the city. They represented very different architectural solutions, reflecting the transition from traditional materials and methods to a concrete-based architecture that has been called the "Roman architectural revolution."[10] Like the Flavians, Trajan built on a grand scale, favoring projects that would directly raise the standard of urban life.

The Forum Traiani was built to provide more open space in the center of the city and to serve the needs of the Romans as public administrators and judges (Fig. 10). It was adjacent to the Forum

Iulium and the Forum Augustum, and extended northward all the way to the Campus Martius. To make room for this complex, Trajan's engineers had to quarry away the end of the Quirinal Hill. The largest and grandest of the imperial fora, it was strictly symmetrical, and its columns and marble revetments conformed to traditional taste. Its beauty and richness compelled superlatives—even in the fourth century when the emperor Constantius arrived for the first time in Rome, the Forum Traiani was the most impressive thing he saw (Ammianus Marcellinus 16.10.15).

Tucked in behind the Forum Traiani, Apollodorus designed the Mercatus Traiani, a shopping center of special interest (Pl. 5). It served the commercial needs of the Romans as consumers and had space for the central offices of the reorganized annona. In contrast to the conservative design of the Forum, it was adventuresome. Instead of marble columns and rectangular symmetry, it used practical brick and concrete in its vaulted spaces as they curved around the sides of the Quirinal on four separate levels. It set the fashion in secular architecture for the next generations.[11]

The residential wing of Nero's Domus Aurea burned down in A.D. 104, and public baths, the Thermae Traiani, were built right on the brow of the Esquiline Hill, to complete the scheme of converting Nero's villa to public use (Pl. 10). The Thermae Traiani echoed the design of the Thermae Titi just down the hill, but they were much larger. Their central hall, roofed with a concrete vault and flanked by a series of symmetrical bathing and meeting rooms, set the style for all the great public baths that were built in Rome and the provinces for the next two hundred years.

Trajan also regularized the distribution of water in the city. One enduring monument of this concern is the Aqua Traiana, an aqueduct that brought water to the Trans-Tiber region (Fig. 11). Another is Frontinus's book *The Aqueducts of Rome,* which reports on a survey of the aqueduct system and its maintenance procedures.

From Augustus to Trajan, a series of plans addressed practical needs such as water and food supply, political and legal business, recreation, and circulation of pedestrian traffic. Monuments like the Theatrum Marcelli, the Colosseum, and the Forum Traiani gave monumental architectural focus to the junction of separate regions of the city. There were plenty of variations, but construction during the Augustan Age was largely made coherent through the use of white marble or travertine columns; that of the Flavians was characterized by arcades; that of Trajan by brick and concrete.

When Hadrian (A.D. 117–138) became emperor, he was confronted with hostility on the part of many senators who had respected Trajan and were suspicious that he had not in fact designated Hadrian as his heir. Perhaps to allay such hostility, and perhaps to circumvent it, Hadrian seems to have used his building program to carry several messages. First, he was loyal to tradition, and the traditions he emulated were those not of the old republic but of the principate, in particular its founder, Augustus.[12] Second, he was loyal to the memory of Trajan, his adopted father. Third, while celebrating continuity, he also claimed a new beginning, parallel to Augustus's new era. He issued coins that showed a phoenix rising out of ashes to new life.[13] Similarly, Hadrian early in his reign retraced the sacred boundary of the pomerium, restored its boundary markers, and inaugurated an official birthday celebration, the Natalis Urbis Romae, on April 21.

The specific buildings of Hadrian's program extended from the Velia to the upper Campus Martius. For the most part they avoided previously built-up locations, but by means of their scale and conception imposed new, distinctly Hadrianic features on the city.

On the Velia, the small hill between the Colosseum and the Forum Romanum, Hadrian constructed an immense artificial podium to support the largest temple ever built at Rome, that of Venus et Roma (Pl. 10, 12C). Its floor plan was as innovative as its size, with two cellas facing away from each other, one toward the Colosseum, the other toward the Forum.[14] Outside, it had the continuous surrounding colonnade of a Greek temple, though it was dedicated to the two most Roman of goddesses. Given its bulk and site, it must have forced comparison with the Temple of Iuppiter over on the Capitoline: together they framed the old sacred soil of the Forum Romanum.

Beside the Capitoline, where the Forum Traiani pushed out into the Campus Martius, Hadrian honored his predecessor by burying him at the base of his column, and by erecting the temple of the

Deified Traianus on the axis of Trajan's forum.

Farther out in the Campus Martius, on undeveloped land beyond the Saepta,[15] other structures proclaimed Hadrian's loyalty to his predecessor: a Temple of the Deified Matidia (Hadrian's mother-in-law and Trajan's sister), a Basilica Matidiae, and a Basilica Marcianae (Marciana was Trajan's sister).

When fire destroyed Agrippa's Pantheon on the Campus Martius around A.D. 126, Hadrian redesigned and rebuilt it, producing what is still probably the most breathtaking structure in the city of Rome (Pl. 6, 8). Approached from the north, the direction in which the Campus was being developed, the new temple presented a traditional rectangular temple porch, eight columns across. But as soon as visitors passed through the porch into the cella, they found themselves in a round space surmounted by an immense coffered dome that suggested the perfect sphere of the universe ruled by "all the gods," whose temple it was. The low slope of the dome's exterior, with its open oculus in the center, was covered with gold foil. It was, and still is, an impressive landmark when viewed from any of the hills,[16] visually recalling the mound of the Mausoleum of Augustus.

Farther north, recent archaeological discoveries show that Hadrian raised the ground level of the upper Campus Martius, probably to prevent floods. In the process, he made space available for building (an extensive apartment complex is known to have been built in this period on the east side of the Via Lata[17]), and also enclosed Augustus's Ara Pacis in a small sunken park. An east-west street from the Via Lata passed north of the Temple of Matidia, the Pantheon, the Thermae Neronianae, and the Stadium Domitiani (Pl. 8). Near the far end of this street, where the Tiber makes its bend, Hadrian built a bridge, the Pons Aelius. It led northward across the river to his tomb, the Mausoleum Hadriani, which consisted of an immense square supporting a cylinder. Clearly visible from anywhere on the Campus Martius, Hadrian's tomb invited comparison with the (smaller) Mausoleum of Augustus, across the river about a kilometer upstream.

The thrust of most of Hadrian's building in Rome is formal and religious. Other aspects of Hadrianic architecture appear in his palace, which, perhaps significantly, was built not in Rome but in the suburban municipality of Tibur (Tivoli), at the base of the Sabine hills about 25 kilometers (15 miles) from Rome. Whereas Nero's Domus Aurea had brought a country villa into the middle of the city, Hadrian's villa was in some respects an attempt to bring the city into the country. It was located at the base of the hill at Tibur, lower than most of the earlier villas, slightly too low to have a view of Rome (Pl. 13). This low site offered a refuge, a relief from the concerns of Rome, and perhaps made the architectural experiments at the villa less of a direct challenge to the city itself. As Hadrian returned from travels all over the empire, he added follies to remind him of the places he had visited (S.H.A., *Hadrian* 26.5). The villa became an idealized model world, with its Canopus representing Egypt, its Vale of Tempe representing northern Greece, its Poecile representing Athens, its temple of Aphrodite representing Cnidus in Asia Minor, even its cryptoporticus representing the entrance to the underworld. Like the Pantheon, the villa was a stylized image of the known world, but it drew the image in a different medium: here there was no overarching architectural unity; instead, unity was imposed by the imaginative stylistic innovations present in every corner. The total design resembled a museum, each element designed for maximum effect in its own terms, but without any strict axial symmetry.

As a utopian expression of a multifaceted world that worked with efficient beauty, its closest analogy may be Disneyland. Just as Disneyland represents not only an ideal, romanticized world but also the technology of a new, sanitized city, Hadrian's villa was a careful, three-dimensional representation of Rome as world-city. Merely to house the imperial household required the physical plant of a small city, and the architectural inventiveness of the emperor created a model urban environment without the unpleasantness that was so hard to avoid in Rome itself. Hadrian's ideal city had private residential quarters ranging from elegant bedroom suites and outdoor dining rooms and reception rooms, to comfortable guest chambers with mosaic floors, to barracks for soldiers and slaves. It had open spaces that could serve as models for forums and public gardens (with fountains and ponds), as well as colonnades in all traditional and several original architectural orders. It had temples of several shapes, two theaters, libraries, indoor baths, an outdoor swimming pool, aqueducts, and police and fire stations. By the time of Hadrian's death, his stately pleasure complex had become a full image of his idiosyncratic vision of the kind of city he would have liked the world to be.

In terms of his temperament, Hadrian often seemed to be a most untypical Roman. Yet in many ways the structures he erected at Rome and at Tibur incorporated all the most important developments in Roman civic and domestic architecture of the high empire: new, imaginative uses of concrete to vault easily over large spaces, a delight in sheer size, a fascination for enclosing space and for taming the natural outdoors through technology, the cultivation of gardens, and carefully exploited water fountains and natural vistas.

After Hadrian, the pace of monumental building projects slackened perceptibly, and it was not until Constantine that Rome enjoyed another overall urban plan. Most of the building in the later second century continued the growth of the city northward into the Campus Martius.

Antoninus Pius (A.D. 138–161) built a temple to the deified Hadrian which faced the Via Lata just east of the Temple of Matidia. In the Forum Romanum, tucked into a corner where the Argiletum entered, he also built a temple to his wife, Faustina, when she died in A.D. 141. After his own death and eventual deification this was renamed the Temple of Antoninus et Faustina. The dedicatory inscription is still legible, in front of the baroque façade of the Church of Saint Lawrence in Miranda, which was built into the remains of the temple.

Marcus Aurelius (A.D. 161–180) was so preoccupied with the practical needs of maintaining the threatened boundaries of the empire and with his own philosophical reflections that he had little energy or inclination for urban development. The only monuments of his reign were the Ustrinum Antoninorum, where Antoninus was cremated, and a column in his memory, the Columna Antonini Pii, both of which were built alongside the Via Lata. Nearby, another column, the Columna Marci Aurelii Antonini, was erected to commemorate Marcus's wars on the German frontier. This still stands, the focal point of the Piazza Colonna.

Marcus's son Commodus (A.D. 180–192) was reputed to be a sinister megalomaniac, and this is reflected in his decision to change the name of Rome to "Colonia Commodiana." His only new construction consisted of baths, the Thermae Commodianae, and the Temple of the Deified Marcus, dedicated by the Senate in honor of his father. We also know that he spent money lavishly on public games (S.H.A., *Commodus Antoninus* 11, 16).

The Later Empire

After Commodus was assassinated in A.D. 193, a brief period of chaos ensued. Then Septimius Severus (A.D. 193–211) became emperor and founded the Severan dynasty. A soldier from Africa, Septimius replaced the Praetorian Guard, reinstituted free distributions of grain, and added distributions of olive oil. In his reign the city received the official designation *urbs sacra*, "sacred city," which seems to be an indication of Rome's complete transformation from independent city-state to administrative capital of an empire. Septimius restored aqueducts, river embankments and temples, and built baths (S.H.A., *Severus* 19.5).[18]

Two monuments in the center of the city represent a deliberate attempt on the part of this African dynasty to turn its official back on the remnants of republican traditions. In the Forum Romanum an arch, the Arcus Septimii Severi, was erected in A.D. 203, sited at the northern corner of the Forum in such a way as to cut off completely the Curia of the Senate from the main area of the Forum. (It still stands, one of the most imposing features of the modern archaeological zone.) On the Palatine, Septimius added a new wing to the southern end of the imperial palace. The monumental façade of this wing, the Septizodium, faced south, toward the Via Appia and Africa. An ancient biographer (S.H.A., *Severus* 24) tells us that the emperor was planning to move the official reception rooms to this end of the palace, but was outmaneuvered by the prefect of the city, who installed the emperor's statue in the middle of the façade, thereby making it useless as an entrance.

Septimius's interest in the southern entrance to the city was continued by his son, Caracalla (A.D. 211–218). He concentrated on the stretch of the Via Appia just outside the city wall, a region of thinly distributed middle-class housing. Beside the road, on the slope of the smaller end of the Aventine, he built another in the series of great imperial baths, the Thermae Antoninianae (Fig. 23). It was approached by a monumental avenue parallel to the old road and three times as wide. On the crest of the Quirinal Hill he built a temple to the Egyptian god Serapis, approached from the Via Lata by a long series of ramps which transformed the side of the hill into a monumental façade facing the Campus Martius.

The reign of Elagabalus (A.D. 218–222), a Syrian cousin of the Severi, was short and bizarre. As high priest of Elagabal, the Syrian sun god, he brought a sense of oriental sumptuousness to the city, erecting the Temple of Elagabal close to the palace on the Palatine. In the garden zone at the eastern end of the Caelian, he built a large private villa that included baths, an amphitheater (the Amphitheatrum Castrense), and a circus.[19]

The third century was a time of political confusion. After Alexander Severus (A.D. 222–235), who rebuilt many temples and public structures, there was a rapid succession of emperors—twenty-five, according to one count, in the fifty years between 235 and 285. Military, political, and economic problems afflicted the empire and the city, and few building schemes attracted much attention. Decius (A.D. 249–251) celebrated the millennium of the founding of Rome by building baths, the Thermae Decianae, on the Aventine. Aurelian (A.D. 270–275) built a huge Temple of Sol ("Sun") in the Campus Agrippae. He also enclosed the city in a new circuit of walls, the Muri Aureliani, nineteen kilometers (eleven miles) long. The city had long since outgrown the old wall of the fourth century B.C. During the tranquil days of the High Empire, the capital had had no need of defenses, but in the middle of the third century, even Rome's security was threatened by the growing pressures along the boundaries of the empire.

The chaos came to an end with the elevation of Diocletian (A.D. 284–305), who imposed a new order on the empire with two "Augusti" as heads of state, assisted by two "Caesares." Diocletian

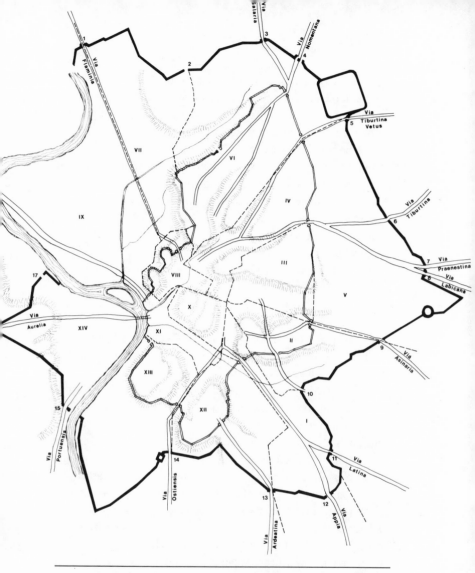

Fig. 6. Rome: The Imperial City, showing the fourteen regions of Augustus and the Walls of Aurelian. *Regions:* **I** Porta Capena, **II** Caelimontium, **III** Isis et Serapis, **IV** Templum Pacis, **V** Esquiliae, **VI** Alta Semita, **VII** Via Lata, **VIII** Forum Romanum, **IX** Circus Flaminius, **X** Palatium, **XI** Circus Maximus, **XII** Piscina Publica, **XIII** Aventinus, **XIV** Trans Tiberim. *Gates:* **1** Porta Flaminia, **2** Porta Pinciana, **3** Porta Salaria, **4** Porta Nomentana, **5** "Porta Chiusa," **6** Porta Tiburtina, **7** Porta Praenestina, **8** Porta Labicana, **9** Porta Asinaria, **10** Porta Metrovia, **11** Porta Latina, **12** Porta Appia, **13** Porta Ardeatina, **14** Porta Ostiensis, **15** Porta Portuensis, **16** Porta Aurelia, **17** Porta Septimiana.

spent much of his time on campaign defending the frontiers, but he did mark the beginning of his reign by building a new set of baths in Rome. These were the Thermae Diocletiani on the Quirinal, in a heavily populated area where a large amount of private property had to be bought up (*CIL* 6.1130).

In A.D. 305 the "Augusti" Diocletian and Maximian abdicated, and Constantius and Maximinus took their place. Maximian's son, Maxentius, had been passed over, and attempted to set himself up as emperor in A.D. 306. Although his claim was hotly contested, he did control Italy, and like a good Roman noble used buildings to solidify his claim. One was the Basilica Maxentii, part of which still stands on the Velia, overwhelming even as a fragment. On the Via Appia, beyond Aurelian's wall, in what must have been a suburban garden area with tombs lining the road, he built a villa with a race track as big as the Circus Maximus.[20]

For his part Constantine (A.D. 312–337) defeated Maxentius at the battle of the Mulvian Bridge, a short distance north of Rome where the Via Flaminia and Via Cassia meet to cross the Tiber. He then celebrated the beginning of a new era in the traditional way. He built, in a crowded residential quarter of the Quirinal, the Thermae Constantinianae, smaller than the baths of Diocletian, and much closer to the center of town. Near the Colosseum, he erected a triumphal arch, the Arcus Constantini, composed of bits and pieces of sculpture expropriated from monuments of earlier emperors, a museum display of the imperial city's artistic history.

Of greatest importance was his introduction to Rome of a new architectural form, the Christian church, based on the basilica but serving the special needs of the Christians, who were given official recognition by the Edict of Milan in A.D. 313. At the east end of the Caelian, on the site of the barracks of the Equites Singulares (the emperor's mounted bodyguard, disbanded by Constantine), distinctly removed from the pagan center of Rome, Constantine began work on the church of Saint John Lateran. It was to serve as the cathedral of Rome and the residence of its bishop. Nearby, on the grounds of the Severan palace, Constantine's mother, Helena, built the Church of the Holy Cross in Jerusalem as a shrine for the true cross and for other sacred relics she had brought back from the

Holy Land. Across town and across the river, the Church of Saint Peter was built on an immense scale over the site of Peter's tomb, among upper-class graves near the Circus Gai et Neronis. Other churches rose over the tombs of other martyrs: Saint Sebastian on the Via Appia, Saint Lawrence on the Via Tiburtina, Saints Marcellinus and Peter on the Via Labicana, and Saint Agnes on the Via Nomentana.[21] But these represent a tradition that is beyond the scope of this book.

The sudden appearance of Christian churches does show, however, that Rome's role was changing along with its appearance. One result of Diocletian's division of the empire into eastern and western sectors was that the focus of activity tended to shift away from Rome. Certainly the establishment of Constantinople in A.D. 324 as a "New Rome" diverted attention and prestige from the city on the Tiber. Hence, when Constantine's son and successor, Constantius II (A.D. 337–361), arrived in Rome in 357, he was visiting it for the first time. The description of his entrance is preserved by Ammianus Marcellinus, who makes it perfectly clear that even if the city had by now lost its unique political function as capital of the empire, it still retained its cosmopolitan appearance and bearing, and could still dazzle an imperial visitor (16.10.13–15).

URBAN LIFE
IN ROME

Six

Population

As we turn from the city as a whole to the people who lived in it, it would be good to know such facts as how many of them there were; the relative numbers of rich and poor, male and female, old and young; birth and death rates; population density and residential patterns; and trends of immigration and emigration. Unfortunately, we do not have enough information to give precise answers to any of these questions. The best that scholars have been able to do is to make some educated guesses. We can at least start with a bland statement on which everyone, ancient and modern, agrees: Rome was very large.

At the end of the republic, it had about 250,000 adult male citizens.[1] If we double or triple that to take account of their wives and children, and add several hundred thousand slaves and foreigners, we can estimate a total population of between 750,000 and 1,000,000.[2] We can assume that the poor vastly outnumbered the rich; that there were more men than women in the city (because men would migrate in search of work, and because poor parents might be more inclined to abandon a baby girl than a boy); that in the city there were fewer children in relation to adults than in the country or in less-crowded municipalities (because it cost too much for the poor to raise a family); and that people died earlier in the city than outside it (because of the poor sanitation, the dirt and the noise, and the general lack of medical care). These statements seem likely, judging by the accounts of urban life in the sources, but there are no reliable statistics to support them.[3]

If we assume a population of about a million, we must conclude that Rome in the early principate was one of the most densely populated cities the world has ever known—as crowded, probably, as modern Bombay or Calcutta.[4] The space for building was restricted by the green belt of gardens surrounding the city, and (a reasonable guess) about half was occupied by public buildings, which necessitated an even greater spot density in the residential areas.[5] The Regionary Catalogue, compiled in the fourth century A.D., gives the total number of residential units in each of the fourteen regions, separated into *domūs* and *insulae*. A domus is an independent house, an old-fashioned mansion or town house for the wealthy; the total number (1,832) corresponds approximately to the number of senators and equestrians at the top of the socioeconomic pyramid. *Insula* usually means "apartment house," and although its precise definition in the Catalogues is disputed, it clearly refers to a type of housing with multiple occupants.[6] It is therefore interesting to note that there was relatively little mass housing either in the lower Campus Martius, with its plethora of public buildings, or in the more exclusive neighborhoods atop the Oppian, Esquiline, and Aventine. The number of insulae was proportionately higher in the valleys between the hills, in the eastern, nonmonumental part of the Campus Martius along the Via Lata, on the slopes of the Palatine, and in the slums of the Trans-Tiber section.[7]

Viewed chronologically, there were certain times of marked increase in Rome's population. The traditional accounts mention the synoecism of the Latins and Sabines as the first real spurt of growth. From better-documented times we can be sure of a sudden expansion in the second century B.C., caused by small Italian landowners dispossessed from their farms by the Hannibalic War, who once in Rome probably found work on the docks and in construction. Another increase seems to have taken place in the middle of the first century B.C., when the rural poor were encouraged to come into the city by the expanded grain dole and the generosity of Roman politicians in the market for large retinues of clients.[8] There may have been another large influx under Augustus and the Julio-Claudians as merchants, teachers, tourists, and slaves from all over the empire poured into the city that had now assumed its proper role as imperial capital.

The Ruling Class and Its Clients

The pinnacle of Roman society was the small group of families of the senatorial order, defined by the men who had held one of the important magistracies and entered the Senate—perhaps six hundred at a time. Within this group an even smaller elite, the *nobiles*, could count a consul somewhere in the family's past or present.[9] This senatorial aristocracy represented the great families who ruled Rome and its empire, and whose intense pride in their traditions fueled the patriotism and competitiveness we noticed in Chapters 2 and 3. In the republic, they provided the leadership for politics and war, and so dominated the life of the city and the state that they could not help but think of themselves as *the* city and *the* state, as the only Romans who really counted. They received honors and status symbols from the state,[10] and they earned them with their devotion, time, and skill, along with contributions of money, games, and buildings.

They competed with each other for position and prestige, and they cooperated with each other in bonds of *amicitia*, "friendship" (Cicero, *De Officiis* 1.92), as private and family interests dictated. They dealt with each other on the basis of village values of mutual reliance, with extensive intermarriage, and they regulated their behavior and that of their neighbors by means of a small-town concern for what their peers would think.

When changed social conditions forced them to recognize the existence and interests of the lower orders, especially in the second and first centuries B.C., their attempts to resist or exploit the trends brought them into armed conflict with each other, and this involved the whole state in the chaos of the Roman Revolution. Many of the old families died out, victims of some temporarily victorious enemy faction, and when the principate was established under Augustus and his Julio-Claudian successors, the old families of the senatorial order found themselves living in a world where their proud traditions had very little relevance. Emperors like Caligula and Nero systematically humiliated and harassed the old aristocracy. New families entered the Senate, many of them from the provinces, and quickly assimilated the values and life-style of the old senatorial families.[11]

Wealthy freeborn men who did not participate in politics were listed, if their property amounted to 400,000 sesterces, as members of the "equestrian" order, a name derived from their ability, in early Rome, to buy and maintain a horse. Since many of them collected taxes on behalf of the state, and used their influence with senatorial friends to ensure that their widespread business interests were protected (Cicero, *Against Verres, Part Two,* 5.149; *Pro Lege Manilia* 11, 14–19), it is appropriate to consider them as part of the ruling class.[12]

A third influential group was drawn from the local aristocracies of the municipalities and colonies of Italy and the empire. Many of these aristocrats owned enough land to hold equestrian status, and many came to Rome, became active in public affairs, and entered the Senate,[13] drawing on bonds of friendship and dependency with the senators and equestrians already in Rome.

Such a relationship between persons of unequal social status was known as *clientela,* one of the most pervasive and characteristic elements of Roman society. A person became the client of a patron in several ways. He might be a municipal aristocrat working for the political interest of a senator. Or he might be a former soldier who had served under the patron, or the son of a father who had been his patron's client, or a tenant farmer who moved into the city, or a freed slave. The client looked to the patron for legal protection, occasional food and money, and a sense of contact with some sort of power. In turn he owed the patron obligations that varied with the individual but that almost always included the duty of being present in his toga each morning to greet the patron and accompany him in a formal walk to the Forum, to display the great man's retinue to the whole city (Juvenal 1.96–139; 5). The client also owed the patron support at election time, and he could represent the patron's financial interests in the long-distance trade in which the senator could not participate in his own name.[14] The client was explicitly protected from a neglectful patron as early as the Twelve Tables, and the clientela system continued well into the principate. It was the mechanism by which the great politicians of the late republic gained vast political followings, and the model by which Augustus and his successors claimed to sponsor the whole city and empire. It was the typical device of a village extended family, magnified and modified to permit this small aristocracy to run its immense hometown and empire.

Citizens and Foreigners

The lower economic classes did not necessarily share the principled, small-town values of the aristocracy. They were exposed to them through public proclamations, political speeches, and the public-relations panoply of buildings and statues. But life could be too spare, too brutish, and the vast numbers of the lower classes no doubt adopted the more cynical, street-smart urban habits and attitudes expressed by Plautus's slaves and the denizens of Petronius's *Satyricon*. Still, status distinctions were important among these lower classes, too, and one of the most valuable distinctions was that between citizen and noncitizen.

Roman citizenship belonged by birth to the child of two citizen parents, or of one citizen and one foreigner who possessed the legal right of marriage to a Roman (*connubium*). Citizenship was also extended to Rome's allies under certain conditions, and after the Social War (91–87 B.C.) it was granted to all residents of Italy. Occasionally individual residents of the provinces, or entire communities, received citizenship from a general or a governor.[15] When a citizen manumitted a slave, the slave received Roman citizenship along with his or her freedom. In A.D. 212, Caracalla extended citizenship of the world-city to all free inhabitants of the empire.

Citizenship during the republic carried the responsibilities of military service and the privileges of marriage, voting, and holding office. In the provinces it also entailed exemption from the jurisdiction of the Roman governor. These privileges were mostly of tangible benefit to the rich, but citizenship carried a certain social prestige and the very real right of appeal to the people or, later, the emperor.

The badge of citizenship was the *tria nomina,* the "triple name." It consisted, basically, of a *praenomen* (e.g., Gaius), a *nomen* (e.g., Iulius), and a *cognomen* (e.g., Caesar). The praenomen was the personal name, and there were so few of them (Gaius, Lucius, Marcus, and Titus were most popular) that they were nearly always abbreviated in writing. The nomen was the family name, the name of the *gens* (e.g., Cornelius, Tullius, Licinius, Ovidius). The cognomen was originally a distinguishing descriptive epithet such as Scipio ("Staff"), Cicero ("Chickpea"), Calvus ("Bald"), Naso ("Nose"), and was usually inherited along with the nomen.[16]

Roman citizens spread out from the city along the lines of conquest: first as soldiers, but also as veterans, merchants, shippers, and tax agents. At the same time, foreigners crowded Rome's streets and enriched the texture of urban life. Attempts have been made to estimate the proportion of foreigners in the city's population, but beyond the usual lack of statistics, the problems of defining when an individual stops being "foreign" and becomes "Roman," and of determining whether an individual foreigner had already received Roman citizenship before coming to Rome, add further complications.[17] It was an old Roman tradition, starting with Romulus, to extend Roman citizenship to foreigners. Foreign princes, municipal aristocrats, citizens of certain allied towns, even freed slaves, all received citizenship. At the top of the social pyramid, the senatorial order itself included members not only from Italy but also from Spain and Gaul by the first century of the principate, and from Greece, Syria, and Africa by the second.

Yet as Rome became more and more a world city, the influx of foreigners aroused resentment. We glimpse it in the periodic expulsions of foreigners during the republic, and in the text of Juvenal, who complained constantly that Rome was becoming an oriental bazaar.[18] Certainly, foreigners came to Rome from every corner of the empire, bringing with them their native dress and language.[19] Greek, for example, must have been heard everywhere, spoken by ambassadors, teachers,[20] businessmen, and slaves.

Merchants from the Syrian coast offer a typical case. From an inscription (*IG* 14.830), we know of an organization of Tyrians at the harbor town of Puteoli and in Rome expressing some of the special anxieties they felt as foreign businessmen. Yet some Syrians adapted well to life in Rome. Marcus Antonius Gaionas, for example, became a member of the civic administration, holding the minor office of *cistiber* (*CIL* 6.32316). He did not lose track of his Syrian heritage, however, for a handful of other inscriptions describe him as a devoted member of a cult society that met in the sanctuary of the Syrian gods on the Janiculum. Apparently he derived the greatest satisfaction from continuing to worship his ancestral gods as he presided over banquets and contributed a basin for holy water in a social atmosphere that reminded him of his ancestral home.[21]

The Jews formed an important minority, as we can tell from occasional references in literature and from grave inscriptions. Jews were already in Rome in 139 B.C. (Valerius Maximus, *Memorabilia* 1.3.3), and when Pompey brought back captives from Palestine in 61 B.C., they were bought and set free by Jews who were already there (Philo, *Embassy to Gaius* 155). Some of these may have been Roman citizens, perhaps the descendants of manumitted slaves, and they in turn would have bestowed citizenship on the slaves they bought and set free. By 4 B.C., there were 8,000 adult male Jews in Rome (Josephus, *The Jewish War* 2.6.1.80–81), and more were brought in as captives after Vespasian and Titus crushed the Palestinian revolt. During the principate we know of eleven separate synagogue congregations, principally in the crowded, ethnic Trans-Tiber region. Most of the inscriptions from the Jewish catacombs are written in Greek, which shows that the Jews in Rome had their roots in the diaspora communities of the Hellenistic world.[22]

Masters, Slaves, and Freed Slaves

The institution of slavery—present at every level of Roman life— was full of contradictions. Slaves had virtually no legal rights, although as thinking human beings they were often entrusted with important responsibilities, including those of nurse, teacher, and physician. Hierarchies of differential status existed among slaves, both within a given household and among various groups of slaves, depending on the status of the master. The emperor's slaves, especially those who worked in the palace, enjoyed high prestige and, under the later Julio-Claudians, handled the bureaucratic work of the imperial administration, doing the work of their master. Domestic slaves in town houses and country villas served as cooks, personal attendants, nurses, tutors, entertainers, and seamstresses; or they worked in the master's business enterprises, sometimes with a sum of money (*peculium*) to invest and use at their discretion. Lower on the scale, public slaves were assigned to clean the streets, repair aqueducts, stoke fires in the baths. The most miserable lot was that of the chattel slaves, who worked in chain gangs on the farms and in the galleys, quarries, and mines.

At Rome, even members of the upper class referred casually to shopping for slaves, in person or through an agent (Cicero, *Pro Plancio* 62; Pliny, *Letters* 1.21.2, 3.19.7).[23] Individuals came into slavery as prisoners of war, mainly, but captives of pirates and kidnappers could also become human merchandise, as the plays of Plautus and Terence show. With the decline of extensive overseas warfare in the principate, slave dealers on the fringes of the empire, and even in the central areas of Asia Minor like Phrygia, Lydia, and Caria, probably maintained their stocks through raids.[24] Some slaves were born and raised in the master's family, and as *vernae* had special status. A few may have been taken into the family as foundlings (*alumni*).

Slaves in the urban household, with their opportunity for interaction with the master and his family, may have been treated well and respected for their skill and intelligence, but the comments of slaves in the writings of the comic poets can quickly remind us that the threat of harsh brutality was all too real in their lives (e.g., Plautus, *Menaechmi* 966–977).

A remarkable aspect of Roman slavery was the frequency with which masters manumitted their slaves, especially those with skills.[25] Once manumitted, the slave became a *libertus,* a "freed man," and the client of his former master, to whom he owed certain obligations. A master might manumit a slave because the slave had saved enough from his (or her) peculium to pay the price of freedom; or because it was cheaper for a freedman to live outside the family than to pay for full maintenance. The manumission might be a potlatch-like sign of wealth and power, or a simple gesture of gratitude for faithful service. Female slaves were occasionally freed so that they could marry the master, since marriages between free and slave were not legally recognized. Any children born before manumission remained slaves, as did spouses who were not specifically manumitted. But children born after manumission were considered full citizens.[26]

In general, freedmen were inclined to be loyal to their patron and to the institutions of the city.[27] For them, after all, the system had worked, and some of them assumed important roles in Rome. Ex-slaves of the emperor formed a bureaucratic elite.[28] More humble freedmen and women found work as small manufacturers, craftsmen,[29] shopkeepers, butchers, perfumers, sellers of purple dye, metal workers, day laborers. Many served as the business agents of their patrons, and some were very successful. The most vivid example is probably Trimalchio, the fictional, boorishly rich freedman whom Petronius lampoons in the *Satyricon*. As Petronius has Trimalchio tell his life story (*Satyricon* 76), aping the cultured conversation of the aristocracy while at the same time openly acknowledging his servile origin, Trimalchio inherited a vast fortune, and freedom, when his master died. He invested his new wealth in shipping, but lost it in shipwrecks. His wife (apparently set free at the same time) contributed her jewelry, and he raised enough to outfit another ship. This time, he made enough to buy farmland (the traditional source of wealth), and also to make commercial investments (slaves, cattle, moneylending), which made him fantastically rich.[30]

Examples of real life *liberti* are the baker Eurysaces and his wife, whose grandiose tomb, the Sepulcrum Eurysacis, stands beside the Porta Praenestina (Pl. 11), still proclaiming their commercial success and his appointed position in the city's bureaucracy as an *apparitor*.[31] Others are the wealthy brothers Aulus Vettius Restitutus and Aulus Vettius Conviva, whose house is known to all modern visitors to Pompeii (Fig. 15). We know from a graffito (*CIL* 4.3509) that Conviva, at least, was an *Augustalis*. Since the Augustales were organized as a kind of parallel order to that of the freeborn aristocratic decurions, Conviva belonged to the highest status group among freedmen.[32]

Women and Men

Women usually appear in Roman literature and art in terms of their relationship to men. As daughters, they received no personal name, but only the name of their father's gens—for example, Tullia was the daughter of Marcus Tullius Cicero—and kept it throughout their lives.[33] They were treated with special affection by doting fathers, but they were also unsentimentally married off to their father's political friends and potential allies.

As wives, they are mentioned with both stereotypical affection (e.g., *CIL* 6.1527; 15346; Pliny, *Letters* 4.19, 7.5)[34] and stereotypical disdain (Plautus, *Trinummus* 40–63; Aulus Gellius 1.6; Juvenal 6). They had no legal rights except through their husbands or fathers, to whose power they were subject[35]; and one old-fashioned phrase that was still used in the principate referred to marriage as "buying a wife" (Gaius, *Institutes* 1.113). Yet there were good marriages, in which husband and wife loved and respected each other. Indeed, the Romans were proud that their women had more respect than Greek women, and also proud that they were not as loose as Etruscan women.[36]

As mothers, women were highly regarded, and were charged with rearing their children in the ways of Roman respectability. The model was Cornelia, younger daughter of Scipio Africanus, who referred to her sons, Tiberius and Gaius Gracchus, as "my jewels." She illustrates the truism that Roman women, though they sometimes had an opportunity to influence political events, did so only indirectly, through the men in their families.[37]

Upper-class women responded to the increased opportunities of the late republic and the principate by acquiring more freedom of activity. In the second century B.C., a major "women's issue" was a law to restrict the amount of jewelry they could wear. Cato spoke against the practice of using elaborate clothes, jewelry, and carriages, and the women demonstrated in favor of it, but in any case they were acting as wives, showing off their beauty and their husbands' wealth (Livy 34.1–8).[38] By the end of the republic, the women in our texts appear in much more independent capacities. Clodia was attacked by Cicero (*Pro Caelio* 35–38; *Letters to His Friends* 5.2.6), for example, for dealing in real estate, commanding slaves, conducting semipublic liaisons with young men, and influencing political decisions, not always discreetly behind the scenes. More public-spirited were Afrania and Hortensia, who took on the role of lawyer and orator in the late republic (Valerius Maximus, *Memorabilia* 8.3; Quintilian, *Institutio Oratoria* 1.1.6). In the Augustan period, Sulpicia wrote love poetry, and upper-class women could be depicted as the love partners of elegiac poets. Horace (*Satires* 1.2) commented on the tendency of free women to demand the attentions traditionally given to mistresses and prostitutes. Later in the principate, Juvenal (6) spewed out tirades against women who spoke Greek in public, became gladiators, attended the public baths, wore tons of cosmetics, and divorced and remarried wholesale.[39]

But these are exceptions. Normally even strong-willed upper-class women, to the extent they appear in our sources, exercised their influence for and through their men. This was true of Livia, wife of Augustus, and of Agrippina, mother of Nero. It was also true of the Arria who killed herself as an example of bravery to her husband (Pliny, *Letters* 3.16). Among the aristocracy of Pompeii, a woman like Eumachia (who dedicated the large building that bears her name in the Forum) could hold a position of public prominence, as priestess of an important official cult and as patroness to the guild of Pompeii's fullers. But she owed her position to the fact that she was daughter and wife of local aristocrats.

Among the working class of free and freed, women must have taken on their share of the work. Graffiti from Pompeii, tomb carvings from Ostia, and occasional references in the literature show us women at work as weavers, dressmakers, copyists, midwives, physicians, grocers, innkeepers, barmaids, entertainers, and barbers.[40] Such women would have been free of some of the constraints of traditional rectitude: their economic contribution to the family was too important, and their background, whether in the slums or the dormitories of a house where they had been slaves, would not have socialized them to the niceties of aristocratic femininity.

Cynthia, the love of the poet Propertius, provides us with an interesting example, even if a woman who could hold such a spell over Propertius would not, almost by definition, have been very typical. We cannot be sure whether she was an unmarried prostitute, perhaps a freedwoman, or a citizen married to a neglectful husband, but in any event Propertius depicts her as unavailable for him to marry (2.7).[41] She lives in the Subura (4.7.15) with her women slaves (3.6.15). She is courted by many, including an important politician (2.16), wears the newest eye makeup from Belgium and Britain (2.18.26), strolls about in porticoes and the Campus Martius (2.23), visits the Temples of Vesta (2.29.27) and Isis (2.33), and takes frequent trips out of town—to country resorts near Rome (2.19, 32; 3.16; 4.8), to Baiae (1.11), and even to the Caspian Sea (2.30).

Seven

City Government

The administration of Rome was slow to keep pace with the phenomenal growth in the political power of the city, from sheepherders' village in the eighth century B.C. to capital of a world-scale empire in the second century B.C. Institutions that had originated in the regal and early republican periods, when Rome was a modest city-state, were still in existence at the end of the republic, stretched to the breaking point by the administrative demands of a far-flung empire as well as the local operations of the city of Rome. One of the ways in which the principate marked a new era was in its attempts to devise more rational, appropriate structures for making the city work.

Urban Administration under the Kings

We know very few details of political arrangements in early Rome, but it seems as if the kings ordinarily took the initiative for building projects, and that construction was often done by corvée labor. According to tradition, the Senate was a council of senior advisors to the king, and the population was organized into three tribes (Ramnes, Luceres, and Titienses), each of which was divided into ten *curiae* for purposes of voting and military mustering. Each of these curiae had its own meeting place, where it worshiped its par-

ticular gods and joined in communal meals (Dionysius of Halicarnassus, *Roman Antiquities* 2.14.3; 2.23.1–2).

Urban Administration under the Republic

After the expulsion of the kings, the administration of the city lay
primarily with the senators, who represented the aristocratic traditions of the leading families. The official designation *Senatus Populusque Romanus* reflects the spirit of this time, when the handful of
senators reckoned themselves as equal and more than equal to the
remaining mass of the citizen population. The weighty business of
running an empire, and the political battles in which the senators
were constantly occupied, left little energy for the details of local
administration. The Senate retained control of finances and state
contracts, but other matters of day-to-day administration were the
responsibility of regular groups of magistrates, elected for one-year
terms.

Two *consules,* the chief civil and military officers, presided over
the Senate and led the armies in war. They used the Temple of Castor as their headquarters, convening the assembly and conducting
other official business on the podium, within view of the crowd in
the Forum (Plutarch, *Sulla* 8, 33.4; Cicero, *Pro Sestio* 79).

The title *praetor,* "one going in front," was probably at the beginning a title of the consul, as head of state. But in 366 B.C. a separate
office was established, that of *praetor urbanus,* who could command
the army, convene the Senate and the assemblies, and preside over
the law courts, especially those concerning debt. A *praetor per-
egrinus* was added in 242 B.C., to supervise lawsuits concerning
foreigners, who had become more numerous by that time. As
Rome extended its domain during the third and second centuries,
more praetors were added, bringing the total to eight in 80 B.C.

Consuls and praetors served only single-year terms, but *censores*
were elected every five years to take the census. The position of
censor carried considerable moral authority, for it involved not
only counting the citizen population but also arranging it according to wealth, into units called "centuries." In drawing up the lists
of senators and equestrians, censors had the discretion to strike off

the names of those who had given false statements or had behaved inappropriately at home, on military service, or in provincial or public administration. They also controlled the public treasury, and thus were intimately involved in running the city. They supervised the leasing of public land, granted water rights, constructed and maintained public buildings, and arranged for the construction of roads and sewers. Their office and archives were in the Atrium Libertatis, near the Forum.

The plebeian assembly had its own officers, the *tribuni plebis*, "tribunes of the plebs." Originally charged to defend the lives and property of the plebeians, they exercised their power chiefly by obstructing legislation that ran counter to their interests. Since their authority was limited to the city of Rome and the mile-wide space outside it, they were perceived as the special officers of the urban population. Once the plebeian assembly gained the power to make laws that were binding on the whole state (around 287 B.C.), the tribunes came to be regarded as regular magistrates, and by the second century B.C. anyone who held the tribunate was admitted to the Senate on the completion of one year of service.

The *aediles* were the magistrates most responsible for the daily administration of the city. They maintained the archives, public buildings, roads, and sewers, supervised the grain supply, and provided for the celebration of festivals (Cicero, *Against Verres, Part Two*, 5.36).

The *quaestores* served as the state's chief financial officers. Four urban quaestors administered the state treasury, in the temple of Saturnus in the Forum; others administered the grain supply at Ostia and in the provinces. By the 80s B.C. there were twenty of them, and Julius Caesar found it convenient to add another twenty.

This shows that the machinery of the republic had to keep stretching to keep up with the demands of administration. On many occasions, the traditional magistracies could not handle certain specific jobs, and—especially in the second and first centuries B.C.—special commissions were created to do them.[1]

Another administrative problem during the republic was the one-year term of elected magistrates, which ensured a constant supply of relatively inexperienced officials. To help them with the details, a bureaucracy of *apparitores*, "assistants," developed. It included *scribae* to act as secretaries, *lictores* to attend consuls and praetors as bodyguards, *viatores* and *praecones* to carry and announce official messages, and various experts in the sacrificial procedures over which magistrates had to preside.[2]

Although muted by the hierarchical, status-conscious quality of so much of Roman life, ordinary citizens also played their part, arranging themselves in different configurations to play different roles in the pageant of civic life (Cicero, *Pro Sestio* 106–127). At public games in forum, circus, or theaters, unofficially but often effectively, and often at the instigation of a claque leader, they cheered their favorite politicians and jeered unpopular ones. Or they gathered at a *contio*, an informal rally, to hear politicians argue for their legislative proposals. Such meetings were held wherever space permitted, in the Circus Flaminius (Cicero, *Letters to Atticus* 1.14.1), elsewhere in the Campus Martius (Cicero, *Pro Sestio* 108), or in the Forum Romanum, either at the Rostra in the Comitium or in front of the consuls' headquarters at the Temple of Castor. As passions rose in the hothouse politics of the 50s and 40s B.C., violence often broke out at these meetings, as Cicero attests (*Pro Sestio* passim, *Letters to Atticus* 4.3.2, and *Letters to Quintus* 2.3.2; cf. Plutarch, *Cato the Younger* 42). In the months before important elections, political agents moved among the citizens in the Forum, lining up votes among members of tribes and clubs, and candidates in their chalk-whitened togas walked about (the process was called *ambitio*), shook hands (*prensatio*), showed off their retinues of clients, and made deals.[3]

At official meetings of the various *comitia*, the people voted for laws and candidates. Although the thirty curiae of early Rome lost most of their powers, their representatives gathered throughout the republic as the *comitia curiata* to perform certain religious functions (Cicero, *Contra Rullum: De Lege Agraria* 2.27–31) and to confirm the election of consuls and praetors by formally voting to grant them *imperium*, the power to command.

The *comitia centuriata* were meetings of all the (male) citizens in their role as soldiers. They were grouped into 193 "centuries," military units based on the wealth and age of each individual. Voting power was weighted in favor of the few richest citizens, while the poor, surely a majority of the population, were massed together in the lowest five centuries. As the assembly of Rome's citizen army, the comitia centuriata elected military commanders (consuls, praetors, and censors), declared war and peace, and heard charges of high treason.[4] Meetings were held on the Campus Martius, the traditional military parade and exercise ground; elections were held in the Ovile, "sheepfold," where movable fences could be arranged to herd the voters into orderly groups.

In addition to a military century (assigned on the basis of wealth or lack of it), each citizen was born into or assigned to one of thirty-five tribes. For most of the ordinary public business, the citizens assembled according to tribes as the *comitia tributa,* or as the *concilium plebis,* which also voted by tribes.[5] The tribal assemblies met at the Comitium in the Forum Romanum to vote serially, tribe by tribe, on legislation. As the bodies responsible for electing aediles, quaestors, and other minor magistrates, they convened in the Campus Martius, where the Ovile was arranged to accommodate simultaneous voting.

The most common activity in the Forum Romanum, however, was legal. Seated on an elevated tribunal and attended by lictors and advisors, the urban praetor heard preliminary arguments, summarized the issues to be decided, and appointed judges and juries. On a typical busy day, praetors and lesser judges presided over civil and criminal cases, the jury seated on benches on the Forum paving, while arguments were intoned by luminaries like Cicero and Hortensius, as well as by an unending supply of lesser rhetorical lights. We do not have enough evidence to locate the various courts precisely, but one good informed guess puts the praetors on various permanent raised platforms in the Forum—the platform between the Comitium and the Curia, the Rostra, the Tribunal Aurelium, and the porches of various temples.[6]

It is in literature, as usual, that we get our best sense of the animation with which speakers and spectators filled the Forum. Limiting ourselves to a few passages in Cicero, we glimpse people crowding into the Forum, pushing up onto the steps of temples to get a better view (e.g., *Pro Lege Manilia* 44, *In Catilinam* 4.14, *Pro Caelio*

21, *Pro Milone* 3, *Pro Sulla* 28); the Catilinarian conspirators and the witnesses against them being led across the Forum to where the Senate is meeting in the Temple of Concordia (*In Catilinam* 3.22); or the *scribae* gathering for the allotment of posts at the Temple of Saturnus, and shifting their attention to the debate in the Curia (*In Catilinam* 4.15).

The Forum Romanum during the Republic

Cicero, in his more rhetorical moments, uses the Forum to summon the patriotic impulses of his listeners, both aristocrats and ordinary citizens. The gods looked out from their temples to bless the political activity (*Pro Lege Manilia* 70). The Forum was the "seat of all justice," the Curia "the mighty protection of all nations" (*In Catilinam* 4.2), "the shrine of holiness and majesty and wisdom and statesmanship, the very center of the city's life" (*Pro Milone* 90). Throughout the republic, the Forum Romanum was the stage on which the drama of political life was played. Politicians and lawyers took the leading roles, delivering well-rehearsed speeches or indulging in extemporaneous give-and-take. The Senate played a supporting—or sometimes antagonistic—role, and the formal and informal assemblies of citizens provided the background chorus. As a stage, the Forum displayed many of Rome's greatest treasures, and expressed its values and priorities, a focus of civic pride and historical consciousness.

Here the Senate, the comitia, and the law courts convened, politicians spoke at informal contiones, sacrifices were offered in front of temples, statues commemorated great men, and arches recalled great triumphs. For triumphal processions, the steps of the temples served as reviewing stands. Funerals of distinguished men—and women—were held here. Gladiators fought here (Vitruvius 5.1.1; Livy 23.30.15; Augustus, *Res Gestae* 22), and when a Crassus (in 183 B.C., Livy 39.46.2) or a Caesar (in 46 B.C., Plutarch, *Caesar* 55) treated the Romans to a public banquet, the tents and tables were set up here too. Moneychangers made their deals, which guaranteed a smooth flow of commerce throughout the empire (Cicero, *Pro Lege Manilia* 19). Shakers, movers, hacks, and loafers of every description lounged about, striking appropriate deals and poses.

The Forum started as a flood-prone low-lying area of cemeteries in the eighth century B.C. By the seventh century some residential huts had been built at the upper edges, and the first evidence of monumental treatment as a public space came in the early sixth century, when it was paved with small stones. A brook flowed through the Forum and out through the Velabrum to the river. Under the Etruscans the channel of this brook was walled in to form the core of a sewer system, the Cloaca Maxima.

From the fifth to the third centuries B.C., the Forum was the central stage of the city's commercial, political, and social life. Figure 7 illustrates it in the early republic, a paved space with shrines and small shops. The private houses surrounding it were mostly owned by aristocratic families taking advantage of a prestigious address.[7] At the southeastern end (Fig. 7, upper right), dominating the point where the Via Sacra led down from the Palatine villages to enter the Forum, on the site of the king's residence, the infant republic built several structures. One was the Regia, a rectangular building of three rooms lying to the south of an irregular, partially columned courtyard. Here were sanctuaries of Mars and Ops, as well as relics of Rome's sacred and political traditions.[8] Across the street, the round shape of the Temple of Vesta recalled the huts in which Rome's original inhabitants had lived. The Vestal Virgins tended its sacred hearth, and lived next door in the Atrium Vestae (shown in plan in Fig. 7). Close by stood a small, sacred grove and the Lacus Iuturnae, a sacred spring where, legend said, Castor and Pollux watered their horses after the battle of Lake Regillus (Dionysius of Halicarnassus, *Roman Antiquities* 6.13.1–2). The Temple of Castor, dedicated in 484 B.C. to commemorate their divine aid, appears in Figure 7 as a typical Italic temple of moderate size. The wooden columns on its porch and along its sides punctuated this corner of the Forum with a sense of mass. Stretching along the southern side of the Forum were the Tabernae Veteres (Old Shops), which housed moneychangers, and beyond them, at the southwestern corner, was the Temple of Saturnus. One of the earliest building projects of the republic, this temple was dedicated in 497 B.C. and contained

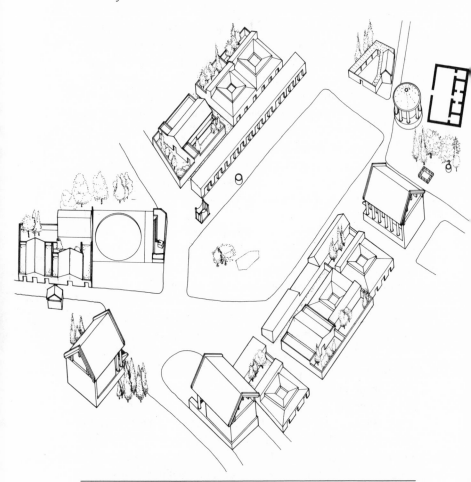

Fig. 7. Rome: Forum Romanum, fourth century B.C. *Clockwise from the southeast (upper right):* Regia, Temple of Vesta, Atrium Vestae (plan), Lacus Iuturnae, Temple of Castor, Tabernae Veteres, Temple of Saturnus, Temple of Concordia, Carcer (along road to the north), Curia, Comitium, Rostra, Shrine of Ianus, Shrine of Venus Cloacina, Tabernae Novae.

the Aerarium, the city-state's treasury. Across the short, north-western end of the Forum were a number of small monuments, in-cluding the Volcanol, an enclosure with an ancient altar dedicated to Vulcan. Above, on the axis of the Forum, was the Temple of Con-cordia, erected in 367 B.C. to commemorate a pact between patri-cians and plebeians. At the northern corner of the Forum an area was set aside for public business. The Curia, built on rising ground so as to dominate the whole long space of the Forum Romanum, was the normal meeting place for the Senate. In order for its busi-ness to take place with full access to the will of the gods, meetings could be held only in a space that had been formally "inaugurated" as a place from which priestly officials could read the skies for omens (Aulus Gellius 14.7.7).[9] The original building that was set aside in this way and devoted to the use of the Senate was the Curia Hostilia—built, tradition said, by King Tullus Hostilius himself, and therefore even older than the republic. It was apparently large enough to accommodate the 300 or so men who made up the Sen-ate during most of the republic. Below and in front of the Curia, and always under its influence, was the Comitium, where the peo-ple stood to hear announcements and speeches, and to vote. It is restored as a circular area with several steps, on analogy with the Curia at Cosa (Pl. 15).

Next to the Comitium is a sacred precinct known as the Lapis Niger, which contains an archaic inscription referring to the king and which may have been a hero shrine to Romulus (Festus, p. 117L).[10]

On the long, northeastern side of the Forum a second series of shops stretched from the Comitium to the Regia,[11] and several small shrines recalled moments in prerepublican history. At the point where the Argiletum entered the Forum, perhaps originally in the form of a bridge across the brook, was the Shrine of Ianus, a gate in honor of the god of passages.[12] It had an important symbolic function because its doors were solemnly opened when the state was at war, and closed during peacetime.

Smaller monuments included the small, open-air Shrine of Venus Cloacina; a tree rumored to be as old as Rome itself; other trees (Pliny, *Natural History* 15.78, 16.236); and a fenced-off depression called the Lacus Curtius, associated with the patriotic heroism of a citizen named Curtius.

In the late fourth and third centuries B.C., the Forum Romanum acquired more of the look appropriate to a cosmopolitan city. The butchers and grocers, with their common activities, moved to their own markets (Nonius, *Compendium* 12.853L). The platform from which speakers spoke to the people in the Comitium was rebuilt. Bronze prows (*rostra,* "beaks") captured from enemy ships were built into the front of the platform, giving their name to it. The admiral in charge of that victory was Gaius Maenius, and to claim his share of the credit, he erected a memorial column, the Columna Maeniana, just west of the Comitium. Several years later, in 318, when this same Maenius was censor, he built two-storied porticoes, thenceforth known as Maeniana, over the shops along one or both sides of the Forum. Such projects made the Forum Romanum a more gracious, leisurely place, and lent it a new symbolic function, that of a museum containing souvenirs of conquests and memorials of the noble families whose members had won the victories. Statues and paintings went up everywhere, most thickly around the Comitium (Pliny, *Natural History* 34.20–25, 30; 35.25). By 158 B.C. there were so many that a law was passed requiring that all statues that had not been approved by the Senate and the people be removed.[13]

Still, these developments were slow, and at the end of the third century B.C. the Forum Romanum remained an irregular open space marked by nothing more monumental than a handful of average-sized temples. It was in the following century that the Forum began to acquire the dignity befitting a really important city.

The physical expression of that dignity was the *basilica,* a unique contribution of the Romans to architectural history. When Italy is sunny, it can be intolerable to stay in the heat and glare; when Italy is not sunny, the rain also is intolerable. Such mundane considerations, along with an increase in legal business, led to the invention of the basilica, an enclosure that was a roofed extension of the Forum, intended to permit the businessmen, politicians, and lawyers to conduct their business in any kind of weather. To maximize the available space, rows of columns or piers created several aisles, often left open to the Forum (cf. the basilica at Cosa, at the upper right of Plate 15). Balconies over the aisles added to the usable space, and porches marked the entrances (Vitruvius 5.1.4–5).[14] Cato, when he was censor in 184 B.C., built the Basilica Porcia, the first one for which we have explicit references.[15] It probably stood at the northern corner of the Forum, and is represented on Figure 8 as adjacent to the Curia, on the road leading to the Campus Martius.

The censors in 179 B.C. followed Cato's lead and built the much larger Basilica Aemilia-Fulvia along the northeastern edge of the Forum, behind the Tabernae Novae.[16] This was balanced in 170 B.C. by the Basilica Sempronia behind the Tabernae Veteres on the opposite side of the Forum.

All this tended to make the Forum a more pleasant, convenient place in which to be, and an alarmed Cato was moved to argue that it should be paved with sharp stones in order to discourage people from loitering there (Pliny, *Natural History* 19.24). Such sentiments could not prevail against the Mediterranean propensity to gather in public spaces, however, and a passage from a play of the early second century conveys a vivid picture of the somewhat disreputable types to be found working and lounging about the Forum. In Plautus's account (*Curculio* 470–483), perjurers, naturally enough, hang out at the Comitium, while liars and braggarts are farther along at the Shrine of Venus Cloacina, and prostitutes and pimps encounter rich married men and their money in front of the basilica. Outside the Forum proper, in the Forum Piscarium (the Fish Market), are members of dining clubs. The middle of the Forum had three parts: in the lower part, near the Temple of Concordia, are men of quality and wealth, Plautus says; phonies are higher up, near the sewer ditch; gossips farther still, by a cistern (*lacus*), "gratuitously shouting abuse at other people." Moneylenders are at the Tabernae Veteres, but dealers in more suspect goods would be

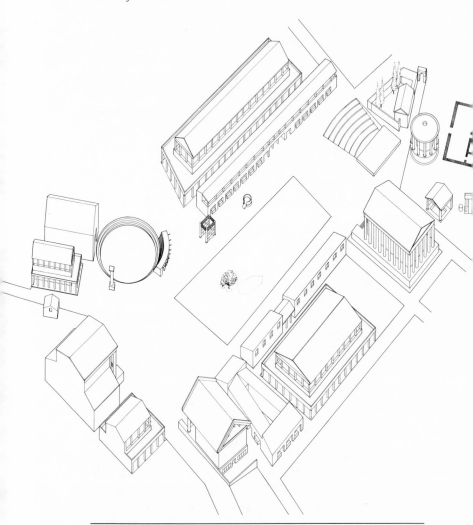

Fig. 8. Rome: Forum Romanum, second century B.C. *Clockwise from the southeast (upper right):* Tribunal Aurelium, Regia, Fornix Fabiorum, Temple of Vesta, Atrium Vestae (plan), Lacus Iuturnae, Temple of Castor, Tabernae Veteres, Basilica Sempronia, Temple of Saturnus, Basilica Opimia, Temple of Concordia, Carcer, Basilica Porcia, Curia, Comitium and Columna Maeniana, Rostra, Shrine of Ianus, Shrine of Venus Cloacina, Tabernae Novae, Basilica Aemilia.

around behind the Temple of Castor; there, too, in the Vicus Tuscus, are male prostitutes. In the Velabrum are the butcher, the baker, and the prophecy maker.

The second half of the century was busy as well. To celebrate the victory of the optimates over the Gracchi in 121 B.C., the consul Lucius Opimius enlarged the temple of Concordia, adding at its side a new basilica. The façades of the two buildings gave new definition to the northwestern end of the Forum. That same year Quintus Fabius celebrated his conquest of the Allobroges by erecting the Forum's first triumphal arch, the Fornix Fabiorum, at the southeastern corner, just beyond the Regia. In 117 B.C. the old Etruscan-style Temple of Castor was rebuilt on a larger scale; as Figure 8 shows, it now had the tall surrounding colonnade that was characteristic of a Greek temple. This, with a new, larger Regia and the Fornix Fabiorum, formed a monumental entrance to the southeastern end of the Forum which balanced the construction at the other end and reflected the new taste for Hellenistic elegance.

Until about the middle of the second century B.C. the Comitium was the site of voting and jury trials, but then the legislative activity moved out into the Forum Romanum. There the citizens, after listening to speeches, filed by the tellers according to their membership in the 35 tribes. People noticed and talked when Licinius Crassus in 145 and Gaius Gracchus in 123 B.C. made a political issue of the spatial arrangements by turning their backs on the senators in the Curia and speaking directly to the people out in the Forum Romanum, in violation of parliamentary etiquette (Cicero, *De Amicitia* 96; Plutarch, *Gaius Gracchus* 5).

The Senate continued to meet in its old Curia, but when Sulla expanded its membership (to 600), he had to enlarge the building as well. It was kept in the same location and orientation as its predecessor because it was completely in line with Sulla's pro-senatorial policies that the Senate House should stand in this dominating position, in view of the whole Forum and above the Comitium, where the people voted, and the open square where they gathered to listen to speeches. This was the Curia in which many of Cicero's speeches were delivered, where debates over the fate of Catiline or the distribution of commands were held. After the death of Sulla, in 78 B.C., his spirit was kept alive by a large number of his old allies. Therefore, it was grimly appropriate that in 52 B.C., when Publius Clodius Pulcher (one of the strongest rivals to Sulla's heritage) was killed, his supporters carried his body into the Curia, piled up the furniture and set fire to it all as a funeral pyre. Within a few years, Sulla's son, Faustus, was commissioned to rebuild the Curia, but Julius Caesar tore it down before it was ever completed, in order to make way for his own Forum Iulium.

Administration under the Principate

In the last years of the republic it was all too evident that traditional institutions were no longer capable of efficiently running a city with a population near a million. Julius Caesar increased the numbers of quaestors, aediles, and praetors, and sponsored legislation (the *Lex Iulia Municipalis*)[17] in an attempt to instill some order into the city's administrative mechanism. It was Augustus, however, who, after restoring order to the empire, was able to give the city an orderly administration. The framework of his innovation was a re-organization of the city into fourteen administrative regions. Each was presided over by one of the praetors, tribunes, or aediles chosen by lot. The regions in turn were organized into *vici,* existing streets that functioned as small neighborhood wards. The officers of the vici[18] were appointed by the emperor, who also controlled the appointment of a new bureaucracy. At the head of this bureaucracy was the *praefectus urbi* ("prefect of the city"), appointed from the senatorial class for an extended term. The prefect commanded the soldiers of the urban cohorts and presided over his own court.

The powers of the traditional elected officials quickly eroded as the imperial bureaucracy grew. The praetors' jurisdiction was reduced to relatively minor law cases. The emperor himself assumed the duties and power of the republican censors. The tribunate lost all its powers, but remained as a stepping stone to higher office. The aediles kept their responsibility to maintain the physical fabric of the city, but gave up the administration of the grain supply and festivals. The quaestors lost their fiscal duties and became cere-

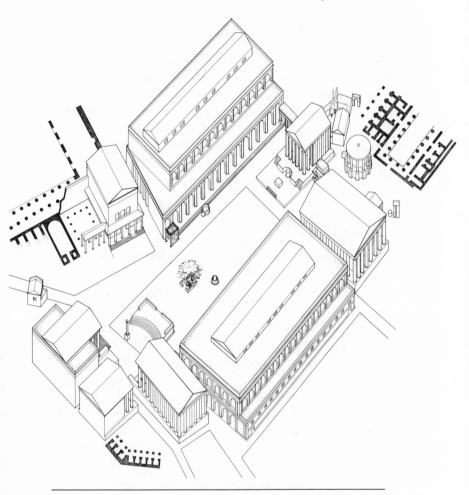

Fig. 9. Rome: Forum Romanum, first century A.D. *Clockwise from the southeast (upper right):* Temple of the Deified Iulius, Regia, Fornix Fabiorum, Atrium Vestae (plan), Temple of Vesta, Arcus Augusti, Lacus Iuturnae, Temple of Castor, Basilica Iulia, Rostra, Temple of Saturnus, Porticus Deorum Consentium (plan), Temple of the Deified Vespasianus, Temple of Concordia, Carcer, Curia Iulia, Basilica Aemilia.

monial bodyguards to the emperor and consuls. The consuls retained their position of prestige, although this too was diluted because they tended to serve for only part of the usual one-year term, to make the office accessible to more people. And of course it did not take long for the consulships to be occupied only by people of whom the emperor approved. For a while Augustus made a great show of going about the Forum soliciting votes for the candidates he was supporting (who were always elected, of course), but by the reign of Tiberius, elections of magistrates had been taken away from the people's comitia and put into the more easily controlled hands of the Senate (Tacitus, *Annals* 1.15). As the traditional magistrates declined in authority, the responsibility of running the city shifted to the emperor and others directly responsible to him.[19] Many routine duties were entrusted to the emperor's freedmen and slaves.

The Forum Romanum in the Principate

By the end of the reign of Domitian, the Forum Romanum had assumed the form shown in Figure 9. Along both sides the two major basilicas had been rebuilt. The Basilica Aemilia, on the northeastern side, had been enlarged in 55 B.C., and when it burned down in 14 B.C., was rebuilt with marble paving and columns. On the southwestern side, Julius Caesar had replaced the Basilica Sempronia and the adjacent shops with a grand new Basilica Iulia. It too was damaged in a fire, in 12 B.C., and was rebuilt on an even larger scale by Augustus: triple rows of piers surrounded the central space, creating a double-vaulted ambulatory. On one side the space opened out to present a monumental façade to the Forum, mirroring that of the Basilica Aemilia across the square. The Basilica Iulia housed the Centumviral Court, a panel of 180 jurors which usually met in four sections to hear civil lawsuits such as inheritance disputes. Literary references of the late first century A.D. give us a good picture of the Basilica when these courts were in session: a speaker at one court, popping loud rhetorical fireworks, distracting the attention of spectators at the other courts as well, to the embarrassment of any other speakers. For important cases, all 180 jurors sat together as a single panel, as they did once when Pliny the Younger, on an exceptionally good day in his career as a lawyer, attracted an enthusiastic crowd of men and women who hung over the balcony railings and pushed their way onto the presiding officer's tribunal

(Pliny, *Letters* 6.33; cf. Quintilian, *Institutio Oratoria* 10.5.6).

Bankers also set up their tables in and beside the basilicas. An inscription commemorates one "Lucius Marcius Fortunatus, banker from the Basilica Iulia."[20] In front of the Basilica Aemilia were the Tabernae Argentariae (Moneychangers' Shops), and in the ruins of the Basilica Aemilia, fused into the marble pavement, are remains of coins spilled by moneychangers scrambling to safety when the building burned down in late antiquity.

In addition to the Basilica Iulia, Julius Caesar planned an elaborate rearrangement of the northern corner of the Forum Romanum when the Curia burned in 52 B.C. The senatorial Curia was pushed back from its former prominence and tucked behind a corner of the Basilica Aemilia. Even though it was less conspicuous, the Curia Iulia was large enough to accommodate most of the senators, who now numbered nearly a thousand. Although the Curia, which is still in a very good state of preservation, was rebuilt by the emperor Diocletian after a fire in A.D. 283, it seems to have retained the basic floor plan of the Curia Iulia, and this allows us to visualize a meeting of the Senate during the principate. A broad aisle led from the door to a platform on which the presiding officers, usually the consuls, sat. On each side of the aisle were three low steps, where the senators sat on wooden benches. When a large number of senators turned out for a meeting, there was not quite enough room for all to sit down (which is true of the British House of Commons as well). The most distinguished members, especially former consuls and praetors, sat on the front benches. The youngest or least prominent had to stand near the back on the top step: they were known as *pedarii* ("footmen"), not only because they had to stand but also because they would walk to a speaker whose position they favored. The Senate did not normally take formal votes; when the presiding officer saw a majority gathered on one side of the aisle or the other, he declared the issue settled. Meanwhile, except in rare executive sessions, the doors of the Curia were kept open, and the space just outside them was reserved for the sons of senators to observe the conduct of business.[21] With this rebuilding of the Curia, the old Comitium was largely obliterated, an echo of the historical realities of Roman politics under the principate, when elections were taken away from the republican assemblies and placed in the hands of senators and emperor.

Between Julius Caesar and Tiberius, the whole northwestern end of the Forum Romanum received a new face. We have already mentioned the construction of the Basilica Iulia by Caesar and its enlargement under Augustus. The Temple of Saturnus next to it was refurbished by Munatius Plancus in 42 B.C. It had been the last building in the Forum to retain the old Etruscan-Italic type of architecture. Now it, too, took on the enclosing colonnade and tall proportions characteristic of a Greek temple. The Rostra were moved, to define a new axis running the length of the Forum, well separated from any obvious connection with the Curia; here speakers could address a large crowd, and magistrates could preside over trials. Tiberius rebuilt the Temple of Concordia and erected a triumphal arch for himself.[22] Later the Temple of Deified Vespasianus was built next to the Temple of Concordia, facing the Clivus Capitolinus as it started up the hill. Two final monuments were the Arcus Septimii Severi, at the northern corner of the Forum, next to the Rostra, and the Porticus Deorum Consentium, just up the hill from the Temple of Vespasianus.[23]

At the opposite, southeastern, end of the Forum lay a jumble of small monuments—the Regia and the Temple of Vesta, and the Lacus Iuturnae tucked in behind the Temple of Castor. Augustus effectively removed all these from the monumental part of the Forum by composing a new façade. On the spot where Julius Caesar's body had been cremated, the small Temple of the Deified Iulius was built on a high podium. Its six columns reflected those of the temples already standing on the other sides of the open Forum.[24] On each side of this temple, to mark the entrance into the Forum Romanum from the Sacra Via, Augustus erected arches commemorating his victory over Antony and Cleopatra at Actium, his victories (and those of all the consuls and triumphant generals of Roman history) over foreign enemies, and the dynastic promise for the future embodied in his grandsons, Gaius and Lucius.[25] In this way the southeastern end of the Forum became a dynastic monument, dominated by three generations of Augustus's family. The old landmarks—Regia and Vesta—were placed quite literally in their shadow, reduced to rather quaint antiquities. The Forum Romanum itself, meanwhile, changed from an informal jumble of buildings to a coordinated space. A strong axis led from the Temple of the Deified Iulius to the new Rostra. If you stood in front of the Temple of the Deified Iulius and looked along that axis, you saw the colonnades and porticoes of temples and basilicas on each side, and as a backdrop at the far end, the façade of the Temple of Concordia and, higher on the Capitoline Hill, the vaults of the Tabularium.

The Imperial Fora

The tendency to make the Forum Romanum more regular paralleled similar trends elsewhere in Rome—for instance, the influence of the traditional marketplace, with its rows of shops, the regular axiality of Italic temple precincts, and the colonnaded agoras familiar in the Greek cities of the Hellenistic world. Within the city, the clearest expressions of this tendency were the imperial fora. These lay to the north and northeast of the Forum Romanum, eventually forming a contiguous series of enclosed areas, each with a temple placed axially at the back and flanked by porticoes on each side (Fig. 10).[26]

The Forum Iulium illustrates the basic shape. Begun by Julius Caesar in 54 B.C. and dedicated in 46 B.C., its architectural focus was the Temple of Venus Genetrix (Pl. 12A). The enclosed space in front of it contained an altar, a fountain with statues of nymphs, and other statues and paintings displayed as in a museum. With its border of porticoes and shops, the Forum Iulium was intended to provide additional space for the legal business that had severely taxed the old Forum Romanum (Appian, *Civil Wars* 2.102).

The Forum Augustum was intended from the beginning (begun in 37 B.C., dedicated in 2 B.C.) for more specific ceremonial functions, but it also increased the space available for routine legal business by means of two hemicycles along its sides, behind the columns of the porticoes. In Chapter 4 we analyzed the iconography of its architecture and sculpture, which served as an eloquent advertisement for Augustus's policies.

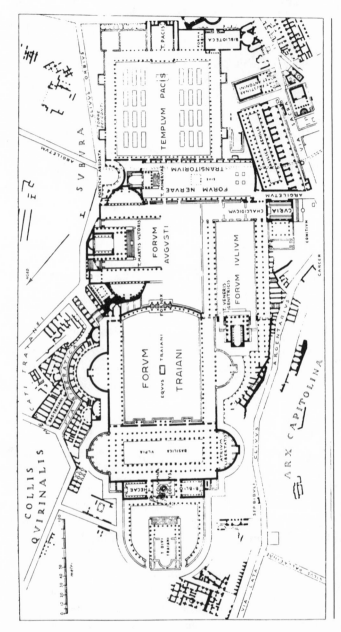

Fig. 10. Rome: Imperial Fora

Even larger was the Forum Pacis, erected by Vespasian to commemorate the return of peace after the chaos of the year A.D. 69. Here the Temple of Pax was reduced in visual importance, placed behind a colonnade at the eastern end of the precinct. On each side of the temple were libraries and a museum, and the central space was filled with flower beds and elegant statuary. This forum functioned more as a quiet place of refuge than as a place for official business.

Vespasian's son Domitian planned an additional forum between the Forum Pacis and the Forum Augustum. It was known as the Forum Transitorium, since it accommodated those who passed through the Argiletum on the way between the Subura and the Forum Romanum. Here the problem was to occupy the narrow space available while using the traditional vocabulary of the Forum Iulium and Forum Augustum. The problem was solved by emphasizing the façade of the temple, dedicated to Minerva, although little room was left for the porticoes on each side. In their place, engaged columns were added to suggest the architectural iconography of the earlier fora while introducing a baroque element—the projecting cornice—which was dear to the hearts of Domitian's architects. This forum was completed by Nerva and is often called the Forum Nervae.

The last and grandest of the imperial fora was the Forum Traiani. Its original plan did not include a temple as a focal point, but instead combined a great open space flanked by two hemicycles, and closed on the northwest by the gigantic Basilica Ulpia. Beyond this basilica, a pair of libraries surrounded the Columna Traiani, a monumental column covered with reliefs celebrating Trajan's conquest of Dacia. Hadrian then added a temple on the northwestern end to make at least the ground plan of the Forum Traiani correspond more closely to that of its predecessors.

These five fora, erected between 54 B.C. and A.D. 113, so vastly increased the space available for public business in the center of the city that the old Forum Romanum was left without its original function. The food merchants had moved out long ago, and now the lawyers had also found more agreeable quarters. So the Forum Romanum became a symbol, a stage for pageantry, a museum of past and present glories. Triumphal arches accumulated: for Augustus in 29 and again in 19 B.C., for Tiberius in A.D. 16, for Drusus in A.D. 23, for Septimius Severus in A.D. 203. New temples were built, in honor of Vespasianus and Antoninus et Faustina. Monuments such as the Equus Domitiani, a statue of Domitian to which Statius devoted the opening poems of his *Silvae,* or from the very end of antiquity the Columna Phocae, which still stands next to the remains of the Basilica Iulia, celebrated the exploits of the emperors.[27]

Eight

Services, Public and Private

The public world of showy buildings, political speeches, and legal proceedings is normally no more than an interesting backdrop in the lives of both ancient and modern city dwellers, who tend to play out their roles on the stage of smaller social groups—family, friends, and colleagues. The public world impinges on the private one only when an individual and his or her immediate group look beyond themselves for security, food, water, medical care, and the like, and find either help, hindrance, or indifference.

In ancient Rome the interactions between urban government and private residents shaped a very different profile of services from that which is familiar in modern industrialized cities, and so the section headings of this chapter are self-consciously "modernizing." They are the categories for which a modern city planner would expect to make some provision. As we shall see, they were not necessarily what the Romans considered essential issues, but they nevertheless help us frame the question, What resources were at hand to help individuals cope with the day-to-day problems of living in the ancient city of Rome?

The most basic need was for security, which the republic had provided for several centuries, even when faced with Hannibal's invasion. In the last century of its existence, however, as the institutions of the republic failed to provide even the basic security of peace in the streets and food in the markets, the traditional Senate-centered government yielded control of essential services to the institutions of the principate. Under nearly all our headings, the proposals of Julius Caesar and the reforms of Augustus are crucial factors in the reorganization and regulation that took place.

Finances

To provide public services was generally a responsibility, and an opportunity, of the ruling class, which not only sponsored much of the building in the ancient city but also established endowments, supplemented the grain supply, or paid for games as a kind of *munus,* "public obligation." A problem with depending on the usually self-interested generosity of an upper-class sponsor was the potentially haphazard way in which "services" were "delivered."[1] When the emperors assumed responsibility for construction or other public services, they used their own purse, the *fiscus,* in much the same way that members of the aristocracy had traditionally used their family fortunes to pay for their donations to the public good. They worked on a much larger scale, however, and in theory a more systematic one.

Funds belonging to the state treasury flowed into the *aerarium* in the Temple of Saturnus in the Forum Romanum. Taxes and tolls, produce and rents from public land, generated this revenue. The money was available to aediles and censors, who used it to construct and maintain public buildings and roads. Sometimes the army supplied the manpower, but more often, especially in and around Rome, city officials depended on private contractors to supply slave or free labor.

Police

The state did its best to provide peace and security through its military policy, but during the republic, law enforcement and police protection were left in the hands of private individuals. The Twelve Tables make it clear that although the state took responsibility for conducting trials and passing judgment through its magistrates, the praetors, it was the job of the victim or his or her family to apprehend and prosecute the lawbreaker. The only specific law enforcement officers mentioned in the Twelve Tables are the *quaestores paricidii,* whose duty it was to investigate "parricide." In the traditional Roman legal vocabulary, this was the premeditated murder of a free person (Festus, p. 247L), the one crime in which the state took an explicit active interest. The Twelve Tables recognized private suits between citizens, though often these were arbitrated by some third party—*iudex unus*—whom both parties trusted.[2] Starting in the second century B.C., separate tribunals were established to judge crimes against the state,[3] although it still remained the responsibility of private citizens to gather evidence and conduct the prosecution.

Routine police activities were distributed among several of the annually elected magistrates. The aediles had general responsibility for keeping public order, and three minor magistrates, the *triumviri capitales,* were in charge of arrests, prisons and executions.[4] The latter were relatively inexperienced junior magistrates just starting their public careers. They had a staff of public slaves to assist them and to do the dirty work of torture and executions,[5] but they did not really have the capacity to deal with major disturbances. This led to tremendous difficulties in the late republic, when political gangs roamed the streets and nocturnal violence was an unavoidable fact of urban life. The powerful needed their retinue of clients to act as bodyguards; the ordinary citizens had no real defense.

The rule was that if you wanted justice, you had to get it for yourself. If you had a grievance, you had to get satisfaction, or persuade or hire someone to help you get it. To help, contractors stood ready with the equivalent of hired guns and hoodlums. The gang warfare of the last generation of the republic, spearheaded by Publius Clodius Pulcher and Titus Annius Milo, was only one example of the general tendency to take the law into one's own hands, with the understanding that the state was not usually concerned.

Such was the situation when Augustus assumed control. He assigned the aediles to continue their duties of policing roads, taverns, baths, and the like, and the triumviri capitales to continue administering the Carcer, the old prison in the Forum Romanum. For more effective police capabilities, Augustus turned to the army, a move that had considerable impact on the texture of city life. Under the republic, soldiers bearing arms had not ordinarily been permitted within the city, but Augustus stationed several military contingents in and around it, even at the risk of offending republican sensibilities.

The *cohortes praetoriae* became a pervasive military presence in the city.[6] An elite corps, these praetorians were installed by Tiberius in the Castra Praetoria on the Viminal. They were responsible, under the command of the praetorian prefect, for the security of the emperor. As such they formed a ceremonial honor guard, but they also probably provided riot control.[7]

Three *cohortes urbanae* performed general police duties under the command of the praefectus urbi.[8] They were lodged with the praetorian cohorts on the Viminal until in the third century A.D. Aurelian built them a camp of their own, the Castra Urbana, in the Campus Martius.

Seven *cohortes vigilum* patrolled the streets of the city at night as watchmen (Dio Cassius, *Roman History* 55.26.4–5), but dangers persisted. Torches carried by pedestrians provided the only light, the streets and alleys were full of places in which to hide, and if a rich man went out at night, he took private bodyguards with him. The poor man took his chances.[9]

Two detachments of sailors were stationed in Rome to supervise navigation and patrol the military harbors on the Tiber, as well as work the sail-like awnings at the amphitheater and tend the Naumachia Augusti.[10] Criminal investigations were often undertaken by private entrepreneurs known as *delatores,* who brought information to the courts of the urban praetor and the emperor. Their uncontrolled activities, documented in literature of the principate, show why the upper classes viewed them as a threat until they were restrained by Trajan and other emperors. In the second century A.D., the task of supplying information to the emperor was entrusted to *frumentarii.* These were originally, to judge from their name, involved with supplying grain to the legions. Their awareness of logistics eventually led to more sinister duties, gathering information, performing assassinations, and conducting prisoners to Rome.[11]

Criminal trials were conducted before the appropriate praetor or the emperor. Punishments were administered according to the social rank of the convicted person. Men and women of the upper classes were punished with loss of status, exile, or a private execution, usually by beheading in the Carcer, a small, stone-walled, subterranean prison at the base of the Capitoline. Under some emperors the upper classes also felt the fear of cruel tortures. Seneca (*De Ira* 3.18–19; cf. *Epistulae* 14.4–6) lists the fears of a public official faced with the emperor's suspicion or displeasure: sword, fire, chains, wild beasts, the cross, the rack, the hook, the impaling stake, chariots to tear a victim apart, or shirts smeared with pitch and set ablaze.

The lower classes were more generally subject to beatings and public execution, and slaves and war criminals could suffer the most horrendous public torture. This public display of the instruments and procedures of official cruelty would most shock a modern visitor, yet it seems to have been taken for granted by ancient writers. Plautus makes comic allusions to the punishments awaiting slaves (*Asinaria* 301–305); *Curculio* 689–690; *Mostellaria* 56–57); and other sources show that slaves suffered their punishment in full public view, in the streets (Tacitus, *Annals* 14–45), the Circus Maximus and Forum (Livy 2.36.1; Dionysius of Halicarnassus, *Roman Antiquities* 7.69.1; Valerius Maximus, *Memorabilia* 1.7.4); the theaters, or in the atrium of the house, with the doors wide open (Suetonius, *Augustus* 45.4). Contractors rented out *carnifices,* whose job was to execute slaves for their masters; Martial (2.17.2) mentions their blood-stained whips (knotted around sharp pieces of metal or bone to inflict maximum pain) hanging where the Subura entered the Forum Romanum. The place of flogging and execution—by crucifixion or impalement—was on the Via Tiburtina, outside the Porta Esquilina, near the public burial dump (Plautus, *Miles Gloriosus* 359–360; Tacitus, *Annals* 2.32).[12]

Fire

The Romans knew all too well the dangers of fire, and yet the responsiblity for fighting fires remained in the hands of individual owners. Their wood-frame buildings of *opus craticium* were crisply inflammable and packed close together, and conflagrations recurred frequently in the history of the city.[13]

In the late republic, Marcus Licinius Crassus made a profitable enterprise of appearing at a fire in time to buy the burning building at a low price from its desperate owner, whereupon his gang of 500 trained slaves extinguished the fire (Plutarch, *Crassus* 2.4). Marcus Egnatius Rufus, aedile in 22 B.C., used another approach, prompted by public spiritedness or, more likely, ambition to appear as a benefactor. He offered his own slaves and other men hired at his expense to help owners whose houses were burning. This made him so popular that Augustus became suspicious, and issued a curt edict encouraging the aediles to spend more time preventing fires rather than extinguishing them (Dio Cassius, *Roman History* 53.24.4–6).

The watchmen in Augustus's cohortes vigilum became responsible for preventing and fighting fires.[14] Each of the seven cohorts was responsible for two of the city's regions. The personnel included officers—tribunes, centurions, and *principales*—and men specially trained as *siphonarii* (pump mechanics and engineers), *aquarii* (who had to know the location of water supplies within their regions and organized the bucket brigades), *centonarii* (who apparently smothered fires with mats), *falciarii* and *unciarii* (who wielded the demolition hooks), *ballistorii* (who manned the catapults that knocked down buildings adjacent to the fire), and physicians. Each cohort had its headquarters (*statio*) in one of its regions,[15] and a subsidiary dormitory (*excubitorium*) in the other.[16]

Water

At first, Romans took their water supply from the Tiber, or from springs and wells. By the end of the fourth century B.C. this seemed inadequate, and during the censorship of Appius Claudius Caecus

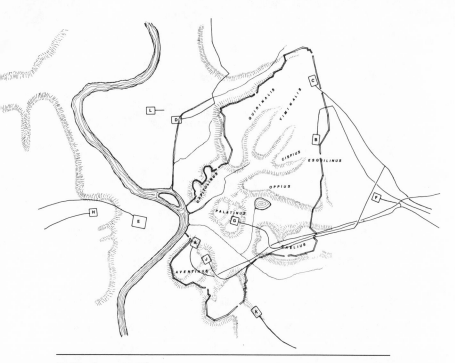

Fig. 11. Rome: Aqueducts

A *Aqua Appia:* 312 B.C. Appius Claudius Caecus (censor). From springs on the Via Praenestina (eighth/ninth milestone) across the Aventine to the Porta Trigemina. 11,190 paces (16,561 m.) long. Underground except for 60 paces on arches at the Porta Capena. Capacity 1,825 quinariae (75,737 m.³/day). Augustus added a new supply channel near the source.

B *Anio Vetus:* 272 B.C. Manius Curius Dentatus (censor). From Anio (between Vicovaro and Mandela) to the Esquiline (near Termini Station). 43,000 paces (63,640 m.) long. Underground except for 221 paces on supporting walls. Capacity 4,398 quinariae (182,517 m.³/day).

C *Aqua Marcia:* 144 B.C. Quintus Marcius (praetor). From upper Anio (the thirty-sixth milestone of the Via Valeria) to the Viminal, with branches to the Quirinal, Capitoline, Campus Martius, Caelian, and Aventine by the late first century A.D. 61,710 paces (90,000 m.) long. In the country, 463 paces on arches; near the city, 528 paces on substructures and 6,472 paces on arches. Capacity 4.690 quinariae (194,365 m.³/day). Augustus added a new supply channel, 800 paces long, at the source. Caracalla added a channel (K) to supply his baths.

Aqua Tepula: 125 B.C. Gnaeus Servilius Cepio and Lucius Cassius Longinus Ravilla (censors). From the Villa of Lucullus (tenth milestone of the Via Latina) to join the Marcia near the city. Length unrecorded. Capacity 445 quinariae (18,467 m.³/day).

Aqua Iulia: 40 or 33 B.C. Agrippa (praetor in 40, aedile in 33). From springs near the twelfth milestone of the Via Latina, it absorbed the Tepula and joined the

Marcia near the city. 15,426.5 paces (21,677 m.) long. 528 paces on substructures and 6,472 paces on arches. Capacity 649 quinariae (31,576 m.³/day).

D *Aqua Virgo:* 19 B.C. Agrippa. From springs below the Villa of Lucullus (eighth milestone of the Via Collatina), past the city on the north, under the Pincian to the Saepta and the Thermae Agrippianae on the Campus Martius. 14,105 paces (20,571 m.) long. 540 paces on substructures and 700 paces on arches. Capacity 2,504 quinariae (103,916 m.³/day).

E *Aqua Alsietina:* 2 B.C. Augustus. From Lake Alsietinus (Martignano) and Lake Sabatinus (Bracciano) to the Trans-Tiber region, mainly to supply the Naumachia Augusti. 22,172 paces (32,815 m.) long. 358 paces on arches. Capacity 392 quinariae (16,228 m.³/day).

F *Aqua Claudia:* A.D. 38–52. Caligula and Claudius. From the Caerulian and Curtian springs at the thirty-eighth milestone on the Via Sublacensis to the Esquiline. 46,406 paces (68,681 m.) long. 604 paces on substructures and 6,491 on arches. Capacity 4,607 quinariae (191,190 m.³/day). Nero added a branch to the Caelian, which was extended by Domitian to his palace on the Palatine (G).

Anio Novus: A.D. 38–52. Caligula and Claudius. From the upper Anio (forty-second milestone of the Via Sublacensis), then along the course of the Claudia to the Esquiline. 58,700 paces (86,876 m.) long. In the country, 9,400 paces on substructures; near the city, 609 paces on substructures and 6,491 paces on arches. Capacity 4,738 quinariae (196,627 m.³/day).

G *Arcus Neroniani:* A.D. 52–68. Nero. See F.

H *Aqua Traiana:* A.D. 109. Trajan. From Lake Bracciano to the Janiculum. 32,500 meters long. Too late to be recorded by Frontinus.

J *Rivus Herculaneus:* Augustus, Nero, Trajan. An extension, much rebuilt, of the Aqua Marcia over the Caelian to the Aventine.

K *Aqua Antoniniana:* A.D. 212–213. Caracalla. An extension of the Aqua Marcia to serve the Thermae Antoninianae.

L *Aqua Alexandrina.* A.D. 226. Alexander Severus. From the fourteenth milestone of the Via Praenestina over the Esquiline (?) at or near ground level to the Campus Martius and the Thermae Alexandrinae.

(312 B.C.) Rome's first aqueduct was built. The Roman engineers adapted the technology of the underground sewer, learned from the Etruscans, to construct a conduit from springs beyond the eighth milestone on the Via Praenestina. To maintain a gradual downgrade toward the city, the underground channel followed a twisting course and entered the city on the high ground of the Caelian Hill. It crossed over a series of low arches to the Aventine, under which it tunneled to an outlet near the river.[17] In 272 B.C. a

second aqueduct, the Anio Vetus, was built from the Anio River to supply the growing population on the Esquiline, using the same kind of underground channel.

With the tremendous growth of the city in the second century B.C. a new aqueduct was needed. After an unsuccessful attempt in 179 (Livy 40.51.7), the Aqua Marcia was constructed in 144 B.C. This also tapped the Anio, but from a spot farther upstream, where the water was fresher. To keep the route of the water channel as short as possible, the engineers, when they encountered a valley, built a bridge of masonry arches to carry the channel from the hill on one side to the hill on the other. Similarly, when they reached the point where the ground level dropped off, at the seventh milestone from the city, they built a series of arches that allowed a gradual drop in elevation. These arches are still visible, marching across the landscape along the Naples railway line at Capanelle, east of Rome.

Once inside the city, the water was received in a settling basin (*lacus*) and passed through a distribution tower (*castellum*) into a smaller channel (*rivus*), and then to a public fountain. Public baths received a special supply of water, delivered through pipes of terracotta or lead.[18] Private individuals with enough money or prestige could obtain the Senate's permission to tap into the public water supply, additional evidence of their clout. The less-exalted folk fetched water from the public fountains, or hired an *aquarius,* a contractor who delivered water to customers. These aquarii carried jars of water up the steps of insulae or hauled them up in nets to apartment windows.[19] If a line in Juvenal (6.332) is any indication, their rounds brought them in contact with lonely women, and the aquarius was as good a source of off-color jokes as the milkman has been more recently.

We know about the water supply system in great detail because in A.D. 97 the emperor Nerva appointed Sextus Julius Frontinus to be water commissioner of the city. Frontinus had served as praetor urbanus, as consul, and as governor of Britain, and he brought to his new office a sense of public duty in combination with a general's ability to organize, an engineer's love of gimmicks, and a bureaucrat's passion for detail. As a result, through his work *The Aque-*

ducts of Rome, we know the building history, length, and capacity of each of the nine aqueducts in service at the time, as well as the organization of the corps of workmen assigned to the aqueducts and some of the major legislation regarding the administration of the water supply.

During the republic, the construction was paid for by the censors out of their general funds. They hired private contractors who used gangs of slaves to keep the aqueducts in repair. Censors and aediles inspected the work. Legally, the water was to go to the public fountains for the common good, and only the Senate had the prerogative of assigning water rights to private individuals. Householders of course found ways to bribe slaves and their supervisors, and when Cato was censor in 184 B.C. he tried to impose some discipline by disconnecting the private supply pipes (Livy 39.44.4). Under Augustus, Agrippa established a more orderly administration. Using his staff of 240 skilled slaves, Agrippa improved supervision and enforcement, built the Aqua Iulia and the Aqua Virgo, and added elaborate public fountains (*nymphaea*) to the urban scene. When he died, in 12 B.C., he left his staff to the emperor, who organized it as a new commission to maintain the aqueducts. A series of laws passed in 11 B.C. provided for the maintenance of public fountains, regulated the diversion of water for private uses, and mandated a right-of-way on each side of the aqueducts (Frontinus, *Aqueducts of Rome* 2.98–111).[20]

Sanitation

The disposal of waste water was a concern of the community, especially for one with a site like Rome's, where the civic center occupied a low-lying area prone to floods and marshiness. The solution was the construction of a channel, at first open but later roofed over, along the line of the brook running down through the Forum Romanum and Velabrum to the Forum Boarium. Tradition held that the Etruscan kings built the first sewer, the Cloaca Maxima, in Rome (Livy 1.38.6, 1.46.2; Dionysius of Halicarnassus, *Roman Antiquities* 3.67.4; 4.44.1; Pliny, *Natural History* 36.106),[21] although the earliest remains in the Forum Romanum seem to be from the fourth century B.C. We know that Cato, as censor in 184 B.C., arranged for sewers on the Aventine and elsewhere (Livy 39.44.5). By the first century A.D., the capacity and efficiency of the system was so impressive that Pliny, ever the technocrat, managed to express the thought (*Natural History* 36.104) that of everything in Rome, the sewers were "the most noteworthy thing of all."[22]

Archaeology provides almost our only evidence of the existence of latrines. No commemorative inscriptions record the construction of public toilets, and we really have no archaeological evidence for the period of the republic. Examples from the principate are usually rectangular rooms with mosaic pavements and a long stone bench along several sides. A row of keyhole-shaped openings indicate a decided lack of privacy, and suggest that these activities were, whether intentionally or not, social occasions. Below, running water passed through a trench as a flushing mechanism; to provide it, latrines were usually located at or near public baths.

Additional conveniences were offered by managers of shops, especially the fullers. Since urine was needed for their cloth-working, they often installed a large jar in the floor of a closet near the front of the shop, and men were free to use it as they passed by (cf. Macrobius, *Saturnalia* 3.16.15–16). Other small latrines were often located, both in public places and in private houses, in the odd space under a staircase.

Welfare

It was traditional for the aristocracy in Greco-Roman cities to make contributions or bequests in the form of banquets, entertainments, or distributions of grain, olive oil, or money. The object of these bequests, it seems, was recognition and honor, and so, more often than not, the greatest share was stipulated to go to those who could bestow honor, and consequently had the least need—town councillors and Augustales, for instance—although the poor did usually receive something, even though it was calibrated to take account of their lower rank. In Rome, the casual munificence of private patrons or ambitious aediles was complemented in 123 B.C., when as tribune Gaius Gracchus carried a motion to supply a regular ration of grain to each citizen (not to each resident) of Rome at a subsidized low price (Plutarch, *Gaius Gracchus* 5; Cicero, *Tusculan*

Disputations 3.48). Sulla may have abolished this provision, but in 58 B.C. the tribune Publius Clodius Pulcher improved on the Gracchan subsidy by providing a fixed amount every month completely free of charge. The model of the *clientela* is useful in understanding the shift. Politicians like the Gracchi used their own funds, and those of the state, to appeal to voters among the people. In effect, they made them their clients, and this model helps explain the success of Clodius's measures as well as those of Julius Caesar later in the first century.

Under the principate, the emperor became the patron of the whole city, and took on the responsibility of supplying food to the citizens, both in the regular monthly distributions of grain and in *congiaria,* handouts of money on special occasions. It is clear that in this period the populace acquired some expectation that the state would make minimal provision for its welfare, as seen in its complaints about the scarcity of grain or wine and in its demands for cash distributions.[23]

In Rome and other cities of Italy, *alimenta,* state-sponsored systems of loans to landholders, provided interest income to support annual payments to children. These began with Nerva or Trajan, and typically provided 16 sesterces a year for a boy if he was legitimate, 14 if he was illegitimate; 12 for a girl if legitimate, 10 if illegitimate. This is a small enough amount to suggest that it was aimed primarily at the poor, to subsidize their basic sustenance or encourage them to have children, but the qualifications clearly show that once a family got its child admitted to the dole, status was more significant than need.[24]

Such subsidies apart, the poor did what they could. Traditionally they became the clients of patrons who provided food or money in exchange for political support or other help. If that did not work— and the sources show that the process could involve an intensely competitive scramble—there was begging, stealing, or starving. Beggars are not mentioned much in classical literature, probably because the upper-class bias of our authors sailed over the head of poverty in the streets. In the Roman sense of values, predicated on a morality of reciprocal favors granted and expected, helping the poor and homeless was simply not the traditional way. That kind of charity was an Oriental concept codified by Jews and Christians who became conspicuous and a little suspect in their zeal for taking care of the sick and the poor.[25]

Health

In the Roman tradition, medical care, too, was a private matter. The duties of the *paterfamilias,* the father of the household, included tending the sick of his *familia.* Cato the Elder speaks for this tradition, as he knowledgeably lists cures for a wide variety of ailments. He was particularly fond of cabbage, which he prescribed as a tonic for indigestion, colic, fever, headache, constipation, insomnia, and deafness; prepared as a salve, he noted, it could be used for sores, scabs, and skin wounds (Cato, *On Agriculture* 156–158). The paterfamilias could also recite magic charms or offer prayers to such gods as Carna, who specialized in the internal organs, or he could call in specialists like the Marsian hill-people, who knew the herbs and spells that cured snakebite (Vergil, *Aeneid* 7.750–760; Silius Italicus, *Punica* 8.497–501). When a wife, son, or daughter took sick, the traditional Roman father administered remedies like these directly; lower-ranking members of the household would be cared for by slaves.[26]

Some medical problems were too serious to be handled within the household, and when a serious epidemic struck, the state reacted in the ways that were open to it, through the apparatus of the official priesthoods. Prayers were said, vows were made, and when the plague was averted, the deity was solemnly thanked: Apollo received a temple in 431 and games in 208 B.C.; Aesculapius was brought from Greece around 291 B.C. and given a temple on the Insula Tiberina. The city also took an active part in preventive medicine: Roman writers knew and appreciated how much aqueducts, sewers, and public baths contributed to public hygiene.[27]

Greek learning and culture made its impact in medicine just as much as elsewhere in Roman life. Lore from the medical schools in Greece and in the southern Italian Greek city of Croton may well have filtered into Rome for centuries, but the first Greek physician we know of in the city was Archagathus, who arrived in 219 B.C., during the hard times of the Hannibalic War. In subsequent centuries doctors of every persuasion converged on Rome, lecturing on their favorite theories, demonstrating their surgical techniques and elegant equipment (Plutarch, *Moralia* 71A; Dio Chrysostom 33.6), and arguing with each other about methods.[28] Some of these Greek immigrants became rich and influential by attracting the attention of the ruling class; Galen, physician to the imperial family of the Severi, is a particularly successful example. In some places, the city appointed a well-respected physician to an endowed position as *archiatros*.[29] The career of the younger Pliny's medical advisor, Harpocras, is perhaps a typical variation of the success story; an Egyptian who had learned the skills of an *iatraliptes,* specializing in certain kinds of physical therapy, Harpocras was so successful that Pliny (*Letters* 10.5–7) asked the emperor to grant him citizenship. From Seneca (*De Beneficiis* 6.16) we learn that the doctor-patient relationship could be more than professional, that a sincere and devoted bedside manner was appreciated and could ripen into friendship.

More often, the image of the *medicus* ("physician") in Roman literature is negative. He and his female counterpart, the midwife, tended to be slaves or ex-slaves.[30] They worked with their hands, and often stooped to dubious methods of attracting attention. Frequently the cures did not work, and visits of the medicus were stereotyped and parodied: drain some blood, apply a dressing, administer an enema (Pliny, *Natural History* 29.17–28; Galen, *Commentary on Hippocrates' De Alimento* 3.15).[31]

Other sources of medical help included the neighborhood barber, who knew something about herbs and knew how to handle sharp instruments.[32] The Temple of Aesculapius on the Insula Tiberina offered medical lore, a retreat from the city crowds, and an atmosphere of faith in the god's healing powers, reinforced by inscriptions and dedications testifying to cures.[33] Many turned to purveyors of magic charms amd amulets. Pliny (*Natural History* 20–32), when he discusses plants, earths, and animals, devotes most of his attention to their medicinal properties. Business in drugs and curative minerals was brisk.[34]

It is not hard to imagine that an invalid in Rome was faced with a bewildering variety of options, and no reliable guidance in finding treatment. Celsus, a Roman writer who apparently practiced medicine in the first century A.D., gives what seems to be a typically Roman response; after listing how each of the Greek medical schools would treat a fever, he advocates trying them all (*De Medicina* 3.14), and elsewhere he combines modern surgery with such folk cures as drinking the blood of a gladiator (for epilepsy, 3.23.7) or eating a snake (for swollen glands, 5.28.7).

Compared with a modern city, sickness was more visible on the streets of ancient Rome, a function of haphazard medical care and the nonexistence of hospitals and rest homes. Swollen eyes, skin rashes, and lost limbs are mentioned over and over again in the sources as part of the urban scene.[35] Certain virulent diseases would appear suddenly, cause consternation and panic, then subside (Pliny, *Natural History* 26.1). The sources do not allow us to quantify any meaningful statistics, but inscriptions and literature indicate that the mortality rate among children and young adults was high. Grief was a frequent emotion in ancient Rome.[36]

Education

The traditional Roman pattern of education was private and privileged. Cato is a paradigm again, representing the all-sufficient paterfamilias who takes on the responsibility of teaching his son, composing the *Origines* as a made-to-order textbook of Roman history (Plutarch, *Cato Major* 20).

A systematic curriculum in literary classics entered Rome in the third century B.C., in the person of a Greek slave from Tarentum who was later manumitted as Livius Andronicus. As tutor to his patron's children, Livius translated Homer's *Odyssey*, adapting the Greek classic to a Roman audience. Literature then continued as a major component in elementary education. Horace, for instance, mentions that when he went to school he had to memorize Livius's poems (*Epistles* 2.1.69–71); and in a later generation, a schoolboy at Pompeii practiced his Vergil assignment by scribbling the opening words of the *Aeneid* on a wall (*CIL* 4.5002; cf. 7131, 9131).

Some upper-class families used their own trained slaves as teachers; others, and the lower classes, hired teachers or sent their children out to a *ludus,* where reading, writing, and rote learning formed the basis of the curriculum and discipline was a proverbial and constant problem. The early morning noise of one of these *ludi* is the subject of a famous epigram by Martial (9.68). from which we also learn that boys and girls went to school together, in a rented shop, or the portico of a public square, or a courtyard.[37]

After the basics were acquired at home, an upper-class young man would spend several years in the company of his father's friends, observing and helping as they attended the Senate, campaigned for office, spoke in assemblies and law courts, and went on military campaigns. These political activities generated a demand for instruction in public speaking, and by the second century B.C., Greek rhetoricians were teaching their skills to an eager aristocratic audience. In the first century Cicero took a leading role in adapting Greek rules to the practical needs of Roman oratory, and he did the same for philosophy, stressing the parts of Greek speculative thought that provided practical moral guidance to an aristocratic statesman-politician.

To supplement this literary training and restore a neglected Roman tradition, Augustus instituted *collegia iuvenum,* clubs paid for by the state in which young Romans were taught military discipline and loyalty (Dio Cassius, *Roman History* 52.26.1–2). Significantly, such training was limited to the sons of the two highest orders, the senators and equestrians. These collegia reinforced Roman class consciousness, trained future leaders, and produced one of imperial Rome's most characteristic sights: boys drilling and exercising on the Campus Martius (Vergil, *Aeneid* 7.162–165).

By the early principate, freelance educators representing different schools of pedagogical content and method sought customers in an atmosphere of cut-throat competition.[38] Some teachers benefited from having important patrons, and during the principate no patron was more important than the emperor. Augustus paid Verrius Flaccus 100,000 sesterces a year to set up his school on the Palatine, and later under the Flavians a public chair of rhetoric was established in Rome, occupied first by Quintilian, and paid for from the emperor's fiscus (Suetonius, *Vespasian* 18; Dio Cassius, *Roman History* 65.12.1a.146).[39]

As Roman society became more complex during the late re-public, it needed additional forms of education. Slaves, for instance, were sent out to ludi to learn the skills necessary to their jobs as teachers, bookkeepers, secretaries, shoemakers, weavers, physicians, musicians, cooks, and carvers.[40] Both slaves and children of the poor studied crafts as apprentices; as such they were subject to corporal punishment, which could become so extreme as to be noted in legal opinions (Justinian, *Digest* 9.2.5.3).

As attested by anecdotes of women quoting poetry and by the surviving poems of Sulpicia, who wrote elegies in the late first century B.C., upper-class women acquired a literary education. In addition, public libraries, first opened under Augustus, and facilities for lectures and readings in the baths, provided opportunities for continuing education for large numbers of the city's residents.[41]

Communication

Life in the modern world, with its electronic technology and diz-zying succession of media revolutions, makes it especially difficult for us to imagine how messages were conveyed in ancient times. Long-distance communications strike us as painfully slow and uncertain. When Cicero, for instance, sent a letter outside Rome, he had to send a slave, or find some acquaintance who would carry it.[42] It often took a month or more for a message to be delivered in this way, and the only faster means of communication was the *cursus publicus,* a service whereby the army delivered messages between the central authority in Rome and commanders and governors in the provinces. It was a relay system of riders and mounts which, with the help of the well-maintained Roman road system and stopping places at regular distances, permitted a message to be delivered to the frontier within a few days.

Sending messages within the city, or between the city and its suburban hinterland, was of course easier. Again, private communications were often entrusted to slaves, or to a network that passed messages orally around upper-class dining rooms and lower-class tabernae. Social networks kept patrons, clients, and slaves alike informed of gossip and news, and even private events could quickly become public knowledge,[43] a phenomenon of small-town life that magnified itself to the scale of the ruling class in Rome, as attested, for example, in Cicero's not-so-subtle innuendos about the immoral behavior of Clodia (*Pro Caelio* 31–36), or in the backstairs gossip that Suetonius so confidently reports throughout his *Lives of the Caesars.*

State officials conveyed formal announcements to the people. On the *Kalendae*, the first day of each month, for instance, the pontiffs announced (*calare*) in the Curia Calabra on the Capitoline the significant days for the people to anticipate (Varro, *De Lingua Latina* 6.27). And each day an apparitor of the consuls ascended the steps in front of the Curia in the Forum Romanum to announce the hour of noon (Pliny, *Natural History* 7.212). Various types of heralds, sometimes assisted by trumpeters, issued the summons of censors, consuls, praetors, or dictators to public meetings (Varro, *De Lingua Latina* 6.86–95; Livy 4.32.1), and they also advertised races and games, where the audience could hear proclamations and read billboard-like signs (Aulus Gellius 5.14.29; Dio Cassius, *Roman History* 69.16.3).

In 304 B.C., as part of a populist program, Gnaeus Flavius, an aedile, posted copies of the laws and important dates on an *album* of white boards in the Forum Romanum, to inform the general populace about legal procedures (Livy 9.46.5). In 59 B.C. Julius Caesar arranged that official decisions of the Senate and the assemblies be written up and posted daily in the Forum Romanum (*acta diurna* or *acta urbana*—Suetonius, *Julius* 20.1), and although Augustus stopped the publication of the Senate's business, the acta diurna continued to list legal actions and decisions, public events, new buildings, donatives to the people, edicts and birthdays of the emperors, imperial ceremonies, and information about citizens' births, marriages, divorces, and deaths.

This all implies a fairly high degree of literacy, and indeed, it seems that writing was everywhere. The walls shouted out at passersby: "Aufidius was here!" "Elect Cerrinius aedile!" "Marcus Agrippa dedicated this temple." Graffiti were scribbled over all sorts of accessible surfaces, expressing electoral, romantic, and artistic preferences. Propertius (1.16.10) depicts a door scribbled over with obscene messages. On another occasion (3.23.23) he sends his slave off to post a lost-and-found notice on a column where everyone can see it. Political slogans covered porticoes, buildings, and houses (Plutarch, *Tiberius Gracchus* 8). Pompeii is a casebook of writing on the wall. Painted signs advertised election campaigns, upcoming gladiatorial exhibitions (*CIL* 4.3884), price lists (*CIL* 4.8566), and accommodations at inns (*CIL* 4.807). Poets could deliver the message of political programs in baths or lecture halls, and orators in forum or basilica.

Important deeds and benefactions were recorded in official inscriptions on temples, in lists of consuls and triumphs, and on the statues that proliferated all over the city. The profiles, names, and slogans on coins commemorated achievements and policies, and advertised them in even the most trivial financial transactions of the populace.

Triumphal arches, covered with inscriptions and sculpture and topped with the triumphant general in a chariot (accompanied by the goddess of victory), served as "billboards" to proclaim to the urban world the glorious achievements of this or that general or emperor.[44]

The arrangement and details of the city streets spelled out other implicit but clearly readable messages. The juxtapositions of crowded streets and spacious gardens, of teeming tenements and vistas into the interiors of gracious homes, emphasized the great disparity of wealth in Rome, and reminded everyone how difficult it was to leap the gap from one social level to another. At the same time, the great public monuments—the fora, temples, and baths—stood open to rich and poor, citizen and noncitizen, proclaiming the beneficence of the aristocracy and emperors who had constructed them, and giving all the residents of the city a share in their grandeur. The ordinary citizen, the visitor from abroad, even an emperor who had never been to Rome before (Ammianus Marcellinus 16.10.13), could not help but be impressed by the physical monuments of Rome's greatness: trophies of foreign conquests, statues of great benefactors, architectural reminders of the city's complex heritage from all the peoples it had absorbed into its empire and citizenship.

Nine

The Commercial City

In a short set piece, Livy (6.25.9) describes how Camillus entered the town of Tusculum in 382 B.C. to find a busy scene of peaceful small-town commerce: open doors, shops with merchandise on display, craftsmen intent on their work, schools with students reciting their lessons, and streets crowded with men, women, and children. A city the size of Rome had many times more mouths to feed, backs to clothe, and bodies to house than Tusculum, yet even in the metropolis, trade was generally conducted on the small scale typical of preindustrial cities, regardless of size.[1]

Individual farmers or artisans sold their own goods, in small shops or from temporary stands or carts. As for goods that had to be carried over longer distances, private contractors (*negotiatores*) arranged to ship them and to sell them at their destination to small merchants who came down to the docks or markets for that purpose. At every stage, from production to transport to sale, small and large owners used their own slaves or hired free labor or gangs of slave or free labor assembled by other contractors.[2]

Even when the state took control of some industries, much of the work was contracted out to individual entrepreneurs. In the absence of any central office for collecting taxes, for instance, individuals and corporations undertook the responsibilities, risks, and profits. Other examples are the grain and marble trade, where the state used private shippers and agents to supply the annona and the public building projects.

The flow of food, cloth, money, marble, and countless other commodities into Rome from every corner of the empire suggests the extent to which Rome, as early as the second century B.C., had become a "consumer city," even a "parasite," on its ever more immense hinterland. It also exploited its empire by collecting taxes and by selling the produce of state-owned farms for profit. Furthermore, the ruling class of the empire owned properties all over the Roman world, and spent the surplus on their homes in the capital and in the suburban estates that surrounded it.

But there is, the economists remind us, no free lunch, and the city paid its grocery bills to the rest of the empire at least partly in the services it provided. Administrative expertise, military defense, legal codes, market opportunities for trade, and the cultural and architectural gifts acquired from Greece and elsewhere, filtered through its own very special civic experience and urban pattern.[3] It has even been argued, on tentative and theoretical but plausible grounds, that the taxes and rents the provinces paid to Rome resulted in more productive agriculture, more abundant trade, and a more flexible, monetized economy in the principate.[4]

Feeding the City

In antiquity, the supply of grain and other food was a precarious matter, for agriculture barely supported the farmers even in a good year, and surplus population or excessive cold or drought could drive families or whole societies to the brink of starvation.[5] Supplying food to Rome, especially as it grew to the vast size it became under the principate, was a constant challenge to Roman organizing skills. Our sources tell us of frequent severe food shortages, which occasionally led the people to riot.[6]

At first, each family supported itself from its own farmland and from its own flocks. The list of tradesmen which is ascribed to King Numa (Plutarch, *Numa* 17.3) does not, significantly, mention any purveyors of food. Later tradition remembered that emmer wheat, a hardy strain, was cultivated by the first Romans, who used it to make a kind of cereal gruel known as *puls*—easy to cook up over a simple fire in a coarseware pot (Pliny, *Natural History* 18.83–84). Fish came from the river and the sea. Meat from home-grown sheep, cattle, and pigs was available at sacrifices. Fruits and vegetables, carried in from nearby farms or grown in kitchen gardens in back of town houses, provided variety in the Romans' diet. The remains of third-century houses in Cosa show such gardens (Fig. 14), and Pliny also mentions them as typical of early Roman society, where even the Tarquin kings cultivated a garden (Pliny, *Natural History* 19.50). (In the imaginative drawing of the early Forum, Fig. 7, the nobles' houses surrounding the public square are shown with attached gardens.)

Pliny's researches convinced him (*Natural History* 18.107–108) that professional bakers first appeared in Rome during the Third Macedonian War, 171–168 B.C., though he is aware that even earlier Plautus and his audience knew a whole inventory of cooks and bakers who could be hired for special events (*Aulularia* 397–402). The late third century B.C., a time of intensified contact with the Greeks and of Hannibal's invasion, seems to have been the significant turning point. The Romans became more sophisticated about food, and they developed a taste for imported cuisine which paralleled their taste for Greek architecture and literature. Cookery was more universal than art, however, and the Romans imported and consumed delicacies from all over their world: grain from Africa, special breads from Parthia, walnuts from Persia, dried fish from Spain, and wine from Gaul and the Greek islands (Pliny, *Natural History* 18–19; Martial 13).[7]

As a source of complex carbohydrates, grain—chiefly wheat and millet—was the essential item of nutrition. As long as enough could be cultivated at home, or in the immediate vicinity of Rome, grain could be bought and sold in an open market. Fluctuating supplies and prices, however, could cause consternation, and the state had to step in. The first instance of state intervention dates from 299 B.C., when high prices provoked the aediles to improve the supply and lower the price of grain (Livy 10.11.9).[8] In subsequent centuries the aediles continued to take care of the grain supply, coordinating the delivery of the imported grain to the retail markets and controlling its quality and price.

During the second century B.C., a shift to cash crops meant that the large Italian farms produced less grain and more vines, olives, and cattle. At the same time, the population of Rome was growing, increasing the need for grain. The simultaneous growth of Roman power around the Mediterranean gave Rome the opportunity to fill the need, bringing wheat from Sicily and Sardinia at first, and later (after 146 B.C. and the final destruction of Carthage) from Africa. The greater volume of grain coming into the city was the main impetus for the construction of the Porticus Aemilia along the Tiber in the second century and of the adjacent Horrea Galbae in the early first century B.C. However, importing grain was still a hazardous business, and shippers had to deal with adverse winds, storms, pirates, and natural fluctuations in the production of grain at the sources. In the free enterprise markets of Rome, the supply and the price varied greatly from year to year and season to season. To alleviate this problem, Gaius Gracchus in 123 B.C. passed a law that permitted all Roman citizens who were residents of Rome to buy a certain ration of grain at regular monthly distributions for a fixed and artificially subsidized price—6.33 *asses* for a *modius* (about a peck, 6.5 kilograms). The grain was thus available to all citizens, but naturally it was the poor who benefited most from it. During his dictatorship in the 80s, Sulla abolished the subsidy along with other populist legislation, but in the last decades of the republic the grain supply became a major political issue as each of the magnates attempted to win favor through some adjustment of the system.[9] Augustus, in reorganizing the city administration, appointed a *praefectus annonae* to administer the distribution of grain (the *annona*) and arrange contracts with private shippers. By now the seas were safe from piracy, even if storms were still a danger and sailing was virtually impossible during the winter months. During the first century A.D., when Claudius built his harbor at Ostia, it became more efficient to unload grain there, and the emperor assigned a member of his household to work with the praefectus annonae.[10] In subsequent centuries, the importance of the grain supply was recognized more and more openly by the emperors, and eventually it was extended (under Aurelian) to include distributions of oil, pork, wine, and baked bread.[11]

The real workings of the annona can be shown by tracing the path of grain, during the principate, from its overseas source to the mouths of Rome. The grain came principally from Egypt, Africa, Sicily, and Sardinia, as well as from Spain and Gaul, and most of it was bought from private landowners. It was threshed and winnowed in the fields, transported to local barns and then to the harbors, where it was stored until it could be loaded onto ships. Samples of the shipment were taken and sealed in leather wallets or clay pots to guard against adulteration during the trip. The ship then sailed to Italy, a trip that could take a month or two. At its destination, the cargo was inspected on board by *mensores,* who measured the shipment and checked the samples. Porters then unloaded the grain, either into dockside warehouses or into small boats for immediate transport to Rome. Sacks destined for the open market were sent to private warehouses[12] and were eventually distributed to wholesalers and retailers. The warehouses (*horrea*), were carefully designed to protect the grain from insects, rodents, moisture, and heat; rooms were arranged in rows or around courtyards. Access was by ramps; the tile floor was raised on foot-high foundations to allow the circulation of air; the walls were of heavy masonry (tufa in the republic, concrete or brick in the principate) carefully plastered; lighting was minimal. Official mensores saw to the transport of the free grain to the public distribution points. Here the citizens lined up on their appointed day of the month at their assigned gates, presented their identity tokens (*tesserae*), and received their ration of grain.[13]

For daily consumption, most residents of the city seem to have bought their bread in round flat loaves, although various specialty shapes also were available (Pliny, *Natural History* 19.53). Bakeries at Pompeii and Ostia help us evoke the process, as do the comments of slaves, who fear work in the mill and bakeshop as the most grueling job in the city, and the narrative frieze along the top of the Baker's Tomb (Sepulcrum Eurysacis) in Rome. Millstones (Pl. 18) were turned by small donkeys, while slaves took wheat, poured it into the top, and after the hard outer husk had been ground away, extracted the flour from the bottom. Different grades could be milled by repeated grindings and the use of sieves. Water and yeast, and sometimes flavorings like wine or seeds, were added, and the dough was kneaded and shaped by hand or machine (Pliny, *Natural History* 18.104). Kneading and shaping took place in a back room, and the loaves were placed into the large oven with a long-handled wooden scoop. The bread was then sold at retail in the front of the bakery or at portable street-side stands, or was packed in large baskets for wider distribution.[14]

Apart from grain, an individual's diet depended on his or her resources. Some urban residents—and the archaeological evidence from Pompeii indicates that this was more common than has usually been assumed—had gardens in back of their houses to provide fruits and vegetables. Other items were available at market, whether in the informal vegetable market that gave its name to the Forum Holitorium, or in more elaborate structures: the *macellum*,[15] or food market, mentioned by Livy (27.11.16) near the Forum in 209 B.C.; the Macellum Liviae, built under Augustus on the Esquiline; or the Macellum Magnum, built under Nero on the Caelian. At a poultry vendor's shop, for instance, represented on a sarcophagus from Ostia, we see the proprietress selling prepared food to a customer, while trussed birds hang on racks behind and two pet monkeys play at the side (Pl. 23). The earliest markets were open spaces surrounded by simple shops (*tabernae*) (Livy 40.51.5). Examples are known at Pompeii, Thamugadi (Fig. 28), and elsewhere. Usually these markets consisted of a columned rectangular space, in the middle of which there was a circular construction made of an open colonnade and a pitched or domed roof. The design seems to owe something to the rectangular Greek agora surrounded by colonnades and shops, and also something to bazaars built by the Phoenicians in their North African colonies.[16]

Of the produce that was for sale, olives were an essential source of fat. They were grown on the commercial farms of Italy, and several passages of Cato's essay *On Agriculture* (64, 144–147) explain how a contractor (*redemptor*), sometimes in association with partners (*socii*), bought the crop, supplied men (free or slave) to gather the olives, and then presumably transported them to market in the towns and cities. Luxury varieties were also imported from the other shores of the Mediterranean, and were sold fresh, pickled, or processed into olive oil, which in turn was used as salad dressing, cooking oil, lamp fuel, and detergent. Since olive oil does not keep very well, presses in and near the city produced supplies to be sold at retail. Wine, however, once sealed in its storage amphoras, could be shipped long distances, and inscriptions and graffiti record the names of the growers and contractors responsible for shipping; a significant number of them were women.[17]

Other crops may have been marketed, like olives, with the help of a contractor's labor, by speculation in a kind of futures market, by auction, or by individual sale by farmers and tenants trekking into town like a farmer in Vergil (*Georgics* I.273–275).[18] Honey, the primary sweetening agent, was produced on small farms.[19] Beans and peas, important in lower-class diets, were grown in Italy and sold either dried or, in tabernae (Pl. 24) and by street vendors, hot. Onions, radishes, turnips, and other roots and bulbs also were home-grown on farms near the city, though the demand for onions was apparently high enough that they were imported from Pompeii, Africa, and Gaul. Because they are perishable, most green vegetables must have been grown locally, but artichokes, asparagus, broccoli, and leeks were more expensive and were transported farther. Fruit was eaten fresh in season, dried or preserved in winter: apples, pears, figs, grapes, quinces, and pomegranates were popular; cherries, apricots, oranges, lemons, and dates were more exotic and were not cultivated in Italy until the principate. Dairy products were produced near the city. Fresh milk would hardly have been expected, but cheese and various types of commercially soured milk were available.

Meat (pork, mutton, beef) was scarce except at sacrifices and the dinner parties of the rich. Fish was more common, and special markets were set aside for its sale. Some types of fish took on special sophistication and brought big prices: mullet, for example, of the type raised in the fishery excavated at Cosa, could fetch absurdly high prices, and elaborate means were invented to assure its freshness.[20] There were industries devoted to the cultivation of oysters, snails, and oak grubs on a large scale. Dormice and chicken also were available, as were sausages, which would keep without refrigeration.

As for condiments, salt was harvested from the beds at Ostia. Pepper and other spices were imported from the East in small quantities, which made them a luxury for the rich. The pervasive seasoning agent was *garum*, a briny fish sauce that could be made at home or, more usually, bought already prepared. A processing plant has recently been excavated in the southeast part of Pompeii, with a courtyard available to spread the fish to dry in the sun, and amphoras to hold the fermenting sauce.[21] A great variety of wines was available, from the fine vintages such as Falernian (from Etruria) and Chian (from the Aegean), praised by Horace, to simple local types, to the Spanish varieties that dominated the Roman market in the first century A.D. (Pliny, *Natural History* 14.62, 71; 17.213). It could be bought by the cup in a taberna (Pl. 22, 24) or in amphoras to stock the cellar of a large household.

To imagine what the Roman diet was like, we might indulge in some culinary parochialism and consider what was missing. There were no tomatoes, potatoes, bananas, or peanuts. Nor was there any rice, maize, butter, cane sugar, chili pepper, chocolate, coffee, or (except on the fringes of the empire, where it was regarded as a distinctly barbarian beverage) beer.

Crafts and Trades

The small taberna, which consisted of a rectangular room with a wide front that could be secured by a grill or a folding door, and often a rear room or upstairs mezzanine where the workers lived, was the setting of most commerce. In some tabernae, slaves tended shop on behalf of their master. A collection of legal opinions from the first century B.C. (Justinian, *Digest* 14.3.5) lists various jobs for responsible slaves and freedmen: the mule driver and the stable hand; the *insularius,* who managed an insula for the owner; the *institor* or agent, who even though a slave could make binding business deals in his master's name; the baker's slave, who could go out to sell bread and make contracts for daily delivery; the *circitor,* who peddled at retail the clothes or fabrics distributed by *vestiarii* and *lintearii;* the *pollinctor,* a slave sent by the undertaker to wash and prepare corpses for burial. These talented and clever slaves belonged to the same breed as those who inhabited the comic stage, wheeling and dealing, bargaining and browbeating.[22] They were generally trustworthy, although the legal writers worried that a *pollinctor* might rob the corpse he was sent to tend, or that a fuller's slave might take in a load of laundry to be cleaned and then run away, taking the customer's clothes with him. If they did well and were manumitted, they might continue to operate the shop under their patron's sponsorship. This reminds us of the importance of slaves in the economy of ancient Rome, the small scale on which these businesses operated, and the importance of a network of self-supporting clients to a patron.[23]

Elsewhere, in other tabernae, independent men or women did the selling, helped by spouse and children and perhaps a few slaves. These craftsmen and shopkeepers were often descended from slaves or were foreign immigrants to Rome. In any event, they did not admit to the kind of bias against retail trade and manual work which aristocratic authors like Cato and Cicero regularly expressed; instead, whereas the nobility listed their offices and military honors, these lower-class shopkeepers and artisans proudly expressed on their tombstones their pride in their trade, and even listed their place of business (e.g., Pl. 22, 23).

A good location was an important asset to a businessman or businesswoman, and tradespeople who shared a neighborhood dealt with one another in a spirit of cooperation rather than cutthroat competition.[24] It may be the fault of our sources, but we hardly ever hear about the economic failure of a small business;[25] instead, neighbors involved in the same trade tended to band together in *collegia* (see Chapter 12, page 209), for social contact and the good of business. The atmosphere was probably similar to that of Rome's modern flea market at Porta Portese, or the market of a medium-sized city in the Arab world. Book dealers—many of them Greek freedmen—set up shop in rows of tabernae north of the imperial fora, in the Argiletum and Vicus Sandalarius (Martial 1.2, 1.117), or at the Sigillaria in the Campus Martius (Aulus Gellius 2.3.5, 5.4.1). Dealers in gold and pearls worked in temporary booths along the Sacra Via.[26] *Argentarii,* who may have been money-lenders or silver workers, concentrated in the Velabrum (*CIL* 6.9184) and the Clivus Argentarius, between the Forum Romanum and the Campus Martius. In the principate, the old voting halls of the republican Campus Martius were turned into luxury shops where serious and casual shoppers could find young slaves, expensive furniture, Corinthian bronzes, classical statuary, fine jewelry, and precious goblets and vases (Martial 9.59; Juvenal 6.153–155). Wine and garum merchants concentrated around the docks and the Forum Vinarium, or around the Castra Praetoria on the Esquiline.[27]

Clothing was a typical item of retail trade. Although pious tradition held that every good Roman wife would spend her time spinning and weaving, the custom was only a memory by the time of Augustus. He, in fact, made an ostentatious attempt at wearing garments spun by his wife and daughter, although they seem to have been no more eager for the task than other upper-class women of the period (Suetonius, *Augustus* 73; Columella 12.praef.9). Instead, from the late republic on, the wool of sheep raised close to Rome was woven by slave women for use within the household or was made into cheaper grades of togas and cloaks for sale.[28] At Pompeii, slaves worked as weavers, and literary sources tell us of poor women working wool night and day at home in a kind of cottage industry (Apuleius, *Metamorphoses* 9.5; Juvenal 8.42–43).[29] Finer and stronger grades of wool came from the Po Valley in Cisalpine Gaul (Strabo 5.1.7, 12), in the form of togas, tunics, blankets, and carpets.[30] The coarse brown wool that slaves in Rome wore came from Canusium, in southern Italy (Martial 9.22.9; 14.127, 129), and cheap woolen blankets and tunics were imported from Gaul. Sources of still cheaper clothing were the *centonarii* ("rag pickers"), who gathered up worn garments, recycling what was usable into patchwork tunics, blankets, and saddle cloths (Cato, *On Agriculture* 59, 135; Petronius 14.7; Seneca, *Epistulae* 80.8; Livy 7.14.7).

The *fullones* ("fullers") played an essential role in the clothing industry, for their shops had the facilities to make felt, dye cloth, and wash and dry clothing. This was important because the white wool toga, which Romans wore on all formal occasions, stained easily and must have needed frequent cleaning. Examples at Pompeii and Ostia show that fullers' establishments (*fullonicae*) were somewhat larger than most businesses, for they required considerable investment in space, money, and labor. According to one estimate, 19–27 skilled workers were needed to do the washing, dyeing, rinsing, and finishing in an average fullonica.[31] If we take the fullonica on the Via degli Augustali at Ostia (V.vii.3) as an example, we find a central courtyard filled with four large tanks (Pl. 25). For washing, urine was a common detergent; it was obtained from receptacles all over town, and was even imported. Dye came from plants and shellfish, and depending on its rarity was an important item in luxury trade. After rinsing, the cloth was hung out to dry. In Plate 25, indentations are visible on the piers; wooden beams were inserted in these indentations, and the cloth was then hung on them. At other fullonicae, such as that of Stephanus at Pompeii (I.vi.7), the roof was built flat so as to allow drying racks to be set out in the sun. Because of the more crowded conditions in Rome, fullers were permitted to set their wares out on the streets to dry (Justinian, *Digest* 43.10.1).

Shoes were available in every part of town and in great variety. We read about specialists in sandals, military boots, slippers, women's shoes, and light papyrus slippers. Wholesale dealers in soles formed a collegium that met in the Trans-Tiber district, where the smelly, dirty leather tanneries were concentrated along the river.[32]

Finished clothing and luxury fabrics were specialties of the merchants in the Horrea Agrippiana, on the western edge of the Palatine along the Vicus Tuscus (*CIL* 6.9972). In this large tufa structure, apparently sponsored by Agrippa before his death in 12 B.C., the tabernae surrounding a rectangular courtyard were rented out to individual businessmen.[33] Plate 2 shows an imaginative reconstruction of the complex at work; it is based on the Forma Urbis (frag. 37), archaeological remains, and several inscriptions.[34]

The Horrea Agrippiana exemplifies one architectural facility for retail sales. Elsewhere, tabernae lined the streets, often behind colonnades (Pl. 7). Their wares tended to spill out on to the streets, and from time to time the aediles had to step in and clear a way for passers-by.[35] At other places rows of tabernae faced each other across a wide passageway, or surrounded a courtyard. The whole is easy to envision at Ostia, where the remains of tabernae line the streets and squares in various combinations, but examples are also known in Rome.[36]

In Rome, space was used most imaginatively in the Mercatus Traiani, Market of Trajan, which covered the side of the Quirinal Hill next to the Forum Traiani (Pl. 5). This was a severely practical complex, its brick-faced concrete contrasting with the marble revetments in the adjacent forum. The shops, arranged with great subtlety and sophistication on five different levels, integrated several streets and made use of ordinary rows of tabernae, a large semi-circular hall roofed by a concrete half-dome, and an elaborately vaulted main hall (entered from the modern Via Quattro Novembre) with two stories of shops on each side.[37] This was built by the emperor, and it seems likely that it housed the offices of the administrators of Trajan's alimenta. It could also have provided spaces for auctions and lectures. But the rows of tabernae clearly suggest that space was rented out to individual tradesmen operating on the small scale common throughout the city and the empire.

The auction was a frequent means of sale, a way to dispose of whole estates or specific items, whether a slave or two, fine linen, or shrubbery. The father of the poet Horace was an auctioneer (*coactor*), and Horace (*Satires* 1.6.70–88) expresses a certain determined pride in his industriousness.[38] We know a great deal about the business affairs of an auctioneer, Lucius Caecilius Jucundus, because we have 138 of his business receipts, preserved on wax tablets from his house at Pompeii (V.i.26). They show that he extended credit to purchasers and also contracted to collect taxes on behalf of the municipality.[39]

Prices

When the Romans talked about prices, they usually spoke in terms of the *sestertius*. This was a bronze coin, as were the smaller denominations: the *dupondius* (two to the sesterce); the *as* (four to the sesterce); the *semis* (two to the as); and the *quadrans* (four to the as).

Larger denominations were the silver *denarius* (four sesterces) and the gold *aureus* (four denarii).[40]

It would be foolish to try to translate these into modern equivalents, but we can get some sense of financial realities in, say, Rome of the early principate from frustratingly sparse references in literature and inscriptions. A laborer might expect to earn 2–4 sesterces a day (Cicero, *Pro Roscio Comoedo* 28), which means that in a good month five days' wages would buy enough grain to feed one person for a month.[41] A loaf of bread seems to have cost 1 or 2 asses, and a given quantity of wine could vary from an as to a sesterce, depending on its quality. In the late first century A.D., Martial, perhaps exaggerating, complained that 6.25 sesterces—a typical amount for patrons to distribute to clients—would not buy a decent dinner. A typical price for a tunic was 15 sesterces, and the price to clean it was 4 sesterces.[42] If we turn to the more luxurious price ranges, we find that they were astronomical in comparison with the necessities, and that that was in keeping with the tremendous disparity in income levels between the privileged and the unprivileged.[43] Quotations of slave prices ranged from a low of 750 sesterces to an astounding 700,000, with 2,000 a legally recognized norm.[44] Houses in Rome could sell for as much as 3.5 million sesterces, and a minimum yearly rent for an apartment might be, at a guess, 400–500 sesterces a year in Rome. At the upper end of the scale, renters could expect to pay many times that, especially in Rome, where prices seem to have been much higher than elsewhere.[45]

The Building Industry

Suetonius (*Vespasian* 18) tells a story about Vespasian in which an engineer approached him with some labor-saving device to make the building of the Capitoline temple easier and quicker. The emperor refused to hear anything about the device, however, because he did not want to deprive "his little plebs" of the opportunity to earn its daily bread.[46] The incident is instructive for many reasons, not least because it reminds us of the workmen whose muscle and sweat constructed the buildings of ancient Rome.

Like most Roman commercial activity, the building industry was organized around the efforts of *redemptores,* contractors who depended both on a permanent staff of slaves and on free labor, hired on demand. The state depended on such contractors for most of its construction, and on really big projects such as roads, aqueducts, and amphitheaters, the censors, or in the principate the emperor's staff, had to coordinate the activities of a large number of redemptores (Polybius 6.17; Frontinus, *Aqueducts* 2.119, 124).[47]

The supply of materials also was a job for contractors, even in the case of timber from public land or marble from imperially owned quarries. Trees became door frames and roof trusses. Tufa from Veii, travertine from Tibur, colored or veined marble from the Greek islands, and pure white marble from Luna, near Pisa, were all transported. Many of the marble quarries were imperial property, and seem to have been efficiently administered: poorer grades were used near the quarries, while only the finer grades were shipped to Rome. Much initial work was done by sculptors on the spot, and sizes were frequently standardized. Roof tiles were made, presumably by contractors, near the sources of the clay, often on the property of some member of the landed gentry.[48] Other contractors, *fabri tignarii,* were in charge of the actual construction. They were an important group in Ostia, as we know from inscriptions of their collegium in the second century A.D., when there was constant building activity. These building contractors were equally important in Rome, as attested by literary sources and tomb inscriptions.[49] In the third century A.D., over 1,300 fabri, presumably owners of small firms, were counted among the members of their collegium.[50] Legal texts imply that the typical builder had a small permanent staff, but turned to free labor when he had a big job to do.[51] For large projects like the Colosseum or a road, the appropriate officials divided the work and made the necessary arrangements with the contractors.[52] The well-known sculpture from the Tomb of the Haterii, now in the Vatican museum, shows a crane operated by a large tread-wheel powered by slaves; it seems to indicate that the family of the Haterii made their money as successful contractors in the building industry.

Big jobs were expedited when concrete was introduced into the repertory of construction, with the discovery of the tremendous binding properties of the volcanic dust called *puteolanum,* from Puteoli on the Bay of Naples. It could even be used under water, and the earliest such use we know of in Italy was at the harbor works at Cosa, in the late third century B.C. It was tremendously strong, and could be poured into any shape desired. A wooden form was built and the puteolanum was mixed with water, stones, and any small bits of available building debris. Stones or, later, bricks were placed along the form, to serve as the facing when the concrete dried and the wood was removed. This was a labor-intensive technique, but not much of the labor needed to be very skillful, and the quick popularity of concrete construction in Rome, and in all of central Italy, starting in the second century B.C., may well have been a sign of the availability of a larger supply of unskilled laborers, slave and free, who could be taught to do the relatively simple carrying and pouring operations.[53]

Ten

Households and Housing

To the extent that the traditional Roman house was a castle, it was a safe refuge from rivals and the whirl of public life outside. It was a separate world, mirroring in domestic space the relationship between the family and the other worlds outside its boundaries. But even though these boundaries were real, they were not impermeable, and the relationship between what was private and what was public was fluid, pervasive, and less distinct than it is in a large city today.

In the republic, housing reflected the great gulf between the upper classes and the lower—the extended aristocratic familiae living in their mansions (domūs), and the plebeians living in small rooms arranged in rows of tabernae or, later, piled on top of each other in tenements (insulae). The more complex society of the principate developed in turn a residence pattern that was appropriate to its nature, both highly stratified and more socially mobile; in the developed insula of the imperial city, the roomy apartments of the rich were near street level, and quarters became progressively smaller and humbler as one climbed higher, to a fourth or fifth story.

The Family

Depending on its wealth and prestige, the Roman *familia* could include hundreds of persons. At the head of the family unit was the *paterfamilias,* who represented the family in its dealings with the world and at least in theory had absolute power over the other members. His wife, the *materfamilias,* enjoyed prestige corresponding to that of her husband. Within the household, she had formal custody of the keys, and directed the daily lives of children and household slaves.

The nuclear family tended to be small, at all levels of society. Few families seem to have had even as many as three children, and when the emperors tried to encourage an increase in the birth rate, they gave special rewards and status to those who produced that many.[1] Sons usually moved to their own house when they married, but remained under the authority of the paterfamilias as long as he lived. Daughters also, except under certain rare types of marriage contract, remained under their father's authority even after they were married. The family's slaves were considered a part of the familia, as were its liberated slaves and other clients. All shared, in various degrees, in the social life and religious observances of the familia.

We usually think of the great households of the rich when we talk about the extended Roman family—the hundreds in the *familia urbana* of Livia, Augustus's wife, for example, or the 400 belonging to the senator Lucius Pedanius Secundus in the first century A.D. (Tacitus, *Annals* 14.43). But even a relatively poor man like Martial had a slave or two, and a relatively small house in Pompeii (I.xii.16) had benches for clients outside the front door.

Evidence is most abundant, and has been most thoroughly studied, for the very large households at the pinnacle of Roman society.[2] These immense staffs give us a model and reflect, on a large scale, the jobs that slaves and freedmen may have played in a more modest upper-class household: the *dispensator,* who acted as major-domo or steward (Cicero, *Letters to Atticus* 11.1.1); *ostiarii,* who tended the door, controlling the entry of visitors and checking slaves as they went out on errands (Seneca, *De Constantia* 14.1–2;

Fronto, *Epistulae Graecae* 5.1); *atrienses,* who cleaned, swept, and scrubbed the public and private rooms (Cicero, *Paradoxa* 37); personal attendants who looked after the bedrooms and served as footmen, entertainers, barbers, hairdressers, messengers (Plautus, *Trinummus* 250–252), doctors, wet nurses, teachers, and "pets"; cooks and waiters; maintenance men and gardeners. Available statistics show that among household slaves, males outnumbered females two to one or three to one, which indicates that there were fewer jobs for women.[3]

Working-class families were less structured than richer ones. Women did more physical labor and earned more of the family's income, and children went to work early in their lives; masters and slaves lived in greater proximity than in the great houses of the rich.[4] Even in the most highly structured households, however, there was opportunity every day to interact with a wide variety of people. The various social classes came in contact the moment the appointed slave went to wake the master, and again at the formal *salutatio,* when clients waited outside, were admitted to the house by one slave, identified by another slave, and received—individually or in groups, depending on their importance—by the paterfamilias. Often the clients were dismissed with some kind of handout (*sportula*), which might be a basket of food or a small number of coins. When the patron, attended by slaves and clients, set off to the Forum, he was able to show the world how large and devoted his familia was.

Important events in the family's life brought its members together, and also gave the family an opportunity to display its wealth, traditions, and status to the city outside.

Ritual surrounded the birth of a child, and extended it to the world of public life: the father formally acknowledged it;[5] on the eighth day girls, on the ninth boys, received their names; within thirty days the birth was registered at the temple of Saturnus. At some point in his teens (the exact age varied between fourteen and nineteen), every young man celebrated his formal coming of age, usually on March 17, the festival of Liber and Libera. The family celebrated with him, escorting him in the new white *toga virilis* (which symbolized his status as a full citizen) to the Tabularium to

be registered, and then to the Forum Augustum for further ceremonies. All the family's important friends, and all its clients, were
invited to dinner to conclude the event (Juvenal 3.187–189,
8.166).

At weddings, another occasion for general celebration, ceremonies began in the morning when the groom arrived with his
family and friends at the bride's family home. A sacrifice was
held—at home or at a sanctuary, since slaughtering a ewe or an ox
was a messy business. The couple took their vows and then joined
the guests in food, dance, and song. In the evening all accompanied
the couple in a procession to their new home, amid noisy celebration and off-color good humor.[6]

Birthdays offered more opportunities for a party, with friends
and clients bringing presents and joining the family in the house
for a sacrifice of food and wine on a small earthen altar dedicated to
the protective spirit (the *genius* or *juno*) of the celebrant, and for
dinner (Martial 10.87; 12.60).

When a member of the family died, the body was prepared for a
lying-in-state, which lasted as long as seven days and concluded
with a procession of family and friends. In the case of very important people, masks of the family's ancestors were worn in the procession so that many generations of the extended family would be
present (Polybius 6.53–54), strengthening the family's identity
and displaying its pride and grief to the whole city. The funeral
procession of those active in politics wound down to the Forum
Romanum, where some member of the family gave an appropriate
commemorative oration. This honor was usually reserved for men,
but Julius Caesar extended it to his Aunt Julia when she died, in 69
B.C., and it became customary in the principate to give full funerary
honors to distinguished women. Finally, the procession walked out
through the city gates. If the body was to be cremated, it was placed
on a pyre at an *ustrinum,* and the ashes were carried to the tomb
along one of the highways leading out of the city. Poor people and
less-distinguished members of rich families were buried more
simply, after a period of mourning that usually lasted just one
night. In all cases the corpse was accompanied by mourners outside the walls to the final resting place. Normally a pig was sacri-

ficed and a meal was eaten at the grave. When the family returned home, it performed a rite of purification by fire and water. Nine days later the family returned to the grave for another ceremonial meal, poured a libation, and concluded the official period of mourning.[7] The family might also return to the grave for a sacrifice and a memorial meal at regular intervals, such as on the birthdays of deceased members; these do not seem to have been particularly solemn or grim occasions, but were rather like a family outing with picnic.

Some of the city's religious events each year were really family festivals.[8] On the Parentalia (February 13–21), offerings were set out for the dead at their tombs (Ovid, *Fasti* 2.537–540). On the Caristia (February 22), the family celebrated its solidarity with a common meal (Ovid, *Fasti* 2.631). The first of March was the Ma-tronalia, "Mother's Day," when the ladies of the households dressed up in their finest outfits, husbands gave gifts, and the streets were full of people delivering presents to relatives and the wives of their patrons ([Tibullus] 3.1.1–4). From the seventeenth to the twenty-third of December, every Roman family celebrated the Saturnalia. Vendors set up canvas booths in the Porticus Neptuni and elsewhere to sell *sigillaria* (little dolls given to children) and *cerei* (wax candles given to friends and patrons) (Juvenal 6.154 and scholiast). There was a public banquet at the Temple of Saturnus and general merrymaking in the streets (Seneca, *Epistulae Morales* 18.1). Families celebrated together. One of the lesser members of the familia was chosen Saturnalian *princeps,* with freedom to give orders to everyone, and masters waited on slaves.[9] The celebration could become pretty raucous, and a paterfamilias who was too self-conscious about his position might, like Pliny (*Letters* 2.17.24), slip quietly away so that he could preserve his Roman dignity while the rest of the familia enjoyed its holiday.

Beginnings of Domestic Architecture

The remains of the earliest Palatine village (Pl. 1) show that the Ro-mans of the eighth century B.C. lived in simple rectangular or oval huts made of a wooden-post frame and wickerwork sides daubed with mud. The roof was pitched, and often covered an entrance porch at one end.

We see evidence of more grandeur in the remains of two houses dating from sixth-century Rome, the city of the Etruscan kings, at the eastern end of the Forum Romanum. The foundations of one, excavated along the north side of the Sacra Via, just next to the archaic necropolis, show a long house with porches, parallel to the street. It has been restored with three rooms on each of two stories, an external staircase in back, and, facing the street, a balcony where the family could watch and be part of events below.[10] The other house, probably a part of the palace of the kings, lay under the later Regia, which seems to have duplicated its plan. A large rectangular room with a hearth was preceded by two antechambers, and an irregular colonnaded courtyard adjoined on the north.[11]

A more standard form of domestic architecture was the *atrium,* which the Romans firmly believed was part of their Etruscan heritage (Varro, *De Lingua Latina* 5.161).[12] The atrium was a central reception or family room with private chambers—sitting rooms and bedrooms—placed around it. Etruscan tombs seem to indicate two different types of atria. One was the "impluviate," in which the four sides of the roof sloped inward toward a central rectangular opening, the *compluvium,* to admit light and rain water; some of the rain water was collected in a shallow basin known as an *impluvium,* while overflow was often stored in a basement cistern. The other type was the "displuviate," in which the outward sloping hip roof carried away most of the rain water from the opening in the roof (Vitruvius 6.3.1–2).[13]

Upper-Class Housing under the Republic

The atrium remained the central ceremonial space of the Roman house throughout the republic. A semipublic waiting room, its doors usually left open to the street, it welcomed guests and contained the finest tokens of the family's prestige. It was identified as the symbolic heart of the household. When, for instance, later Romans remembered the sack of Rome by the Gauls in 390 B.C., they recalled how the heads of the noble households sat unmoving in their atria, quietly and solemnly confronting the barbarians as they entered (Livy 5.41.5–10). Vitruvius, writing in the early principate but reflecting the use and standards of the late republic, emphasized the principle that a house needed to reflect the social status of the owner. Members of the ruling class, he said, needed atria and peristyles of royal dimensions in order to perform all their social obligations to their friends and clients (Vitruvius 6.5.2).

The House of Sallust (VI.ii.4) at Pompeii is an example of a comfortable atrium house built around 300 B.C.[14] Its façade was built in the typical Pompeiian fashion of the period, of regular rows of tufa blocks, conventionally called *opus quadratum*. Its floor plan (Fig. 12) is typical of the private houses of the republican period. Originally six shops opened onto the street, flanking the central door-

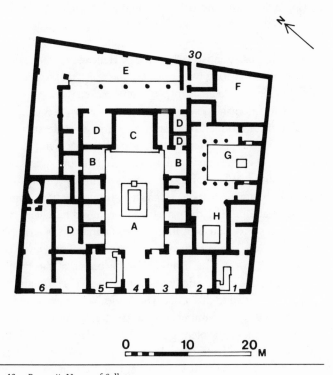

Fig. 12. Pompeii: House of Sallust

way. Through the front door one entered the *fauces,* an entrance corridor leading into the *atrium* proper (A). Small *cubicula* (sleeping rooms) surrounded it, and two projections (B) known as *alae* ("wings") extended the atrium at its back end and may have served as sitting areas. The *tablinum* behind (C) was open both to the atrium and to the garden (E) at the rear of the house. Dining rooms (D), known as *triclinia* (see Chapter 12, page 206), were arranged for seasonal use: interior ones would be more comfortable in the winter, those facing the garden would be appropriate for warmer seasons, and an open-air triclinium at the northern corner of the garden permitted dining under the stars. A service courtyard (F) and rooms upstairs defined the servants' quarters. Along the south side are the remains of a smaller house with atrium (H) and garden peristyle (G); at some point this house was bought by the owner of the House of Sallust and converted into a subsidiary garden and dining room, with a small kitchen off the northern corner of the garden. The walls of the rooms were decorated in what is called the "First" or "Incrustation" style, inspired by Hellenistic interior decoration. A plaster coating was applied to the walls, then carved and painted to look like regular rows of stone masonry.

The street-door-fauces-atrium-tablinum-garden sequence is normal in these republican houses, and marks a progression from public to private space. Yet the formal axial arrangement, and the tendency to keep the door open, gave a certain public access deep into the house.[15] What happened in the atrium was visible to the street, and the atrium marked a characteristic intersection of public and private affairs. Here the paterfamilias received his clients, and the family displayed busts of ancestors and reminders of its importance (Varro, *De Lingua Latina* 5.125; Vitruvius 6.3.6; Pliny, *Natural History* 35.6–7). The atrium was the center of the family's world: the shrine of the family gods stood here (Pl. 20), and the house faced inward to this space where, ideally, the women of the household did their spinning and the children played, under the authoritative and benevolent gaze of the paterfamilias. His office (originally also his bedroom—Propertius 4.11.85) was the tablinum, which because of its slightly elevated position on the main axis of the house dominated everything that happened within the home (Pl. 19). Subordinated to the semipublic domain of the pater-familias in tablinum and atrium were the dark little cubicula that served as bedrooms and individual sitting rooms and could be closed off with doors or curtains. Even here true privacy was diffi-cult to find, though, for the slaves who were all over the house would be aware of comings and goings.

As an expression of the wealth and dignity of the upper classes, these houses inevitably came to express the refined taste and living standards that penetrated Roman life so dramatically in the second century B.C. Marble entered the decorative repertory, in columns or in paintings that imitated the colorful grain of rare stones (Vitruvius 7.5.1). Copies of Greek paintings and statues appeared, as wall paintings, floor mosaics, and garden bric-a-brac. Marble columns and pilasters affected the design of the traditional atrium (Pliny, *Natural History* 36.48–50): old, dark, displuviate roofs were rebuilt with impluviate designs, or columns were added to create grander spaces.[16] The garden became a Greek peristyle, complete with Ionic or Corinthian columns, mosaic floors, formal plantings, and an array of rooms which Vitruvius (6.3.8–10) calls by the gen-eral (Greek) name *oecus,* "house."

We can see the results in a house like the House of Pansa (VI.vi.1; Fig. 13) at Pompeii, where to a typical Tuscan atrium plan was added, between 140 and 120 B.C., a formal Ionic peristyle with rooms all around; this case is unusual only in that there was a swimming pool in the middle of the peristyle instead of the more predictable formal garden. The inspiration was Greek, yet the product had a distinctly Italic air, demonstrated in the formal ax-iality of the arrangement of rooms. Hellenistic and Italic taste were both apparent in the vista a person received while standing at the front door and looking through the carefully and symmetrically ar-ranged atrium, tablinum, and peristyle to a distant green garden (Pl. 19).

This taste is apparent in the few surviving remains of republican houses in Rome, such as the House of Livia, the House of Augustus, and the House of the Griffins on the Palatine. Their walls, like those of houses in Pompeii decorated between about 80 B.C. and the end of the century, are covered with paintings in the "Second Style."

Fig. 13. Pompeii: House of Pansa (Insula Arriana Polliana)

Whereas the effect of the "First Style" had been to make plaster look like regular rows of ashlar masonry, the artists of the "Second Style" painted a wall in fresco to simulate a three-dimensional scene of a garden, a landscape, or a mythological vignette; columns and other architectural details were painted in fresco as a frame. This was a more complicated, sumptuous kind of wall covering, which clearly appealed to the upper classes of Rome in the first century B.C. Its inspiration lay partly, no doubt, in all those newly imported columns and the vistas they created, and also in the increased popularity of gardens.

Lower-Class Housing under the Republic

While the aristocrats and the upwardly mobile lived in ever-grander atrium houses, ordinary citizens lived in small tabernae of one or two rooms. These were open to the street, except for folding wooden shutters (Isidorus of Seville, *Etymologies* 15.2). They served as shops and workrooms as well as houses, and were usually grouped in attached rows.

Another type of simple house is represented at Cosa (Fig. 14). Built on a long, narrow lot with a garden behind, it was entered through a fauces (corridor) with a room on each side. The fauces led to an unroofed courtyard, which perhaps served some of the humbler functions of an atrium. A series of spouts and pipes conducted rain water into a cistern below. Behind, under a lean-to roof, a tablinum-like room faced south to pick up the winter sun; beside it was a cubiculum. At the rear a long, transverse room over a drainage pit functioned as kitchen, toilet, bathroom, and storeroom. From it, steps led down to a vegetable garden.[17]

In republican Rome, as the population increased, houses were

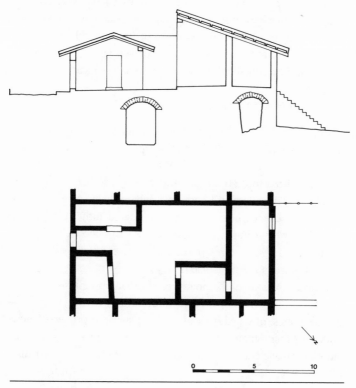

Fig. 14. Cosa: House V-D

built in new areas such as the Aventine and Trans-Tiber. In the third and second centuries B.C., however, the influx was so great and the area bounded by the walls and gardens was so limited that residential units had to be extended upward. At first Roman landlords built fragile, combustible buildings of wood-frame wickerwork (*opus craticium*), though in the second century the introduction of concrete (*opus caementicum*) permitted builders to produce somewhat more solid apartment blocks called *insulae* ("islands"). Vitruvius (2.8.17), from his Augustan perspective, gives a rosy and optimistic account of insula construction, but the realities of plebeian life under the republic were much grimmer than his upbeat discussion suggests (cf. Diodorus 31.18.2).[18] As the number of poor people crowded into miserable housing kept growing, some efforts were made to reduce the pressure by encouraging emigration. Thus the Gracchi sent many of the poor abroad as colonists, and Pompey in 61 B.C. proposed a redistribution of land which among other things was intended to encourage the poor to leave the city and presumably live like their predecessors at Cosa.

Upper-Class Housing in the Principate

During the principate the traditional forms of domestic architecture gave way to other forms. As the republican family traditions and values became less important, the atrium and tablinum, which had symbolized those traditions and values, also became less important. Older houses still had atria, where their owners still received their clients, but they were considered rather quaint and old-fashioned.[19] A fragment of the Forma Urbis shows, in the late second century A.D., three traditional houses side by side in the midst of more modern insulae (Pl. 7).

In Rome, of course, the pressures of urban space restricted the construction of ceremonial rooms, but both in Rome and in less-crowded cities, those who acquired more spacious properties now tended to focus their family life and social entertaining on the garden peristyle and the dining rooms rather than on the atrium. Where space allowed, there was a new emphasis on gardens, and the ultimate example was Nero's Domus Aurea, with its acres of landscaped gardens, meadows, and trees imitating the "paradise" or pleasure garden of the old Persian kings. In more limited space, the wealthy imitated Nero's example by arranging formal gardens in back of their houses; in place of the vegetables and fruit trees, which were characteristic of republican domestic gardens, there were now boxwood hedges, shrubs, statues, and pools and fountains fed by improved aqueduct systems. Smaller gardens were expanded visually by means of paintings and mosaics, sometimes arranged to produce an impressive vista from the front door even in a limited space.[20]

The House of the Vettii (VI.xv.l) at Pompeii illustrates the new taste in town houses (Fig. 15). Originally built during the second

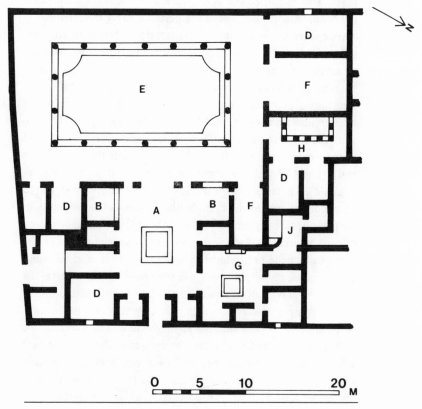

Fig. 15. Pompeii: House of the Vettii

century B.C., the house came into the possession of two freedmen
who had become wealthy enough to buy such a large house. They
did not reject the old aristocratic form of their house, but they remodeled extensively to reflect the most up-to-date taste. The
atrium (A) was retained, with its impluvium covered in marble and
two strongboxes at each side; the walls were carefully decorated
with paintings, one of which showed a sacrifice to the Penates, the
household gods traditionally worshiped in Roman atria. Toward
the rear on each side were the canonical alae (B). Tastefully decorated with mythological scenes, a winter dining room (D) and four
small cubicula opened onto the atrium. Presumably the house
originally had a tablinum, but if so, it was removed when the peristyle, with its garden (E), was installed. In the house's last phase
the columns and plantings of the peristyle drew the attention of
anyone entering the atrium, as they still do in their restored forms
today. Twelve statues and two basins served as fountains, with water supplied through lead pipes from the municipal aqueduct; marble tables and busts completed the furnishing; flowers and shrubs
were formally arranged; and the walls of the portico were decorated
with architectural views, still lifes, and literary figures. On two
sides the triclinia and oeci (D, F) were open to the peristyle and
were covered with fine wall paintings of several mythological cycles
and a series of Hellenistic *putti* busily engaged in business activities—all portrayed in great and practical detail. Women played
an important part in the household: the commercial activities in
the paintings are performed by both girls and boys, Amazons play a
role in the decorative schemes, and a small suite of rooms off the
north side of the peristyle has a small garden (H) and paintings
with feminine mythical themes; this suite has been identified as the
gynaeceum, or women's quarters. As was fairly common in the mansions of Pompeii, a secondary atriolum (G) was located to the north
of the atrium. The atriolum has an impluvium of tufa and, on the
wall, a shrine of the family Lares. Opening from the atriolum were
several cubicula, a kitchen (J), and a staircase leading to upstairs
rooms, probably quarters for the slaves. Other upper-story rooms
(no longer preserved) were approached by a staircase on the south-

ern side of the atrium (A). At the southeastern corner of the house was the stable, which had a latrine.

The House of the Vettii illustrates an important development in the Pompeiian real estate market in the decade or so before Vesuvius erupted in A.D. 79. Old houses were bought up and remodeled by new elements in the population as the traditional aristocracy apparently moved out of town and sold or leased their old town houses. Even the Insula Arriana Polliana, which we have already met as the House of Pansa (Fig. 13), was converted into apartments and rented out (*CIL* 4.138), and the House of Sallust (Fig. 12) was converted into a hotel. At Rome, too, in two of the three traditional houses on the Forma Urbis (Pl. 7), the atrium seems to have been split up into smaller rooms, which may indicate that it had been converted into apartments.

New social forces in the principate had changed the composition of the group that could afford "upper-class housing." The old families of the republic had died out, and although some members of the new aristocracy and the rich freedmen may well have expressed their public spirit and political ambition in an old-fashioned atrium house,[21] most of the houses of the principate were inspired not by the narrowly Roman tradition of the atrium but by the more widespread Mediterranean tradition of the central courtyard.

At Ostia, the House of Fortuna Annonaria (V.ii.8) provides a second-century example (Pl. 29): a taberna-like vestibule led directly into the north side of a peristyle—a courtyard surrounded on three sides by a portico of travertine columns. Several small rooms opened from the portico, but of major architectural interest were the two rooms that faced each other across the peristyle—a dining-room on the east, and a somewhat larger sitting room (to which a semicircular apse was added in the third century) on the west. The floor of one small room was raised so that hot air could circulate beneath it, and this seems to be the earliest known example of radiant heating in Ostia. With the shift of architectural focus from traditional atrium to open courtyard, the sitting room became the place to receive guests. It was no longer on the main axis from the front door, and the explanation for this may have been a desire for greater privacy.[22] The owner of this house was well-to-do, and must have had a large retinue of clients, but he was probably not as constantly involved in public life as his republican predecessors, and could enjoy his wealth without so much preoccupation with impressing the neighbors. The wealth was displayed in the mosaics on the floor, the marble revetments on the walls, the travertine columns, and an interesting collection of sculpture, mostly copies of old Greek masters, but with a pair of portrait busts from the third century A.D.

The House of the Round Temple (I.xi.2), built in the third century A.D., offers a similar ground plan. The same kind of entrance hall leads into the southern side of a courtyard, which here is surrounded by a masonry arcade rather than columns; the courtyard is paved with colored marble and has a marble basin in the center. On the northern side, separated from the courtyard by two Corinthian columns, is a large sitting room. The plans of these two houses are very similar, as was the domestic life within them. But one significant difference is that above the House of the Round Temple there were additional stories—it was not an independent domus but the desirable ground-floor apartment in a multistoried insula.

In Rome and in Ostia, the insula reflected the social realities of the principate, both the mobility and the highly stratified nature of its population. In modern apartments, elevators make the rooftop penthouse the most desirable and expensive in the building; in a Roman insula, however, as Juvenal among others makes plain, the poor lived in the small rooms and apartments in the upper stories, the well-to-do in the lower stories. A very common apartment plan appears throughout the city of Ostia—on the Via dei Vigili (II.iii.3; Pl. 27), for example, and in the so-called Garden Houses (III.ix.11–20; Pl. 28). They have in common an exterior wall with many windows, which light a long central room (*medianum*) and, at one or both ends, a deep sitting room (*exedra*). Along the back wall of the medianum are two or more cubicula for sleeping.[23] The Garden House complex was surrounded by its own wall for security, and by an open space that probably had topiary plantings. There were eight apartments on the ground floor of two central buildings, and more along the enclosure wall. Each apartment had the plan just described; the exedrae at both ends were two stories high, so the upstairs apartments must have been smaller than those on the ground floor. At Pompeii a similar plan appears three times, with variations, along the eastern side of the Insula Arriana Polliana (Fig. 13), and these may have been the rental apartments "fit for an equestrian" mentioned in an advertisement graffito (*CIL* 4.138).

The evolution away from the traditional atrium was complete by the third and fourth centuries. The House of Amor and Psyche (I.xiv.5; Fig. 16) and the House of the Nymphaeum (III.vi.1) at Ostia are typical of later houses. Both were built into the shells of older buildings, but most of the exterior windows were bricked in to focus attention on an interior garden with an elaborate fountain. These houses had fewer but larger rooms than their Ostian predecessors, and they were better provided with heating and with

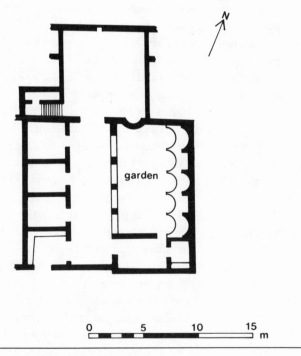

Fig. 16.   Ostia: House of Amor and Psyche

paving in colored marbles (*opus sectile*). They seemed to reflect a decline in community life, a tendency to look inward to the family and the self.

Lower-Class Housing in the Principate

Under the principate the basic units of housing for the poor continued to be the tabernae. They line the streets of Rome on the Forma Urbis and the streets of Ostia in the excavated ruins. The basic room opening onto the street sometimes had a back room or a mezzanine that offered some privacy, but not much.

Somewhat more elaborate were the "strip houses," a form that was widespread in the medieval and early modern cities of Italy and that was probably very common in antiquity, although Ostia and Pompeii did not produce very good examples of it. The best illustrations are in Herculaneum. In one such house (Herculaneum IV.8) a taberna faces the street; beside it on one side is a stairway to the upper story; on the other is an entrance to a corridor running most of the length of the narrow strip house, giving access to several rooms and a small courtyard/light well.[24] The wood-frame house built of opus craticium and known as the Casa a Graticcio at Herculaneum (III.13–15) has a similar plan on the ground floor, but it is larger and (since the upper story is well preserved) we can see that it was divided into several separate apartments (Pl. 21). In addition to the street-side taberna with its back room, the ground-floor corridor visible on the section drawing led to a porter's room and a small sleeping room on the right, and to a set of rooms that might have had residential use, or else were workrooms connected with the taberna; three courtyards provided light and (in the first courtyard reached by the entrance corridor) space for a cistern. Between two of the courtyards a staircase led up to an apartment (*cenaculum*) with a sleeping room (the bed was preserved and is indicated on the drawing), a dining room (the couches, arranged in an **L**, were preserved), and a latrine down a corridor at the rear of the upper story (not shown on the section drawing). The front half of the upper story was a separate apartment, entered by its own staircase from the street; it had several attractive features, including a large sitting/dining room opening off a balcony that provided air, light, and a view of what was going on in the street below. Cooking was done on a chimneyless hearth in the central hallway.

The people who lived in such apartments must have had some money with which to pay the rent, but the many who could not afford to rent a whole apartment sometimes shared one. We know, for example, from several legal passages that separate tenants occupied the sleeping and sitting rooms opening off a shared medianum (Justinian, *Digest* 9.3.5.2). At Ostia, one type of residence that may have been shared in this way is in a project-development in the northwestern part of Ostia known as Casette-tipo (III.xii and III.xiii). In plan they resemble the Garden Houses (Pl. 28), but are of much flimsier construction, and have smaller rooms, with only one common sitting room in each unit.

Most characteristic of Ostia and Rome, however, was the multi-storied insula, in which apartments were available for many economic sorts and conditions.[25] At Ostia, the House of Diana (I.iii.3, 4; Fig. 17) had the usual tabernae along the street façade (A), two of them with back rooms (B). An interior courtyard (C) provided light and air, and contained a masonry cistern (D) to supply water. Access was from two entrance corridors (E). On the ground floor, a corridor and several suites of rooms (F, G, H; I, J; K) surrounded the courtyard. One of the rooms (K) connected with the two shops with back rooms (B) and was later converted to a stable. A latrine (L) and porter's lodge (M) apparently served the whole building. On the second story, reached by stairs (N, P, Q), rooms were grouped into apartments, some lighted from the street (S, Y, Z), others from the courtyard (S, T, U, V, X).

Normally, the best apartments were on the ground floor, unless that was taken up entirely by shops. The farther tenants climbed up the increasingly narrow stairs, the more rickety and cramped were their rooms. Martial's apartment in Rome, on the third floor of an insula on the Quirinal, sounds reasonably comfortable (1.117, 5.78), but higher up in a neighboring insula, and lower on the social scale, we might meet Juvenal's Codrus (3.203–211), who lived with his wife in an attic apartment furnished with a too-short bed

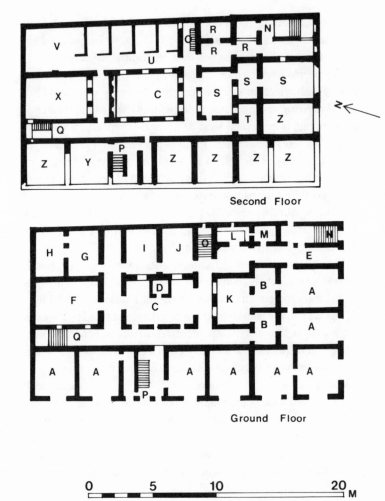

Second Floor

Ground Floor

0   5   10   20 M

Fig. 17. Ostia: House of Diana (first and second floors)

and a few poor possessions: six small souvenir jugs, a marble stat-
uette, a few frayed books.

One surviving insula in Rome itself is well enough preserved to
confirm what the literary sources tell us about middle- and lower-
class housing in the capital. It stands in the shadow of the Capitoline Hill, below the medieval Church of Saint Mary in Aracoeli,

on Via Giulio Romano (Pl. 9). What remains is probably the east wing of a courtyard insula like the House of Diana; we do not know anything about the west wing, which was located under the present street. The main stairs were at the north end. The remaining façade opened onto the interior courtyard, which at ground level probably served as a shopping mall, for the lowest story was the usual row of tabernae with mezzanine living quarters above. The upper stories were devoted to rental apartments (Fig. 18). The second floor seems to have contained two spacious apartments reached by a bal-

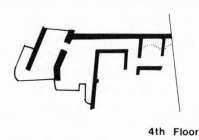

4th Floor

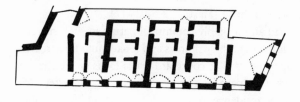

3rd Floor

2nd Floor

Fig. 18.   Rome: House on Via Giulio Romano (second, third, and fourth floors)

177

cony along the front of the building. On the third floor were three suites of small rooms arranged in parallel rows, each row reached by a corridor. Only the front rooms received any significant natural light, and were probably sitting rooms. One of these apartments was more elaborate, because it had a large corner room lighted by several large windows. The fourth floor is poorly preserved, but the flimsy walls indicate the cheap apartments we would expect this high up. There are no identifiable kitchens—the residents must have used charcoal braziers for cooking, or have gone out for hot meals. There are no identifiable latrines—they used the small spaces under the stairs, and chamber pots.[26]

The layout of the insula made privacy a hard thing to find. The apartment itself might well be full of neighbors, since several unrelated individuals or small familiae might share a cenaculum, taking turns cooking in the medianum, trying not to violate the law by throwing refuse out the window, and retiring for privacy or sleep into an individual cubiculum. The rituals of insula life must inevitably have been different from those in the aristocratic domus. Street noises probably penetrated even to the interior cubicula and made sleep difficult (Martial 12.57.3–17).

Life had an inevitably communal nature in such surroundings. People leaned out the windows and looked into the street and into other apartments. The courtyard was a focus of socialization. The windows were perhaps the most important characteristic—they opened the residence to the world outside, unlike the old atrium houses which looked inward to the family unit.

The Insula of Serapis and the Insula of the Charioteers at Ostia (Pl. 30) are examples of a well-developed insula neighborhood, with shops and courtyards at each end and a public bath between. Such a complex, like the insula below the Capitoline, must have had regular service personnel: a slave or freed *insularius,* who managed the building on behalf of the owner; an *officinator* (superintendent); and attendants at the shops, who were fixtures of the social life of the insula.[27]

Inns

When the upper classes of society traveled, they were well attended
by slaves and clients. Whenever possible they stayed in the country
villas or town houses of friends.[28] The rest of society also found it
necessary to travel, often renting horses or mules for transport;
when night fell they could approach a city for lodging in an inn—a
stabulum or *hospitium*. Pompeii once again offers us a representative
variety. About two-thirds of this town of 20,000 inhabitants has
been excavated, and eighteen inns have been identified inside the
walls.

One of the more luxurious inns had been installed in the House
of Sallust (VI.ii.4), discussed above (Fig. 12). Evidence for its con-
version to a public house is shop number 5, in which the counter
has been arranged to serve guests in the lobby (A) as well as people
passing by on the street, and also the profusion of dining facilities
(D), which seem clearly intended to accommodate a large number
of parties. The bakery at number 6 presumably supplied bread and
sweets for the inn's guests.[29]

The Inn of Albinus (Insula Occidentalis 1–2; Fig. 19) was located up the street, immediately on the right as one entered the city
by the Herculaneum Gate. It is typical of inns at the edge of town,
which would have been used chiefly by travelers, usually of the
lower classes, who were driving mule carts. The curb in front of the
inn was beveled to permit the wheeled carts to enter its courtyard.
Stables were located along the north side of the court, and a staircase led up from them to what was probably a dormitory for the
hired mule drivers. Bases for a line of posts near the center of the
courtyard show that there was a balcony covering part of it, which
would have given access to guest rooms upstairs. Opening onto the
street just south of the carriage entrance was a room that could
serve as a snack bar; behind it was a more private room, where
customers could drink and eat seated at small tables. Next to it, but
opening onto the courtyard, was a room that could have accommodated couches for more elaborate meals. Food was cooked in an
oven on the other side of the courtyard.[30]

On the street just west of the Stabian Baths are several inns, rep-

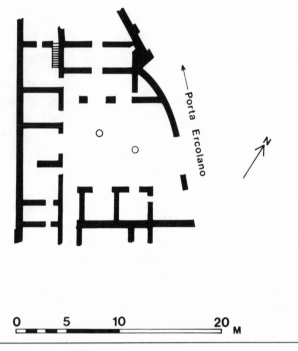

Fig. 19. Pompeii: Inn of Albinus

resenting a wide range of possibilities (Fig. 20). One, quite large (VII.xi.11–14), could accommodate around fifty guests. The big room at the southeastern corner (16–17) may have been a stable for customers' horses; if so, it was completely separate from guest quarters. A traditional atrium at the northern end (A) and the old tablinum (C) probably served as lobbies and reception rooms. Staircases led to guest rooms on the second story, and several dining rooms (D) are in evidence. Weather permitting, most meals were probably served in the large garden (H), where fruit trees, flowers, and vegetables provided pleasant surroundings for dining; arbored enclosures at the northwest corner could be set up with tables and couches for full-scale meals. This kind of garden was a desirable feature, a sign of a certain amount of elegance, and a way to attract customers.[31]

Across the street stands the much smaller Inn of Sittius (VII.i.44–

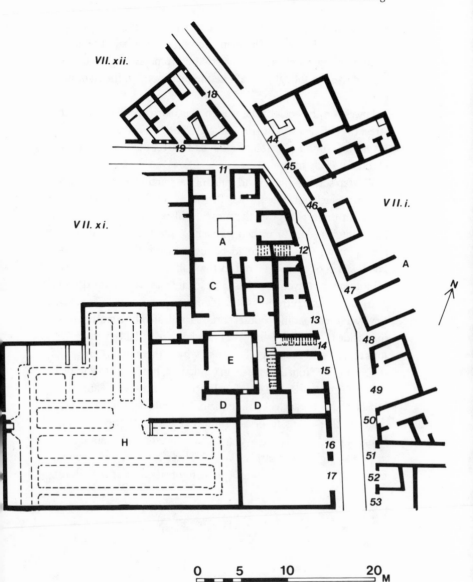

Fig. 20. Pompeii: Inns northwest of the Stabian Baths

45). It lacked a garden, but its sign advertised lodging and a proper triclinium (*CIL* 4.807). The plan shows a normal bar at 44 and a series of guest rooms at 45. The triclinium may well be the room behind the bar, though it could be the first room on the right next door.

Lowest on the social scale was the *lupanar* (brothel) across the street (VII.xii.18–19). Its tiny cubicles, erotic paintings, and boastful graffiti remind us that inns often had the reputation, and reality, of today's seedy motels.

Written sources give a vivid sense of the rough-and-ready quality of life in such establishments. Petronius, in *Satyricon* 91–99, a scene set in an inn, gives the most detail.[32] Encolpius and Giton have rented a room furnished with a bug-infested bed, a table, and a lamp stand. The door could be locked from inside or outside. Food was cooked and served in the building, as was drink. The tenants are portrayed as noisy and excitable, as we might expect in any place where Petronius's low-life heroes would stay. They had, however, their real-life counterparts, as indicated by a graffito in an inn inside the Stabiae Gate. "We pissed on the bed, I confess it. Yes, innkeeper, we did wrong. If you ask why—there wasn't any pot!" (*CIL* 4.4957). From Aeserniae, in Campania, not far from Pompeii, the tombstone of Lucius Calidius Eroticus and his wife, Fannia Voluptas, shows a traveler settling the bill, supplemented with a brief dialogue that seems to be an innkeeper's joke: "'Innkeeper, let's figure the bill.' 'You have—wine, 1/6 *as:* bread, 1 *as;* main dish, 2 *asses.*' 'All right.' 'The girl is 8 *asses.*' 'That's all right too.' 'Hay for the mule, 2 *asses.*' 'That mule is going to break me!'" (*CIL* 9.2689).

Eleven

City and Suburbs

The Romans' image of themselves as citizen-farmers, cultivated by legends such as that of Cincinnatus at the plow, writings in praise of agriculture, and poems praising the simple life of a country villa, often conflicted with the realities of urban life. Poets and moralists voiced contradictory feelings, complaining about the noise and confusion of city life, but admitting the attraction of its excitement and cultural richness. City and country depended on each other: the city concentrated people, experiences, and monuments of Roman greatness; the country supplied food, water, and fresh air.[1]

Neighborhoods

A person walking through the streets of ancient Rome was assaulted by impressions in every sense. There were landmarks, statues, buildings, and varied colors and textures to see; sounds of construction and vehicles, shouts and conversations in Latin, Greek, and several barbarian languages to hear; the fragrance of bakeries and food shops and the stink of smoke, sewage, sweat, and urine to smell; jostling crowds to touch; and a kinetic sense of movement through many types of urban environment.

An episode in a play by Terence (*Brothers* 573–585) gives a lighthearted inventory of urban landmarks. One character is sending another on a senseless mission to the other side of town, and although his directions are meant to be confusing, they list the main features of the city scene. Near the center are a portico behind the market, a big fig tree, a temple, a small neighborhood shrine, the house of a rich man, wide streets, and little dead-end alleys. Farther out, toward the city gate, he conjures up a business district with a cistern to supply public water, a mill to grind grain, and a workshop where luxury furniture is available.

The tenants of damp, smoky, dark apartments could lean out windows and talk to neighbors across the street, or they could go down into the streets and squares, where along with a breath of air and a glimpse of sky, they would find a muddy, crowded, smelly, shoving, noisy, colorful scene (Seneca, *De Ira* 3.35.5), populated by peddlers selling water, matches, cooked beans, sausages, or salt fish, vagabonds charming snakes or reciting poetry, pimps and transvestites hustling the crowds (Martial 1.41), and dancing, begging priests of one or another exotic divinity (Lucretius 2.618–628; Ovid, *Fasti* 4.183–190).

It was all very colorful and exciting, but it also had its brutish aspect. Juvenal (3.240–267) warned of the danger of being trampled in the crowd or run over by a passing construction cart, or struck by crockery and slop buckets falling from upper-story windows. Legal decisions also acknowledged this danger (Justinian, *Digest* 9.3), as well as the possibility that trash, animal skins, and human corpses might be left in the street (*Digest* 43.10.1.5).[2]

The urban unit was the *vicus*—a street and the neighborhood spreading around it into alleys and little squares. The residents and shopkeepers here shared a common urban landscape, and in spite of differences in status and wealth, they must have developed certain common interests. The vicus provided a natural unit for organization, for political partisans stirring up the population at the end of the republic, or Caesar organizing a new census. Augustus arranged that each of the fourteen regions be administered by vici, through two *vicomagistri,* each vicus symbolized by a central shrine of the Lares Compitales, deities of the *compitum,* "crossroads."[3] Some vici took their name from a prominent landmark, like the

Vicus Aesculeti, named for an oak grove, the Vicus Apollinis at the Temple of Apollo on the Palatine, or the Vicus Rostratae near some monument decorated with ships' beaks. Others were named for residents, like the Vicus Caeseti, or the Vicus Tuscus where the Etruscans once lived. Still others commemorated the tradesmen who worked there, like the Vicus Frumentarius at the grain market, or the Vicus Lorarius of the harness makers.

The different regions of Rome had separate personalities. As early as the fourth century B.C., there were perceptible differences between the sacred acropolis of the Capitoline, the plebeian quarter on the Aventine, and a developing upper-class enclave on the Palatine (Livy 8.19.4).[4] By the first century B.C., the Palatine was the most exclusive neighborhood in Rome. Here were the old monuments of earliest Rome, the Casa Romuli and the Temple of Magna Mater, and here lived the great and near-great of the late republic, in spectacular mansions like the ancestral home of the Gracchi, or those belonging to Lucius Licinius Crassus, famous for its marble columns and six lotus trees, Quintus Lutatius Catulus, adorned with its own semipublic portico, and Gaius Octavius, where his son, who would later become Augustus, was born.[5] Here, too, lived the occasional social climber, like Chrysogonus, the freedman of Sulla, active in politics and a target of Cicero's scorn (*Pro Roscio Amerino* 133–134). After his term as consul in 63 B.C., Cicero himself decided to buy a house on the brow of the hill looking down into the Forum Romanum, and he was willing to put himself into a straightjacket of mortgages to be able to pay the 3.5 million sesterces the house's prestigious location demanded (*Letters to His Friends* 5.6.2). This literary record is supplemented by the archaeological remains of the House of Augustus, bought from the estate of the orator Hortensius. The House of Livia next to it (Fig. 5), and the House of the Griffins, buried under Domitian's palace, both presumably had a traditional atrium at the top level of the hill, but since they were located on sloping ground, additional rooms were built on lower terraces. It is these lower, partly subterranean rooms that survive, with their barrel-vaulted ceilings and elegant paintings.

We can reconstruct a more mixed neighborhood on the Quirinal, thanks to the comments of several authors. We know that at the end of the republic Cicero's friend Atticus lived there, in a house that was relatively simple but comfortable, and had room for a garden with trees that was big enough to be called a "wood" (Nepos, *Life of Atticus* 13). This was also the site of such landmarks (listed in the fourth-century A.D. "Notitia of the XIV Regions") as the Temples of Salus, Serapis, Flora, Quirinus, and (on the site of Vespasian's family home) the Gens Flavia. There were statues and fountains and, at the outer end, the Horti Sallustiani, the suburban villa that once belonged to Gaius Sallustius Crispus, the historian, and was later taken over by the emperors for their own use. In the first century A.D., Martial lived on the Quirinal, in a walk-up apartment on the third floor of an insula (1.117; 5.78) near the landmark the Tibur Column (5.22). His poems allow us, in our imagination, to take a walk down through the Subura, where his list of things worth mentioning includes the residence of Lucius Arruntius Stella, poet and (in A.D. 101) consul (a grand town house near the Forum which had a large garden, a fountain, and statues [6.47; 7.15; 12.3]); shops where Martial could find any groceries he needed (7.31.12; 10.94); barbers, shoemakers, and the contractors who punished criminals (2.17); and lots of prostitutes (6.66; 9.37; 11.61, 78). Climbing the Clivus Suburanus to the edge of the Esquiline, he complains about the wet, muddy steps, and the trains of mules hauling marble for some building project (5.22). (This road appears in Plate 10, in the lower right-hand corner, passing the rectangular Porticus Liviae, just next to the Thermae Traiani.)[6] On the Esquiline he points out a theater-shaped fountain decorated with statue groups representing Orpheus singing to the animals and the rape of Ganymede by the eagle, a small house with an eagle carved over the door, and the large house belonging to Pliny the Younger (10.19).

Several pieces of the Forma Urbis (Pl. 7) combine to show us a neighborhood somewhere in Rome in the late second century A.D. which confirms the impression of a mixture of many kinds of buildings and functions.[7] A main street runs straight along the top of the fragment; tabernae line up along both sides. If, in our imagination, we walk from right to left along this street, the plan seems to indicate on our right (the upper side of the fragment) a series of small tabernae grouped around the open courtyards of insulae. On the other side of the street, we would pass on our left an arcade in front of the shops; from it a passageway leads back into a small courtyard, also surrounded with shops. Next along the main street on the left are more shops, in front of three traditional atrium houses, at least two of which are cut up into smaller spaces. Next door to these houses there appears to be an open courtyard with some kind of construction in the middle, and a series of rooms along the back wall. One of these is wider than the others, and the layout suggests that it may be a *schola,* the meeting place of a *collegium* or cult group. Next along the street is another long arcade, two bays deep, with a series of shops and stairs leading up to, perhaps, the second floor of an insula. (Stairs are indicated by **V**-shaped marks.) Part way along this arcade is a broad staircase leading up (or down?) to an open space at a different level. In the lower left-hand corner of the fragment we can make out a large hall, its roof supported by square pillars and surrounded by shops, and next to it a large, open park, laid out with rows of trees surrounding three **U**-shaped elements that may be hedges or water channels.

Such open public spaces had been an important part of the Roman scene since Pompey constructed his garden-filled Porticus Pompeii next to his theater, and the open parts of the city offered opportunity for casual contacts, for business and pleasure. Horace, on a famous walk through the Forum (*Satires* 1.9), encounters a friend with nothing to do, an acquaintance who tortures him with boring chatter, and a determined litigant at the praetor's tribunal. Catullus, too (55.1–8), looks through all the public spots— Campus Martius, Circus Maximus, Capitoline, and Porticus Pompeii—when searching for his friend Camerius. And in the park on the Capitoline, a politician "works" the crowd as it promenades there, enjoying the view and shopping among the displays of silk and jewelry (Sidonius, *Letters* 1.7.8). These are all examples of the irrepressible Mediterranean tendency to get out into the sun and enjoy the company of other human beings. There were opportunities, too, for romantic meetings: in streets no longer quiet where (to hear the elegiac poets tell it) whole bands of young men serenaded desirable women and assaulted their thresholds;[8] in the Campus Martius and temple precincts all abuzz with amorous whispering (Horace, *Odes* 1.9.18–20); and at the Circus Maximus or the Subura, where the streetwalkers walked.

Streets

The neighborhoods were joined by streets that were seldom perfectly straight, as they followed the route of tracks that joined the villages of earliest Rome, and seldom very wide. The Twelve Tables specified that a *via* should be eight feet wide on the straightaway and sixteen feet wide on curves (Varro, *De Lingua Latina* 7.15), and inside the city only two streets were imposing to qualify for the title. One, the Sacra Via (Sacred Way), carried traffic into the Forum Romanum from the Velia. The Nova Via (New Way) ran parallel to it along the base of the Palatine.

Apart from these, the term *via* was used only to designate the major highways that fanned out between the city gates and all of Italy. Two streets outside the pomerium in the Campus Martius also claimed the term: the Via Lata, the final mile of the Via Flaminia as it entered the city, and the Via Tecta, cutting across the lower part of the Campus.

The term *vicus* was used for the street that defined a neighborhood, but was sometimes extended to major thoroughfares, like the Vicus Longus and the Vicus Patricius, which ran along the valleys on each side of the Viminal (Fig. 2). A sloping street that climbed the edge of a hill was known as a *clivus,* like the Clivus Suburanus. *Platea,* which means "wide" in Greek, was applied to major streets and probably to squares as well, and *angiportum* usually referred to one of the many narrow streets, whether dead-end or not.[9] *Semita* also referred to a narrow street, though the name was retained as a quaint, old-fashioned designation for the Alta Semita (High Path), a major artery along the top of the Quirinal.

We should imagine the streets of early Rome as made of dirt, with an occasional surface of pebbles. Our first evidence for paving is that of the Clivus Publicius from the Circus Maximus to the Aventine in 238 B.C., and then we read (Livy 41.27.5–8) that in 174 the censors paved streets throughout the city, using large, flat blocks of *silex* (a generic term for hard stones like flint, granite, and basalt). Most streets had raised sidewalks; rain water and trash would wash down streets with a slope, and some of these were built over arched drains that connected with the sewers.

At Pompeii, the Via dell'Abbondanza (Pl. 17) lets us imagine a business street with stone paving, raised sidewalk, stepping stones, shop after shop, and the windowed façades of town houses above. The Via dei Vigili in Ostia (Pl. 27) typifies a back street of the city in the principate, with the brick walls and windows of apartment houses. In Rome itself, the tall façades and projecting balconies of insulae gave the streets a narrow, hedged-in feeling, and often put the streets themselves in the shade. For much of the Italian year, that would be a blessing, and when Nero widened the streets as part of his reconstruction program, people complained that it made them too hot (Tacitus, *Annals* 15.43). The front doors of shops were folded back during business hours so that customers could see their wares, which often spilled out onto the streets themselves (Livy 6.25.9; Martial 1.41 and 7.61; Pl. 16, 17). Some buildings of-fered colonnades or arcades to shelter the sidewalk and to add some architectural interest (Pl. 7). An occasional tree also relieved the monotony, although there were not very many of them—those that are mentioned in the sources seem to have been regarded as something special. In open spaces one might find a statue depict-ing some distinguished Roman or a hero from Greek mythology. Perhaps there would be the columned porch of a temple, or foun-tains delivering water into simple troughs, or elaborate nymphaea. A street scene might come to a dramatic climax with an arch—either the arch of an aqueduct passing over the road, a triumphal arch (carefully arranged for maximum effect), or one of the gates in the city wall.

Walls

According to Vergil (*Aeneid* 7.156–159), the first real action taken by Aeneas after he arrived in Latium was to dig a ditch and erect defensive walls. According to Livy (1.7.3), the first thing Romulus did in founding Rome was to fortify his city on the Palatine; the physical protection of the walls and the sacred boundary of the pomerium theoretically coincided and reinforced each other. Rome's first walls were probably simple wooden palisades enclosing the Palatine, but as the city grew and came into conflict with its neighbors, a larger defensive circuit was a practical necessity.

Tradition says that King Servius Tullius enclosed his "city of the four regions" (Fig. 2) within a defensive ditch and wall that enclosed the Quirinal, Viminal, and Esquiline hills. The problem was to protect the long stretch where geologically the hilltops continued on into the surrounding countryside, in contrast to the Palatine and Capitoline hills, whose steep sides offered a natural defense. The solution was an earthwork embankment, the *agger,* preceded on the outside by a defensive ditch, the *fossa.* Stretches of masonry wall were built of a local friable stone known as *cappellaccio.*[10]

These defenses proved inadequate against the Gallic invasion in 390 B.C., and during the fourth century the Romans built the elaborate circuit of the wall known (erroneously) as the "Servian Wall," using large blocks of the hard, strong *Grotta oscura* stone from Veii. The wall defended Rome successfully against Hannibal's threat of attack, and it also defined the city for six and a half centuries. (Legislation, for instance, refers to the *urbs,* "city," as the space within this wall.) The wall continued to serve that symbolic function even after urban activities and structures were sprawling outside it, when Italy and the empire were so secure that Rome itself needed no defensive wall.

In time, however, the need returned, and in A.D. 271 the emperor Aurelian started a new circuit of walls, the Muri Aureliani (Fig. 6), now nearly 19 kilometers in length, which shows how much the city had grown. These walls were about 6 meters high, and built mostly of brick, although where possible they incorporated existing structures. Rectangular towers reinforced the wall at intervals of 100 feet. The general design was rather conservative, which has been taken to be evidence that the walls were built by the urban collegia rather than by up-to-date experts from the army's corps of engineers.

Suburbs

For all its symbolic value, the wall built in the fourth century B.C. could not contain the city in its centuries of growth. By the Augustan period, when Dionysius of Halicarnassus visited Rome, the city had grown in such a ragged fashion and was so bound up with the surrounding countryside that it gave the onlooker "the impression of a city stretching out into infinity" (*Roman Antiquities* 4.13.3–4). In fact, Roman laws regularly included "the city and the mile outside" within the urban jurisdiction. The "mile outside" was a kind of aura around the old city, and corresponded approximately both to the area that was built up during the principate and to the circuit of the Muri Aureliani.

Along the outer edge of this suburban area, the rich bought small farms and built private villas and gardens on them, creating a broad green belt that sometimes threatened to choke the city and prevent its outward growth. To the masters of these villas, however, a semirural environment was available within easy reach of the city's Forum, temples, and markets. The attraction is expressed most clearly by Martial in a poem in which he describes the comfortable but relatively modest estate of his cousin, overlooking the city from the top of the Janiculum: "While the crooked valleys are clouded in mist, it basks in the clear sky and shines with a special radiance of its own. . . . From here you can see the seven lordly hills, and can survey all of Rome, the Alban hills and those at Tusculum, every cool suburban spot. . . . The traveler on the Via Flaminia or the Via Salaria appears in his chariot, noiseless, the wheels incapable of disturbing sleep's sweet embrace" (Martial 4.64; cf. 7.17). The owner of such a place was able to indulge the desire to get away from the city's hubbub. But for a Roman aristocrat it did more; it indulged his traditional addiction to the soil, to the ideal of the citizen-farmer like Cincinnatus. No noble Roman had done any serious farming since the third century B.C., of course, but that did not dim the appeal of a quieter, more pastoral life than could be found in the city.[11]

In the immediate area of Rome, a good example of a suburban villa was excavated, but then covered up, under the Villa Farnesina on the right bank of the Tiber. The rooms that were excavated were decorated with mosaic floors, "Second Style" paintings, and fine stucco reliefs showing pastoral and Dionysiac scenes. We can visualize a large building with a cryptoporticus along the river; above would have been gardens and walks arranged around a great semicircular belvedere. The view included the river, and the hills and buildings of the city on the other side.[12]

As if to demonstrate architecturally that life in the country was the reverse of life in the city, the parts of villas were arranged, from the point of view of a town house, backwards. Instead of being closed in from the urban street, they were wide open to the surrounding landscape. The atrium, freed from its city role as a semipublic reception room, was set back as a private living room. The peristyle was in front, where guests entered (Vitruvius 6.5.3).

The best-known example of such a suburban villa is the Villa of the Mysteries (Fig. 21), located a short distance north of the Herculaneum Gate in Pompeii and built early in the second century B.C. A visitor entering from the east (not from the modern tourist entrance) came first into a peristyle (E) surrounded by sixteen Doric columns. (When the villa was changed from a country residence to a working farm in the first century A.D., a wall was built between the columns, the residential wing to the west was largely abandoned, and a wine press was installed in a room off the northeastern corner of the peristyle.) In the gracious days of the late republic and early principate, a visitor standing among the columns of the peristyle enjoyed a magnificent vista out through the formal, Tuscan-style atrium, a *tablinum* (C, later walled off), and a curved belvedere onto the fields near Torre Annunziata and the Bay of Naples, which would have been visible in antiquity. The peristyle was surrounded by rooms of various sizes, including several bedrooms; an apsidal room (F), which may have been a shrine or a reception room;[13] the formal atrium (A); a smaller *atriolum* (H), which gave access to a bathing complex just to the east; and a kitchen yard (G) with two ovens. The rooms of the western wing, around the formal atrium (A), had floors paved with cut stones and mosaics, and walls painted in the "Second Style." The most famous painting at Pompeii is surely that in room D, which shows scenes relating to Di-

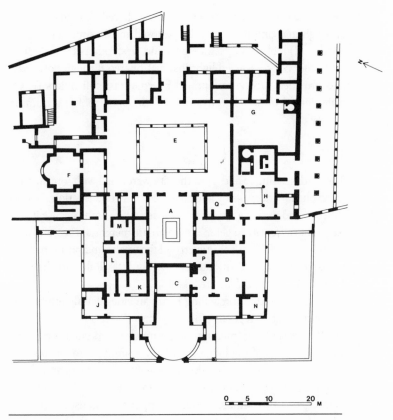

Fig. 21. Pompeii: Villa of the Mysteries

onysus and his attendants in front of a bright red background.[14] To judge by its size and shape, and its location at the southwestern corner of the house, commanding an impressive view along the outskirts of the town and the coastline, it was the formal triclinium. A cryptoporticus ran under the main floor to the north, west, and south, and along the edge of the platform on which the house rested were two terraces planted with hanging gardens, arranged symmetrically around the belvedere and reached by a series of porticoes. The rest of the space in the western wing was occupied by suites of sitting and sleeping rooms. Some of them (K, L, M) were entered through small anterooms; some (J, P) had alcoves for one

193

bed, some (O, Q, M) for two beds. They offered all kinds of views and lighting: one (N) was fully exposed to the south and west; another (J) looked out to the north and west; others (K, L, M, O), set farther back, received light that was filtered through porticoes, and provided nice vistas framed by columns; still others (P, Q) were lighted only indirectly, through the open roof of atrium or peristyle.[15]

Tombs

The roads leading to and from the city were lined with tombs, relegated outside the walls by ancient custom. A good location, next to the road and near the city gates, was desirable, both because it was easier for the family to get to it to celebrate memorial rites, and also because it more effectively advertised the wealth and position of the tomb's occupant. Death had remarkably little ability to slow the constant competition for prestige and status.

Along the roads approaching Etruscan cities, family tombs had been arranged in regular, often rectilinear, streets as a city of the dead (*necropolis*), in imitation of the much less permanently constructed houses of the living (Pl. 11, 31). Similarly, tombs outside the walls of Rome reflected the variety of the living city and of the empire's traditions, imitating Etruscan mounds, Syrian towers, even Egyptian pyramids, as well as upper-class houses decorated with stucco moldings, engaged columns, and even the busts of the deceased looking out, as if through a window on the travelers passing by. Tombs proclaimed the political accomplishments of prominent families, the successful upward mobility of freed slaves, and the business connections of traders. They accommodated the whole familia, from paterfamilias to slaves, and often provided a triclinium in which the survivors ate memorial meals.

Polybius comments at length (6.53–54) on the way the upper-class Roman families used the funeral to remind themselves, their peers, and the city at large of their noble heritage and their contributions to the city. The family tomb was a logical extension of this process of commemoration, and no family in the republic had prouder traditions, or a more impressive tomb, than the Cornelii

Scipiones. This was located on a side road just off the Via Appia, about 1 kilometer from the Porta Capena, carved in the tufa where the ground level rises. On an imposing façade added in the second century B.C., engaged Corinthian columns framed doorways in which statues of distinguished Scipios stood, looking out toward the city. A series of six galleries carved in the rock gave access to about thirty sarcophagi, the oldest from the early third century B.C.[16]

The Mausoleum Augusti (Pl. 8) introduced a new order of conspicuous funereal architecture. Located in a prominent position between the Via Flaminia and the river, it consisted of a tall masonry core of concentric vaulted passages around which earth was piled and planted with cypress trees, the whole crowned with a statue of Augustus. The effect was that of a great mound 87 meters in diameter and about 45 meters high, of the type that is characteristic of the Etruscan cemetery at Cerveteri, about 50 kilometers north of Rome. It served as the tomb for the whole family of Augustus and his successors, and apparently stressed the native Italic tradition within the Augustan social program. It also inspired a fashion, and members of the imperial entourage built circular tombs for themselves, unmistakable Augustan landmarks along several of the roads leading to Rome.[17]

A similar showpiece was the pyramid-tomb built by Gaius Cestius on the Via Ostiensis, about 500 meters south of the Servian Wall. It was built of concrete faced with slabs of marble, about 22 meters square and 27 meters high, and it seems to have been an expression of the mania for Egyptian artifacts which swept Rome in the decades after Augustus defeated Cleopatra in 31 B.C.

Probably the most remarkable expression of funereal bravado is the Sepulcrum Eurysacis, the tomb of the baker Marcus Vergilius Eurysaces, erected around 30 B.C. just inside the gate (the modern Porta Maggiore), where the Via Labicana and the Via Praenestina diverge (Pl. 11). On the side of this small, trapezoidal monument, facing travelers as they approached the city, was a relief of Eurysaces and his wife, Atistia. At the bottom of the tomb vertical cylinders are represented, and above them the openings of horizontal cylinders—usually interpreted as grain silos and/or baking ovens. A frieze along the top displays a relief showing the whole process of bread-baking. We can imagine Eurysaces planning with his colleagues, wife, and architect a monument that would rivet the attention of everyone passing the spot and clearly declare how successful he had been at his trade.[18]

These examples, all exceptional in some way, were intended to preempt the attention and make a statement about the tomb owner's accomplishments. Such emphatic architectural statements could be successful, of course, only when they stood out over a mass of more ordinary structures (cf. those depicted along the Via Labicana and Via Praenestina at the right of Pl. 11). Typical assemblages of tombs from the late republic and early principate are preserved outside the gates of Pompeii, where tombs take the form of altars, semicircular exedrae, open-air enclosures, and canopies supported by rings of columns.[19] For the second and third centuries, the road at Isola Sacra leading north from Ostia to the Trajanic port offers a representative sample. In the background of Plate 31 we see the house-shaped tombs that accommodated urns containing the remains of members of the whole familia, from masters to slaves. Visible in the two tombs at center left are the small arches of the niches for ash urns, and the broader arch enclosing an *arcosolium*, in which a body could be laid. At the entrance to such tombs was a triclinium, an inscription, and often a relief showing the deceased at work. Less prosperous folk, who did not belong to a familia with a common tomb, were buried farther back from the road in simple brick-lined chambers sunk in the ground, indicated by a half-round mound toward the left of the photograph. Bodies of the poorest were placed in the simple ceramic coffins shown in the left foreground, or their ashes were placed in urns sunk in the ground.

Burial rather than cremation became relatively more common from the second century A.D. on, and the rich bought marble sarcophagi, often elaborately carved with standardized mythological scenes, presumably denoting some aspirations to a happy afterlife. Jews and Christians always preferred burial to cremation, and to accommodate their dead they dug corridors into the soft rock of suburban estates belonging to well-to-do members of their communities. These corridors were extended as the need arose, thereby producing the extensive catacombs found along every road.

Burial plots were privately owned, and the inscriptions on them were often precise in giving the dimensions of the plot and conditions of inheritance, and asking the reader to respect their sanctity. Paupers with no resources were unceremoniously dumped into a common grave, but the poor could hope to avoid that by being included in the family tomb of a patron or by joining a *collegium funeraticium,* a club that provided funerals for its members out of a common treasury; an inscription from Lanuvium (*CIL* 14.2112) records the charter of such a collegium, with membership requirements, schedules of dues, and rules governing behavior at the monthly banquets.

Twelve

Social Life in the City

As Rome grew to become the largest, most important city in the world, it became more cosmopolitan and sophisticated in its diversions, occupations, distractions, and pleasures. Its inhabitants were constantly assaulted and enticed by the variety of stimuli, and while some observers of the urban scene were delighted by the city and celebrated its diversity, others decried its decadence. In an eloquent passage reflecting moral rectitude Seneca, who was well acquainted with the dangers and pleasures of Nero's Rome, put the many options of city life in their social and physical context:

> Virtue is a lofty thing, exalted and royal, invincible, inexhaustible; pleasure is a low thing, servile, feeble, transitory—its home and office are the brothels and wineshops. Virtue is encountered in temple, forum, curia; it stands before the walls, covered with dust, well tanned, holding out callused hands. Pleasure is always hiding out, skulking in the darkness around baths and saunas and places that are afraid of the aedile—soft, effete, soaked in wine and perfume, pale as a corpse or painted and embalmed as for a funeral. (Seneca, *De Brevitate Vitae* 7.3)

Seneca's preference for the open air was characteristic, for Roman cities tended to conduct their activities outdoors—parades and promenades, of course, but also trials, political meetings, elections, funerals, plays, buying and selling. Dinner at a restaurant or at home was always more pleasant under a trellis than a ceiling. Even though some activities had to take place under a roof—legal business during a rainstorm, for example, or taking a bath—Roman architects seemed determined to devise ways to paint their walls with such realistic vistas or build their roofs with such wide spans that the indoor scene became an almost acceptable substitute for the outdoor one.

The Daily Round

The Roman day, from dawn to dusk, was divided into twelve equal hours. The first hour began at sunrise, the seventh hour at noon, and the twelfth ended at sunset. In the middle of summer, each hour in Rome was about 75 minutes long; in the middle of winter, about 45 minutes.[1]

The city's day started early, and the hours before dawn must have been busy and noisy: wagons from the country rattled along, making deliveries, gangs of porters lugged building material and debris to and from construction sites, herdsmen drove animals to the meat markets, slaves were hard at work in the bakeries (Pl. 18), and clients bustled through the streets to greet their patrons.

During the first two hours, we can assume that small shopkeepers were getting ready for the day's business, that the public slaves were at work cleaning streets or repairing aqueducts, that restauranteurs and wandering peddlers were selling light breakfasts of rolls, and perhaps a little cheese, to the crowds passing by (Martial 14.223; Apuleius, *Golden Ass* 1.18). The ancient literary sources insist that the most noticeable activity at these early hours was the *salutatio,* the morning ritual that required clients to put in an appearance at their patrons' houses, to be received in the atrium and to present, as a group or as individuals, their formal greetings (Juvenal 3.184–189 and 5; Martial 10.10; Seneca, *De Brevitate Vitae* 14.3–4). All through the city, you could see clients hurrying through the streets, or standing or sitting in small groups outside their patrons' homes, waiting to be admitted.

This ritual was finished by the beginning of the third hour, when the important people proceeded, on foot or in a litter, to the fora and basilicas, attended by as many clients as they could muster. Clients with shops to tend dropped away, but some stayed in attendance while patrons in the ruling class attended meetings of the Senate, presided over a court of law, defended a client in a lawsuit, or addressed one of the assemblies of citizens. Negotiatores were busy by the third hour, meeting in their stationes to close deals, see to paper work, and arrange for shipping (Martial 8.44.8). The shops were open, and housewives and household slaves bought supplies. The hungry slipped into a taberna for a snack of bread soaked in wine. Schools were in session—in an atrium, a taberna, or the upstairs room of an insula. Libraries were open for business during the morning hours.[2]

Most Romans had thus put in a hard day's work by the sixth hour, and so at that point nearly everyone stopped for lunch (*prandium*), a light meal traditionally eaten alone at home (Plutarch, *Moralia* 726E). In the days of the early principate, however, many people must have taken a quick lunch at a *popina* (Pl. 15, 22), or a more leisurely one in the shady garden of one of the better inns (Pl. 24).[3] By then—at least in summer, when nights were short and mornings were long—it was time for a nap.

Shopkeepers and food sellers were back at work in the afternoon, but ordinarily no more official business was transacted, and the sources give the impression that the streets were quieter then. Those with leisure moved out and enjoyed the panorama of the city or spent a quiet afternoon at home. These were the hours when a Mamurra went window-shopping in the luxury shops in the Saepta Iulia (Martial 9.59), or a Horace sauntered around the greengrocers, watched the gamblers at the Circus Maximus, listened to the fortunetellers (*Satires* 1.6.111–128). Those who wanted more strenuous relaxation went to the Campus Martius to exercise (Horace, *Satires* 1.6.126; Martial 4.8), or visited the baths. After the bath, dinner.

The working classes ate meals, mostly of legumes and bread, cooked (if at all) on braziers in back of their shops or in the courtyards or on the balconies of their insulae. Some grabbed a hot bowl of something at a neighborhood popina or restaurant. Among the upper classes, a simple dinner at home began around the tenth hour, but a more formal party began at the ninth (Martial 4.8)—it was a sign of amusing decadence that Nasidienus's dinner (Horace, *Satires* 2.8) began at the seventh hour. This in theory allowed the guests time to eat, talk, be entertained, and go home before it was too dark to navigate the streets safely. The literature, however, is full of references to parties that went on long into the night: for example, Cato reeling home drunk so late that he runs into clients going to a salutatio (Pliny, *Letters* 3.12); Propertius partying into the night and being attacked by Cynthia as she charges in and disturbs the whole Esquiline in her fury, upsetting lamps and smashing heads (Propertius 4.8); Trimalchio exhorting his guests to drink until dawn, and eventually waking the whole neighborhood and attracting the attention of the firemen (Petronius, *Satyricon* 73.6; 78.6–7). Propertius seems particularly proud of his knack for disturbing the neighbors with raucous parties (3.10.25–26), and Juvenal (3.232–236, 268–314) lists the nocturnal hazards: rattling carriages, brawling herdsmen, falling crockery and slop buckets, and roaming gangs of toughs. These muggers might be professional thieves, renegade slaves, a group of desperately poor people, or a band of upper-class youths out for thrills (Suetonius, *Nero* 26.1; S.H.A., *Lucius Verus* 4.6–7).

An individual could spend a lifetime in the city without friends or significant social contacts, lonely in the crowd. But nearly always there was a crowd of some sort. Philosophers and misanthropes may have sought the seclusion of a country villa or an urban garden peristyle, but in general, it should be clear that life in a Roman city was a very *social* life.

Baths

The bath, with its pleasant distraction from the cares and squalor of ordinary life, became a way of life for the Romans. It was the setting in which they washed themselves, took their exercise, spent their leisure time, were exposed to art and cultural programs, made business and political contacts, and conducted their social activities. In the beginning, of course, things were simpler (Seneca, *Epistulae Morales* 68.9). Private houses, like those at Cosa, had

modest bathrooms (Fig. 14), and the poor probably washed in the
river.

Public baths entered the Roman social and architectural vocabulary in the second century B.C., along with other borrowings
from the Greeks, and examples of an early type of bath building are
preserved at Pompeii. The earliest were the Stabian Baths, but the
Forum Baths (Fig. 22) show the elements of the arrangement: an
open courtyard derived from the Greek palestra forms the focus,
and along one side are rooms arranged in a series. Entering from

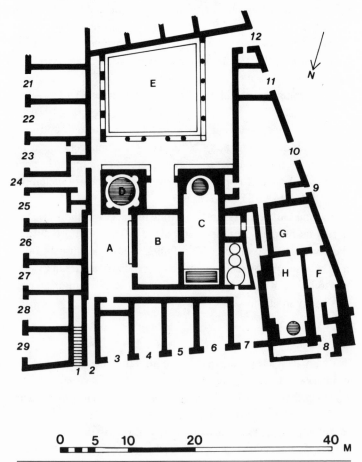

Fig. 22. Pompeii: Forum Baths

the street, one passed into a barrel-vaulted dressing room (*apodyterium,* A), then moved to the warm room (*tepidarium,* B), and eventually to the hot room (*caldarium,* C), which had a bathtub at one end and a splash basin in an apse at the other. The heating of these rooms involved the use of brick pillars, which by raising the floor created space through which hot air from the furnace could circulate; in practical fashion, the hot room was closest to the furnace. After the hot bath, a customer would go back for a cold plunge in the domed *frigidarium* (D). A *palestra* (E) was available for taking exercise and sun; in an open room facing the palestra, lectures or readings could be held. The Forum Baths also had a set of women's baths, with apodyterium (F), tepidarium (G), and, nearest the furnace, the caldarium (H), as well as conveniently placed shops (3–6). The Stabian Baths, which were larger, also offered a swimming pool flanked by rooms with splash basins, offices, supply rooms, cubicles with individual baths, and a latrine.

A more elaborate conception of public baths entered the Roman repertory in 25 B.C., when Agrippa constructed his baths in the Campus Martius, on a scale so large that he had to build a new aqueduct, the Aqua Virgo, to supply enough water for it. The distinctive architectural feature of the new building was a domed room over 20 meters in diameter, part of which is still visible on the Via della Ciambella, south of the Pantheon. The old word for bath, *balneum,* was not deemed adequate for such a grand structure, and so it was known as the Thermae Agrippianae, from the Greek word for "hot." From the Augustan Age onward, hot baths were an indispensable part of the Romans' life-style. Vitruvius paid a great deal of attention to arrangements for central heating (5.10.1), and moralists like Seneca (*Epistulae Morales* 86.6–13) decried the luxury of latter-day baths, contrasting it with the simplicity of the old republic. Certainly heating brought a change in the mystique of the bath; it became a more comfortable place, and people tended to spend more of their waking hours there.

The Thermae Agrippianae stood alone until Nero constructed his Thermae Neronianae nearby on a still-grander scale. But not all Romans used the great public thermae. Smaller baths under private ownership were scattered throughout the city. For example, the

Balneum Surae on the Aventine, which appears on the Forma Urbis, had the same basic design as the baths in Pompeii, with palestra and a series of bathing rooms.[4] We have only the plan of the Balneum Surae, but we know from literature something about the fittings and luxury of another privately owned bath, opened near the end of the first century A.D. by Claudius Etruscus, a freedman. Radiant in alabaster and colored marbles from Greece, Asia Minor, and Africa, it offered head-on competition to the standards of the great public baths. *Balneum* was considered to be too common a word to describe these baths. Indeed, Martial (6.42) called them *thermulae,* "little thermae," and Statius (*Silvae* 1.5) also described them effusively. Either they were something extraordinary, or Etruscus had invested in a very high-powered advertising campaign.

For the Flavians and many later emperors, building baths was an easy way to demonstrate the emperor's concern for the welfare of the common people. On the slope of the Esquiline above Nero's Domus Aurea, for example, Titus built his Thermae Titi. Their plan, known from a sixteenth-century sketch of Palladio, was to become the standard form of the imperial baths: a central axis flanked by symmetrically arranged halls. (They are visible in Pl. 10, to the right of the Colosseum, just above the hemicycle of the much larger Baths of Trajan.) The plan was followed in the Baths of Trajan, in those of Caracalla, Diocletian, and Constantine, and in many of the baths constructed throughout the empire. The Thermae Antoninianae (Baths of Caracalla) are the best preserved, and illustrate the design and immense scale of such projects (Fig. 23).[5] The axis of the central building ran through a triple-bayed open-air swimming pool, a transverse hall with a great vaulted ceiling (D), a smaller tepidarium with two tubs (B), and a circular caldarium (C) roofed with a dome 34 meters in diameter. Flanking the rooms on the central axis were dressing rooms (A), steam baths, and unroofed peristyle courts (E). This main building was surrounded by a great courtyard over 300 meters square which contained a stadium, libraries, and lecture halls. The grand scale, the imposing technology, the marble revetments, the Greek architectural details applied to Roman concrete walls, the copies of Greek sculpture distributed throughout, made of such baths a museum, a cultural cen-

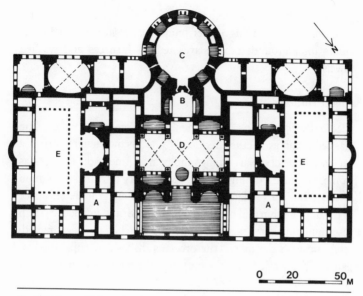

Fig. 23.   Rome: Thermae Antoninianae (Baths of Caracalla)

ter, a political statement that declared the glory of Rome and its emperors as eloquently as the monuments in the Forum.

For a minimal admission fee, all this luxury was available for anyone who wanted to enjoy it. In these "villas of the poor," the commoner found opportunities for exercise, swimming, steam baths, saunas, sex, gossip, lectures, and poetry readings. The towel-draped nudity of the bathers must have contributed considerably to a perception of social leveling, although a rich man could find ways to show off his wealth, by means of the crowd of his attendant clients and slaves and by means of the quality of his towels (Petronius, *Satyricon* 27–28).

Customers had a wide variety of exercises to choose from, from lifting weights and playing ball to swimming and receiving a massage. The ruins of the Baths of Caracalla suggest a variety of spectator activities as well, from sprints at the stadium track to literary readings in the hemicycles. Service personnel were available to give massages, to pluck hair, and to sell cakes, sausages, and bath oil (Seneca, *Epistulae Morales* 61.1–2). In the changing-room, slaves guarded their masters' clothes, not always successfully (Plautus, *Rope* 382–385; Catullus 33; Petronius, *Satyricon* 30.8, 93). In corridors underground, other slaves tended furnaces and washed towels.

Dinner Parties

Cicero (*De Officiis* 2.64) recommended that members of the ruling class entertain each other frequently, and his own letters portray a busy schedule of social comings and goings. Among the Romans, as in most cultures, dining was an opportunity to express common interests and consolidate social cohesion through the shared space of the dining room and the shared food and drink. But it also set up discriminating barriers, excluding those who had not been invited, while through the menu, the precious dishes and cups, the elegance of the service, and the beauty of the room asserting the status, wealth, and taste of the host.

Every house of any pretension had at least one dining room, and the more elaborate houses had several. The dining room was called a *triclinium* ("three-couch place") because couches for diners were normally arranged in rows around three sides of the room.[6] Vitruvius (6.4.2) recommended that a dining room used in the summer should face the north, and one for spring and autumn should face east, so that the sun would warm it and have it ready for an evening's socializing. A winter dining room, however, should be relatively enclosed, and decorated simply, in a way that will not be spoiled by the smoke from the braziers and oil lamps (Vitruvius 7.4.4; cf. Varro, *De Lingua Latina* 5.162). Since the dining room was a semipublic space, it was decorated with the finest mosaics and wall paintings. The decorations of the "Second" and "Fourth" styles seem to have been modeled on scenes from the stage, and suggest that the triclinium was a stage on which the dramas of social intercourse and social climbing were played.

Dinners were studied exercises in conspicuous consumption, over which the cook and other slaves worked for days (Plautus, *Braggart Warrior* 738–762; Juvenal 14.59–67). The guest list often included a sampling from several social strata; this, at any rate, is the impression we gain from the satirists, who of course looked for opportunities to comment on incongruities. The dinner of Nasidienus reported by Horace in *Satires* 2.8 is typical of what we have to work with. The guest of honor is Maecenas, who has brought along a couple of his clients, his "shadows," who drink too much for the host's comfort. Three literary types representing the intelligentsia provide witty conversation, and two clients of Nasidienus help with his hosting duties and are careful not to drink too much.

The gradation of guests according to social status was often carried to extremes. In one instance Pliny (*Letters* 2.6) reported on a meal where totally different menus were served—the best food and wine to the host and guests of honor, lower-quality fare to less-important friends, and cheap scraps to freedmen-clients. Pliny found this offensive; so, presumably, did the two lower categories of guests. The ancient documents imply that certain dangers resulted from the presence of guests from different social conditions. Fine manners could not always be expected, and the satirists delighted in portraying outrageous behavior (the dinner of Trimalchio in Petronius's *Satyricon* 28–78 is the classic example). But the problem was not simply the invention of the writers. Mottoes painted on the walls of the triclinium at the House of the Moralist in Pompeii (III.iv.2–3) remind guests to let the slaves wash their feet, not to rumple the slipcovers, to be careful of the linen, not to flirt with someone else's wife, to speak decently, and not to get into fights. "If you can't," they say, "go home" (*CIL* 4.7698). The regulations of a collegium at Lanuvium also make a special point about decent, seemly behavior at the monthly banquet (*CIL* 14.2112).

Most of the guest lists that we have show a preponderance of men, but the Romans were proud of the tradition that wives and other women could be present at formal dinners, in contrast to the Greek custom. Entertainment could be a simple recital by a single slave, or anything the imagination of the host could devise, from Spanish dancers to raucous scenes from pantomimes.[7]

There were simpler occasions, too, when an individual invited a single friend over for something like potluck. Pliny tells us of one such dinner he planned (*Letters* 1.15)—a simple meal of lettuce, eggs, snails, and cake; the only touch of luxury was snow-chilled wine. For entertainment, he arranged for the reading of a play or for a singer. And Martial (5.78) invited a single guest to join him in a plain but filling meal, while a slave played the flute.[8]

Restaurants and Taverns

A wealthy person who lived in a private domus or on the ground floor of a luxury insula was apt to stay at home in the evening. The poorer resident of the city might try to escape from a dank room by seeking out companionship at a *caupona*, a *popina*, or a *taberna*. A caupona was a full-service establishment that offered meals and drinks as well as rooms (Pl. 24). Here we might find a stand-up snack bar, a room with tables and chairs, and in more elegant establishments, an inner garden with private dining rooms complete with couches (Fig. 20). Included among the poems of the *Appendix Vergiliana* is the *Copa,* in which a Syrian freedwoman advertises the elegant facilities of her inn, including greenery, dining couches, musical entertainment, and exotic dancers. In many of these inns, slaves or freedwomen were available as prostitutes, and eventually the word *caupona* took on the connotation of a low-life dive. More respectable terms for an inn with a restaurant and bar were *hospitium, deversorium,* and (if there was a stable for horses or mules) *stabulum* (Fig. 19). Graffiti on the walls of cauponae at Pompeii suggest that booksellers met in one, and fullers in another.[9] A popina, a simpler restaurant, served wine and some hot food. *Popina* is a Sabine word, and perhaps it was introduced to Rome by foreigners who made a living by going into the restaurant business. This type of establishment often had the aura of a "greasy spoon." Martial, for example (5.70), describes a certain Syriscus, perhaps a freedman, who wandered about to table-and-chair popinae, stuffing himself without even being able to lie down for a proper meal. And Juvenal (8.146–178) presents Lateranus, who rose from mule driver to consul, but who still shows his low breeding by crawling around to all-night popinae, where he drinks with muggers, sailors, thieves, runaways, butchers, coffin makers, and eunuch priests. Horace, listing the vaguely disreputable attractions of city life (*Epistles* 1.14.21–25), includes the "greasy" popina and the neighborhood taberna, a simple place where meals were not usually served, and customers stood at the counter or sat on one of the few chairs, as in a modern Italian bar (cf. Pl. 15, lower left, and Pl. 22).[10]

It was natural for neighborhood acquaintances or professional groups to gather in such establishments to drink, gamble, and talk. Catullus (37) shows us a taberna near the Forum Romanum, just nine doors away from the Temple of Castor, where a group of young men about town made a habit of sitting to drink and brag about their sexual successes. This could go on far into the night—one group at Pompeii was known, either among themselves or among their political opponents, as *seribibi*, "late-drinkers" (*CIL* 4.581). The talk could take a political turn, and inns and taverns were often regarded as breeding grounds of political unrest. During the early principate the taverns of Rome were restricted in various ways, apparently to make them less attractive as places to gather. Tiberius (Suetonius, *Tiberius* 34) prohibited the sale of baked goods in popinae. Claudius (Dio Cassius, *Roman History* 60.6.6–7) closed the taverns where collegia had been meeting and prohibited the sale of meat and hot water. Nero (Suetonius, *Nero* 16; Dio Cassius, *Roman History* 62.14.2) enforced the ban on meat and permitted only vegetables and cabbage to be sold. Vespasian (Dio Cassius, *Roman History* 60.10.3) restricted the menu to peas and beans. We cannot be very sure about the purpose or the effectiveness of these regulations, or whether they continued to be enforced during the second century A.D. and later. It is interesting, however, that in Pompeii in the first century A.D. the street-side snack bar almost always had large jars sunk below the counters to hold cooked vegetables and stews, whereas in Ostia in the second century these were usually absent (Pl. 24). This seems to imply a more limited menu at the later popinae of Ostia, and perhaps a more exclusive emphasis on the sale of wine and *calidum*, a popular hot drink made of wine, water, and flavorings.[11]

Collegia

Apart from casual collections of drinking companions, the residents of Roman cities also organized themselves into more formal clubs or guilds known as *collegia, sodalicia, corpora,* or *curiae.* Some of these were professional groups, composed of owners and entrepreneurs. Another type focused exclusively on social (or religious) purposes. This type included cult groups devoted to a specific god, friendly societies of foreigners banding together in a sympathetic atmosphere, clubs of upper-class young men playing sports and doing military drills, associations of veterans who organized for fraternal purposes, and rich freedmen who earned civic distinction by serving the imperial cult as Augustales. A third category included the *collegia tenuiorum,* in which poor people paid dues to a common treasury to guarantee, under the sponsorship of one or more rich patrons, a simple but decent burial.[12]

All these groups met regularly–normally once a month–to hold a sacrifice and share a meal. Their organization often imitated that of the city, with one or more presiding officers, a governing council of decurions, and quaestors to serve as treasurers. The membership at large was called the *plebs.* Smaller or poorer groups met in restaurants or even in private homes; more prosperous ones had their own *scholae* as meeting places.

Ostia offers a wide variety of such scholae. An elaborate version, belonging to the builders (I.xii.l), occupied the ground floor of an insula. Members entered the central courtyard through a wide entrance from the main street. Facing the entrance across the courtyard was a chapel in which typically statues of the patron deity and the presiding *genius* of the collegium, and also of members of the imperial family, were displayed. Along the east and west sides of the courtyard were rooms arranged with couches to accommodate diners at the collegial meals.

A more modest schola (I.x.3) was arranged by the *stuppatores,* the dealers in rope and oakum. During the third century A.D. they moved into a row of five tabernae vacated by a small public bath and converted them into workrooms and a shop (Pl. 26). A narrow alley gave access to the tabernae, and at the back a schola was arranged. It included an assembly room (d), a dining room (c), an open courtyard (a) and a temple (b). The group seems to have run out of money by the time the podium of the temple was finished, so Fructosus, a patron of the collegium, paid to install a temple to the oriental god Mithras inside the podium.[13]

In Rome, inscriptions inform us about the scholae of several collegia, like that of the *praecones,* located just east of the Temple of Saturnus in the Forum Romanum. It was lavishly furnished with marble, a statue of Victoria, and bronze chairs (*CIL* 6.103). In another collegium at Rome, devoted to the god Silvanus, members whose names identify them as freedmen made dedications to furnish the gardens in which the group met (*CIL* 6.642, 671, 675): a temple building, a marble altar, a portico, and statues of Silvanus and the emperor are listed.

These collegial groups had a long history. According to tradition (Plutarch, *Numa* 17), Numa Pompilius himself had instituted professional collegia,[14] and they certainly were known in the fifth century B.C., because they are mentioned in the Twelve Tables. Eventually the desire to associate with people who shared common interests spread to other sectors of society besides businessmen and craftsmen. We hear of collegia of philosophers and cooks, artists and musicians, devotees of foreign gods, neighborhood groups. Such associations had their own interests distinct from those of the larger society, and although they were not necessarily hostile to the larger society, they often aroused suspicion among the defenders of the established order. In 186 B.C. the republic repressed the collegia devoted to Bacchus throughout Italy, on the grounds that they were dangerous and potentially subversive (Livy 39.9–13). In 64 B.C., the Senate outlawed all such collegia, with only a few specific exceptions (Asconius, p. 67 Clark). Publius Clodius Pulcher, when he was tribune in 58 B.C., repealed the law and used collegia as political action committees in his battles with the senatorial aristocracy. As portrayed by Cicero (*Pro Sestio* 34) Clodius's collegia were a sorry rabble of slaves and good-for-nothings. Clodius's opponents organized their own supporters into similar collegia, and their clashes in the streets hurled the city into the violent last years of the republic. Julius Caesar reimposed the earlier ban on collegia (Suetonius, *Caesar* 43), and Augustus required each collegium to be chartered by the emperor or the Senate (Suetonius, *Augustus* 32). Ordinarily, under the early principate, charters were given only to collegia tenuiorum that could meet once a month, and to those that met for religious purposes (Justinian, *Digest* 47.22.1–3). This turned out to be a very wide loophole, and collegia proliferated, all of them proclaiming allegiance to the emperor and to some other deity. Although Trajan was still very worried about the political repercussions of collegia (Pliny, *Letters* 10.34, 93), after his reign emperors tolerated them less guardedly. Alexander Severus actually sponsored the creation of collegia for all the trades and granted them legal representation (S.H.A., *Alexander* 33).

Collegia incurred suspicion, but at the same time they served important functions in the social life, and even in the political life, of the larger community. They organized the energies of many levels of society in ways that could be positive as well as deleterious. Collegia had their assigned seats in the amphitheater, and could turn out to cheer the emperor. They focused their members' attention on the imperial cult. They provided a small environment in which even the humblest member could speak his mind and have an effect on policy. They brought peace of mind to poor men and women, free and slave, who could rely on the group to bury them decently; and in general during the principate, surrounded by an aura of pious devotion to the imperial cult, they channeled the energies of the populace into constructive currents.

Thirteen

The City and the Gods

The ancient Roman city does not easily accommodate our distinction between things "religious" and things "secular." The political and administrative life of the city was conducted in full view of the gods, in buildings consecrated to them. The calendar of the state was determined by the rhythm of religion. Temples were the most prominent landmarks in the city, thickly clustered in public areas like the Forum Romanum, but also located throughout the city's neighborhoods.

Roman religion was, in its origins, agricultural, deeply attuned to the rhythm of the agricultural year and to the farmer's reverence for the mysterious forces that manifest themselves in every aspect of rural life—in the soil that nurtures plants and in the diseases that wither them, in the seed's vegetative power and in the storehouse that protects it until it is planted again in the new year. Divine forces (Roman called them *numina*) also permeated the house, protecting and threatening the family. The traditional Roman recognized the numina present, for instance, in the door, the boundary that guarded the family and through which it dealt with the world outside; even crucial parts of the door, like the hinge and the threshold, were treated reverently with simple rites. Similarly, the hearth represented the sacred power of fire to warm, lighten, and destroy. And the continuing influence of the family's ancestors was acknowledged in a shrine in the atrium of the house (Pl. 20). As the city was forming in the sixth and fifth centuries B.C., it developed a civic religion that was modeled on this simple agricultural and domestic religion. Divinities became more specific and, under Greek influence, were personified: in the Forum Romanum, Ianus guarded the passage across the stream, Venus Cloacina the drainage ditch, Vesta the communal hearth. High above, dominating the civic activities like a paterfamilias in his tablinum, Iuppiter presided over his temple, flanked by Iuno and Minerva, reflecting Etruscan tradition and a more anthropomorphic conception of the gods. The oldest god of the Capitoline, remembered in local tradition, was personified as Saturnus and given a temple at the foot of the hill, where the Clivus Capitolinus descended to the Forum. Greek religious traditions were explicitly adopted in the Temple of Castor, and in shrines of Hercules where Greek rather than Roman ritual was performed.

Templum

The Latin word *templum* did not refer primarily to the temple building that sheltered a god's image; the word for that was *aedes,* "house." *Templum* referred to a ritually defined space, set aside through sacred words and gestures for the purpose of taking the auspices. A priest, called an *augur,* marked out a portion of the sky and then looked in the four quadrants of that portion for omens from the gods. The piece of ground where he stood to "contemplate" the heavens was called the templum, and it had to have an uninterrupted view of appropriate landmarks to delimit the templum of the sky (Varro, *De Lingua Latina* 7.8). Thus the earliest temples in Rome faced southward to the convenient landmark peaks of the Alban hills, and nearly all temples faced away from any nearby natural obstacle such as a hill, to give a broad view in the opposite direction.[1] The essentials of a proper templum were an open viewing space, called the *area,* and some sort of boundary wall, which could be as simple as boards or linen cloths. The next-most-important feature of a templum was the altar on which sacrifice, animal or vegetable, was offered to the gods. The aedes, or "temple" building, when it was added, housed the objects dedicated to the god, including the cult image, if there was one. The site of an Etruscan templum, constructed in the early sixth century B.C., has been excavated at Murlo (Poggio Civitate), in Tuscany; this templum consisted of a small enclosure that formed the focus of a large courtyard, colonnaded on three sides.[2] The Romans always looked to the Etruscans for inspiration in their religious ceremonies and architecture, but the custom of marking out a templum in the sky, and relating it to a rectangular patch of earth, has parallels in the indigenous rituals of Oscans, Umbrians, and Latins. The Romans too made the custom profoundly their own. The resulting "ritualization of space" is perhaps the most characteristically Roman feature of Roman urban architecture; it helps account for the tendency to enclose open spaces, impose human demands on the limitless forces of nature, control earth and sky for practical ends, and bargain with the gods on human terms.[3]

Temples and Urban Architecture

Temples were the most prominent landmarks in the city. Some were located on the sites of age-old, primitive shrines; others were placed on the brow of a hill or as the focal point of an urban vista. Many were situated along roads or in public squares, where large crowds could pass through them and read their dedicatory inscriptions.[4]

The appearance and arrangement of early Roman temples owed a great deal to the Etruscans. Their primary characteristics may be summed up as (1) axiality—the temple building was placed near the back of the rectangular area, centered on an axis running back from the sanctuary entrance; (2) elevation—the building was placed on a relatively high podium of stone; and (3) frontality—the temple was usually set at the back of the sanctuary, approached by a flight of steps, and entered only from the front. The wooden columns of these Etruscan-inspired temple builings supported a low roof with wide eaves to protect the mud-brick walls of the cella (Pl. 14). Roofs were of tile, and colorful revetments of terra cotta were added along the cornices. Brightly painted terra-cotta statues often surrounded the buildings or were placed along the peaks of the roofs or in the pediments, producing an exotic, richly textured effect.

Starting in the fourth century B.C., perhaps under the influence of the Greek cities of southern Italy, some temples were constructed of stone. This brought about a change in the shape of temple buildings. The greater strength of stone permitted higher walls, and the heavier superstructure required that columns be placed closer together. Thus the adoption of Greek building materials and techniques led to the assimilation of Greek proportions and details, and in turn to the appearance of more and more Greek gods and Greek-style divine abstractions like Victoria and Concordia. Although the theological and architectural borrowings from the Greeks did not proceed in lock step, they did follow generally parallel paths.

For example, at the Area Sacra di Largo Argentina (Fig. 4), Temple A and the even larger Temple C both date from the late fourth century B.C. and both are markedly "frontal," with a clearly marked entrance, an altar on axis, and a deep front porch. To the south of Temple C is Temple D, which was built in the second century B.C. Although it had the traditional Italic frontality with a porch three columns deep and an approaching flight of stairs, the increasing impact of Greek aesthetic notions is discernible on the cella wall, on which engaged Ionic half-columns suggest the surrounding peristyle of a Greek temple. At some point near the end of the second century B.C., the three temples were incorporated into a single area; a pavement of volcanic tufa was laid down to define the three temples as an architectural group, and there is some evidence that the space was surrounded on several sides by a Greek-style colonnade. The new paving raised the ground level of the area considerably, and thus provided it with better protection from flooding. It also reduced by half the height of the podia on which the temples were constructed. Lower temple podia are typical of Greek architecture, and Greek influence is apparent in the way Temple D was refaced with stone blocks and Temple A was rebuilt with a much larger podium and a Greek peristyle surrounding it on all sides (visible in the drawing, Fig. 4). Both the facing of the podium of Temple A and the capitals of its columns were made of travertine, a white lime-stone from Tibur (Tivoli) that gave to the temple a lighter look, even a suggestion of the whiteness of Greek marble, introduced into Roman temple architecture in 146 B.C. at the Temple of Iuppiter Stator at the Circus Flaminius. Around 100 B.C. a round temple was added at the Largo Argentina complex, in the space between Temple A and Temple C. The round shape of this temple—Temple B—and its surrounding colonnade of Corinthian columns (made of tufa, but covered with white stucco, and finished with travertine bases and capitals), marked further triumphs of Greek taste.[5] The whole complex was given its final form in A.D. 80, when the ground level was again raised—this time by a travertine pavement—the access stairs to all the temples were rebuilt, a new portico was built around the whole area, Temple A received new Corinthian columns of travertine, Temple B's columns were built into a new wall, and Temple C received a new mosaic pavement.

The four temples of the Largo Argentina illustrate the increasing influence of Greek architecture, and they also typify two other features of later republican architecture in Rome. One was the tendency to group several temples in a row, their front columns more or less on the same plane, creating a more monumental façade than would be possible with a single temple. Other examples of this feature are the three temples in the Forum Holitorium, and the two temples of Fortuna and Mater Matuta at Saint Omobono (Fig. 3). At Ostia, too, four republican temples stood in a row just outside the eastern gate of the castrum (Fig. 26). The other developing feature was the colonnaded enclosure. This was borrowed from Greek architecture, and became especially popular starting in the second century B.C., when colonnades and porticoes appeared in the Forum Romanum and in Roman temple precincts (Velleius Paterculus 2.1.2). In Roman contexts the colonnade tended to be more strictly symmetrical, emphasizing the axiality of the temple buildings. Examples, in addition to the Largo Argentina, are the Porticus Octaviae and Porticus Philippi, next to the Circus Flaminius (Fig. 4), the imperial fora (Fig. 10; Pl. 3, 12A), and, at Pompeii, the Temple of Apollo and the Forum (Pl. 16).[6]

By the end of the republic, marble had become much more common. The round temple in the Forum Boarium (Fig. 3), which has been ascribed to an upwardly mobile merchant,[7] was built in the late second or early first century B.C., with marble walls and columns. Some use of marble, decorative if not structural, became normal for temples built in the capital during the principate. Façades also became more elaborate, with sculptural decoration in pediments, along the peak and at the corners of the roof, and flanking the podium steps (Pl. 12B). An aesthetic of size also came into fashion, as in the immense Temple of Venus et Roma, with its ten columns across each short end, and its gigantic cult image inside (Pl. 10, 12C), or in Hadrian's Pantheon, where the newest technology of poured concrete was put into the service of an architectural idea, creating a vast enclosed space sacred to all the gods of the universe (Pl. 6).

Temples in the City's Life

If we entered a simple temple precinct, we would see the essentials of a temple: the ritually defined *area* (usually bounded by some kind of wall) and the altar. A more elaborate temple area contained an aedes, or house for the gods and for displays of offerings and treasures (Macrobius 3.11.6). Dedications of spectacular booty brought back by triumphant generals would have been most noticeable, and most prominently displayed. But Horace, who celebrated a personal triumph with an offering and a well-known poem, reminds us that more humble objects also crowded the temple walls: "For a long time I have been a fit campaigner with the girls, and fought and won my share of glory; now this wall—which guards the left flank of Venus of the Sea—will hold my weapons and my lyre, which has fought its last war" (Horace, *Odes* 3.26.1– 6). Lamps, columns, and tablets, as well as statues and paintings, were common votive gifts, and the Temple of Ceres on the Aventine, Concordia in the Forum Romanum (Pl. 12B), and Apollo on the Palatine were museums of artworks of many types. Such dedications were placed in the area surrounding the temple, which also contained subsidiary shrines and altars, basins for ceremonial washings, trees and shrubs, and various seats and benches.

The most common religious ceremony was a sacrifice. An ox, pig, sheep, or bird was offered to the deity by an official magistrate of the city-state or by a club, or by a private individual. While prayers were said, the head of the animal was sprinkled with meal, then an attendant stunned the animal with a hammer blow to the head, and cut its throat. As the blood ran out, the animal was cut up, its entrails examined to make sure there were no bad omens, and it was roasted over a fire on the altar. Certain portions were reserved for the god, but the worshipers usually ate the edible portions in a feast held in the temple precinct. Such animal sacrifices were the appropriate celebration of an important occasion. More modest offerings, to accompany an individual's petition or thanksgiving, included cakes, vegetables, flowers, and small clay images.

One of the most solemn rites of the Roman state religion, the *lectisternium,* involved the spreading of tables in the Forum or in a temple and the arrangement of images of the gods so as to allow them to join in the meal. A similar procedure, called a *supplicatio,* was observed when the state had suffered a military setback, had been disrupted by unfavorable omens, or was subject to some kind of good or bad excitement. During the last centuries of the republic such supplicationes occurred almost every year; the temples were opened and the citizens went round to address the gods individually in prayer (Livy 30.17.6).

On such occasions, temples were the sites of official expressions of the civic religion. Temples also served the state in other capacities, as meeting places for the Senate[8] and as offices for important magistrates: the consuls in the Temple of Castor, the quaestors in the Temple of Saturnus, the plebeian aediles in the Temple of Ceres on the Aventine.

Temples served another political purpose; they advertised the generosity and military prowess of rising politicians in the republic, and of the emperor in the principate. One example is the inscription that Lucius Mummius, who crushed Greek resistance to Rome in 146 B.C., placed on the Temple of Hercules Victor: "Lucius Mummius, son of Lucius, consul, since under his leadership, auspices, and command Achaea has been captured and Corinth destroyed, has returned to Rome in triumph; in token of these fine exploits and because of his vow during the war as commander-in-chief, he dedicates this temple and statue of Hercules Victor" (*CIL* 6.31).

The ancient sources show how pervasive temples were in the lives of Roman urbanites. For instance, the area around the Temple of Iuppiter Optimus Maximus on the Capitoline not only contained a number of subsidiary shrines, statues of gods and famous Romans, copies of significant treaties and trophies of important victories, and diplomas of honorable military discharge; it was also a favorite spot for a promenade (Sidonius, *Letters* 1.7.8). The precincts of other temples offered a place to sit and rest (Varro, *On Agriculture* 1.2), or to enjoy the plantings in a formal garden. In these places where crowds gathered, there were opportunities to pick up girls or meet for a tryst (Horace, *Odes* 1.9.18–24; Ovid, *Art of Love* 1.75–88; Juvenal 9.22–25). In some temples, like that of Apollo on the Palatine, poets studied and found a quiet retreat; in others, like that of Hercules Musarum, they assembled for recitations and competitions (Horace, *Satires* 1.10.36–39, and scholia). Businessmen and bankers met and had offices at the state treasury in the Temple of Saturnus in the Forum Romanum. Merchants tended to meet at the Temple of Mercurius, their patron. In fact, the scholae in which many professional groups met also served as temples to the groups' patron deities (Pl. 26).

Similar in nature and function were the many temples consecrated to various Oriental deities from Phrygia, Egypt, Syria, Iran, and Palestine. Some of these, like the Temple of Magna Mater on the Palatine and those of Isis and Serapis in the Campus Martius, were public shrines. Others were the private preserves of specific groups: the temple of the Syrian god Iuppiter Heliopolitanus on the Janiculum, the various shrines of Mithras, the Jewish synagogues, and the Christian house-churches, for example. Originally these temples were founded by immigrants to Rome who gathered to remember the gods of their native lands and to worship them in familiar ways. Although such Oriental cults were often viewed with suspicion (Augustus, for instance, was especially hostile to the cult of Isis, associated as it was with the Egypt of his enemy Cleopatra), they were eventually accepted by the Romans, and were even patronized by the emperors. These cults added color and a touch of the exotic to the religious scene in Rome, and their temples often made some effort to re-create the environment of the immigrants' home countries: obelisks and sphinxes in the Temple of Isis, for example.

A typical occasion when the Roman and foreign religious worlds met was the annual festival of the Phrygian Magna Mater, on April 4. A corps of *galli,* castrated Oriental priests, emerged from their sanctuary on the Palatine and walked through the streets clashing cymbals, blowing pipes, brandishing weapons, and strewing gold, silver, and rose petals before the statue of the goddess (Lucretius 2.600–628; Juvenal 6.511–516). During the republic these cavortings were exotic, vaguely suspicious, and restricted to certain times and places. Under the principate, even though Juvenal included the rites of the Magna Mater in his list of disagreeable urban phenomena, they seem to have been regarded more tolerantly, as just another reflection of the city's cosmopolitan diversity.[9]

Public Religious Life: Festivals

If the temple made urban space sacred, so the calendar made time sacred. Even though the annual cycle of festivals was originally agricultural, the city as it grew appropriated and retained it, without much change. By the end of the republic, however, the festivals had become quaint ceremonies or faint memories, grist for the scholarly mill of a Varro, who regretted the way in which Rome had lost contact with its agricultural roots. Augustus tried to restore some vitality to these old ceremonies.[10]

The civil year started with a festival which, while celebrating the civic life of the urban community, also alluded to the seasons of the agricultural year. Just as the days began to lengthen, promising new life and new beginnings, the two new consuls entered their term of office on January 1.[11] The celebration began before daybreak, when the consuls climbed (probably) to the platform of the *auguraculum* on the Capitoline and took the auspices. They then went to their own houses to prepare for the first parades of the day. Friends and supporters paid a formal *salutatio* to each consul, then accompanied him and his lictors to the Forum Romanum, where the two groups joined. Then, taking the animals that would be sacrificed, the whole human embodiment of Rome's power and glory, arrayed in their togas and cheered by the people, climbed the Capitoline. In front of the great Temple of Iuppiter Optimus Maximus the consuls sat down on their ivory chairs of office and sacrificed a pair of white bulls. The Senate entered the temple to hold its first meeting of the year under Jupiter's supervision, and the day ended with more parades as the senators escorted the consuls to their homes.[12]

Various ceremonies recalled the local groups and rites of the earliest city of sheep-herders and farmers. On February 15 the Luperci, famous because of their appearance in the opening act of Shakespeare's *Julius Caesar,* ran naked along the Sacra Via, striking at women to induce fertility.

On March 16 and 17 the religious dignitaries of the city made a solemn circuit of thirty ancient shrines that housed the *argei,* small effigies made of rush. These shrines were distributed throughout the oldest regions of the city, on the Caelian, Esquiline, Quirinal, and Palatine. On May 14 the dignitaries again made the rounds, gathered the effigies, and solemnly threw them into the Tiber at the Pons Sublicius, in a rite that must have attracted a curious crowd of onlookers along the Forum Boarium waterfront.

The collegium of the Salii marked the springtime start of the agricultural year on March 1, and again on March 19 and 23, by marching through the old parts of the city and stopping at certain stations to leap and skip in a traditional dance, singing an ancient song that was already unintelligible by the end of the republic (Dionysius of Halicarnassus, *Roman Antiquities* 2.70–71; *CIL* 1.28).[13] On October 19 they danced again, to celebrate the ritual cleansing of sacred weapons in honor of Mars.

On October 15, as part of an annual Festival of Jupiter, neighborhood groups from the Sacra Via and the Subura played a kind of rugby game to capture the head of a horse that had just been sacrificed, presumably preserving some agricultural and/or military rite from the early days of the city.

Other agricultural festivals were: a simple one celebrated in early February, when rustic offerings of grain and fruit were made at the old Curiae; the Fordicidia, on April 15, when pregnant cows were sacrificed; the Parilia, on April 21, celebrated officially with sacrifices by the Vestal Virgins and the Rex Sacrorum, but more popularly by building small bonfires and leaping over them; April 23, when the vintners brought their wine to market; and the Vestalia, on June 7, when millers and bakers hung garlands of violets and rolls in their shops (Ovid, *Fasti* 6.309–318).

Scattered throughout the year there were occasions for general relaxation in honor of some god or another. Near the beginning of January (usually between the third and the fifth), the people of the vici celebrated the Festival of the Compitalia, in honor of their local crossroads gods, by taking the day off and relaxing with their families (Dionysius of Halicarnassus, *Roman Antiquities* 4.14.3). On March 17 old women dressed up as priests of Bacchus; crowned with ivy, they set up portable altars and sold little cakes of oil and honey to customers for sacrifice. On June 13, 14, and 15 the flute players celebrated their festival wearing their best outfits, playing their flutes, marshaling at the Temple of Minerva, wandering through the fora and shops, genially disrupting public and private business, and regrouping for a banquet at the Temple of Iuppiter (Livy 9.30; Varro, *De Lingua Latina* 6.17; Ovid, *Fasti,* 6.651–692). The Festival of Fors Fortuna provided an excuse to escape from the gathering heat of the city on June 24, the longest day of the year and the first day of summer. The goddess had two temples on the far side of the Tiber, at the first and sixth milestones. People walked to them across the bridges or sailed to them on the river. Local farmers brought flowers and vegetables to sell, and the inscriptions dedicated by collegia of wool and bronze merchants imply that they too set up shops on the right bank, anticipating today's flea market outside the Porta Portuensis (Ovid, *Fasti* 6.771–784; Columella 10.311–317; *CIL* 1².977, 6.167–169).

The Parentalia in February was a time for families to remember their dead by making private trips to the tombs outside the city walls. In public recognition of this family rite, and in deference to (and fear of) the dead, no temples were open, no sacrifices were offered, no public business was conducted during the whole period from February 13 to February 21.

Finally, the Saturnalia combined the observances of family and city. This festival began on December 17 and continued until December 23. On the first day, the Senate and crowds of citizens gathered at the Temple of Saturnus in the Forum Romanum for a public sacrifice and banquet. Shops and public offices were closed. At home, the ordinary restraints of daily life were relaxed; masters waited on slaves, and families exchanged presents and celebrated the holiday with eating and drinking. The festivities spilled out onto the streets, and people gambled, sang, and danced through the city (Livy 22.1.19–20; Seneca, *Epistulae Morales* 18.1).

During the republic, there were fifty-eight of these *feriae,* when official sacrifices were offered and no legal business could be conducted. During the principate more feriae were added, to celebrate anniversaries of the accessions and victories of the emperors. By the reign of Marcus Aurelius the number of festival days had increased to 135.[14] The central rite on a feria was the official sacrifice at the appropriate god's temple, an event which was normally woven without much trace into the rich fabric of urban activity. The days on which processions of some kind were conducted stood out, and on a few feriae the city population actually broke the strands of its schedule, closing shops for the Compitalia, the Saturnalia, and perhaps the Parilia, or going to the suburbs for a picnic on the feast days of Anna Perenna (Ovid, *Fasti* 3.523–542) and Fors Fortuna.

Fourteen

Roman Holidays

Looking out at the street from their shops or apartments, or passing grand buildings and monuments as they pushed through the crowds, the residents of Rome were assaulted by the spectacular richness we have surveyed—in buildings, open spaces, monuments, statues, and even the people themselves. With so much visual, aural, and tactile stimulation, it was easy to become numb to the grandeur of it all. In compensation, frequently but with an irregular pacing that prevented complacency, the city offered various types of colorful, glamorous, organized pageantry to bring the populace together, affirm the power and stability of the city, and impose a unity of purpose on all the diverse elements of the population.[1]

Annual Games: Ludi

Each year significant chunks of time were dedicated to the gods as official *ludi,* games, which broke into the city's routine as a series of *ludi scaenici,* theatrical shows, followed at the end with one or more days of *ludi circenses,* chariot races. Additional events included solemn public banquets, military parades, animal hunts, athletic contests, and all sorts of wandering entertainments. At the end of the republic 74 days were set aside for ludi. On 17 of them chariot races were held in the Circus Maximus, which could accommodate about 250,000 spectators, men and women alike. That probably amounted to half the free adult population of imperial Rome. Fewer people could be accommodated at the theatrical shows, but there were many other things to do, and the long stretches of ludi in April (17 days, plus 3 in May), July (19 days), September (15 days), October (9 days), and November (14 days) must have disrupted the normal pattern of life to a considerable extent. The games preempted all other official business activities. The senators left the Forum, and the equestrians left their businesses to claim their places of honor at the theater and circus.

The oldest games, the Ludi Romani, originated in the time of the kings, and were celebrated annually in September starting in 366 B.C. In the late third century, just after Hannibal's invasion of Italy, the Ludi Plebeii were added in November. Around the end of the third century B.C. other games were added to propitiate other gods: the Ludi Apollinares in 208, the Ludi Cereales in 202, the Ludi Megalenses in honor of the Magna Mater in 194, and the Ludi Florales in 173 at the latest. Later games were added in honor of the military victories of Sulla (82 B.C.), Caesar (46 B.C.), and Augustus (11 B.C.). Under the principate more ludi were added until, by the fourth century A.D., 177 days of each year were celebrated with games of some sort.

The games filled many important religious and political functions in the city's life. They honored the gods and celebrated Rome's good relations with them. They commemorated political successes like that of the plebeian leader Flaminius, who built the Circus Flaminius (in which to hold the Ludi Plebeii), and military victories like those of Sulla, Caesar, Augustus, and, in time, many other emperors. The administration of the games was entrusted to the aediles, and during the republic politicians who wanted to impress the populace spent vast sums of their own money to make their games memorable. The correspondence of Cicero with Marcus Caelius Rufus lets us glimpse one aedile's zeal in 50 B.C. to give the people something to remember. While Cicero was off in Cilicia as governor and relying on Caelius for information about the political situation in Rome, Caelius kept up a barrage of requests for Cicero to hunt down some panthers in the Cilician mountains and ship them to Rome to be hunted during his games (Cicero, *Letters to His Friends* 2.11.2; 8.2.2; 8.4.5; 8.6.5; 8.8.10; 8.9.3).

The ludi also served economic and social functions. Some workers took the days off and enjoyed the spectacles, while others—actors, charioteers, peddlers of food and souvenirs, prostitutes—found work and opportunity at them. The ludi also provided a well-defined situation in which all the various strata of the population could meet one another. Status distinctions were affirmed—the senators and equestrians had seats down in front, the women were seated in the back rows, and the poor folks had standing room in the gallery at the very top. But status distinctions were also transcended, in that the common citizens had a chance to react to the comings and goings of the nobility, to cheer a favorite or boo an unpopular politician. During the principate, the similar interaction between the crowds and the emperor was the closest approximation to a referendum that existed. The powerful knew what it meant, and the historians recorded it. Furthermore, during the games the routines and standards of life were held in abeyance. The Senate and law courts were in recess. The moneylenders closed their shops, which allowed even the debtor to forget his troubles while he was at the theater (Plautus, *Casina* 23–27).[2]

Theatrical shows came to Rome, according to tradition, in 360 B.C., when a serious plague afflicted the city, and the chariot races, which constituted the main spectacle at the Ludi Romani, did not seem to be enough to make the gods put a stop to the epidemic. So, as they often did during the early republic, the Romans sent off to the Etruscans for help. Help came in the form of *histriones,* dancers who performed to the music of woodwinds and who became a regular feature at the games. In time a plot line was added to these performances, and under the influence of the Greeks, dramatic recitations were included as part of the festivities. The landmark figure is a freedman from Tarentum, Livius Andronicus. Starting in the Ludi Romani in 240 B.C., he translated Greek plays into Latin and performed them at the games for the audience (Livy 7.2; Cicero, *Brutus* 72). The word for a stage, *scaena,* was borrowed

from the Greeks, and the theatrical events were called *ludi scaenici.*
Before long, entrepreneurs assembled troops of actors—slaves,
freedmen, Greeks—and hired writers like Naevius and Plautus to
translate and adapt Greek classics, both tragedies and comedies.
Greek plays were popular for all the reasons Greek art, architecture, and myths were popular, not least because many members of
the audience, starting in the third century B.C., had visited Greek
cities (at least in southern Italy and Sicily) and could appreciate the
Greek words and situations. In addition, the playwrights composed new dramas, based on noble moments in Roman history
(*fabulae praetextae*) or the everyday world of the taberna (*fabulae
tabernariae*).[3]

References in republican and imperial literature help us chart
the tides of changing taste. In the late third and early second centuries B.C., when Plautus was writing and producing his plays, the
audience preferred comedy to tragedy (Plautus, *Amphitryon* 50–
55), and Terence complained that the first production of one play
(at the Megalenses of 165 B.C.) was disrupted by the performance of
a rope dancer, a boxing match, the catcalls of claques, and the out-
cry of women, and at the second production (at the funeral games
for Aemilius Paulus in 160 B.C.), by a gladiatorial show (Terence,
The Mother-in-law 4–5, 29–42). A century later audiences were
just as hard to please, and when they became restive they were apt
to hoot at overacting or yell "Bring on the bears! Bring on the
boxers!" (Macrobius 2.7.12–16; Horace, *Epistles* 2.1.186). By the
time of the late republic, little new material was being written.
Sponsors concentrated on extravagant and luxurious production
values, which reflected the greater luxury in all phases of urban life
at the time. Cicero, for instance (*Letters to His Friends* 7.1), sneered
at Pompey for bringing onstage 600 mules in a revival of Accius's
Clytemnestra and a whole triumphal procession in the *Trojan Horse*
(by Livius Andronicus or Naevius) at the opening of his theater in
55 B.C.[4] Horace joins the lament (*Epistles* 2.1.182–213), complaining that in his time even the more cultured elements in the audience would rather see an exotic visual spectacle than hear a well-
composed piece of literature. In the Augustan Age the official pre-
dilection for traditional forms was reflected in the theater. The clas-

sics were tastefully performed, and the old Italic tradition of the Atellan farce, a cabaret performance of topical humor acted by Roman citizens, was revived. At the same time, the Greek ballet form known as the pantomime was beginning to become popular, and by the second century of the principate it had become, along with a more burlesque variation known as the mime, the main form of theatrical entertainment (Pliny, *Letters* 7.24; Lucian, *The Dance* 35). If a performance described by Apuleius (*Golden Ass* 10.29–34) is any indication, ambitious producers managed to broaden the appeal of their pantomimes by introducing kinky sex or sensational violence, which tended to blur any lingering distinction between the theatrical stage and the gladiatorial arena (Suetonius, *Gaius Caligula* 57.4; Martial, *On the Spectacles* 7).[5]

During the republic the plays were held in the open. The players acted on a portable wooden stage; the spectators sat on the grass or on wooden bleachers. Attempts were made to build more comfortable facilities, but they always aroused conservative opposition. An attempt to build a permanent theater in 154 B.C., for instance, moved Publius Scipio Nasica to forbid the erection of seats for plays, in order to extend the "famous Roman, virile art of standing" from political assemblies to occasions of relaxation as well (Valerius Maximus, *Memorabilia* 2.4.2). In spite of this, some temples that were built in and around Rome in the second and first centuries B.C. had semicircular steps in front to accommodate spectators at dramatic performances.[6] By the middle of the first century B.C., it was usual to spread awnings over the temporary seating to provide shade; Lucretius (4.75–83) calls attention to the patterns made by the sun shining through the yellow, red, and purple canvas. The temporary theaters were often astonishingly elaborate, full of technological virtuosity and moving parts, and they in turn aroused the righteous indignation of traditionalists.[7]

In the midst of these temporary marvels, Pompey the Great erected, and with great spectacle in 55 B.C. dedicated, Rome's first permanent theater building. He circumvented the traditional opposition by constructing a Temple of Venus at the top of the rows of seats, and by placing the complex within the tradition of the theater-temple. Once Pompey had set the precedent, two more theaters were built in short succession in the same general area of the Campus Martius. All three (as we can see from the Forma Urbis for the Theatrum Pompeii and the Theatrum Balbi, dedicated in 13 B.C., and the extensive remains of the Theatrum Marcelli, completed in 17 B.C.) were manifestations of Roman engineering talent (Fig. 4). Unlike their architectural precursor, the Greek theater resting on the slope of a hill, these theaters were freestanding, artificial hills of masonry walls and radiating concrete vaults that supported concentric rows of seats in the *cavea*. The rows of seats formed a semicircle, and at its center, on ground level, the *orchestra* also formed a semicircle. Unlike its precursor (*orchestra* meaning "dancing floor" in Greek), the Roman orchestra provided prestige seating for senators and equestrians. Moreover, the Roman cavea was not separate from the scaena, but joined it to form an architectural unity and enclose the unroofed area completely. In the case of the Theatrum Marcelli, the curved exterior of the cavea was faced with three stories, and the ends of the supporting vaults were masked with arches decorated with Doric columns on the lowest story, Ionic columns on the next, and Corinthian pilasters on the closed attic. According to Vitruvius (5.6.8–9), the stage building itself consisted of a long, narrow platform in front of a permanent background. Here a central door representing the entrance to a royal palace was flanked by two subsidiary doors. Convertible scenery, appropriate to the play, was inserted into openings in the background: columns and statues for a formal tragedy, perspective views of houses for domestic comedies, and country scenes for rustic mimes and satyr plays. These were also the motifs of Second Style wall painting, popular in domestic decoration in Vitruvius's day. At each end of the stage, the background scaena projected forward to meet the cavea, and at each end there was another entrance. One was supposed to lead to the downtown area of the Forum, the other to the harbor.

The day of the ludi scaenici began, not unexpectedly, with a parade. After a sacrifice at the appropriate temple, *exuviae,* tokens of the gods (a thunderbolt or eagle for Jupiter, a shield or helmet for Mars, a dove for Venus, a turreted crown for the Magna Mater) were placed on chairs and carried in solemn procession, heralded by flutes and trumpets, to the theater, so that the gods could enjoy the show held in their honor (Tertullian, *De Spectaculis* 10). The plays themselves reinforced the sense of holiday, especially the comedies with their plots set in far-off Greek cities in which the serious pursuits of the Forum and the shop were mocked openly, young love always triumphed, and slaves could make utter fools of their masters. We do not know the exact performance schedule, except that Atellan farces tended to follow tragedies, and performances could last all day long (Cicero, *Letters to His Friends* 9.16.7). The prologue to Terence's *Mother-in-law* makes it clear that other events were going on at the same time as the plays, creating the atmosphere of a carnival midway. At the end of the day, the exuviae of the gods were returned, in still another procession, to their temples.[8]

At all the games, more days were devoted to ludi scaenici than to other activities. At the two ludi in honor of Jupiter, the Ludi Romani and the Ludi Plebeii, the theatrical days were followed by the Ides (of September and November respectively), on which the Senate went to the Temple of Iuppiter on the Capitoline to partake of a great banquet, the *epulum Iovis,* in the presence of the god. On the next day, the cavalry of the equestrian order paraded in review through the city at the *Probatio Equitum.*

The final days were devoted to ludi circenses, chariot races in the Circus Maximus. These were the most popular and exciting events of the year. The Circus could accommodate a quarter of a million spectators, and everyone, from the emperor to a lowly cook (Suetonius, *Gaius Caligula* 55.2–3; Martial 7.7; Petronius, *Satyricon* 70), had favorite teams, horses, and charioteers. During the republic there were two main *factiones* ("teams"), the whites and the reds. Two more, the blues and the greens, were added during the early principate, when the factiones became major social entities. They were virtual corporations under imperial patronage, managed by *domini*, a board of directors, and investors. Each factio bought and trained horses, bought and maintained chariots, bought or hired drivers. The emperors built stabula for them in the Campus Martius (Suetonius, *Gaius Caligula* 55; Josephus, *Jewish Antiquities* 19.257), with a full staff of coaches, trainers, blacksmiths, farriers, veterinarians, grooms; the teams also had clerks and secretaries, attendants and waiters, and clubhouses with an imperial suite.[9] At least once (Dio Cassius, *Roman History* 61.6.2–3) the factiones formed a cartel and demanded exorbitant prices before bringing their horses to the starting line. To meet the emergency, the praetor in charge threatened to race dogs instead, but Nero came to the rescue with a subsidy.

On the day of the race, a procession was held into the Circus. The crowd cheered their favorites, consulted their programs, placed bets, jostled for places, and watched in rapture as a trumpet was blown and the presiding consul or praetor signaled the start of the race by dropping a napkin (Ovid, *Amores* 3.2; Ovid, *Art of Love* 1.135–170; Pliny, *Letters* 9.6; Juvenal 11.194–202; Sidonius, *Poems* 23.307–427). There were races for chariots with two horses or, more commonly, for those with four. Novelty races with other numbers of horses (as many as ten to a team!), or exhibitions of trick-riding, foot races, or relays also provided variety. Seven laps around the course constituted a race, and a full day's program included 24 races. At the conclusion, the victors received prizes: the victor's palm, crowns, and neck chains of gold. Many of the charioteers started out as slaves, and the successful ones could earn enough in prize money of their own to buy their freedom and become "free agents." One such charioteer was Gaius Appuleius Diocles, who has left us a long inscription (*CIL* 6.10048) listing his many victories and tremendous earnings in the middle of the second century A.D. Martial tells us (10.50, 53) of another famous charioteer, Scorpus, who won over two thousand races before he was killed in an accident at the age of twenty-seven.[10]

In addition to the regularly scheduled ludi (18 days in the republic, 66 by the fourth century A.D.), other games were held on special occasions. It was sometimes necessary to repeat games spoiled by bad omens, or hold new ones to celebrate a military victory, fulfill a vow, or dedicate a new temple. Sometimes, especially during the fourth and third centuries B.C., when the city was under some such stress as a plague or a military defeat, a lectisternium was declared. For one or more days of the observance, the temples were opened and couches were arranged with images of gods reclining and goddesses sitting on them. Food was set in front of them, and as if to join them in their banquet, citizens opened their houses and entertained anyone who dropped in (Livy 5.13.6–8, 22.10.9).[11] Most rarely of all—less frequently than once in a life-time—the Romans celebrated the *ludi saeculares,* "Centennial Games," to mark the stability and progress of the city (*CIL* 6.32323; Horace, *Carmen Saeculare*).[12]

Gladiatorial Shows: Munera

In addition to the ludi, and sometimes in connection with them, upper-class Romans on occasion paid for *munera* in the form of gladiatorial shows. These munera were originally part of the rites owed to the dead. Borrowed from either the Etruscans or the Cam-panians, they became a part of noble funerals, and thus were one of the ways members of the upper classes extended their family life out into the life of the city (Polybius 6.53–54).[13] The first recorded gladiatorial *munus* in Rome was held by the sons of Marcus Iunius Brutus Pera in 264 B.C., in the Forum Boarium. In 216 B.C., 22 pairs of gladiators fought in the Forum Romanum at the funeral of Marcus Aemilius Lepidus, and in 183 B.C., 60 pairs fought when Publius Licinius Crassus was buried, an occasion upon which a great banquet also was given for the citizens at tent-shaded tables in the Forum (Valerius Maximus, *Memorabilia* 2.4.7; Livy 23.30.15 and 39–46).

The popularity and political potential of these games was evident as early as 133 B.C., when Gaius Gracchus used an original grand-stand ploy to win the favor of the plebeians. Enterprising contrac-tors had erected bleachers around the Forum Romanum, intending to sell seats to those who could afford to have a good view of the munera; this meant that the poor would not be able to see anything. The night before the show, however, Gracchus (who as tribune had public workmen at his command) dismantled the seats, thus giving his constituency an unimpeded field of vision (Plutarch, *Gaius Gracchus* 12.3–5).

Meanwhile Roman armies were campaigning in new and exotic foreign lands. It did not take long for them to encounter new and exotic animals, which they captured, shipped back to Rome, and used to impart new excitement to victory celebrations. Leopards, ostriches, lions, hippopotami, and crocodiles were brought to Rome for display, and starting in 186 B.C. were stalked and killed in staged hunts called *venationes*.[14] Such games soon became the occasion for a potlatch of conspicuous consumption, as when Cicero's friend Titus Annius Milo planned to spend what amounted to three fortunes for funeral games in 54 B.C. (Cicero, *Letters to Quintus* 3.8.6; Cicero, *Pro Milone* 95). When Pompey celebrated the dedication of his theater in 55 B.C., he set aside the appropriate number of days for tragedies and Atellan farces in the theater itself, followed by a series of athletic contests in the Greek manner, which turned out to be boring for the Roman audience. The big events took place during the final five days, which were given over to venationes. In the Circus Maximus 600 lions and 400 leopards were killed, working up to a grand climax on the last day. On it, 18 elephants were brought out to be hunted by Gaetulians from Africa armed with javelins. It was all very spectacular, but the huge beasts turned out to be too pathetic—even the tough Roman crowd pitied them —and too dangerous—they nearly stampeded into the spectators' seats (Cicero, *Letters to His Friends* 7.1; Pliny, *Natural History* 8.20–21).

This, however, was a game Julius Caesar knew how to play. When he celebrated his triumphs in 46 B.C., all the resources of the conquered provinces and of his keen sense of showmanship were marshaled to give the city a spectacle it would remember for a long time. In addition to the normal triumphal procession, and the usual sort of gladiatorial duels in the Forum Romanum, Caesar staged events all over town. Plays, including modern mimes composed for the occasion, were performed in each of the four regions of the city. A special wooden amphitheater was built—presumably in the Campus Martius—for the venationes at which Romans got their first-ever glimpse of a giraffe. Another special facility was built at the marshy Codeta Minor in the Campus Martius; there grandstands were erected, some hydraulic arrangements caused the site to be flooded, and Caesar was able to stage a full-scale naval battle, with 4,000 oarsmen and 2,000 armed marines, the first such show ever held in Rome. Mock battles were also held in the Circus Maximus: 400 cavalry, 1,000 infantry, and special troops mounted in turrets on the backs of 40 elephants. (Caesar had learned from Pompey's mistake in staging the elephant battles. At *his* games, the elephants provided transportation, not targets; and to prevent other trouble, a moat 10 feet wide and 10 feet deep was dug all around the Circus between the battle areas and the spectators— Pliny, *Natural History* 8.22; Suetonius, *Julius* 39; Appian, *Civil Wars* 2.102; Dio Cassius, *Roman History* 43.22–23.) In these battles prisoners and condemned criminals fought, as did professionals from the gladiatorial schools and even some distinguished Romans of the equestrian order. Greek athletic contests had become traditional, and must have had some fans among the population, so Caesar included some of them, even though they were not very popular. Other events had a low-key but exotic attraction, such as the Lusus Troiae, a horseback drill executed by young Romans and later described by Vergil (*Aeneid* 5.545–603), and the Pyrrhic war dances, performed in armor by noble youths (Suetonius, *Julius* 39).

The popular appeal of such spectacles was too great for the emperors to ignore. Augustus boasted that on 26 occasions he sponsored venationes in the Circus, the Forum, and a new amphitheater, which Statilius Taurus built in the Campus Martius in 29 B.C. Augustus also constructed a permanent *naumachia* on the right bank of the Tiber, which could be flooded for the performance of naval battles (Augustus, *Res Gestae* 22–23). During the principate these animal hunts and gladiatorial shows were detached from funerals and from the religious ludi. Then the Flavian dynasty built the Amphitheatrum Flavium (the Colosseum), and this marked a significant turning point. In A.D. 80, when Titus dedicated the amphitheater with splendid games that lasted for a hundred days (Dio Cassius, *Roman History* 66.25) and were described with grisly enthusiasm by Martial (*On the Spectacles*), Rome gained a permanent facility that accommodated 50,000 people at a time and proclaimed that the gladiatorial shows were unabashedly performances, entertainments.

The Colosseum recalled the exterior of the Theater of Marcellus, with its three superimposed arcades framed by engaged half-columns—Tuscan at ground level, Ionic on the second level, and

Corinthian on the third (Pl. 10, 12D). The fourth level was an attic decorated with Corinthian pilasters and consoles to support poles from which banners were flown. The exterior dimensions of the ellipse were 188 meters by 156 meters. Through ground-level arches the spectators entered by a carefully engineered system of vaulted passages and stairs. These allowed easy access from ground level to all the different zones of the seats in the cavea and equally easy egress when the show was over. The elliptical rows of seats in the cavea rested on concentric vaulted corridors, and the seats sloped down toward the *arena* (which means "sand") proper. This focused every spectator's attention on the show and magnified the enthusiastic roars of the crowd. Admission to the amphitheater was free (since the shows were invariably the result of the emperor's largess), but the spectators were seated according to a strict protocol that reinforced the class consciousness of Roman society. The best seats, next to the arena but protected by a wall or grating, were reserved for the senators. Also located at this level was the imperial box, from which the emperor presided over the games. The next-higher zone was for the equestrians. Higher still were separate areas identified by inscriptions as reserved for such groups as the Arval Brethren, "public guests," "clients" (i.e., the urban plebs), and, at the very top, women. The amphitheater thus provided a model of the social world of the city, and of the Roman world, with its gladiators and beasts from the farthest ends of the empire fighting to focus and (at the same time) divert the attention of the urban populace— to be, in Byron's famous phrase, "butcher'd to make Roman holiday." It also displayed the prowess of Roman engineers (in the practical arrangements for logistics and crowd control) and the taste for Greek architectural refinement (in the decoration of the external façade). With its imposing bulk, and with its exclusive devotion to aggression, the brandishing of spears and swords, and brute physical courage, it invited a description in Freudian terms, as an image of the Romans' preoccupation with the display of virility (Valerius Maximus, *Memorabilia* 2.4.2).

An industry grew up to cater to the need for gladiators. The emperors built four training schools for them, and a whole catalogue of specialties arose: heavily armed *hoplomachi;* lightly armed

"Thracians"; *retiarii,* who fought with a net and dagger and relied on quick footwork; *essedarii,* who fought from chariots; *equites,* who fought from horseback; *bestiarii,* who specialized in killing animals. Vast sums were spent on training gladiators; on feeding them and outfitting them with weapons, costumes, and medical attention; on capturing animals and shipping, feeding, and storing them; and on supporting the attendants who checked tickets and cleaned up, the vendors who sold food and drink, and the sailors who maneuvered the canvas awnings to shade the spectators. On the day of a spectacle, normally the morning was given over to wild beast hunts, which were often elaborated with scenery suggesting the exotic places where the animals might be at home. At noon, during the lunch break, mock battles or amateur tryouts were held; if criminals were to be executed, this was the time when they were thrust into the arena, unarmed, to face either a gladiator with a sword or a hungry bear or lion. The main event was scheduled for the afternoon, when the skilled gladiators fought in pairs until one in each pair was too seriously wounded to continue. The winner asked the *munerarius,* the sponsor, whether to spare or to kill. The spectators were on their feet by this time, gesturing with their hands to indicate whether the loser should be spared or killed.[15]

The insidious appeal of the gladiatorial shows is conveyed most eloquently by Saint Augustine (*Confessions* 6.8). He tells how his innocent friend Alypius was induced, reluctantly, to go to a show at the Colosseum. To avoid being contaminated by the sight of the bloodshed, he closed his eyes. But a roar of the crowd made him open them, and, says Augustine, once Alypius drank in the carnage, he became drunk with a blood lust that could be satisfied only by going back again and again for more. The program was a ritualized, systematic violence, but because of the skill of the trained gladiators it could be passed off as sport. The average spectator was far enough away from the swords and knives to feel safe, but close enough to see that real blood was being spilled and to realize that in the safety of the seats he had a very real power of life and death over the performance.[16]

Triumphal Processions

The highest honor the Roman state could bestow was the right to march through the city of Rome as a *triumphator*. This was a proud tradition, which Roman historians traced back through a long line of victorious generals to Romulus himself (Plutarch, *Romulus* 16); indeed, the route of the triumphal procession encircled the old city of Romulus on the Palatine. By the third century B.C. the basic ritual of the triumph had been established, and as Roman armies continued their conquests farther and farther away, the triumphal processions became ever-more-spectacular devices for assuring the citizens back home that the military and political affairs of the city-state were being conducted well.

The victorious general returned to the city to ask for the triumph, but he could not enter it. To cross the pomerium was to lose his *imperium,* his power of command, so the Senate went out to meet him, usually in the Temple of Bellona. If a triumph was granted, the general and his army camped out on the old military parade ground of the Campus Martius. For the day of the procession, the triumphant general assumed some of the attributes of Jupiter himself: his face was smeared with the same red paint that was applied to Jupiter's statue on the Capitoline; he wore a tunic embroidered with palm leaves, a symbol of victory; over this he wore an embroidered toga; a golden crown was held over his head as he rode in a gilded chariot. The procession was marshaled in the lower Campus Martius, perhaps in the open space of the Circus Flaminius, and the general made a speech to the troops and presented awards and decorations. Then he mounted his chariot, surrounded by his children and accompanied by a slave who held the crown above his head and was supposed to keep reminding him that he was, after all, mortal. The procession set off: first the spoils captured from the enemy, along with floats and pictures illustrating important battles; then the prisoners of war, with captured princes, kings, or queens as featured attractions; and finally the triumphant general surrounded by his soldiers. It all moved solemnly, impressively, gaudily through the Porta Triumphalis, then past cheering crowds through the Circus Maximus and around the

Palatine to the Sacra Via, the Forum Romanum, where important prisoners were taken off to the prison and executed, and up the slope to the Capitoline, where the rite climaxed with a sacrifice to Jupiter and a banquet in his temple. The long day ended when the general was escorted home to the music of flutes.[17]

The focus of all this was the general, whom the rites surrounded with a holy ambiguity. Wearing the garments of Jupiter, the general was reminded of his mortality by a slave; riding as a commander in a golden chariot, he was surrounded by his soliders, who sang songs that made fun of him; claiming all the honors of a king, he ended the day by losing his military authority. This ambivalence reminds us how suspicious the Romans were of the trappings of kingship during the republic. Such scruples were irrelevant under the principate, when the triumph naturally became the emperor's exclusive prerogative, celebrated rarely but with breathtaking spectacle. The best example is the triumph of Vespasian and Titus after the conquest of Judaea in A.D. 70, described by Josephus (*The Jewish War* 7.119–157) and depicted on the Arcus Titi. Of all the special events, triumphal processions must have made the deepest impression. They condensed the attractions of a parade, conquest, bloodshed, and hero-worship into a single day that occurred no more than once a year in the times of republican conquests and once a generation in the principate. They were the most intense, most spectacular pageant the city had to offer.

Spectacle and the City

The pageantry of color, texture, and masses, the blare of trumpets and the squeal of flutes, the smell of people, sacrificial animals, and blood, the solemn processions and raucous games—all were a kinetic expression of the same grandiose taste that produced fora, temples, and baths. In its festivals, gladiatorial shows, and triumphs the city celebrated itself, its history, its gods, its power. In all these events, Rome was the focal point, the center of activity, the model of order imposed on a compliant world.

The parades of captives and the re-creations of battles were like the inscriptions and paintings on walls. In a city without radio and television, they informed the population about events across the empire. They advertised the power and glory of the aristocracy or the emperor, but they also gave a share in the spoils of empire to the whole population. The spectacle, whether event or building, affirmed the dominant position of the ruling classes, but it was also in a sense accessible to everyone. The poorest immigrant from Egypt could watch the processions and stroll through the fora, enjoying the spectacular panorama of the city just as readily as a senator or an emperor. There were slaves in Rome, and there were desperately poor people, but even they seem to have been able to move through the city with very few restrictions. There was nothing like the laws in Greek cities which allowed no one but citizens into the marketplace. Public areas in the Roman city were open to all, a phenomenon that parallels the way Roman citizenship became more and more accessible during the late republic and the principate. The strength of Rome lay to a large extent in the military discipline the triumphs celebrated, but it also lay—as more than one Roman writer reminds us—in the city's openness to the talents and ideas of other people. The city, with the arches of its practical aqueducts and with its temples of Roman brick encrusted with Greek details, with its gladiatorial extravaganzas drawn from all the corners of the empire, and with its orgiastic processions of the Magna Mater confined to certain days and places, was an ultimate paradigm of the knack for appropriating elements from other peoples and imposing on them the orderliness that was so characteristically Roman.

PATTERNS OF
ROMAN
URBANISM

Fifteen

The Theory and Practice of Building Towns

D uring the Bronze and Iron ages there were no cities in Italy; there were only villages distributed on hilltops or situated well up on the slopes of mountains. During the ninth and eighth centuries B.C. somewhat larger villages appeared on the plains at the foot of the hills, but they lacked any monumental "urban" buildings.

The first cities proper appeared in the eighth century B.C., founded by Greeks from Asia Minor. These Greek colonies, located along the coast of Sicily and southern Italy (which came to be known as Magna Graecia, "Great Greece"), were generally laid out on an orthogonal plan of streets crossing at more or less right angles, surrounded by a defensive wall of irregular ground plan.[1]

In north-central Italy the Etruscan civilization emerged as a recognizable cultural entity in the eighth century B.C. Its exact relationship to the preceding Iron Age cultures is still a matter of scholarly argument, but it seems fair to say that a characteristic feature of the Etruscans was their social organization into cities. It is possible, but not certain, that this urban quality of their culture was in some way inspired by their contact with the Greeks. In any event, the various Etruscan cities, twelve of which constituted a more or less formal "Etruscan League," had certain features in common: a hill-top location, defended by cliffs and walls; an informal, unplanned arrangement of streets; lightly constructed houses, which have not left many archaeological remains; a temple or two; and graveyards outside the walls which often had tombs modeled on the houses of the living, occasionally (as at Orvieto, Cerveteri, and Vetulonia) neatly arranged in an orthogonal plan. In the sixth century B.C. the Etruscans expanded south as far as Campania and north as far as the River Po. The colonies they founded in the sixth century had a more formal appearance than their earlier cities: Capua, Mar-zabotto, and Spina all had rectangular plans, arranged according to the points of the compass.

When the Romans founded new towns and cities as part of their colonizing activity in the fourth century B.C. and later, they inaugurated them with a set of rituals they firmly believed were inherited from the Etruscans, including the ceremonies of plowing the ritual furrow (*sulcus primigenius*) of the *pomerium* (Varro, *De Lingua Latina* 5.143) and placing the first fruits of the earth in a ceremonial pit called the *mundus*, "world." These rituals were an important part of the story of Romulus's founding of Rome (Plutarch, *Romulus* 11), and when performed by the founders of Roman colonies,[2] they symbolically joined the agricultural productivity of the farmland with the defensive and commercial function of the city and its walls.[3]

Within the walls, the Romans laid out the streets and public spaces according to the formal grid plan they seem to have borrowed from their Greek and Etruscan neighbors. Often two main streets, leading directly from the main gates, crossed at the center, and the forum was laid out on or near the crossing.[4] Modern books usually borrow the terms surveyors used when dividing farmland, calling the main north-south street the *kardo maximus* and the main east-west street the *decumanus maximus*.

The Founding of Colonies

During the sixth century B.C. numerous distinct communities of Latin-speaking peoples, called *populi*, emerged to the south and east of Rome. Alba Longa was an important one, Lavinium another.

The populi cooperated with one another and formally acknowledged their common language and kinship by means of a "Latin League," establishing its federal center at Aricia and a major religious shrine on the Alban Mount. According to tradition, the Romans made several early attempts to dominate the Latin League: assuming leadership of the cult on the Alban Mount, establishing a duplicate "federal center" cult of Diana on the Aventine (ascribed to Servius Tullius by Livy 1.45), asserting military primacy at the Battle of Lake Regillus in about 496 B.C. (Livy 2.19), and extracting the Cassian treaty of about 493 B.C., which acknowledged Rome as a partner more equal than the other equals in the League. Many modern scholars believe that these traditions of Roman supremacy were later inventions, a projection backwards by Roman authors who needed to see in the early and poorly documented period some foreshadowing of Rome's eventual rise. In this more modern view, Rome was simply another member of the Latin League for the first several centuries of the republic, and as such joined with the other Latin populi in establishing the oldest Latin colonies. These were fortress communities set up at strategic points all around the Latin territory to control roads, river crossings, and mountain passes. The date of the earliest of them is unknown, but by 380 B.C. these colonies of the Latin League reached north to Sutrium and Nepet, deep in Etruscan territory, and south to Setia and Circeii. All the colonists, regardless of their town of origin, became citizens of the new community and lost their original citizenship; the community became a new member of the Latin League.

Rome began to emerge as a city distinct from the other communities of the League during the fourth century B.C. When the Romans conquered Veii in 396 B.C., they assigned confiscated land only to Roman citizens, not to a colony of all the Latin populi. This produced tensions that occasionally escalated to war, and ended in Rome's victory and recognized hegemony in 338 B.C. Thenceforth Rome dominated Italian colonization, and its colonies were of two main types, "Citizen" and "Latin."

"Citizen" colonies were small groups of about 300 Romans, stationed at strategic points along the seacoast of Latium. The colonists retained their Roman citizenship, and the settlements were viewed as small extensions of Rome. The oldest, and the nearest to Rome, was Ostia, at the mouth of the Tiber.[5] The settlement had the shape of a military camp; it was quadrangular, with a forum at the junction of the two perpendicular main streets. Its walls could have accommodated 300 settlers.

Farther afield, the Romans established larger colonies, similar to the older colonies of the Latin League. Along with a large contingent of Romans, the colonists often included members of other Latin populi and even members of neighboring non-Latin tribes. Such "Latin" colonies were considered politically autonomous, able to make their own laws and administer justice for and by themselves. But their citizens (whether ethnic Latins or not) shared with other Latins the rights of trading and intermarriage with Romans and under certain conditions could even vote when they were present in Rome. They were also liable to Roman military service, and were of great strategic value in consolidating the frontiers of Roman influence (known legally as Latin territory) as it expanded throughout Italy.[6]

In the second and first centuries B.C., citizen colonies were again established, but their purpose served domestic political goals, not military ones. The Gracchi, for instance, helped relieve congestion by proposing to send urban residents out to colonies at Tarentum and Carthage. Sulla rewarded his veterans by settling them on land confiscated from previous inhabitants, and by organizing colonies, of which Pompeii is an example. Julius Caesar established colonies outside Italy for his veterans, at Urso in Spain, Carthage in Africa, and Corinth in Greece. Thenceforth the Roman colony could be established anywhere within the empire.

In the early days, the status of colony was inferior to that of an independent city (*municipium*) because all the original colonists and their descendants were Roman citizens and had no real independence of action apart from the main citizen body in Rome. During the principate, however, when the political action was all in Rome or inherent in Roman citizenship, colonial status became more and more desirable. Many independent cities requested the prestige of the title and citizenship that went with it. Augustus in particular honored the colonies as extensions of Rome, and bestowed special rights and privileges upon them, both in Italy and in the provinces. He, and after him Claudius, Trajan, Hadrian, and the Severi, founded colonies throughout the empire to affirm Roman culture and Roman values in conquered territory (Tacitus, *Annals* 12.32).

The first consideration in founding a colony was its location, and from earliest times its location was determined by strategic considerations.[7] The colony was a Roman presence on the borders of alien territory or in the midst of conquered territory. When necessary, roads were built to assure its communications with the metropolis. Its political and social relationships were with Rome, not with nearby communities, and as far as possible it was economically autonomous. As colonization spread outside Italy into western Europe and northern Africa, the Roman colony stood in the midst of rural peoples, often isolated but always proud, representing urban values cultivated through the centuries in the Italian cities under the influence of Greeks and Etruscans. It was administered by a council and a collegial magistracy modeled on that of the early city-state of Rome itself.[8] And it articulated the message of Roman culture in its buildings—basilica, curia, comitium, and temple dedicated to the Capitoline triad of Jupiter, Juno, and Minerva—which helped make the colony a small-scale copy of Rome.

Laying Out the Farmland and Town

When the colonists arrived at the assigned place, they were led by three distinguished citizens, usually senators, who for a three-year term presided over the necessary tasks of founding and organizing the new colony. They bore the title *tresviri coloniae deducendae,* "commission of three to found the colony." The first thing to do, after attending to the religious rites already described, was to divide the land into individual plots. This was crucial, because the colony had to support itself; etymologically, the word *colonus,* "colonist," is derived from the same verb (*colo*) as the word meaning "cultivation." To survey the land and make fair assignments, there was a virtual town-planning establishment, with professional surveyors and architects. Cicero (*Contra Rullum: De Lege Argaria* 2.32) lists the staff that was needed for a colony: two hundred surveyors (successful professionals of equestrian rank) with a support staff of twenty each, in addition to assorted attendants, clerks, secretaries, heralds, and architects. They in turn needed supplies of mules, tents, food, and cooking utensils. In the above-cited passage, Cicero opposes the proposed colony as too ambitious, so his figures may be exaggerated. But the list itself seems reasonable. Certainly all the ways in which one Roman colony resembled another, and in which each colony evoked the spirit of Rome, implied that standardized procedures were followed by standardized personnel.

We can glimpse this crew at work by reading the technical manuals that survive. A typical one is *De Limitibus Constituendis,* a work of the second century A.D. usually ascribed to Hyginus Gromaticus. The document discusses the patterns of laying out the farmland of a colony, illustrating the variations with specific historical examples. The process of surveying was called "centuriation," and involved the use of a cross-shaped instrument called a *groma,* set up at a central point. From this point the *agrimensor,* "surveyor," extended two lines, the *kardo* (literally a "hinge") and the *decumanus maximus,* at right angles to each other. The four quadrants thus produced were then divided into common land and into long, rectangular plots assigned to individual colonists.[9]

Most of the colonists lived in individual farmhouses on their plots of land, but they all looked to the urban center with its walls as a place of refuge in case of attack and as a focus of commercial, social, religious, and political activity. Some proportion of the colonists lived within the city's walls—those with plots nearby, perhaps, and those with some special skill that could serve the whole community, such as blacksmiths, barbers, carpenters, and shopkeepers. These tradesmen presumably hired native peasants to farm their land for them.[10]

Municipia

Before the Roman domination, Italy was inhabited by Greeks and Etruscans who developed city-states of their own. It was also inhabited by various tribes that were more or less urbanized according to their traditions, the topography of their territory, and the extent of their interaction with other peoples. Among the Oscan-speaking tribes of central Italy, for instance, the Campanians had settled in cities on the fertile plains by the fourth century B.C., while the Samnites remained more nomadic, living in small hamlets in the hills and valleys of the central mountains.[11]

During the fourth and third centuries B.C., the various peoples were absorbed under the Roman hegemony. Since the Romans found city-states easiest to deal with, most of the established cities in the regions acquired by Rome became her allies. Their citizens were generally given partial Roman citizenship. A citizen of the Latin town of Arpinum, for example, was from the Roman point of view a *civis sine suffragio,* "citizen without the vote," but he also retained practical citizenship in his hometown. He was known as a *municeps,* one who "took part" (*capere*) in the exercise of a *munus,* "civic duty." The town, which remained free in theory, was called a *municipium.*

Market Towns

Several inscriptions and graffiti from Campania list the cities of central Italy that held regular market days, although they do not list them in any consistent order. Rome, Capua (Cato, *On Agriculture* 135, recommends its copper, rope, and baskets), Atella, Cumae, Puteoli, and Nola (Cato recommends its oil and copper) seem to have been the most popular spots.[12] In the smaller towns—for instance, towns like Cosa, where most of the citizens lived on individual farms scattered across the colony's territory, market days must have been important events, commercially and socially. Wandering specialty peddlers apparently rode circuit and served several markets in a region; a comment by Julius Caesar (*Gallic War* 4.5) shows how they were pumped for news when they arrived in a town.

In the territory that was settled not by colonies but by individual "viritane" grants, special *fora* were established as sites for rural markets. According to an inscription of A.D. 138 (*CIL* 8.23246), a new market was established at Casae, in the Roman province of Africa Proconsularis. The founding of this market required a specific vote of the Senate in Rome, and granted Lucilius Africanus, a senator, permission to hold a market twice a month on a regular basis. Lurking clearly between the lines of the inscription are the prospect of big profits for Lucilius and the desire of the authorities that the market not become the focus of any political activity.[13]

Another inscription tells us about the settlement of Pizus, a small trading post on a main road in Thrace, which at the beginning of the third century A.D. was chartered as an *emporium,* a market town. Nine gentlemen from the upper classes of the surrounding villages were entrusted with the responsibilities of government (including the protection of supplies from brigands and revolutionaries), and in turn they were granted, as an incentive, immunity from municipal taxes, garrison duty, and the obligation to supply wagons for the imperial postal service. In this community of perhaps 500 inhabitants, we see the imperial government developing a rural market with the essential trappings of Roman civic life, to strengthen morale and tighten the fabric of the Roman presence in the countryside.[14]

Military Camps

An army legion pitching a permanent or semipermanent camp (*castrum*) needed an orderly layout of streets, barracks, chapels, parade grounds, officers' quarters, and a sturdy defensive wall. A standardized plan permitted soldiers to feel securely oriented within camps built at very different locations. Indeed, Polybius wrote that the legionary camps he knew in the second century B.C. were similar to cities.[15] Surveyors' manuals from the principate (e.g., *De Munitionibus Castrorum,* ascribed to Hyginus Gromaticus) and archaeological discoveries of a large number of military camps throughout the empire reveal a reciprocal relationship between the design of camps and the design of cities. The earliest plan of Ostia, dating from the fourth century B.C., is an example of a colony imitating the simple rectangular shape of a military camp.[16]

Like cities, military camps were centers of transportation, habitation, and commerce. Here soldiers lived, fraternized, and grew some of their own food. But they also interacted with nearby towns and cities, making bricks and pottery, working at public construction, and providing police service. They were customers for food, merchandise, lodging, and entertainment. Even military camps that were far from any existing town regularly attracted people to provide essential support services, including drink, games, and girls. (The name for such a campside settlement, *canabae,* seems to be derived from a Gallic word meaning "wineshop.") In time, the business opportunities attracted other tradesmen, and the canabae grew in an orderly fashion with a proper grid of streets and standardized house plans. Eventually cemeteries developed, along with workshops and a recognizable civic life. Veterans discharged from the legions settled down and participated in the community's activities. A forum and its buildings were added, along with temples, baths, an amphitheater, and a market. A town growing up in this way was always closely tied to the military camp and was often located within a few hundred meters of the camp's gates. When the camp near Lambaesis was moved a kilometer or so away in the second century A.D., the military engineers constructed a wide highway to make it easier for the soldiers to get to town.[17]

The military camps and their attendant towns served an important defensive purpose, but they had a more affirmative purpose as well. They bore the message of Rome to the outposts of empire, concentrated its culture within their walls, and beckoned to the surrounding natives with the enticements of its civilization. Tacitus tells us how his father-in-law, Gnaeus Julius Agricola, when governer of Britain, built stockades and castles to pacify the native tribes. He also built temples, law courts, and houses, provided a Latin education to the chieftains' sons, and even encouraged a taste for Roman styles of dress. The result, says Tacitus (*Agricola* 21), was that "little by little they inclined toward the blandishments of decadence—porticoes, baths, and elegant dinner parties. Since they were new at it, they called it civilization [*humanitas*], though in fact it was part of their enslavement."

Urban Patterns in the Countryside

The nonurban Italian tribes subdued by the Roman Republic were organized into rural townships and hamlets that the Romans called *pagi* and *vici* respectively. Local officials continued to supervise things from day to day, but such important functions as the administration of justice were assumed by the Romans, who sent out *praefecti* to act as circuit judges. The judges normally held court in the largest town of a district, and that town came to be known as a *praefectura* (Festus, p. 262L). These praefecturae were often the focal points of market activity in each district.

On many occasions during the republic, Roman citizens were given individual grants of land (called viritane grants) scattered throughout the public land the Romans had confiscated from defeated tribes and states. These citizen-farmers, separated by great distances from Rome, lived in individual *villae*, "farm houses," but gathered occasionally in small villages for market and other social purposes. Such a small village meeting place of Roman farmers was called a *conciliabulum*. It probably had some rudimentary political organization such as a council and local aediles, but important judicial functions were exercised by praefecti sent from Rome. A larger village of this sort located near or on a highway was usually called a *forum*, in recognition of its importance as a market center for the farmers all around.

In the aftermath of the Social War in 90/89 B.C., when Roman citizenship was granted to all Italians, it became necessary to organize these smaller communities into something resembling cities or municipalities, since Romans could live properly only in a recognizably urban setting. The larger fora and conciliabula were chartered as municipia, and the smaller ones were combined for administrative convenience into city-states that sometimes lacked a proper center—they were "urban" only on paper.[18]

At the end of the republic and during the principate the Romans encountered a wide variety of human settlement patterns, ranging from the established urban matrix of the Greek East, to the tribal centers known as *civitates* in Gaul and Britain, to the scattered hamlets of the Berber nomads in northern Africa. In the east, the Romans accepted and utilized the existing urban units. In the west, towns served as forts, markets, transportation centers, or shrines for the scattered tribesmen in their hilltop villages.[19] The Romans encouraged an urban life-style even in the midst of such a rural economy, and many localities in Gaul boasted a temple, a bath, and an amphitheater, but virtually no permanent population. The tribesmen continued to live in their scattered villages, but now came down to the pseudo–urban center for market activities and festivals. Gradually, as Roman influence became more pervasive and peace became more reliable, the natives tended to abandon their hilltop settlements and move down to the plains near the urban centers. In Africa, the Punic and Greek cities along the seacoast provided the framework for development; inland, army camps were established as bastions of Roman cultural and political control.

Throughout the empire, roads played an important role in the location and distribution of the different types of settlements.[20] The villas of farms tended to be set well back from the roads, in order to minimize casual damage from transients (Columella 1.5.7). Nevertheless, the traffic on the roads attracted farmers from the fields: Pliny (*Natural History* 23.95) comments on the farmers at Iguvium (Gubbio), who peddled herbal cures to travelers passing by on the Via Flaminia. Such roadside stands were occasionally turned into somewhat more permanent villages stretched out for a hundred meters or so along both sides of a road, or they were established as proper fora.

According to the evidence, some sort of small village was located every 7–12 Roman miles along the roads. These villages served as relay stations for the cursus publicus, the imperial postal service, and were known as *mutationes* or *stationes*. At wider intervals, corresponding to a day's journey by wagon, there were larger service facilities known as *mansiones*. Normally neither stationes nor mansiones had any discernible civic structure, but were administered by a *manceps*, a private businessman who leased the concession from the imperial bureaucracy that ran the postal service. The manceps' support staff included muleteers, secretaries, blacksmiths, cartwrights, a veterinarian, and some military troops to dispatch and carry messages and to police the road. The buildings at such a roadside village included an inn, which offered lodgings no better than they ought to have been, if we judge from such accounts as Horace's *Satires* 1.5; tabernae, which gave their name to many of these way stations; some sort of bathing facilities; possibly a temple; and the stables and barracks needed to lodge the horses, mules, and soldiers. When a tower was added, it offered protection to the farmers of the district in case of attack, and also an elevated place from which to supervise work in the fields. As the tallest building in sight, it was as conspicuous as the water towers and silos of small towns in the American Midwest, and often gave its name to the settlement. As early as Cicero, we find references to such tower-dominated villages, called *castella, turres,* or *centenaria.* In the later empire, they were frequently called *burgi,* and lined the highways as fortified places of security in unsettled times.[21]

Sixteen

Cosa

I n 273 B.C. a Latin colony was founded at Cosa to guard the coast road and sea, and to maintain a Latin military presence in the territory of the defeated Etruscan city of Vulci. Located about 140 kilometers north of Rome, the site had one of the best harbors on the west coast of Italy. Cosa flourished while the Roman Republic flourished, and since the site was not very important later, the ruins serve as a good, relatively undisturbed example of Roman urbanism outside Rome during the period of the later republic.[1]

Foundation

When the colonists arrived, the first task was to survey the land, divide it into individual plots, and define an urban center. As was typical in the centuriation of new colonies, the augurs built an *auguraculum,* a square platform about 7 meters on a side, cut into the limestone surface at the highest point of the hill on which the town was built. From it they had a clear view of land and sea, and could take the auspices. They could also sight along it to lay out the centuriation of the fields.

Walls about 1,500 meters long, punctuated by square towers, enclosed an area of about 13.25 hectares (33 acres) on the hill top, which included three high points: at the southern corner, the citadel (*arx*) with the auguraculum; at the eastern corner, a steep,

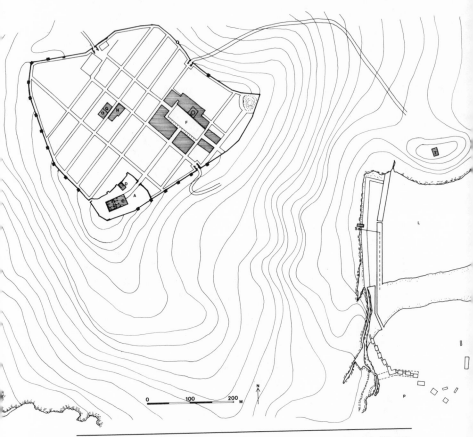

Fig. 24. Cosa: **A** Arx (Pl. 14), **C** Capitolium, **D** Temple D, **F** Forum (Pl. 15), **G** Republican houses (Fig. 14), **H** House of the Skeleton, **L** Lagoon, **P** Port and breakwater, **S** Spring house, **T** Temple (of Portunus?).

small outcropping; and at the northwest corner, an incline where a road ascended from the coast. Streets were laid out on a grid, oriented in practical fashion so that each street remained as level as possible. At the lowest point, in the saddle between the eastern and southern heights, lay the Forum. Two main streets bordered it on northwest and southwest, leading to gates in the northeastern and southeastern walls, and a third main street connected the Forum with the northwestern gate. From the middle of the Forum's long side a wide processional way led up the hill to the arx.

256

Population and Economy

The first settlers numbered between 2,500 and 4,000 colonists with their families, drawn from Rome and several other Latin towns. In the aftermath of the Hannibalic War, a second group of 1,000 reinforced them in 197 B.C. (Livy 33.24.8–9). Only about a quarter of these could be accommodated within the walls, which means that over 2,000 families lived on small farms and in hamlets throughout the *ager Cosanus,* the land assigned to the colony for distribution. During the second century B.C., the patterns of land use changed in a way that was to become typical of Roman Italy: small farms persisted on the land at the margins of the ager Cosanus, but in the richer valleys, larger farms centered on villas became more common. The Villa of Settefinestre, which dominated the coastal plain east of the town, has been excavated as an example of the sort of large country establishment worked by slaves which dominated the economy of the area from the second century B.C. on, particularly after a sack of the town in 60 B.C. removed the area's civic center.[2]

These large villas produced not only grain, grapes, and olives but also containers in which to ship them. Identifying stamps on amphoras show that the family of the Sestii was prominent in trade as well as agriculture. Catullus (44) mentions a wealthy Publius Sestius, presumably the same one Cicero defended on a charge of electoral corruption and violence in 56 B.C.,[3] and it seems likely that this Sestius belonged to the family that shipped vast quantities of amphoras and their contents from Cosa to ports all along the Mediterranean coast during the second and first centuries B.C.[4] (Horace wrote an ode [1.4] to Lucius, Publius's son, quaestor at Rome in 44 B.C. and consul in 23 B.C.)

The good natural harbor at Cosa was used from the very beginning of the colony (Livy 22.11.6; 30.39.1), and during the second century the lagoon in back of it (now silted up) was developed as a commercial fishery. Its brackish waters were perfect for eels and mullets, which fetched extravagant prices in the late republic. Channels were carved out of the rock at the west end of the lagoon and fitted with sluice gates to permit the fish to swim out and in, while fresh water from a spring house regulated the salinity and temperature by means of an elaborate water-lifting mechanism.[5] Even after the town was sacked, the port continued in use, until near the beginning of the first century A.D. (Strabo 5.2.8).

Public Buildings

The first buildings in the Forum of Cosa were those most necessary for the colony's civic life: a Curia for the council, and a Comitium for the assembly, a circular set of steps arranged in front of the Curia just like the Comitium in Rome in front of the Curia Hostilia. These two buildings stood on the axis of the street that led from the Forum to the sacred space on the arx. Toward the end of the third century B.C., a small shrine (along with a small building identified as a prison) was built southeast of the Curia, and during the first decades of the second century eight atrium buildings were erected around the other three sides of the Forum, presumably to serve as meeting places and for official business. Shortly afterwards, the Forum was made more grand with porticoes, paving, drainage, and trees. The elaboration continued when, around 170 B.C., a large commemorative arch was built to mark the northwestern entrance to the Forum, the Curia was enlarged, and a basilica was added in imitation of the new ones in Rome. Toward the middle of the century, a new temple (of Concordia, according to Brown) was built to replace the shrine next to the Curia (Pl. 15).

On the arx, the augural platform stood alone until about the end of the First Punic War, in 240 B.C., when the colonists began to construct, west of it, a small temple to Jupiter. Early in the second century another small temple (Temple D) was built, perhaps in honor of Mater Matuta, to the right of the road as it entered the arx enclosure.[6] In the middle of the second century B.C., the small temple honoring Jupiter was replaced by the Capitolium, one of the largest temples in all of Etruria; it was the colony's crowning glory (Pl. 14). To stress continuity with the colony's past, the terra-cotta plaques of the earlier temple of Jupiter were reused in the decoration of the new one, and to stress the colony's tie to Rome, new decorative details imitated those of the capital. Like the Capitoline temple in Rome, the temple at Cosa was divided into three separate cellas, was laid out on the usual Etruscan plan, faced a terraced temple *area,* and towered over the Forum.

Cosa in the Principate

After the sack of Cosa in the 60s B.C., the town went into decline. Only the port and the large villa-centered farms continued to prosper. The more settled conditions of Italy under Augustus permitted some recovery, attested by terra-cotta plaques of Augustan style on the arx (from a portico, perhaps), and by evidence of renewed habitation. The public atria around the Forum were converted into private houses, and some of the old houses of the republican colonists were removed to allow for roomier atrium houses such as the House of the Skeleton, with its big, comfortable garden.[7] Cosa's active political life declined in the middle of the first century A.D., when the now mostly abandoned basilica was converted to an odeum, where plays could be produced. During the second and third centuries the port was revived as a fishery, and villas flourished along the whole seaside. Cosa disappeared from history in the fourth century, when, according to archaeological evidence in the Forum, both a Christian church and a shrine to the pagan Bacchus were built.[8]

Seventeen

Pompeii

P ompeii is world famous because of its paradoxical preservation through destruction, the result of the eruption
of Mount Vesuvius on August 24, A.D. 79. We can grasp
the human dimensions of the eruption by wandering
through the ruins, seeing the plaster casts of human and
animal victims, and reading the eyewitness accounts by Pliny the
Younger (*Letters* 6.16, 20; cf. Dio Cassius, *Roman History* 66.21–
23). In addition to a sense of immense human tragedy, the ruins of
Pompeii give us insights into the social, political, and commercial
life of a small ancient Italian city. Pompeii is a city whose history we
can trace, sometimes in great and intimate detail, and because of its
sudden destruction it also gives us a glimpse of events that occurred at one specific moment of intense activity.

Samnite Pompeii

Four major roads crossed at the site of Pompeii: northwest along
the coast to the important Greek cities of Cuma and Neapolis (Naples); south along the coast to Stabiae and the Sorrento Peninsula;
north along the east side of Vesuvius to Nola; and east across the
river plain to Nuceria. The agricultural products of the rich volcanic soil in the Sarno River valley were easily brought to market at
Pompeii, where the coast road crossed the river and the river flowed

into the eastern corner of the Bay of Naples at a small but useful harbor.

From scattered archaeological remains, we know that Etruscans and Greeks spent time on the site in the seventh and sixth centuries B.C., and that during the fifth century, Oscan-speaking mountaineers, the Samnites, became dominant throughout Campania. Under the influence of the urbanized Greek cultures, the Samnites organized the city under a magistrate called a *meddix tuticus*, supported by quaestors and aediles. Agriculture—especially the production of olives for oil and grapes for wine—and sheep-herding were major sources of wealth, and a local aristocracy was able to expand the city and build beautiful homes for itself.

At the top of the hill on which Pompeii was built, irregular streets around the Forum suggest paths leading to an early commercial center. Near the center stands a temple built in honor of Apollo in the sixth century B.C., reflecting Etruscan and Greek influence. A tomb, and deposits of Etruscan bucchero vases, have been found under the later Stabian Baths, and show that in the sixth century this site was still outside the inhabited portion of the city. Just southeast of the old core of Pompeii is the Triangular Forum, with its sixth-century Doric temple, which may have functioned as an acropolis and place of refuge.

Walls may have been built around Pompeii as early as the fifth century B.C., but it was after the Samnite Wars in the fourth century and the coming of Roman domination that the walls that still survive were built, along with the grid of main streets and the large space devoted to the Forum, apparently in the third century B.C.[1]

In the second century B.C., Samnite Pompeii consolidated its prosperity. The Forum took on the look of a formal Hellenistic piazza (Pl. 16); a new temple was built on axis at its northern end, a tufa colonnade was added, and public buildings for offices and meetings were built at the southern end. (The basilica at the southwest corner of the Forum, the oldest preserved basilica anywhere, reminds us that it was in the second century B.C. that the Forum Romanum was expanded with basilicas.) At the eastern edge of the built-up part of town, at the junction of roads to Nuceria and Stabiae, the Stabian Baths were constructed. To the south, the old Tri-

Fig. 25. Pompeii: **1** Villa of the Mysteries, **2** Street of the Tombs, **3** Inn of Albinus (*Ins. Occ.* 1–2), **4** House of the Surgeon (VI.i.10), **5** House of Sallust (VI.ii.4), **6** House of Pansa (Insula Arriana Polliana, VI.vi.1), **7** House of the Vettii (VI.xv.1), **8** House of the Faun (VI.xii.2), **9** Forum Baths, **10** Temple of Fortuna Augusta, **11** Forum, **12** Stabian Baths, **13** Inn (VII.xi.11–14), **14** Inn of Sittius (VII.i.44–45), **15** Central Baths, **16** Temple of Isis, **17** Samnite Palestra, **18** Triangular Forum, **19** Theater, **20** Odeum, **21** Gladiators' Barracks, **22** House of Menander (I.x.4), **23** Garum shop (I.xii.8), **24** Bakery (I.xii.1), **25** Via dell'Abbondanza, **26** House of the Moralist (III.iv.2–3), **27** House of Loreius Tiburtinus (II.ii.2), **28** Estate of Iulia Felix (II.iv.2), **29** Palestra, **30** Amphitheater.

angular Forum received a touch of monumentality, an Ionic entrance porch and colonnade, which framed in good Hellenistic style a vista out to the bay and mountains. East of this, a new theater, a colonnaded square, and a gymnasium (the Samnite Palestra) reinforced the Pompeiians' taste for Greek culture. The road leading from the Forum eastward toward Stabiae developed into a busy commercial street, called by modern visitors the Via dell' Abbondanza (Pl. 17).

Prosperity allowed the Pompeiians to rebuild their homes. New houses were built in the open parts of town; the street plan shows a slightly different orientation of streets in the area north and east of the Forum. Some of these houses were large and elaborate. With their First Style decoration, their floor mosaics inspired by Hellenistic paintings, their spacious columned atria, and their axial vistas into colonnaded peristyles, mansions like the House of the Faun and the House of Pansa (Fig. 13) rivaled the palaces of Hellenistic princes.

Roman Pompeii, 80 B.C.–A.D. 62

In the Social War (90/89 B.C.) the Pompeiians joined with other Campanian cities to demand full Roman citizenship, and in the war's aftermath Sulla, in 80 B.C., occupied Pompeii and settled 4,000–5,000 of his veterans there. He gave the name "Colonia Cornelia Veneria Pompeianorum" to the new colony, memorializing both his own family, the Cornelii, and his patron goddess, Venus. The colonists filled new, Roman-style magistracies (two *duoviri* and two *aediles*). The old Samnite aristocracy thus lost its political power, but not its economic influence, and within a generation or so Samnite families gained Roman citizenship, held magistracies, and joined the families of the colonists as members of the Curia. In the Augustan period a new set of family names appeared in the list of magistrates and decurions, which shows that new Roman families were moving to Pompeii and quickly rising to political, social, and economic prominence.[2]

The Roman colonists instituted a building program that gave shape to a more thoroughly Roman expression of city life. The Temple of Jupiter at the north end of the Forum was remodeled to evoke the Capitoline temple in Rome, with separate cellas for Jupiter, Juno, and Minerva; dominating the Forum, this Capitolium gave physical expression to the colony's political role as an extension of Rome (Pl. 16, 20). In the southeast corner of town, which seems to have been fairly free of buildings, the Romans constructed an amphitheater for gladiatorial performances, and they also improved the town's bathing facilities: the Stabian Baths were modernized and the new Forum Baths were built just north of the Forum (Fig. 22). They also completed some of the unfinished plans of the Hellenistic city—for instance, the building of a new small theater (Odeum). In the next century and a half, the physical development of Pompeii continued to reflect the city's integration into the mainstream of Roman urban life. The Palestra was built west of the Amphitheater as headquarters of the collegia iuvenum, the bands of young men organized under Augustus for athletic and quasi-military activities and for patriotic indoctrination in service to the Augustan political settlement. A temple in honor of Fortuna Augusta occupied the corner of a busy intersection north of the Forum, dedicated to the cult of the emperors. The Building of Eumachia, on the east side of the Forum, was dedicated to Concordia and to Augusta Pietas.

The wealthy woman who paid for that building offers us an interesting glimpse into the upper levels of society in Roman Pompeii. Eumachia was born into a Campanian family, the Eumachii, which can be traced back to early Greek settlers who grew rich on the land; wine jars bearing their name have been found in southern France. She was married to M. Numistrius Fronto, a Lucanian who served as duovir in A.D. 2/3, and whose family wealth was based on sheep and the wool trade. Eumachia served as priestess of Venus (patron goddess of the colony) and as patroness of the fullers, who presumably used her building as guild hall and wool market (*CIL* 10.810).

In general, Pompeii ran its own affairs. Samnite and Greek names appear in the lists of magistrates and candidates, which means that under the principate the old native Samnite aristocrats received citizenship and were entitled to hold office, and that descendants of manumitted slaves with Greek names had become prosperous enough to assume the financial obligations of magistracies. The central imperial government did not interfere in the local political or economic affairs of the city, with one important exception. In A.D. 59 a riot broke out in the amphitheater between Pompeiians and visitors from Nuceria—evidence that the amphitheater served a regional audience, not just a local one. People were killed in the melee, and as a result the Roman Senate decreed that the Pompeiians could hold no public gatherings for ten years (Tacitus, *Annals* 14.7).

The Earthquake and Its Aftermath

The most vivid period in the urban life of Pompeii began in A.D. 62, when a serious earthquake inflicted catastrophic damage on the city, and ended in A.D. 79, when the eruption of Vesuvius finally destroyed, buried, and preserved the city. A relief carving in the atrium of the House of Caecilius Jucundus illustrates the first earthquake's damage (Pl. 20): temples, arches, and statues lean crazily on their foundations. Interestingly, the demography of the city seems to have changed significantly between the two eruptions. For various reasons—including, surely, simple fear that more earthquakes would follow—the old landed aristocracy tended to move out of town following the quake of 62. Some private houses were converted to reasonably elegant inns.[3] Others were put to more common uses, which indicate a decline in genteel living standards and a quickened pace of urban life. Gardens were paved over (I.xii.3). Messy, smelly fullers' establishments, and bakeries (Pl. 18), moved into noble houses. The luxurious suburban Villa of the Mysteries (Fig. 21) became a working farm, its elegant chambers divided up into very ordinary spaces. Among Pompeii's total population of between 15,000 and 20,000 there still were wealthy people, of course, but those about whom we have the clearest knowledge were freedmen. With their showpiece of a house (Fig. 15), the Vettii brothers, both freedmen, are a good example of the upper economic class at the time of the eruption in A.D. 79. Another example is the old Samnite family of the Arrii, which is known to have had a major farm in the area, as well as a brick factory. One of their freedmen, C. Arrius Crescens, seems to have lived in House III.iv.2. Another, T. Arrius Polites, is known from a wine jar bearing his name, found in the House of the Moralist (III.iv.3), and from an inscription (*CIL* 4.3152) which records him as a benefactor of the city. It seems likely that both of these freedmen were involved in the wholesale wine business that operated out of the House of the Moralist. The family's old mansion was the Insula Arriana Polliana (VI.vi.1; Fig. 13), but it had become the property of one Cn. Alleus Nigidius Maius, himself a member of an important local trading family, and also known as the sponsor of a pair of gladiatorial spectacles of which he was very proud (*CIL* 4.1177, 1179). By the time the city was destroyed Nigidius no longer lived there. He had entrusted the family mansion as rental property to a slave, Primus (*CIL* 4.138).

At the moment of the eruption in A.D. 79, the Pompeiians were still repairing the damage from the earthquake of A.D. 62, and the progress they had made in those seventeen years gives a remarkable impression of their urban priorities.

In the Forum, they had restored the most necessary buildings first (Pl. 16). At the south end, the Basilica and municipal offices had been thoroughly restored, though the Comitium received more cursory treatment. All the statues had been removed from the Forum, presumably to be repaired, and had not yet been replaced; several new bases had been erected at the southern end, but the statues were never installed. The paving and colonnading of the Forum was only partially completed by 79. Considerable attention had been devoted early on to the eastern side of the Forum. Some repairs had been carried out, no doubt at private expense, on the Building of Eumachia, and two new public precincts, usually identified as the Temple of Vespasian and the Temple of the Lares, were being built to the north, along the east side of the Forum. Both of these were nearing completion in 79, although neither had yet received the final paving and wall decoration. The Market at the northeast corner of the Forum had been thoroughly repaired and was in operation. On the west, the precinct of Apollo was receiving repairs to colonnade, temple, and cult statues, but much remained to be done. The Capitolium temple at the north end of the Forum also was undergoing extensive repairs, but had not yet received its new roof; the cult may have been moved to a temporary site at the smaller and more easily repaired Temple of Jupiter Melichius near the theaters—which would have made it less urgent to finish what in theory should have been the city's most important temple.

In fact, the temple that had been most efficiently and speedily repaired, and even enlarged and elaborated, was the temple of the Egyptian goddess Isis.[4] The devoted activity focused on this Oriental cult contrasts with the more desultory construction work on some of the official cults of the state.

Elsewhere, the top part of the cavea of the large Theater which had collapsed in the earthquake of 62 had not been rebuilt, although the lower rows of seats, along with the stage and the scene building, had been repaired. The collapsed substructures of the Amphitheater had been reconstructed, evidence that the Pompeiians were once more able to enjoy gladiatorial games, and on a more enthusiastic scale than ever. The porticoed square behind the Theater had been converted into a barracks and training ground, and a house close by (V.v.3) into a lodging, for gladiators. The walls of the Palestra had collapsed, and had been quickly repaired; an elaborate swimming pool had been added in the center of the courtyard, although the pipes to supply it with water had not yet been hooked up at the time of the eruption in 79.

An aqueduct had supplied the city—its public fountains, its baths, and many of its private houses—with water ever since the Augustan period, but the earthquake of 62 had severely damaged it. Operations were under way in 79 to expand the system, and the new pool in the palestra was one indication that a better supply was being planned. The new Central Baths, still under construction to serve the growing northeastern residential district, were another. The old Stabian Baths also were being repaired. But while the Pompeiians were waiting for the new water system to be completed, they had to rely on the cisterns and wells that had served the city before the construction of the aqueduct in the first place. As a result, only the Forum Baths (Fig. 22) had been put back into service by 79—partly because they had been less damaged than the Stabian Baths, and partly because they were smaller and could be adequately supplied from the cisterns.

Eighteen

Ostia

According to Roman tradition, King Ancus Marcius established an outpost at the mouth of the Tiber to mine the salt beds there, but no remains of this settlement have been found. The earliest archaeological remains at the site now known as Ostia date from the middle of the fourth century B.C., when the republic established its first military colony there to guard the river mouth against seaborne invaders. During the Second Punic War the colony was useful as a depot for grain being imported from Sardinia, and as the docks and emporium of Rome were developed in the second century B.C., Ostia played an important part in the transshipment of cargoes. The city's main development, however, took place during the principate. First Claudius and then Trajan built large, artificial harbors, which allowed large ships to dock at the port, and soon Ostia replaced Puteoli, on the Bay of Naples, as Italy's most important port.[1] It is our primary archaeological source for the working life of a Roman city in the High Empire.

Commerce and Population

The most important commodity in the economy of Ostia was grain. In the harbor of Ostia it was transloaded onto barges or lighters for immediate shipment upstream to Rome, loaded onto wagons for transfer along the Via Ostiensis into the city, or stored in Ostia to be transferred later. If Meiggs is correct, the population of Ostia during the principate reached approximately 60,000, which implies that there was a considerable local economy based on services— hotels and restaurants, hauling and ship maintenance, and clerical jobs. The heart of Ostia's economic activity was a rectangular precinct of porticoes known as the Piazzale delle Corporazioni. It was part of the theater complex built by Agrippa in the 20s B.C., an ornamental portico of the sort Vitruvius (5.9) prescribed for theaters. Probably it was used under Augustus as a place for commercial activity. Certainly by the time of Claudius, when Ostia was coming into its own as Rome's harbor, this space was elaborated with a Doric/Tuscan colonnade, mosaic floors, and wooden partitions to make *stationes,* office cubicles where the negotiatores could make their business deals and shipping arrangements. A small temple was built on the main axis of the square during the reign of Domitian, and under Commodus the theater and colonnade were rebuilt, the floor level was raised, and new mosaics were laid. Most of these late-second-century mosaics are still in place, and they give us a list of some of the businessmen who worked here: shippers and merchants from many cities of Africa, Sardinia, and Gaul; grain merchants; shippers of timber; river boatmen; tanners; dealers in rope and oakum. The Piazzale was a working place, an exchange built to enable state officials to contact the businessmen who supplied grain to the city and the industries that serviced their ships. It is physical testimony to the importance of shipping in the economy of Ostia, and it and the theater were the material counterparts of those proverbial necessities of Roman city life, bread and circuses.

The inscriptions of the Piazzale help us appreciate the cosmopolitan population of a port city like Ostia, and tomb inscriptions confirm the impression of great variety. We know of individuals from many northern African cities, Spain, Gaul, Asia Minor, Egypt, and other parts of Italy. Many of the foreigners stayed in Ostia only for a while, while their ship was in port, or until they had made enough money to return home. Others stayed, acquired citizenship, and became influential members of the harbor town's civic life. A good example is a certain Publius Lucilius Gamala, a

Syrian who perhaps originally came to Ostia as a slave but was manumitted and gained citizenship. He founded a veritable dynasty of successful businessmen who throughout the principate held public office and contributed *munera* of buildings, games, and banquets (*CIL* 14.375, 376). Others used their money as patrons of the many collegia of businessmen and lower-class folk which formed the focus of urban social life during the principate (*CIL* 14.409).

One touchstone of the cosmopolitan nature of Ostian society is the number and variety of its cults: an elaborate temple complex honoring Cybele, Attis, and Bellona, from Asia Minor, tended by devotees from the upper levels of Ostian society; a more modest temple dedicated to Serapis, from Egypt, built by an individual of private wealth; eleven different temples of Mithras, from Persia, all relatively small and patronized by lower social strata in the late second and the third century A.D.; and isolated dedications to Jupiter Dolichenus, from Syria, and Sabazius, from Thrace. Jews from Palestine had their synagogue near the waterfront. Two interesting anecdotes from the early Christian tradition are set in Ostia.[2] In one, an apologetic essay by Minucius Felix (*Octavius* 2), a Christian and a pagan discuss religion as they stroll along the waterfront. In the other, Augustine (*Confessions* 9.10) remembers the time he stood with his mother in a house at Ostia, looking through a window into an interior garden and talking about faith.

The Early Castrum

The earliest traceable settlement, dated by its tufa walls and pottery to the fourth century B.C., was a rectangular *castrum* of about 5.5 acres (194 m. × 125 m.). Two streets crossed at the center, where presumably the Forum was located. To the east, one of these streets (the *decumanus maximus*) continued toward Rome as the Via Ostiensis. To the west, it split in two just outside the castrum gate. One road, now called the Via della Foce, led northwest to the mouth of the Tiber; the other led southwest toward the seashore. The north-south street extended only a short distance to the north before reaching the riverbank; at the southern gate it connected with a road leading in a southeasterly direction toward the town of Laurentum.

Developments during the Republic

Ostia must have grown considerably in the second century. The part of town northeast of the castrum was declared public property from the decumanus to the riverbank, and given over to public services catering to shippers and traders. To the northwest, houses and temples were built along both sides of the Via della Foce, convenient to the docks at the river. Perhaps the area south and east of the castrum was taken over for residential use by the farmers who owned fields nearby.

At some time in the early first century B.C., perhaps under Sulla, the city received a new set of walls which enclosed 160 acres—not only the construction that had grown up in the past hundred years, but also space for future expansion. Walls of opus reticulatum also allow us to say that during the late second and the first century B.C., many houses of traditional atrium design were built, both within the castrum and in the regions to the west; a marketplace (the Magazzini Repubblicani) was built just inside the eastern gate of the new walls, and it welcomed people arriving from Rome with a portico of tufa piers lining a broad, open square; *horrea,* "warehouses," were built along the south side of the main street (V.xii.2–3); and several temples were built—a sanctuary of Hercules just to the west of the castrum, a row of four small temples along the main street (II.vii.2), and two new temples that gave some regular shape to the northern edge of the Forum.

The Early Principate

Under Augustus, Agrippa constructed the theater and the Piazzale behind it (II.vii), and an imperial freedman named Nymphodotus rebuilt a market outside the west gate of the castrum (IV.v.2). Tiberius added the Temple of Rome and Augustus, which imposed some axial monumentality on the south end of the Forum. It was probably also in his reign that an aqueduct was built to provide a more reliable water supply than had been available from cisterns, a

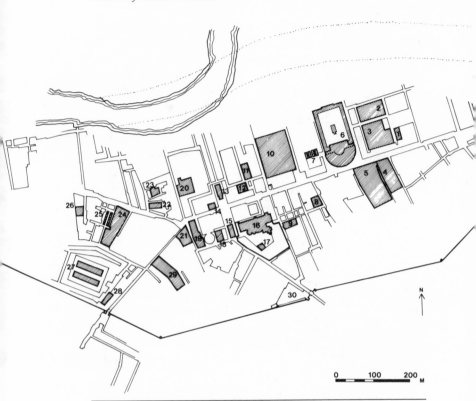

Fig. 26. Ostia: **1** Apartment houses on the Via dei Vigili (II.iii.3–4), **2** Barracks of the Vigiles (II.v.1), **3** Baths of Neptune (II.iv.2), **4** Republican Horrea (V.xii.2), **5** Horrea of Hortensius (V.xii.1), **6** Piazzale delle Corporazioni, Theater (II.vii), **7** Republican temples (II.viii.2), **8** Fullonica on the Via degli Augustali (V.vii.3), **9** House of Fortuna Annonaria (V.ii.8), **10** Grandi Horrea (II.ix.7), **11** House of Diana (I.iii.3), **12** Restaurant (I.ii.5), **13** Capitolium, **14** Curia (or Schola of the Augustales—I.ix.4), **15** Temple of Rome and Augustus, **16** Forum Baths (I.xii.6), **17** Latrine (I.xii.9), **18** House of the Round Temple (I.xi.2), **19** Schola of the Stuppatores (I.x.3), **20** Horrea Epagathiana (I.viii.3), **21** Market (IV.v.2), **22** Temple of Hercules (I.xv.5), **23** House of Amor and Psyche (I.xiv.5), **24** Insula of the Charioteers (III.x.1), Baths of the Seven Sages (III.x.2), Insula of Serapis (III.x.3), **25** Casette-tipo (III.xii–xiii), **26** Temple of Serapis (III.xvii.4), **27** Garden Houses (III.ix), **28** House of the Nymphaeum (III.vi.1), **29** Schola of Trajan (IV.v.16), **30** Temple of Cybele, Attis, and Bellona.

public bath was built east of the theater (under the later Via dei Vigili), and the large Horrea of Hortensius (V.xii.1) were constructed opposite the theater. The elaborate decoration of these Horrea, with Doric columns of tufa both on the street façade and in the inner courtyard, shows how important the grain trade was to ancient Ostia. The emperor Claudius undertook the ambitious project of building a proper harbor, a monument to Roman engineering skill and to his determination to provide a secure grain supply for the Roman populace. He also installed an urban cohort of vigiles to provide police and fire protection. At the same time more warehouse space was added near the docks (the Grandi Horrea, II.ix.7). Under the Flavians we find in Ostia the same kind of practical building activity that characterized their approach to Rome. In the Forum a Basilica was added (I.xi.5), and the building across the street (I.ix.4) was refurbished either as a Curia or, more likely, as a meeting place for the Augustales. Several blocks between the castrum and the Theater were rebuilt, and the ground level was raised to help prevent flood damage.

The Second Century

With the construction of Trajan's new port, Ostia became a boom town (Pl. 22). During Trajan's reign the western end of town, where the road from the port entered, was completely transformed by multistoried insulae built of the brick-faced concrete that was now the standard material of urban construction, at Ostia as well as Rome. During the reigns of Hadrian and Antoninus Pius, building projects were completed at the western end of the city and to the southwest outside the Porta Marina, and the appearance of the city was changed by new brick buildings in every part. Porticoes lined the main streets and added a sense of monumentality. At the northern end of the Forum, the new brick Temple of Jupiter towered over the surrounding apartment houses and completed the formal regularity the Temple of Rome and Augustus had introduced a century earlier. East of the theater, several blocks were rebuilt to produce the Baths of Neptune, new barracks for the vigiles, and a number of apartment buildings (Pl. 27). Antoninus completed these projects of Hadrian and also constructed the grandiose Forum Baths and the so-called Imperial Palace in the northwestern part of town. During these same times private enterprises invested in real estate—the Garden Houses (III.ix; Pl. 28) and other residential units like the House of Diana (I.iii.3; Fig. 17) and the House of Fortuna Annonaria (V.ii.8; Pl. 29), as well as warehouses like the Horrea Epagathiana (I.viii.3) and meeting places like the Schola of Trajan (IV.v.16).

Late Antiquity

By the third century A.D. there were signs that the boom was over. A decline in the population of Rome, the silting up of the old harbor, and the development of Portus as a residential town may explain why buildings in Ostia were not repaired after fires, and why in the fourth century some buildings were converted into single-family dwellings—for example, the House of Amor and Psyche (I.xiv.5; Fig. 16), the House of the Nymphaeum (III.vi.1), and the remodeled House of Fortuna Annonaria (V.ii.8). The life-style of Ostia was changing from the crowded bustle of an active port city to the more restrained pace of an upper-class beach resort.

The development of Ostia during the principate and its decline in the later empire are closely tied to events in the city of Rome. The pace of building in Ostia in the late first century A.D. lagged behind that in Rome by several decades—Rome became a "new city" under Nero; Ostia had to wait until the reigns of Trajan, Hadrian, and Antoninus Pius. But the swampy, mosquito-infested conditions that characterized Ostia at the end of antiquity made it an intolerable place in which to live. As a result, its ruins are so well preserved that they allow us to visualize the streets of imperial Rome better than any evidence we can see in the streets of Rome itself.

Nineteen

Arelate (Arles)

The valley of the Rhone River connects the Mediterranean Sea with the interior of Gaul. On the river in boats, or beside it in carts or on horseback, Roman contacts could spread from the coast to the interior. Where the mouth of the Rhone meanders through a marshy delta, the Greek colonists of Massilia (Marseilles) built the trading outpost Thelinê, and a native Celtic settlement must have been located there too. The Roman general Marius, in his military operations against Massilia and the Teutones in 102 B.C., attempted to provide secure communications with the river by building canals, the Fossae Marianae, through the delta. (No remains of the canals, the Celtic town, or the Greek outpost have been securely identified.) The potential of a site near the mouth of the river to serve as a market and transportation center was first realized by the Romans in 46 B.C., when the colony Iulia Paterna Arelate was founded as a home for veterans of the Sixth Legion, which had helped Julius Caesar in his conquest of Gaul. Like Rome itself, the colony was built on the left bank of the river, at the lowest spot where it could be bridged—in this case about 35 kilometers from the seacoast. This was also the spot where the road connecting Italy with Spain, the Via Iulia Augusta, crossed the Rhone and met the road going north along the east bank of the river toward

Vienna (Vienne), Lugdunum (Lyons), and beyond to the valleys of the Loire, the Seine, and the Rhine. The colony encompassed an exceptionally large amount of land, confiscated from Massilia.

Bridgehead and Market Center

Arelate enjoyed a large and fertile territory, and good communications with its neighbors, so that during its first century the colony's economy was apparently based on agricultural commerce; already in the Augustan period Strabo (4.1.6) called it an important emporium. Another significant economic activity must have been construction, with so many public and private buildings to erect. From the early second century A.D., when Trajan developed Ostia as the major port for bringing grain to Rome, Arelate entered a time of sustained prosperity because of its site at the junction of major land, river, and sea routes. Representatives of Arelate had an office in Ostia, right along with other commercial cities, at the Piazzale delle Corporazioni; the main items of export seem to have been grain, olive oil, and some manufactured items, possibly textiles.

Most of what we know about the city's commercial activities comes from inscriptions. In one (*CIL* 12.672) the imperial *procurator* of the annona for southern Gaul and northwestern Italy is honored as the patron of the five corporations of *navicularii marini,* "overseas shippers," at Arelate. The seagoing vessels of these corporations could continue on up the Rhone as far as Lugdunum, but surely much river-borne cargo was transferred into smaller boats at the Port of Arelate. Many other inscriptions mention corporations of *nautae,* apparently river shippers and barge owners, and *utricularii,* who operated light rafts to make local deliveries and provide ferry service across the river. Service industries also developed; inscriptions mention shipwrights, naval architects, *fabri tignarii* ("carpenters"), and *centonarii* ("ragmen"). Some of these professionals had assigned seating in the amphitheater, and the inscriptions marking their places are helpful in showing their relative status in town (*CIL* 12.714): in the front rows were the decurions and the oil shippers; at the top were the places for the *pastophori,* a religious society, and the *scholastici,* students at the city's important university.[1]

In the fourth century A.D., a technologically unique water mill was constructed at the suburb of Barbegal; it provides hard evidence for an extensive local agricultural industry. Documents of this period also show how active the city's commercial life was. The *Notitia dignitatum occidentis* refers to an imperial mint, a *gynaecium* (official weaving establishment), moneychangers, and the home base of the Rhone River fleet; Ausonius (*Order of Famous Cities* 10) portrays "double Arelate" as Rome on a Gallic scale, enriched by the products of Narbo (Narbonne), Vienna, and the Alps and distributing them across its famous bridge of boats throughout Gaul.

Population: Veterans, Natives, and Freedmen

The veterans who formed the manpower of the original colony of Arelate were for the most part Italians, and we might expect them to form the elite of the political life of the colony. Within a generation of the founding of the colony, however, it is clear that some of the most powerful families were native Gallic ones with rural landholdings throughout the province. In the middle of the first century A.D., for example, we encounter Pompeius Paulinus. His ancestors, says Pliny (*Natural History* 33.143), were from a tribe that wore animal skins, and yet his father was a local notable in Arelate who had enough money to belong to the equestrian order. Pompeius went to Rome and entered the aristocracy there, holding office as imperial legate in Germania in A.D. 55, as consul in a subsequent year, and as administrator of the public revenues in A.D. 62 (Tacitus, *Annals* 13.53.2; 15.18.3). Another important local family was represented by A. Annius Camars (*CIL* 6.449, 12.670), who rose to become praetor in Rome and proconsular legate of the Province of Africa. The career of a certain Titus Iulius shows how a member of the lower classes could rise to the status of the equestrian order; he entered the army, rose through the ranks to acquire the status, and then, when he returned home to Arelate, served as duumvir twice, as augur, and as Priest of Rome and Caesar. Other natives of Arelate, especially in the second century, left home in search of fame and fortune. Favorinus found both: an orator and philosopher, he traveled throughout the intellectual centers of Greece and Asia Minor, a member in good standing of the academic elite; he was not conspicuous for his devotion to his hometown, however, for when the city named him Priest of Rome and Caesar, he tried to evade the honor, which would surely have cost him a lot of money.[2]

Another element in the upper financial class of Arelate was that of the freedmen. We have the epitaphs of two prosperous *navicularii* who were active in civic life and were both freed slaves. Lucius Secundius Eleutherus (*CIL* 12.704) served as a *sevir Augustalis* in Arelate; and Marcus Fronto Euporus (*CIL* 12.982) was *sevir Augustalis* at nearby Aquae Sextiae (Aix), officer of the corporation of the navicularii at Arelate, and patron of several other corporations in neighboring towns. Each of these navicularii had been a slave of an important local family that had connections in many of the surrounding cities, and they illustrate how a loyal and enterprising slave could be manumitted, continue to manage the business affairs of his former master (presumably by marketing the agricultural produce of his estates), and make a lot of money for himself.[3]

As usual, we have less information about the lower classes, which did most of the work in Arelate. There were the sailors, of course, and visitors from overseas. There were bargemen, stevedores, teamsters, shopkeepers, businessmen, and slaves to serve public and private functions.

Double Arelate: Topography

Pottery and architectural finds indicate that a suburb on the right bank of the Rhone, the present-day Trinquetaille, was inhabited from the early days of the colony. Houses with mosaics, warehouses, pottery kilns, a large public building of the first century B.C., and an inscription mentioning the navicularii all indicate a thriving settlement.

The other half of Ausonius's "double Arelate" lay on the left bank. The circuit of its first walls is not known, but it certainly included the hill on which the Theater and Amphitheater stand, and enough of the lower-lying land to the west to accommodate the Forum. In the east, where the road from Rome entered the city, a large gate welcomed travelers. The first public buildings were those that most

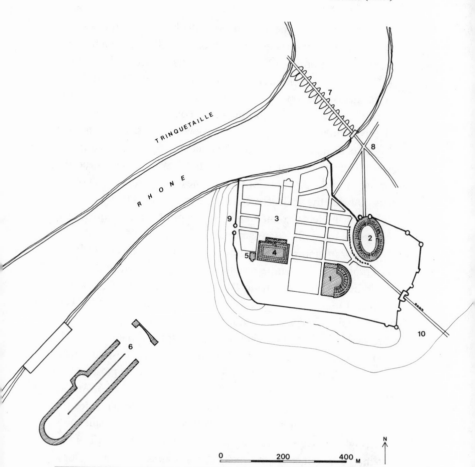

Fig. 27.   Arelate (Arles): **1** Theater, **2** Amphitheater, **3** Forum (?), **4** Cryptoporticus, **5** Apsidal Hall, **6** Circus, **7** Bridge, **8** Site of Arcus Mirabilis, **9** Site of Arch of Constantius, **10** Aliscamps.

clearly characterized a Roman town—the Forum with its Basilica and a temple or two (the exact locations of which are a matter of scholarly guesswork), the well-preserved Theater built to take advantage of the hill, an aqueduct, and the Circus. Under the Forum, or near it, was an underground cryptoporticus, which may have served as a warehouse for grain. During the first and second centuries of the colony's life, the houses of the colony spread far

279

beyond the walls; the Forum was filled with colonnades and statues; the Amphitheater was built on the hill with a slightly different orientation from Forum and Theater, which probably indicates that the grid of streets on top of the hill was slightly different from that on the lower level; a large hall with an apsidal end was constructed west of the Forum; an aqueduct was siphoned across the river through lead pipes; an obelisk was erected in the Circus; a bridge of boats was built across the river; and two triumphal arches were erected, the Arcus Mirabilis, northeast of town near the bridge, and the Arch of Constantius, near the western gate of the city. Outside the walls, cemeteries grew up; that of the Aliscamps, the "Elysian Fields" to the southeast, has produced a uniquely rich harvest of early Christian sarcophagi.

During the fourth and fifth centuries A.D., Arelate enjoyed special prosperity. The emperors often visited it, and contributed new buildings like the surviving Baths of Constantine, which are of standard imperial design. Under the pressure of northern tribes, the capital of Gaul was moved from Augusta Treverorum (Trier) to Arelate in the early fifth century, and in spite of the city's newly acquired importance, new walls enclosed only the most important public buildings on top of the hill, where it would be most easy to put up a defense against attack.[4] Eventually, in A.D. 473, Arelate was captured by the Visigoths. But for almost five centuries the colony was a bright beacon of Romanness in southern Gaul and a thriving entrepôt. Its buildings proclaimed the Roman style of life. Its mosaic pavements, with their scenes from classical mythology, showed the thorough imprint of Roman taste. Its thriving university and its native sons who became famous orators put it in the mainstream of the empire's intellectual life, and the produce of Gaul being exported and the luxury goods being imported through its harbor and its gates bound it economically to the rest of the Roman world.

Twenty

Thamugadi (Timgad)

A s part of his attempt to pacify northern Africa, the emperor Trajan strengthened the armies stationed there and built roads to connect Roman camps and garrisons. The headquarters of the Third Legion, at Lambaesis in Numidia (now southern Algeria), were centrally located to patrol the Aures mountain range and the natives in them, most especially the tribes of the Musulami. The Aures itself was penetrated by a few roads, and on the south side a trading post known as Castellum Dimmidi was built. As a home for soldiers retiring from the Third Legion, Trajan founded Colonia Marciana Traiana Thamugadi, modern Timgad, in A.D. 100. Its location controlled several important valleys leading into the Aures and enjoyed a good source of water, fertile soil, and abundant building stone. A road connected it with Lambaesis, 25 kilometers to the west, and with Thevestis, 100 kilometers to the east.[1]

Population and Commerce

The original colonists were veterans of the legions, and as such they were Roman citizens, although by the second century A.D. only a small percentage of them were native Italians. They had nevertheless become Romanized by their service in the army, and the civic life they led was full of intimations of Rome. They erected the buildings a Roman city needed in order to function properly, and they built altars and temples to such gods and goddesses as Victoria Augusta, Fortuna Augusta, the Genius of the Colony, Jupiter Capitolinus, Mars, and Mercury. Although a city of the second or third rank (with, at its peak, a population of between 10,000 and 15,000), and far removed from the Mediterranean, it could claim an imperial legate, a member of the highest aristocracy in Rome, as its patron. The ruling class, grown rich on agriculture or trade, was honored as the *ordo decurionum;* its members served as magistrates and priests according to the Roman pattern, and donated buildings, games, and banquets to their fellow citizens. The city was full of statues erected to distinguished patrons by clients (*CIL* 8.2393, 2400), a survival of an old Roman institution. Inscriptions introduce us to certain prominent individuals in Thamugadi.

We meet Sertius—whose formal Roman name was Marcus Plotius Faustus and who lived around A.D. 200 and rose to equestrian rank through military service—in the market he constructed at a desirable location just outside the western gate of the castrum. The market was an investment that gave jobs to builders and sculptors and made shops available to small businessmen. It also allowed Sertius to advertise his status and success with multiple statues of himself and his wife (*CIL* 8.2394–2399, 17904–17905). He was a successful businessman, and may have developed a whole tract of real estate along the southwestern edge of the old town. His own house was one of the largest and most elaborate in the colony.[2]

On a statue base found in the Forum we make the acquaintance of Vocontius, whose Roman name was Publius Flavius Pudens Pomponianus (*CIL* 8.2391). He performed, we are told, great military deeds on behalf of his hometown and its citizens. He was also an orator who harmonized Greek eloquence with Roman elegance and expanded the boundaries of literary expression.[3]

Beneath the exalted status of such retired officers who found satisfaction in business and letters was the usual anonymous crowd of small businessmen, manual laborers, and slaves. Some of them were able to afford comfortable houses in the old quarter of town. Some had their own shops, others worked for patrons or as occasion offered. Some were natives, of Berber stock, who came to trade and settled in.[4]

All our evidence for the economic life of this colony is indirect, but we can be sure that agriculture was important. The proliferation of markets, paid for and managed by private enterprises, demonstrates the town's economic vitality. Each colonist received a plot of land to farm, and the town's location guaranteed it some role as a center of trade. An industrial quarter, consisting of small workshops for bronze, glass, and pottery, has been identified just outside the southwestern corner of the castrum.

The Castrum

In the original plan of the castrum at Thamugadi, a wall enclosed a square 355 meters (1,200 Roman feet) on a side. At the north, the main highway from Cirta entered the castrum to become one of the main streets, the kardo maximus. Like the via praetoria of a military camp, it led to the center of town, in front of the Forum, which in turn occupied the position of the praetorium. There the kardo intersected the main east-west street, conventionally referred to as the decumanus maximus, in the position of a camp's via principalis; both the kardo maximus and the decumanus, as well as the main street toward the southern suburbs, were paved in a bluish limestone to distinguish them from the side streets, paved in a more ordinary sandstone.

The Forum was set off from the decumanus maximus by a portico and a row of shops, and it was approached by a broad flight of twelve steps. It too was paved with blue limestone, surrounded by a two-story portico of Corinthian columns and open-fronted exedrae, and filled with altars, inscriptions, and statues. One of these portrayed the satyr Marsyas; his presence recalled the statue of Marsyas in the Forum Romanum, and was the badge of the city's colonial status. The usual necessities of civic life were there. On the east side of the Forum stood the Basilica; on the west, the Curia, civic offices, and an unusually small temple. A latrine was conveniently located outside the main entrance. To the south the Theater, built against the slope of a low hill in the middle of the second

Fig. 28. Thamugadi (Timgad): **A** Arches, **B** Baths, **C** Capitolium, **E** Christian Buildings, **F** Forum, **G** Temple of the Genius of the Colony, **H** House of Sertius, **J** Maison des Jardinières, **L** Library, **M** Markets, **T** Theater.

century, could accommodate about four thousand spectators; above it to the east was a plaza with a couple of small temples.

Private houses tended to be compact, their one or two stories arranged efficiently around a small courtyard. A more expansive tradition in older cities in Africa permitted large colonnaded peristyles, but at Thamugadi only a few houses were so generous. One was the House of Sertius, already mentioned; another was along the east side of the Forum on the decumanus. This Maison des Jardinières, as it is known in the modern literature, was built around an old traditional atrium courtyard filled with plants, and it seems to have been some sort of official residence.

Growth beyond the Castrum

The castrum enclosure may have been adequate for the first contingent of colonists, numbering perhaps several hundred, but almost immediately the town outgrew its original walls. Outside the gates the main roads wandered off in directions of their own, and new construction followed them. By the middle of the second century, the city had already grown about 200 meters eastward, where a new arch was built in A.D. 146. There was corresponding expansion beyond the northern and southern gates, and more extensive development to the west along the Lambaesis highway. The earliest important building outside the walls was the temple to Jupiter known as the Capitolium, an ideological necessity in a city of colonial status. When the community got around to building it in about A.D. 160, there was no room in the grid of the castrum for a temple of the appropriate scale, so it was located in a dominating position about 150 meters south of the western road. A temple to the Genius of the Colony was built north of the road, just outside the western gate of the castrum. By the beginning of the third century, the city had no less than twelve public baths scattered through every part of town; they ranged in scale from intimate to vast, and the larger ones imitated the axial design of the imperial thermae at Rome.

The years of the Severan dynasty (A.D. 193–235) saw much new building, as the Severi encouraged the development of the African cities. One of the most conspicuous landmarks of this period was a triumphal arch built on the site of the old west gate of the castrum, marking the transition between the old town and the newer development along the Lambaesis road. South of the arch the old wall itself, which no longer served any useful purpose, was torn down. The long, narrow plot made available was immediately filled with luxury houses. Since Sertius built his house at the southern end and his market at the northern end of this strip, it seems likely that this was another of his ventures into real estate development.

On the main western road, Sertius's market faced the Temple of the Genius of the Colony across the street. Farther along was a fountain donated by one Publius Julius Liberalis. The whole street was turned into an elaborate showplace, with raised sidewalks and colonnades, stretching about 350 meters westward from the Severan Arch to an older triumphal arch dedicated to Marcus Aurelius and Lucius Verus. South of the Capitolium an open space which probably served as a public market was embellished. Nearby a spring was beautified at public expense in A.D. 214; an inscription (*CIL* 8.2370) mentions bronze grillwork, porticoes, paintings, and marble paving. Farther south, near a medieval fort, was a precinct with a pool, gardens, and shrines to Serapis-Aesculapius, Dea Africa, and some other god with local associations.

The town continued to flourish into later antiquity. The Capitolium was repaired (*CIL* 8.2388) and its fallen columns were re-erected in A.D. 365, and new baths of imperial type were built at the north end of town. Christian monuments are plentiful, including a basilica church, one of the largest in Africa, which may have served as headquarters for the Donatists during the schism that rent the African church in the fourth century A.D. We know from inscriptions that in general the prosperity and political life of Thamugadi continued well into the late empire; like other cities of northern Africa, it remained a bastion of urban culture and the Roman tradition long after what we usually think of as the fall of the empire.

PLATES

List of Plates

Pl. 1.   Rome: Palatine, model of early huts (Davico)

Pl. 2. Rome: Horrea Agrippiana, reconstruction (Gismondi)

Pl. 3. Rome: Forum Augustum, model

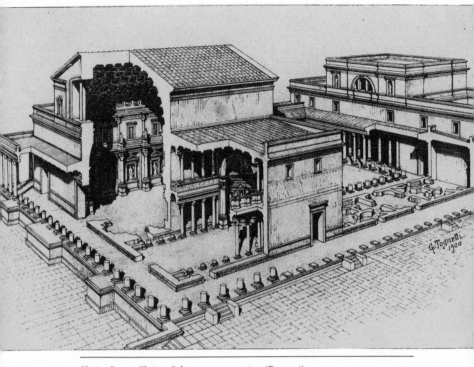

Pl. 4. Rome: Flavian Palace, reconstruction (Tognetti)

Pl. 5. Rome: Mercatus Traiani, reconstruction

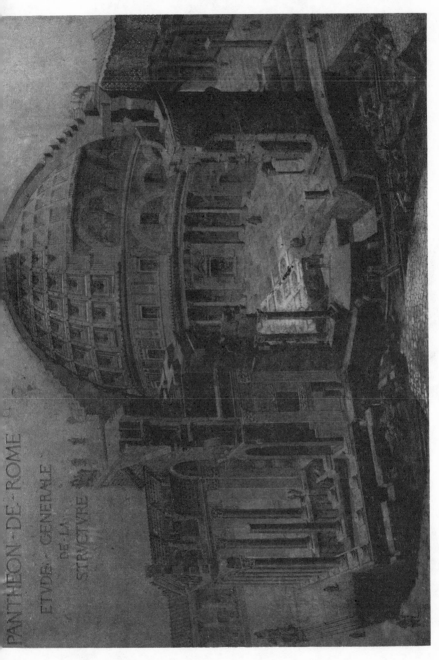

PANTHEON · DE · ROME

ETVDE · GENERALE
DE LA
STRVCTVRE

Pl. 7.   Rome: Marble Plan, residential and commercial zone

Pl. 6 *(opposite)*.   Rome: Pantheon, general view (Chédanne)

Pl. 9. Rome: Capitoline, model

Pl. 8 (opposite). Rome: Model, view from Campus Martius toward Colosseum

Pl. 10. Rome: Model, Amphitheatrum Flavium (Colosseum) and Thermae Traiani

Pl. 11. Rome: Model, zone of the Porta Praenestina

Pl. 12A.　Rome: Temple of Venus
Genetrix, Forum Iulium, coin

Pl. 12B.　Rome: Temple of Concordia,
Forum Romanum, coin

Pl. 12C.　Rome: Temple of Venus et
Roma, coin

Pl. 12D.　Rome: Colosseum, coin

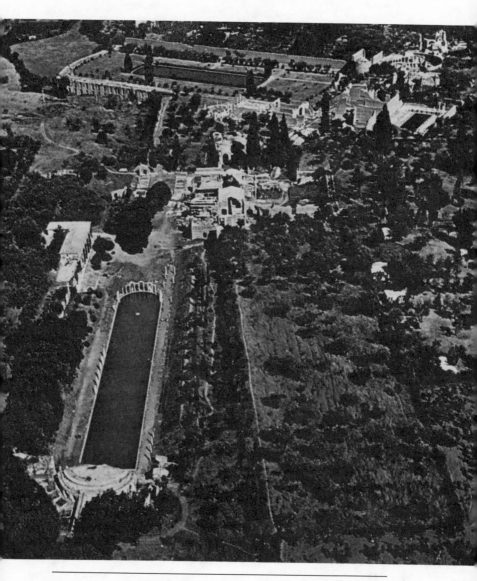

Pl. 13. Tivoli: Hadrian's Villa

Pl. 14. Cosa: Arx, temples in the late second century B.C., reconstruction

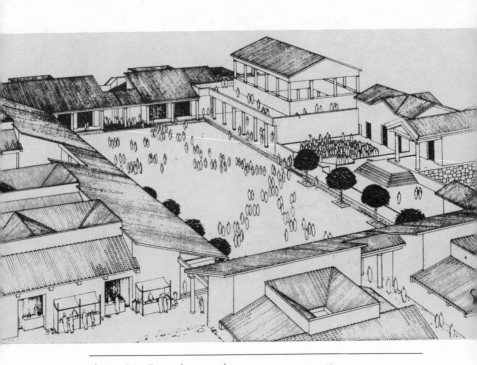

Pl. 15. Cosa: Forum, late second century B.C., reconstruction

Pl. 16. Pompeii: Forum, aerial view (north is at upper right)

Pl. 17.   Pompeii: Via dell'Abbondanza, northern side

Pl. 18. Pompeii: Bakery

Pl. 19. Pompeii: House of Menander, entrance and atrium

Pl. 20.   Pompeii: House of Caecilius Iucundus, lararium

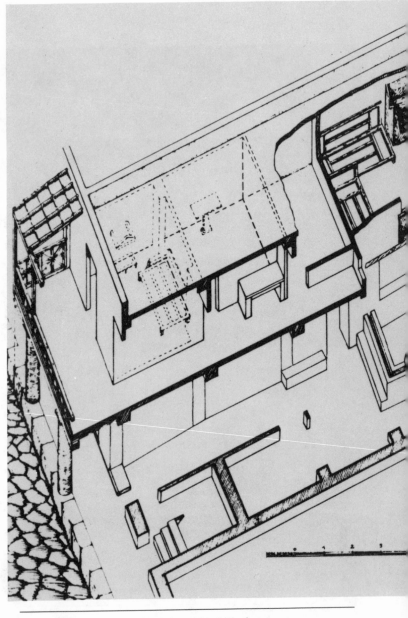

Pl. 21.   Herculaneum: Casa a graticcio, section (Maiuri)

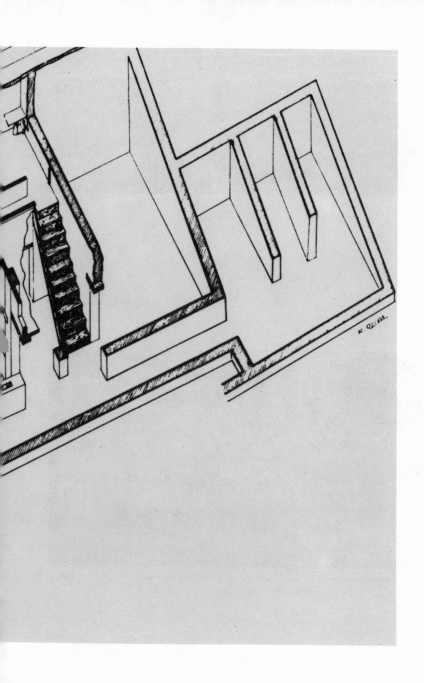

Pl. 22.   Ostia: Sarcophagus with harbor and tavern scenes

Pl. 23.   Ostia: Sarcophagus of poultry vendor

Pl. 24.   Ostia: Restaurant ("Thermopolium")

Pl. 25. Ostia: Fullonica on the Via degli Augustali

Pl. 26 (opposite). Ostia: Schola of the Stuppatores, plan

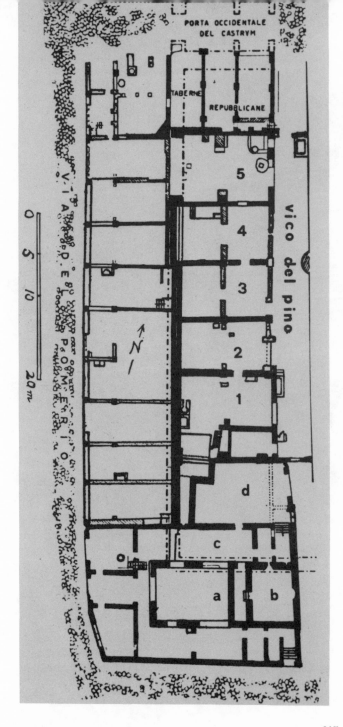

PORTA OCCIDENTALE
DEL CASTRVM

TABERNE

REPUBBLICANE

5

4

3

2

1

d

c

a   b

vico del pino

N

0

5

10

20m

V·I·A ... P·D·E ... P·O·M·E·R·I·O ...

317

Pl. 27. Ostia: Apartment Houses on the Via dei Vigili (II.iii.3–4)

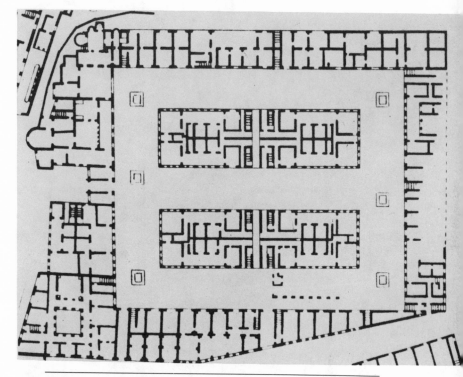

Pl. 28. Ostia: Garden Houses, plan

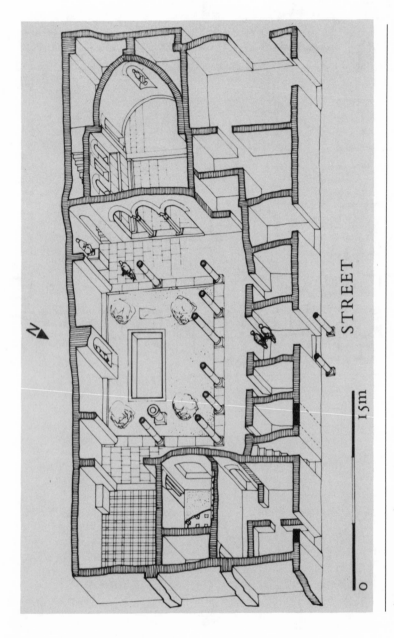

STREET

N

0 ⌐ 15m

Pl. 29.   Ostia: House of Fortuna Annonaria, section

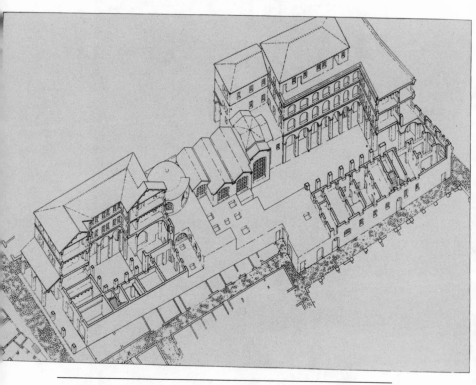

Pl. 30. Ostia: Insula of Serapis, Baths of the Seven Sages, and Insula of the Charioteers

Pl. 31. Ostia: Isola Sacra, graves

Notes

Abbreviations used in the text and notes are as follows:

AJA   *American Journal of Archaeology*

ANRW   *Aufstieg und Niedergang der Römischen Welt*

CIL   *Corpus Inscriptionum Latinarum*

IG   *Inscriptiones Graecae*

JRS   *Journal of Roman Studies*

MAAR   *Memoirs of the American Academy in Rome*

MDAI(R) *Mitteilungen des deutschen Archaeologischen Instituts (Römische Abteilung)*

PDAR   *Pictorial Dictionary of Ancient Rome*

S.H.A.   Scriptores Historiae Augustae

TAPA   *Transactions of the American Philological Association*

Introduction

1. Examples of works in English that have principally a topographical orientation: S. B. Platner and T. Ashby, *Topographical Dictionary of Ancient Rome* (Oxford, 1929); D. Dudley, *Urbs Roma* (Aberdeen, 1967); E. Nash, *Pictorial Dictionary of Ancient Rome* (New York, 1961, 1968), hereafter cited as *PDAR*; P. Grimal, *Roman Cities* (Eng. ed. by Michael Woloch, Madison, 1982). Historical orientation: E. Bacon, *Design of Cities* (New York, 1967); J. B. Ward-Perkins, *Cities of Greece and Italy: Planning in Classical Antiquity* (New York, 1974); the individual articles in *The Princeton Encyclopedia of*

Classical Sites, ed. R. Stillwell, W. L. MacDonald, and M. H. McAllister (Princeton, 1977). Typological orientation: E. Nash, *Roman Towns* (New York, n.d.); A. Boëthius, *The Golden House of Nero* (Ann Arbor, 1960); M. Wheeler, *Roman Art and Architecture* (Oxford, 1964); W. L. MacDonald, *The Architecture of the Roman Empire* (New Haven, 1965, 1986); G. Rickman, *Roman Granaries and Store Buildings* (Cambridge, 1971). Demographic orientation: P. A. Brunt, *Italian Manpower 225 B.C.–A.D. 14* (Oxford, 1971); K. Hopkins, *Conquerors and Slaves* (Cambridge, 1978); C. Nicolet, *The World of the Citizen in Republican Rome* (Eng. tr. Berkeley, 1980). Institutional orientation: N. D. Fustel de Coulanges, *The Ancient City* (Eng. tr. London, 1873; repr. Baltimore, 1980); L. Homo, *Roman Political Institutions from City to State* (Eng. tr. New York, 1962); M. Hammond, *The City in the Ancient World* (Cambridge, Mass., 1972, with a long annotated bibliography); M. I. Finley, *The Ancient Economy* (Berkeley, 1974). Semiotic orientation: K. Lynch, *The Image of the City* (Cambridge, Mass., 1960); D. Preziosi, *The Semiotics of the Built Environment* (Bloomington, Ind., 1979). More rounded social analyses in L. Homo, *Rome impériale et l'urbanisme dans l'antiquité* (Paris, 1951); M. Clavel and P. Lévêque, *Villes et structures urbaines dans l'Occident romain* (Paris, 1971); F. Castagnoli, *Topografia e urbanistica di Roma antica* (Bologna, 1969); P. Veyne, ed., *A History of Private Life: From Pagan Rome to Byzantium* (Eng. tr. Cambridge, Mass., 1987).

2. To give just one example, we can begin to understand the place of the Pantheon in the life of Rome in the second century A.D. because of detailed studies of the physical fabric (how does the dome stay up?), the intellectual context (what does a dome symbolize?), the architectural tradition (was Hadrian himself the architect?), and the historical evidence, gleaned from documents and discovered in excavations, for the plan of its predecessor (what did Agrippa have to do with it?).

3. G. Carettoni, A. M. Colini, L. Cozza, and G. Gatti, *La pianta marmorea di Roma antica* (Rome, 1960); cf., for example, our Plate 7.

Chapter 1. Earliest Rome

1. Archaeological evidence from the valley between the Palatine and the Capitoline shows that Rome was indeed inhabited as early as the fourteenth century B.C. The remains are typical of central Italy at this time, and do not in themselves support the legend's emphasis on immigrants from Greece and Asia Minor. Yet the Romans themselves pointed to the cult of Hercules in the Forum Boarium, which even in historical times used Greek rather than Italic ceremonial. See J. Heurgon, *The Rise of Rome to 264 B.C.* (Eng. tr. Berkeley, 1973), pp. 72–75, 128–132; and in general M. Pallottino, ed., *Naissance de Rome* (Paris, 1977).

2. Plutarch says that the founding ritual was Etruscan. Excavations at the Latin colony of Cosa have revealed a *mundus* beneath a rectangular viewing platform for taking the auspices. See F. E. Brown, "Cosa II," *MAAR* 26 (1960): 9–16; Chapter 16, page 255, of this volume; and Plutarch, *Romulus* 11.

3. It was from this spot that the young men known as *Luperci* started their ritual race every February 15; this celebration of the *Lupercalia,* familiar from the opening of Shakespeare's *Julius Caesar,* recalls a type of rustic religion concerned about fertility, for in it young men ran about naked, striking women with leather thongs. The route of the Luperci probably followed the *pomerium* of Romulus's city. A. K. Michels, "The Topography and Interpretation of the Lupercalia," *TAPA* 84 (1953): 35–59, argues that at least in historical times the route did not go around the Palatine, but started from the Lupercal, ran to the Forum Romanum, and then dodged up and down the Sacra Via. H. H. Scullard, *Festivals and Ceremonies of the Roman Republic* (Ithaca, 1981), p. 77, suggests that the course originally circumscribed the old settlement on the Palatine, but had been shortened by Caesar's time to include only the Forum Romanum and Sacra Via.

4. G. Pugliese Carratelli, "Lazio, Roma e Magna Grecia prima del secolo quarto a.C.," *Parola del Passato* 23 (1968): 321–347; C. Ampolo, "Su alcuni mutamenti sociali nel Lazio tra l'VIII e il V secolo," *Dialoghi di Archeologia* 4 (1970): 37–99, esp. 46–48.

5. These early finds at the church of Saint Omobono were found in fill of a later period. F. Coarelli, *Guida archeologica di Roma* (Rome, 1974), pp. 281–284, suggests that they are from an early settlement on the Capitoline.

6. Sources included archaeological remains, family historical memories, inferences from then-current knowledge of customs and neighboring peoples, and folk tale motifs.

7. The tradition saw Romulus (and his Sabine coregent, Titus Tatius) as chiefly concerned with the basic social and political organization of the city, Numa Pompilius (whose name is Sabine) as concerned with the introduction of religious customs, and Tullus Hostilius as concerned with wars over neighboring Alban tribes. Ancus Marcius won further victories and settled the defeated peoples in the outlying hills. See Heurgon, *The Rise of Rome,* pp. 128–155, 244–250.

8. On these festivals, see Scullard, *Festivals and Ceremonies,* pp. 90–91, 120–121, 203–204.

9. On the economy of Rome in the period of the kings, see the brief discussion in R. Bianchi-Bandinelli, *Rome: The Center of Power* (Eng. tr. New York, 1970), pp. 17–20. Bakers did not appear, it seems, until the second century B.C.

10. The literary tradition asserts that King Tullius Hostilius built the

first Senate House, named in his honor the Curia Hostilia. In front of it were the curved steps of the Comitium, where the citizen assembly gathered. See Chapter 7, page 109. The precinct of the Lapis Niger near the site of the Curia seems to memoralize some royal holding.

11. The earlier dates are those of H. Müller-Karpe, *Zur Stadtwerdung Roms* (Heidelberg, 1962), adopted by J. Heurgon, "Archéologie et critique historique: La Rome des Rois," in *Naissance de Rome,* ed. Pallottino. The later dates are those of E. Gjerstad, *Early Rome,* vol. 4 (Lund, 1966).

Chapter 2. Expansion under the Republic

1. On these early temples, see G. Pugliese Carratelli, "Lazio, Roma e Magna Grecia prima del secolo quarto a.C.," *Parola del Passato* 23 (1968): 321–347; C. Ampolo, "Analogie e rapporti fra Atene e Roma arcaica," *Parola del Passato* 26 (1971): 443–460; and in general I. Dondero and P. Pensabene, eds., *Roma repubblicana fra il 509 e il 270 a.C.* (Rome, 1982).

2. On the institution of the *clientela,* see Chapter 6, page 92.

3. The chronological distribution of Greek pottery at the site of Rome in the sixth and fifth centuries B.C. is significant: 575–530, 103 fragments of Greek pottery; 530–500, 203 fragments; 500–450, 145 fragments; 450–400, only 11 fragments. Cf. E. Gjerstad, *Early Rome,* vol. 4 (Lund, 1966), pp. 514–518; and F. Coarelli, *Roma medio repubblicana* (Rome, 1973), pp. 96–99.

4. The temples of Fortuna and Mater Matuta at Saint Omobono in the Forum Boarium, associated with Servius Tullius, one of the Etruscan kings, seem to have been destroyed in this period.

5. M. G. Morgan, "Villa Publica and Magna Mater," *Klio* 55 (1973): 231–245; G. Tosi, "La Villa pubblica di Roma nelle fonti litterarie e numismatiche," *Atti Istituto Veneto* 135 (1977) 413–426.

6. The more important families provided a model for the republic even in such matters as the conduct of war; cf. the independent foreign policy against Veii waged in the fifth century B.C. by the *gens* of the Fabii (Livy 2.48–50).

7. The near-total physical destruction of Rome by the Gauls is asserted by the ancient sources (Diodorus 14.116.6–9; Livy 5.55, 6.1; Plutarch, *Numa* 1), and most scholars, accepting this, have identified certain ruins with the Gallic sack: Gjerstad, *Early Rome,* vol. 3 (Lund, 1960), p. 220. F. Castagnoli, "Topografia e urbanistica di Roma nel IV secolo a.C.," *Studi Romani* 22 (1974): 425–427, calls all this evidence into question.

8. Literature tells us of Iuno Regina on the Aventine, Iuno Lucina on the Esquiline, Iuno Moneta on the Capitoline, Salus on the Quirinal (on which, see Castagnoli, "Topografia e urbanistica di Roma," pp. 429–430), and Vica Pota on the Velia. Archaeology shows us Temple C at the Largo

Argentina, the largest temple built since the founding of the republic (Fig. 4).

9. Mars on the Via Appia, Fortuna Muliebris on the Via Latina, and Fors Fortuna on the Via Portuensis.

10. Venus, Aesculapius, Iuppiter Victor, Victoria, Minerva, Hercules, Neptunus, Magna Mater.

11. On triumphal painting, see M. Borda, *La pittura romana* (Rome, 1958), pp. 149–151.

12. On the Hellenistic derivation of the Victory gods, see S. Weinstock, "Victor and Invictus," *Harvard Theological Review* 50 (1957): 211–247.

13. On the career of Marcus Fulvius Flaccus, who brought 2,000 statutes from Etruria to decorate Rome, see Coarelli, *Roma medio repubblicana,* p. 104, and M. Torelli, "Il donario di M. Fulvio Flacco nell'area di S. Omobono," *Quaderni dell'Istituto di Topografia* 5 (1968): 71ff.

14. For Rome, we have only the names and an occasional stray literary reference, but there are architectural remains of such atria surrounding the forum at the colony of Cosa. See our Plate 15 and F. E. Brown, *Cosa: The Making of a Roman Town* (Ann Arbor, 1980), pp. 35–37. K. Lehmann-Hartleben, "Maenianum and Basilica," *American Journal of Philology* 59 (1938): 280–296, suggests that these atria were some surviving part of the houses of the nobility that stood near and around the Forum Romanum as late as the second century B.C.

15. The records mention dedications on the Aventine, Circus Maximus, Porta Capena, Palatine, Caelian, Carinae, Velia, Esquiline, Quirinal, Forum Romanum, Capitoline, Campus Martius, Forum Holitorium, and Tiber Island; see H. H. Scullard, *Festivals and Ceremonies of the Roman Republic* (Ithaca, 1981), pp. 277–279.

16. Many experts now accept the identification of the rectangular temple in the Forum Boarium as that of Portunus, originally vowed in 260 B.C. and rebuilt in its present form in the early second century. See F. Coarelli, *Guida archeologica di Roma* (Verona, 1974), pp. 278–279.

17. Here the plebeian assembly met, the Plebeian Games were celebrated, and ambitious politicians soon built three new temples, to Volcanus, Hercules Custos, and Neptunus. See T. P. Wiseman, "The Circus Flaminius," *Papers of the British School at Rome* 42 (1974): 3–26.

18. Servius on *Aeneid* 9.52. The historical accuracy of the Bellona anecdote has been called into question; see J. W. Rich, *Declaring War in the Roman Republic* (Brussels, 1976), pp. 57 n. 3, 127 n. 35.

19. During the second century B.C., even the names of these noble generals became billboards advertising their military conquests—for example, Publius Cornelius Scipio Africanus, Quintus Caecilius Metellus Balearicus, Quintus Caecilius Metellus Macedonicus, Quintus Caecilius Metellus Numidicus, Gnaeus Cornelius Lentulus Gaetulicus, Lucius

Mummius Achaicus. On the competition among generals in 146 B.C., see J. E. Stambaugh, "The Functions of Roman Temples," *ANRW* 2.16.1 (1978): 584.

20. It has been tentatively identified with the temple of the Lares Permarini, vowed by Marcus Aemilius Regillus after a victory over the Greek king Antiochus in 190 B.C., and dedicated in the Campus Martius by M. Aemilius Lepidus during his censorship in 179. See F. Coarelli, "L'identificazione dell'Area sacra dell'Argentina," *Palatino* 12 (1968): 365–378.

21. On the urbanism of the Circus Flaminius area, see P. Gros, *Architecture et société à Rome et en Italie centro-méridionale aux deux derniers siècles de la république* (Brussels, 1978), pp. 37–39; M. J. Boyd, "The Porticoes of Metellus and Octavia, and Their Two Temples," *Papers of the British School at Rome* 21 (1953): 152–159; M. G. Morgan, "The Porticus of Metellus: A Reconsideration," *Hermes* 99 (1971): 480–505; B. Olinder, *Porticus Octavia in Circo Flaminio* (Stockholm, 1974), pp. 83–124.

22. The Porticus Octavia, built in 168 B.C. by Gnaeus Octavius, had two rows of columns, their Corinthian capitals sheathed in bronze. The Porticus Metelli was built in 146 to surround the Temples of Iuno Regina and Iuppiter Stator.

23. One still reached the Tiber Island by boat or ford, although it is worth noting that two new temples were built there in 194 B.C., both presumably small, to Vediovis and Faunus. They joined the third-century temples to Aesculapius and Tiberinus.

24. These arches celebrated Lucius Stertinius's victories in Spain in 196 B.C. (Livy 33.27.4).

25. Hellenistic façades, decoration, and porticoes also appeared on the Capitoline in this period. The great temple was gradually refurbished: in 193 B.C., golden shields were added to the pediment; in 179 the old wooden columns were refinished or replaced to produce an impression of Greek marble (Livy 40.51.3); in 149 a mosaic pavement was installed (Pliny, *Natural History* 36.185); in 146 the ceiling was gilded (Pliny 33.57). In 174 the Clivus Capitolinus was paved and a portico was built beside it (Livy 41.27.7). In 159 other porticoes were added by Scipio Nasica (Velleius Paterculus 2.1).

26. Artists came to Rome in the train of generals and politicians in the first half of the second century B.C.: Livy 39.22.1–2, 10; Diodorus 31.18; Pliny, *Natural History* 34.34; 35.115, 135; Plutarch, *Aemilius Paulus* 6.5; F. Coarelli, "Classe dirigente romana e arti figurative," *Dialoghi di Archeologia* 4 (1970): 241–265, esp. 245–257.

27. During and after the Hannibalic War, the government had to step in to distribute grain to a hungry population in 203, 201, 200, and 196 B.C.— A. Toynbee, *Hannibal's Legacy,* vol. 2 (London, 1965), pp. 337–339. Shortages are also documented in the 130s B.C.—H. C. Boren, "The Urban

Side of the Gracchan Economic Crisis," *American Historical Review* 63 (1958): 890–902; and idem, *The Gracchi* (New York, 1968), pp. 42–45.

28. Livy 34.2–4 reports Cato's speech in 195 B.C. against the repeal of a sumptuary law, the Lex Oppia of 215 B.C., which restricted the jewelry women could wear. Other laws in 182 and 179 B.C. limited expenses at games (Livy 40.44.11–12). In 181 B.C. the Lex Orchia limited the number of guests at a single dinner party (Macrobius, *Saturnalia* 3.17.2), and in 154 B.C. a law forbade the erection of a permanent stone theater (Valerius Maximus, *Memorabilia* 2.4.2.).

29. This is the type of gentleman-farmer addressed by Cato in his work *On Agriculture*, and also the type that seems to appear in the comedies. An example is Sostrata in Terence's *Mother-in-Law*, an upper-class wife who is prepared to get out of the city and retire to a simple life in the country (586–612).

Chapter 3. The Late Republic, 146–44 B.C.

1. M. G. Morgan, "The Introduction of the Aqua Marcia into Rome, 144–140 B.C.," *Philologus* 122 (1978): 25–58.

2. F. Coarelli, "Public Building in Rome between the Second Punic War and Sulla," *Papers of the British School at Rome* 45 (1977): 1–23, reviews the extensive building in the second and early first century B.C. and sees it as a symptom of a growing population; he denies that the reforms of the Gracchi can be viewed as make-work projects to contend with unemployment.

3. Up until this time, service in the legions was reserved for men of rural property.

4. D. E. Strong and J. B. Ward-Perkins, "The Round Temple in the Forum Boarium," *Papers of the British School at Rome* 28 (1960): 7–32; F. Rakob and W. D. Heilmeyer, *Der Rundtempel am Tiber in Rom* (Mainz, 1973); F. Coarelli, "Classe dirigente romana e arti figurative," *Dialoghi di Archeologia* 4 (1970): 241–265, esp. 254–255, 263–264. Attempts to interpret the adoption of a classicizing, Neo-attic style for Roman monuments around 100 B.C. are necessarily speculative. For example, Coarelli, ibid., pp. 264–265, sees it as a conscious choice of the ruling class, the cultivated art of an elite determined to set itself apart from the plebeian traditions of Italic art; cf. R. Bianchi Bandinelli, "Arte plebea," *Dialoghi di Archeologia* 1 (1967): 7–19. With a different emphasis, P. Gros, *Architecture et société à Rome et en Italie centro-méridionale aux deux derniers siécles de la République* (Brussels, 1978), pp. 39–41, suggests that the taste for Greek style was fostered by equestrian *negotiatores,* while the senatorial aristocracy tended at this period to build more conservative temples of old-fashioned material and design.

5. L. Richardson, "Honos et Virtus and the Sacred Way," *AJA* 82 (1978): 240–246, locates this temple on the Velia, just off the Forum Romanum, and suggests that its architect may have been Q. Mucius Scaevola.

6. Pliny, *Natural History* 36.45 says that Sulla took the Athenian columns for the temple on the Capitoline. We know that the Athenian columns were Corinthian, however, and since a coin of 43 B.C. shows the Capitoline temple with Doric columns, it is possible that they were never actually installed—M. E. Blake, *Ancient Roman Construction in Italy* (Washington, D.C., 1947), pp. 51, 52, 140. Even if we should trust the coin rather than Pliny, the point remains the same: Sulla and Catulus changed the look of the Capitoline temple from Etruscan to Greek.

7. In addition, Sulla or his lieutenants also built smaller temples: to Hercules Custos at the Circus Maximus, and to Hercules Sullanus on the Esquiline.

8. On the importance of the Tabularium, see G. Ch. Picard, *Rome et les villes d'Italie, des Gracques à la mort d'Auguste* (Paris, 1978), pp. 94–96; A. Garcia y Bellido, *Arte romano* (Madrid, 1979), pp. 61–63.

9. On the rebuilding of the Forum Romanum under Sulla and Catulus, see E. B. Van Deman, "The Sullan Forum," *JRS* 12 (1922): 1–31.

10. Aulus Gellius 10.1.7–8 tells us that when Pompey was preparing for the dedication of his theater, he was not sure how to write the Latin phrase "consul for the third time"—whether with an accusative, "consul tertium," or with an ablative, "consul tertio." He turned to the experts for help, and Cicero's advice was that he should abbreviate it "consul tert."

11. The space for public works was severely limited by the encroaching residential areas: cf. the trouble Caesar, Cicero, and Oppius had in buying property for the Forum Iulium. Furthermore, Caesar is criticized (Dio Cassius, *Roman History* 43.49) for demolishing numerous houses and the temple of Spes to make room for his theater next to the Forum Holitorium. So it was clear that more space was needed, both for the public buildings the developing empire would need and for housing the growing population. It would have been dangerous to sacrifice the healthful and attractive gardens—private property, at that—which ringed the city; Trans-Tiber was too small and already overpopulated; the space south of the Aventine was full of warehouses next to the port. The Campus Martius, however, was available, measured almost 10 square kilometers (4 square miles), was reasonably empty, and was near the city center.

12. Local parallels to the ground plan of the Forum Iulium are the Porticus Octaviae, Porticus Metelli, and Porticus Minucia, and the temple complexes at Tibur (Hercules Victor) and Gabii. The connection with the ruler-cult shrines of the Greek East, particularly of the Ptolemaic territories at Alexandria and Cyrene, is developed by E. Sjöqvist, "Kaisareion," *Opuscula Romana* 1 (1954): 86–108.

13. See M. Cary, "The Municipal Legislation of Julius Caesar," *JRS* 27 (1937): 48–53. The concept of the city as a collection of random pieces in distinction from the concept of the city as an entity with an overall unifying design is developed by C. Rowe and F. Koetter, *Collage City* (Cambridge, Mass., 1978).

14. E. Rawson, "Cicero the Historian and Cicero the Antiquarian," *JRS* 62 (1972): 33–45.

15. H. Cancik, "Rome as Sacred Landscape, Varro, and the End of Republican Religion in Rome," *Visible Religion: Annual for Religious Iconography* 4–5 (1985–1986): 250–265.

16. For a discussion of Catullus's place in his social milieu, see T. P. Wiseman, *Catullus and His World: A Reappraisal* (Cambridge, 1985), esp. pp. 92–129.

17. T. P. Wiseman, "The Two Worlds of Titus Lucretius," *Cinna the Poet and Other Roman Essays* (Leicester, 1974), pp. 11–43.

Chapter 4. The Augustan City

1. Surveys of Augustan Rome are found in P. MacKendrick, *The Mute Stones Speak* (New York, 1960), ch. 6; H. T. Rowell, *Rome in the Augustan Age* (Norman, Okla., 1962), esp. ch. 4; G. Ch. Picard, *Rome et les villes d'Italie, des Gracques à la mort d'Auguste* (Paris, 1979); J. B. Ward-Perkins, *Roman Imperial Architecture* (Harmondsworth, 1981), pp. 21–44. For a more detailed account, see F. W. Shipley, "Chronology of the Building Operations in Rome from the Death of Caesar to the Death of Augustus," *MAAR* 9 (1931): 7–60.

2. F. Millar, "Triumvirate and Principate," *JRS* 63 (1973): 50–67, shows that we should not overstate the case: the *res publica* was "restored" (*restituta*), in the sense that the state was set once more in a situation where it could function, but nothing in the literature of the period allows us to conclude that Augustus promised to bring back the republican style of goverance.

3. Augustus of course was never able to be sure that he would have a long life in which to exercise power. He had a frail constitution and was often sick. As a result he was preoccupied with having an heir who would be a sympathetic collaborator in his program and would continue it after his death: Marcellus until he died in 23 B.C., Agrippa until he died in 12 B.C., Agrippa's sons, Lucius and Gaius, until they died in A.D. 2 and 4, and finally Tiberius.

4. On the use of marble in buildings of the late republic and the Augustan periods, see M. E. Blake, *Ancient Roman Construction in Italy* (Washington, D.C., 1947), pp. 50–60 and the index, esp. pp. 390–391.

5. Behind the enclosed space of the Forum Augustum, for instance,

radiant with marble, bronze and gold, lay the notorious slum of the Subura.

6. Augustus's use of a republican façade is the theme of G. Ch. Picard, *Augustus and Nero* (Eng. tr. London, 1965), pp. 15–48; Rowell, *Rome in the Augustan Age*, pp. 55–68, 82.

7. R. A. Cordingley and I. A. Richmond, "The Mausoleum of Augustus," *Papers of the British School at Rome* 10 (1927): 24–35. E. Kornemann, "Octavians Romulusgrab," *Klio* 31 (1938): 81–85, derives the shape from that of Etruscan tombs, such as the parallels at Cerveteri. R. Holloway, "The Tomb of Augustus and the Princes of Troy," *AJA* 70 (1966): 171–173, derives the round shape from the supposed royal tumuli near the site of Troy, from whose princes Augustus claimed descent. K. Kraft, "Der Sinn des Mausoleums des Augustus," *Historia* 16 (1967): 189–206, interprets the mausoleum as a response, based on the Italic tradition, to the great Hellenistic tomb in Alexandria of Antony and Cleopatra, whereas J.-Ch. Richard, "Mausoleum," *Latomus* 29 (1970): 370–388, places the tomb in the tradition of the royal tombs at Halicarnassus and Alexandria. M. Eisner, "Zur Typologie der Mausoleen des Augustus und des Hadrian," *MDAI(R)* 86 (1979): 319–324, stresses the novelty of the monument.

8. The ubiquitous statues of Augustus showed a strong tendency toward the classicism of the fifth century B.C., the time during which the Roman republic had been founded and had gone from strength to strength (at least according to Livy's canonical version): the relevant monuments are the *Augustus of Prima Porta,* which copied the pose of Polyclitus's *Doryphorus;* the frieze of the Ara Pacis, which alluded to the frieze of the Parthenon; the ground plan and arrangement of the sculptural panels at both ends of the Ara Pacis, which imitated the fifth-century Altar of Pity in Athens; and the architectural carvings in the Forum Augustum, copied from those of the Erechtheum, on the Athenian Acropolis. Cf. D. E. Strong, "Observations on Early Roman Corinthian," *JRS* 53 (1963): 73–84; G. Sauron, "Aspects du néo-atticisme à la fin du Ier siècle avant J.-C.," *L'art décoratif à Rome* (Ecole Française de Rome, 1981), pp. 285–319. R. Bianchi-Bandinelli, *Rome: The Center of Power* (Eng. tr. New York, 1970), pp. 177–208, is inclined to view the Augustan sculpture as derivative, by way of Hellenistic Neo-Attic works, whereas P. Zanker, *Klassizistische Statuen* (Mainz, 1974), connects the popularity of Polyclitus's youthful athletes with the Augustan collegia iuvenum and the theme of renewal.

9. H. T. Rowell, "Vergil and the Forum of Augustus," *American Journal of Philology* 62 (1941): 261–276, analyzes the Forum Augustum in terms of the program of Vergil's *Aeneid,* and points out parallels between the arrangement of the Forum and the description of the vestibule of King Latinus's palace in the *Aeneid* (7.170–189). See also P. Zanker, *Forum Au-*

gustum: Das Bildprogramm (Tübingen, 1969).

10. Greek paintings had been prestige items of interior decoration since the second century B.C., and during the last half of the first century they became more common, reproduced by commercial artists directly on the walls. Julius Caesar, as an innovation, placed several Greek originals in the Forum Iulium, and during the Augustan Age, Agrippa made an issue of mounting great paintings in public places rather than private homes (Pliny, *Natural History* 35.26–28, 94).

11. O. L. Richmond, "The Augustan Palatium," *JRS* 4 (1914): 193–226; A. J. Marshall, "Library Resources and Creative Writing at Rome," *Phoenix* 30 (1976): 252–264; G. F. Carettoni, "Le costruzioni di Augusto e il tempio di Apollo sul Palatino," *Quaderni del Centro di studio per l'archeologia etrusco-italica* 1 (1978): 72–74.

12. We are reminded once again of Augustus's ironic deathbed comment implying that much of his career had been no more profound than the plays to be seen on the comic stage.

13. As travelers from the north on the Via Flaminia approached, there was the Ara Pacis, the "Altar of Peace." At the Porta Capena, the main entrance from the south along the Via Appia and the Via Latina, stood the Ara Fortunae Reducis, the "Altar of Fortune the Bringer-Back."

14. The classical reference to Maecenas's gardens is Horace, *Satires* 1.8. The gardens are discussed in P. Grimal, *Les jardins romains* (Paris, 1969), pp. 152–157.

15. E. Buchner, *Die Sonnenuhr des Augustus* (Mainz, 1984). F. Coarelli, *Roma sepolta* (Rome, 1984), pp. 72–91, emphasizes the long-standing connection of the northern Campus Martius with funeral monuments of triumphatores, converted by the Augustan projects into a Hellenistic gymnasium; the Horologium alluded to the hero cult at the tomb of Alexander the Great in Alexandria.

16. R. B. Lloyd, "The Aqua Virgo, Euripus, and Pons Agrippa," *AJA* 83 (1979): 195–200; F. Coarelli, "Il Campo Marzio occidentale: Storia e topografia," *Mélanges d'Archéologie et d'Histoire de l'Ecole Française de Rome* 89 (1977): 807–846; W. Loerke, "Georges Chédanne and the Pantheon: A Beaux-Arts Contribution to the History of Roman Architecture," *Modulus,* 1982, pp. 40–55.

17. P. Gros, *Aurea Templa: Recherches sur l'architecture réligieuse de Rome à l'époque d'Auguste* (Rome, 1976), pp. 81–84.

18. Future additions were to be the arches of Tiberius to the southwest and of Septimius Severus to the northwest, and the temple of Vespasian just below the Tabularium.

19. Coarelli, *Roma sepolta,* pp. 106–115; G. Carettoni, *Das Haus des Augustus auf dem Palatin* (Mainz, 1983). On the House of Livia, see *PDAR*, s.v. "Domus Augusti."

20. It has been usual to regard much of Augustan poetry as conventional stuff, based on Greek literary models, quite distinct from the actual life of the poets. G. Williams, *Tradition and Originality in Roman Poetry* (Oxford, 1968), passim, advocates this view. J. Griffin, "Augustan Poetry and the Life of Luxury," *JRS* 66 (1976): 87–105, presents a sensible argument that the Augustan poets lived in an actual social world that was permeated with Greek influences: "They are not transposing the reader into a realm of pure fantasy, but making poetical (and that includes making it more universal, less individual) a mode of life familiar to their readers" (p. 102).

21. M. J. McGann, "The Three Worlds of Horace's *Satires*," in *Horace*, edited by C. D. N. Costa (London, 1973), pp. 59–93, comments on passages in the *Satires* on society as a place of sanity, vice, and artistic creativity.

22. Rowell, "Vergil and the Forum of Augustus."

23. In one poem (2.3) Tibullus finds himself in the city and does actually curse the country for taking his girl away from him, but this seems to be a hollow pose, in which city values have corrupted even the simplicities of rustic existence. Another poem is set in the new temple of Apollo Palatinus, but the only landmarks Tibullus describes are those of primitive Rome, where Aeneas visited, Ilia and Mars loved, and Romulus and Remus settled (2.5.21–38).

24. When Romulus and Remus were washed up on the riverbank, Livy reminds us, they came to rest at the spot where the fig tree known as the Ficus Ruminalis still grows (1.4). The Sabine women's intervention to stop the fighting between their Roman husbands and their Sabine fathers, Livy carefully notes, took place on the site of the temple of Iuppiter Stator (1.12). Navius defied Tarquin and defended the integrity of the augury ritual, Livy adds, on the left-hand side of the steps to the Curia, where a statute of Navius used to stand (1.36).

25. On Cynthia, see Chapter 6, note 41.

Chapter 5. Rome under the Emperors

1. Pliny, *Natural History* 36.111, says that the whole city was surrounded by the villas of Caligula and Nero. See the discussion in J. B. Ward-Perkins, *Roman Imperial Architecture* (Harmondsworth, 1981), pp. 48–49.

2. F. Coarelli, "L'identificazione dell'Area Sacra dell'Argentina," *Palatino* 12 (1968): 365–378, argues that this Porticus Minucia is the travertine colonnade surrounding the temples at the Largo Argentina, dated on stylistic grounds to the second half of the first century A.D. Bits of Claudian legislation show the emperor attempting to deal with various abuses in the

real estate market (*CIL* 6.919 and 10.1401).

3. It was here that many Christians met their death, including (according to tradition) the apostle Peter, who was buried in a cemetery nearby.

4. Several isolated portions of the Domus Transitoria have been preserved in the foundations of later buildings, including a domed intersection of vaulted corridors under the Temple of Venus et Roma and a nymphaeum pavilion encrusted with stucco, glass, and marble under the Domus Augustiana. See the discussions in W. L. MacDonald, *The Architecture of the Roman Empire,* vol. 1 (New Haven, 1965), pp. 21–25, and Ward-Perkins, *Roman Imperial Architecture,* pp. 57–59.

5. For the importance of the architectural innovations of the Domus Aurea, see A. Boëthius, *The Golden House of Nero* (Ann Arbor, 1960), pp. 94–128, and MacDonald, *Architecture of the Roman Empire,* 1:31–46. We might expect the tremendous area of the Domus Aurea to disrupt the traffic patterns of the ancient city, but no ancient source includes that among the considerable number of complaints and grumblings about Rome. Apparently the inconvenience was not very great. To get from the Forum Romanum to the Via Tiburtina or Via Praenestina, for instance, the normal traffic pattern would be to go through the Clivus Suburanus and along the top of the Esquiline (Pl. 10). To get to the Via Latina or Via Appia, one would go well to the south of the area of the Domus Aurea, between the Caelian and the Little Aventine. The only residents who might have been seriously inconvenienced were those who lived on the Caelian (a very small percentage of the whole city).

6. Perhaps this style of painting was a result of the Egyptianizing tendencies of Caligula. It was widely imitated in private houses throughout Italy, as can be seen in the houses of Pompeii.

7. R. B. Lloyd, "Three Monumental Gardens on the Marble Plan," *AJA* 86 (1982): 91–100; J. C. Anderson, "Domitian, the Argiletum, and the Temple of Peace," *AJA* 86 (1982): 101–110.

8. The Colosseum replaced the Amphitheatrum Statilii Tauri in the Campus Martius, which had been dedicated in 30 B.C. and was destroyed in the fire of A.D. 64.

9. Only the most important monuments of Domitian's reign are mentioned in the text. For a more complete list, with references to primary sources, see F. C. Bourne, *The Public Works of the Julio-Claudians and Flavians* (Princeton, 1946), pp. 64–67. MacDonald, *Architecture of the Roman Empire,* 1:47–74, discusses the architectural importance of Domitian's palace.

10. On the Roman architectural revolution, see MacDonald, *Architecture of the Roman Empire,* 1:41–46, 167–183; Ward-Perkins, *Roman Imperial Architecture,* pp. 97–120.

11. On Trajan's Market, see MacDonald, *Architecture of the Roman Empire,* 1:75–93. On his buildings in general, see M. E. Blake and D. T. Bishop, *Roman Construction in Italy from Nerva through the Antonines* (Philadelphia, 1973), pp. 10–39.

12. In accordance with Augustan precedent, Hadrian acquired Senate sponsorship of most of his building projects; see M. T. Boatwright, *Hadrian and the City of Rome* (Princeton, 1987), ch. 1.

13. J. P. Martin, "Hadrien et le Phénix: Propagande numismatique," *Mélanges . . . W. Seston* (Paris, 1974), pp. 327–337.

14. Dio Cassius (69.4.2–6) says that Hadrian himself designed this temple building.

15. The Saepta, an Augustan building, was reconstructed by Hadrian, as were the old traditional Temple of Bona Dea and the Auguratorium, such Augustan monuments as the Porticus Argonautarum, the Thermae Agrippianae, and the Pantheon, and the Flavian Divorum Templum. In general, see Boatwright, *Hadrian and the City of Rome,* ch. 2.

16. On the Pantheon, see W. L. MacDonald, *The Pantheon: Design, Meaning, Progeny* (Cambridge, Mass., 1976).

17. This residential quarter is discussed by G. Gatti, "Caratteristiche edilizie di un quartiere di Roma del II secolo d.Cr.," *Quaderni dell'Istituto di Storia dell'Architettura,* fasc. 35–48 (1961): 49–66.

18. These were the Thermae Septimianae in the Trans-Tiber region. A special aqueduct to supply water to these baths was built so hastily that it collapsed before it was ever put into use.

19. This Severan complex had an interesting subsequent history as the site of the imperial palace in later antiquity and as the place where Saint Helena built the Church of the Holy Cross. The amphitheater and other buildings have been incorporated into Aurelian's city wall and are still visible north of the Church of Saint John Lateran. The remains of the complex are discussed by A. M. Colini, "Horti Spei Veteris, Palatium Sessorianum," *Memorie della Pontificia Accademia Romana di Archeologia* 3, no. 8 (1955): 137–177. See also *PDAR,* s.v. "Amphitheatrum Castrense," "Circus Varianus," "Thermae Helenae," and "Sessorium."

20. On the building projects of Diocletian and Maxentius, see A. Frazer, "The Iconography of the Emperor Maxentius' Buildings in Via Appia," *Art Bulletin* 48 (1966): 385–392.

21. For Rome under Constantine, see R. Krautheimer, *Rome: Profile of a City, 312–1308* (Princeton, 1980), pp. 17–31.

Chapter 6. Population

1. The figure 250,000 is derived from the numbers cited as receiving grain doles in 46 B.C. (320,000), 45 B.C. (150,000), 44, 29, 24, 23, and 12

B.C. (250,000), 5 B.C. (320,000), 2 B.C. (200,000), and A.D. 14 and 37 (150,000). The age at which a boy became eligible for the annona was perhaps ten. See W. J. Oates, "The Population of Rome," *Classical Philology* 29 (1934): 101–116; P. A. Brunt, *Italian Manpower*, 225 B.C.–A.D. 14 (Oxford, 1971), pp. 376–388; K. Hopkins, *Conquerors and Slaves* (Cambridge, 1978), pp. 96–98.

2. The lower figure is from Brunt, *Italian Manpower*, p. 383, who argues that the vast hordes of the poor would not be able to afford a wife and family. The higher figure is from Hopkins, *Conquerors and Slaves*, p. 98.

3. The difficulties of obtaining reliable statistical information are illustrated by looking at attempts to use tombstone inscriptions to calculate average life expectancy. A. R. Burn, "Hic Breve Vivitur," *Past and Present* 4 (1953): 2–31, uses Roman tombstones to estimate an average expectancy of 20–30 years. Other studies, from the western provinces, produce an average of 35–50 years—R. Etienne, "A propos de la démographie de Bordeaux," *Révue Historique de Bordeaux* 4 (1957): 189–200; and J. G. Szilágyi, "Beiträge zur Statistik der Sterblichkeit in den westeuropäischen Provinzen des römischen Imperiums," *Acta Archaeologica Academiae Scientiarum Hungaricae* 13 (1961): 125–156. Such divergent results have made people skeptical, and several recent studies argue that such results are at variance with demographical probability. See K. Hopkins, "The Age of Roman Girls at Marriage," *Population Studies* 18 (1965): 309–327. J. Harper, "Slaves and Freedmen in Imperial Rome," *American Journal of Philology* 93 (1972): 341–342, concludes that if a city slave survived to maturity, his chances of being manumitted were relatively high; since both slaves and freedmen in Italy outside Rome show an average tombstone age that is seven years higher than their counterparts in Rome, Harper concludes that conditions were healthier outside the city and also that manumissions there were probably made at a later age.

4. The built-up area of imperial Rome corresponded more or less to that enclosed by the third-century walls of Aurelian, 1,373 hectares (1 hectare = 2.47 acre), which implies a population density of about 730 per hectare (300 per acre). This compares with an overall density of 452 per hectare in modern Bombay, 364 for Dublin, 295 for Calcutta, and 224 for Mexico City. Most of these modern cities have upper-class residential areas and parks, which decrease the density. The highest spot densities recorded are for Hong Kong (1,656 per hectare), Bombay (1,169 per hectare), and Calcutta (1,018 per hectare). Modern figures are taken from the United Nations' 1977 *Compendium of Social Statistics* (New York, 1980).

5. At Pompeii, 35 percent of the excavated area inside the walls was given over to public buildings and open spaces (gardens, forums, etc.)— W. F. Jashemski, *The Gardens of Pompeii* (New Rochelle, N.Y., 1979), pp.

10–24. At Ostia, the figure is 43 percent—R. Meiggs, *Roman Ostia* (Oxford, 1973), p. 532.

6. The "Regionary Catalogue" of the fourteen regions of imperial Rome (cf. Fig. 6) is preserved in a pair of documents of the fourth century A.D. entitled *Curiosum Urbis Regionum XIV* and *Notitia Regionum Urbis XIV*. A convenient text is printed in H. Jordan, *Topographie der Stadt Rom im Altherthum*, vol. 2 (Berlin, 1871), pp. 539–574. G. Calza assumes that *insula* refers to a large Ostia-style tenement and calculates the population of Rome at 1,800,000 in "La statistica delle abitazioni e il calcolo della popolazione in Roma imperiale," *Rendiconti della reale Accademia dei Lincei* 26 (1917): 60–87, and at 1,200,000 in "La popolazione di Roma antica," *Bullettino della Commissione Archeologica comunale di Roma* 69 (1941): 142–165. There is, however, hardly room inside Rome for 47,000 such buildings. E. Cuq, "Une statistique de locaux affectés à l'habitation dans la Rome impérial," *Mémoires de l'Academie des Inscriptions et Belles-Lettres* 40 (1915): 335, suggests "apartment" as a definition. A. von Gerkan, "Die Einwohnerzahl Roms in der Kaiserzeit," *MDAI(R)* 55 (1940): 160, argues that *insula* simply means one floor of a tenement. F. G. Maier, "Römische Bevölkerungsgeschichte und Inschriftenstatistik," *Historia* 2 (1953): 318–351, esp. 331–333, suggests the concept "surveyor's unit." J. P. Packer, "The Insulae of Imperial Ostia," *MAAR* 31 (1971): 79, regards *insula* as a loose term covering any type of "multiple dwelling." F. Castagnoli, "L'insula nei Cataloghi regionari di Roma," *Rivista di Filologia e di Istruzione Classica* 104 (1976): 45–52, interprets it as any unit of habitation.

7. The Palatine seems out of place in the list of regions having a high proportion of *insulae*; the region must have included the adjacent valley of the Velabrum; on top of the hill there would have been relatively few large *domūs* left after the emperors destroyed them to make room for their palaces. The following list, derived from the Regionary Catalogue, presents the regions in order of increasing ratio of *insulae* to *domūs*: IX (Circus Flaminius, 15:1), III (Isis et Serapis, 17:1), XIII (Aventine, 19:1), V (Esquiline, 21:1), XII (Piscina Publica, 22:1), VI (Alta Semita, 23:1), VIII (Forum Romanum, 27:1), I (Porta Capena, 27:1), II (Caelian, 28:1), XI (Circus Maximus, 29:1), XIV (Trans-Tiber, 29:1), X (Palatine, 30:1), IV (Templum Pacis, 31:1), VII (Via Lata, 32:1).

8. H. Boren, *The Gracchi* (New York, 1968), pp. 77–79; Brunt, *Italian Manpower*, pp. 379–381. Brunt also uses the growth of the aqueduct system as evidence: "The fact that the supply was enormously increased in four stages, 312–273, 144–127, 40(?)–27, and finally under Claudius, suggests that on the eve of each new development (except perhaps the last) it was grossly insufficient" (p. 384).

9. The ruling class of the original republic was made up of the patricians, and the first two centuries of republican history were dominated by

the struggle of the plebeians—presumably wealthy plebeians—to gain the privileges and prerogatives of the patricians. This struggle was over by the fourth century B.C., when plebeians won the right to intermarry with the partricians and to occupy all the magistracies and most of the priesthoods. Wealthy plebeians were then in a position to enter the Senate, and through the rest of the republic and into the principate, the senatorial aristocracy was composed of both patricians and plebeians. On the irresistible force of family tradition on an aristocratic youth, cf. R. MacMullen, *Enemies of the Roman Order* (Cambridge, Mass., 1966), pp. 8–20 (on Brutus), and D. C. Earl, *The Moral and Political Tradition of Rome* (Ithaca, 1967), pp. 11–43.

10. They were entitled to wear the "wide stripe" on their togas, and a special type of shoe, and could sit in the front rows at the theater and circus. During the principate, certain administrative offices were reserved for members of the senatorial order, notably the *praefectus urbi* and the *praefectus alimentorum*.

11. On social mobility into and out of the senatorial order, see T. J. Wiseman, *New Men in the Roman Senate, 139 B.C.–A.D. 14* (Oxford, 1971); K. Hopkins, *Death and Renewal* (Cambridge, 1983), pp. 31–198.

12. Cicero's friendship with Gaius Pomponius Atticus, documented in his *Letters to Atticus,* is a good illustration of a positive relationship between a senator and an equestrian who devoted himself to a relatively quiet life of discreet moneymaking (Nepos, *Atticus* 13) and observation of the political scene.

13. Even in the republic, the most eloquent paradigms of the values of the senatorial aristocracy were men who were newly arrived in it: Cato, in the second century B.C., was from Tusculum; Cicero, in the first century B.C., was from Arpinum. Pliny the Younger, who came from a provincial family in Cisalpine Gaul, expressed corresponding ideals at the end of the first century A.D. throughout his *Letters.*

14. Livy 21.63.3–4. An early example of a senator who organized corporations of clients to invest in long-distance trade was Cato (Plutarch, *Cato* 21). On the phenomenon in general, see J. H. D'Arms, *Commerce and Social Standing in Ancient Rome* (Cambridge, Mass., 1981).

15. The first grant of citizenship seems to have been to Spanish and Sicilian deserters from Hannibal in the late third century B.C. On the subject of such "viritane" grants, see E. Badian, *Foreign Clientelae* (Oxford, 1958), pp. 309–321; and A. N. Sherwin-White, *The Roman Citizenship,* 2nd ed. (Oxford, 1973), pp. 245–246.

16. The most formal version of the name indicated the names of ancestors and the tribe to which the gens belonged: M(arcus) Tullius M(arci) f(ilius) M(arci) n(epos) Cor(nelia tribu) Cicero was "Marcus Tullius Cicero, son of Marcus, grandson of Marcus, of the tribe Cornelia." In cases of adoption, the adopted son took the name of his adoptive father, but

often added a cognomen derived from his original nomen; thus, when Gaius Octavius was adopted by Gaius Julius Caesar, he entered the Julian gens and became Gaius Julius Caesar Octavianus. In cases of manumission, the freed slave took the praenomen and nomen of his former master, and usually retained his slave name as cognomen: thus Gaius Julius Polybius was presumably a slave Polybius who belonged either to Julius Caesar or to Octavian/Augustus, and was then freed. Sons of freedmen sometimes retained their father's cognomen, so we cannot be sure whether Polybius was a freedman himself or the freeborn son or grandson of a freedman; if we had the full, formal nomenclature, we would know, for freedmen were recorded not, for instance, as M(arci) f(ilius), "son of Marcus," but as M(arci) l(ibertus), "freedman of Marcus." The same pattern was followed with a viritane grant of citizenship: the new citizen took the praenomen and nomen of the patron. Thus there are dozens of Pompeii (the recipients of citizenship granted by Pompey the Great throughout the western and eastern provinces), and all the multitudes enfranchized by Caracalla in A.D. 212 took the name Aurelius, the emperor's gens. By that time the cognomen had become the personal name, since nearly everyone in the same area would have had the same nomen and, usually, the same praenomen; cf. Sherwin-White, *Roman Citizenship,* pp. 386–388.

17. The apostle Paul is an example of a Roman citizen who appealed to the rights he possessed, yet whose experience of the city must have been those of a foreigner.

18. E.g., Juvenal 3.58–125. In *To Helvia* 6.2–4 Seneca lists what he thought were the reasons foreigners were drawn to Rome in the first century A.D.: ambition or a diplomatic mission; the attractions of vice and decadence, liberal learning, or the shows; friendship; a desire to sell physical beauty or oratorical skill.

19. Meiggs, *Roman Ostia,* pp. 214–216, lists traders at Ostia from Africa, Spain, Gaul, Asia Minor, Egypt, and Syria. Other free immigrants are from Thrace, Pannonia, Sardinia, Corsica, and several Italian towns. An important useful survey is G. La Piana, "Foreign Groups in Rome during the First Centuries of the Empire," *Harvard Theological Review* 20 (1927): 183–403. J. P. V. D. Balsdon, *Romans and Aliens* (London, 1979), pp. 59–71, catalogues the elements in the stereotypes that Romans held about other races: Germans and Gauls (tall, fair, with long blond or red hair and blue eyes), Africans (short, dark), Arabs (wearing earrings). A systematic survey of the national origins of slaves and freedmen in the first century B.C. is given in S. Treggiari, *Roman Freedmen during the Late Republic* (Oxford, 1969), pp. 1–11, 246–249. F. Snowden, *Blacks in Antiquity* (Cambridge, Mass., 1970), esp. pp. 182–195, stresses the lack of color prejudice.

20. On Greek and Greek-speaking scholars attached to prominent Ro-

mans, see Balsdon, *Romans and Aliens,* pp. 48–58. On the Greek philosophers and rhetoricians, see R. MacMullen, *Enemies of the Roman Order* (Cambridge, Mass., 1966), pp. 46–94; and G. Bowersock, *Greek Sophists in the Roman Empire* (Oxford, 1969). Juvenal's third satire expresses one Roman's resentment at the social progress of these Greeks; the other side is represented by Lucian, who expresses the disdain felt by a cultured Greek for his boorish Roman patrons in the essay "On Salaried Posts in Great Houses."

21. The texts of the inscriptions are given, with an interpretation of Gaionas's career, in S. M. Savage, "The Cults of Ancient Trastevere," *MAAR* 17 (1940): 26–56, esp. 37, 45–46. On the sanctuary, see N. Goodhue, *The Lucus Furrinae and the Syrian Sanctuary on the Janiculum* (Amsterdam, 1975).

22. An analysis of the inscriptions from the Jewish catacombs in Monteverde, on the hill just above the Trans-Tiber region, suggests that the Jews who lived there tended to be more conservative, while groups buried in catacombs on the Via Appia and Via Nomentana, nearer the center of old Rome, show a relatively higher degree of Hellenization and Romanization. Almost half of the Jewish tombstones indicate Latin names (the result of citizenship acquired on manumission or, as in the case of Saint Paul, by heredity), while only about 15 percent have Semitic names; the rest are Greek. See H. J. Leon, *The Jews of Ancient Rome* (Philadelphia, 1960).

23. Augustus imposed a 2 percent tax on the sale of slaves, to raise money for war and for the corps of *vigiles* (Dio Cassius, *Roman History* 55.31), on which see Chapter 8, page 128, of this volume.

24. W. V. Harris, "Towards a Study of the Roman Slave Trade," *MAAR* 26 (1980): 117–140.

25. K. Hopkins, "Why Did the Romans Free So Many Slaves?" *Conquerors and Slaves,* pp. 115–132; Treggiari, *Roman Freedmen;* A. M. Duff, *Freedmen in the Early Roman Empire* (Oxford, 1928).

26. A remarkably large number of freedmen's sons rose to the municipal aristocracies of Italy. In Ostia, 33 percent of the known decurions have the Greek cognomina that normally indicate servile origin—M. L. Gordon, "The Freedman's Son in Municipal Life," *JRS* 21 (1931): 65–77.

27. A sense of the mutual trust that could develop between patron and freedman is expressed in Terence, *Lady of Andros* 31–39, and in grave inscriptions like *CIL* 6.9222.

28. P. R. C. Weaver, *Familia Caesaris* (Cambridge, 1972).

29. In the pottery factories of Arretium, for instance, most of the workmen were slaves (a normal ratio was 16–19 slaves for each freedman laborer), though several owners and managers were freedmen—Treggiari, *Roman Freedmen,* pp. 91–94.

30. The social world of a rich freedman like Trimalchio is discussed

by P. Veyne, "Vie de Trimalcion," *Annales (Economies—Sociétés—Civilisations)* 16 (1961): 213–247. Because of their wealth such freedmen exercised an influence in the life of the city out of all proportion to the prerogatives of their juridical status; this "status dissonance" is discussed in terms of social mobility by K. Hopkins, "Elite Mobility in the Roman Empire," *Past and Present* 32 (1965): 12–26, and by T. Reekmans, "Juvenal's Views on Social Change," *Ancient Society* 2 (1971): 117–161.

31. For the tomb, see also Chapter 11, pages 195–196; on the office of apparitor, see Chapter 7, page 104.

32. Inscriptions show that these Augustales took their privileges and responsibilities very seriously, as justification for their wealth and success (e.g., *CIL* 9.2128.8–9). R. Duthoy, "Les *Augustales," *ANRW* 2.16.2 (1978): 1254–1309; S. E. Ostrow, "Augustales along the Bay of Naples: A Case for their Early Growth," *Historia* 34 (1985): 64–101.

33. Nuclear families tended to be small, and normally there would be only one daughter. If there were two, they would be distinguished by the adjectives "Maior" for the elder and "Minor" for the younger. A third would be "Tertia," etc.

34. Cf. R. Lefkowitz and M. B. Fant, *Women's Life in Greece and Rome* (Baltimore, 1982), pp. 133–156.

35. The old aristocratic model of marriage *cum manu* transferred the woman to the *patria potestas* of her husband's family. This gave way during the later republic to marriage *sine manu*, in which the wife remained under the patria potestas of her own father. See J. F. Gardner, *Women in Roman Law and Society* (London, 1986); and E. Cantarella, *Pandora's Daughters: The Role and Status of Women in Greek and Roman Antiquity* (Eng. tr. Baltimore, 1987), pp. 113–124.

36. L. Bonfante Warren, "The Women of Etruria," in *Women in the Ancient World: The Arethusa Papers,* ed. J. Peradotto and J. P. Sullivan (Albany, 1984), pp. 229–239.

37. Plutarch, *Tiberius Gracchus* 1.4–5 and *Gaius Gracchus,* 4, 19; Cicero, *Brutus* 211; Tacitus, *Dialogus* 28; M. Lefkowitz, "Influential Women," in *Images of Women in Antiquity,* ed. A. Cameron and A. Kuhrt (Detroit, 1983), pp. 49–64.

38. On the independence of Cicero's wife and daughter, see T. Carp, "Two Matrons of the Late Republic," in *Reflections of Women in Antiquity,* ed. H. P. Foley (New York, 1981), pp. 343–354.

39. On the extent of upper-class "women's emancipation," cf. R. O. A. M. Lyne, *The Latin Love Poets from Catullus to Horace* (Oxford, 1980), pp. 1–18; J. P. Hallett, "The Role of Women in Roman Elegy: Counter-Cultural Feminism," in *Women in the Ancient World,* ed. Peradotto and Sullivan, pp. 241–262; and Cantarella, *Pandora's Daughters,* pp. 135–155.

40. N. Kampen, *Image and Status: Roman Working Women in Ostia*

(Berlin, 1981); E. L. Will, "Women in Pompeii," *Archaeology* 32 (1979): 34–43; S. Treggiari, "Jobs in the Household of Livia," *Papers of the British School at Rome* 43 (1975): 48–77; S. Treggiari, "Jobs for Women," *American Journal of Ancient History* 1 (1976): 76–104.

41. G. Williams, *Tradition and Originality in Roman Poetry* (Oxford, 1968), pp. 529–535, considers Cynthia a free woman of some standing, like Sempronia (Sallust, *Bellum Catilinae* 25) and Clodia. According to an older view, she was a high-quality prostitute—J. Fontenrose, "Propertius and the Roman Career," *University of California Studies in Classical Philology* 13 (1949): 371–388; cf. J. Griffin, "Augustan Poetry and the Life of Luxury," *JRS* 66 (1976): 87–105, esp. 103.

Chapter 7. City Government

1. Examples include the *quattuorviri viis in urbe purgandis* (commission of four to clean the streets in the city) and the *duoviri viis extra propiusve urbem Romam passus mille purgandis* (commission of two to clean the roads within a mile of the city).

2. On this bureaucracy of the later republic, see A. H. M. Jones, "The Roman Civil Service (Clerical and Sub-clerical Grades)," *JRS* 39 (1949): 38–55; C. Nicolet, *The World of the Citizen in Republican Rome* (Eng. tr. Berkeley, 1980) pp. 326–334; and N. Purcell, "The *Apparitores*: A Study in Social Mobility," *Papers of the British School at Rome* 51 (1983): 125–173. The best ancient documents are *CIL* 1².587, Sulla's reform of the twenty quaestors and their staffs; and *CIL* 1².594, Julius Caesar's charter for a colony at Urso, in Spain, in which section 62 lists each magistrate's attendants, and their pay. Cf. Chapter 15, note 8, of this volume.

3. On the details of assemblies and voting procedures, see L. R. Taylor, *Party Politics in the Age of Caesar* (Berkeley, 1949), pp. 50–75; L. R. Taylor, *Roman Voting Assemblies* (Ann Arbor, 1966); Nicolet, *World of the Citizen*, pp. 207–315; H. H. Scullard, *Festivals and Ceremonies of the Roman Republic* (Ithaca, 1981), pp. 225–232.

4. The comitia centuriata could also pass laws, although that was normally done through the comitia tributa. When the more conservative bias of the comitia centuriata made passage of a law more likely, the proper magistrate could convene them for that purpose. We know of only one case in which they were used in this way, but it was a famous and important case, the passage of the law in 57 B.C. which recalled Cicero from abroad one year after Clodius had used the comitia tributa to force him into exile—Cicero, *Post Reditum in Senatu* 27–28; cf. Taylor, *Party Politics*, pp. 60–62.

5. The concilium plebis included only plebeians. But since, by the later republic, there were relatively few patricians, there was little practical

difference between the concilium plebis and the comitia tributa, except for the historical distinction rooted in the plebeian-patrician tussles of the fourth and third centuries B.C.

6. On topography: L. Richardson, "The Tribunals of the Praetors of Rome," *MDAI(R)* 80 (1973): 219–233. On procedures: J. A. Crook, *Law and Life of Rome, 90 B.C.–A.D. 212* (Ithaca, 1967), pp. 68–97. On permitted and forbidden days: Scullard, *Festivals and Ceremonies*, pp. 44–46. For a description of the people present at a trial, see, for example, Cicero, *Letters to Atticus* 1.16.2–4.

7. Architectural details of these houses in Figure 7 are imaginary, based loosely on the earlier houses in Pompeii and Cosa.

8. This was the resting place of the shields carried by the priests of the Salii in their processions, as well as the official state calendar and annals, and the records of the pontiffs, the most important priests of the Roman state. It was the headquarters of the *rex sacrorum* and the *pontifex maximus,* two officials who shared the sacred duties that in earliest times had been performed by the kings. Their official residence was apparently just above the Atrium Vestae, on the other side of the street from the Regia.

9. On the templum as an inaugurated space, see P. Catalano, "Aspetti spaziali del sistema giuridico-religioso romano," *ANRW* 2.16.1 (1978): 467–479; and Chapter 13, page 214, of this volume.

10. The Lapis Niger itself is a paving of black marble placed over the archaic shrine around 80 B.C., during Sulla's rebuilding of this part of the Forum.

11. They were destroyed by fire in 210 B.C. (Livy 26.27.2), and rebuilt as the Tabernae Novae, probably in 193 B.C.—L. Richardson, "Basilica Fulvia, Modo Aemilia," *Studies in Classical Art and Archaeology: A Tribute to P. H. von Blanckenhagen,* ed. G. Kopcke and M. B. Moore (Locust Valley, N.Y., 1979), pp. 210–211.

12. L. A. Holland, *Janus and the Bridge* (Rome, 1961).

13. The most famous statue represented the satyr Marsyas. It figures prominently in ancient illustrations of the Forum, and seems to have represented liberty. The custom was to crown it with garlands, and during the principate municipalities that enjoyed the special privileges of the *Ius Italicum* symbolized their status by erecting a statue of Marsyas in their own fora. See F. Coarelli, *Il Foro Romano,* vol. 2 (Rome, 1985), pp. 87–123.

14. The word *basilica* is apparently derived from the Greek *basilike stoa,* the "Royal Stoa" in the agora at Athens. This was a small building in which legal cases concerning religious matters were heard by the magistrate called "King Archon," in which the council of the Areopagus met occasionally, and in which official copies of certain laws were preserved. The earliest basilicas in Rome seem to have served similar purposes. Nothing remains of these early basilicas, but the drawings of them in Figure 8 are

based on the excavated remains of the second-century basilica at Cosa (Pl. 15).

15. A still earlier basilica seems to have stood on the site of the later Basilica Aemilia. It is attested in Plautus, *Curculio* 472. See G. E. Duckworth, "Plautus and the Basilica Aemilia," *Ut pictura poesis: Studia latina P. I. Enk oblata*, ed. P. de Jonge et al., (Leiden, 1955), pp. 58–65; and Richardson, "Basilica Fulvia, Modo Aemilia," pp. 209–215.

16. Some tufa remains of the original building indicate that it already had the rectangular outline and interior colonnade that were standard features of the basilica form.

17. *CIL* 1².593; Dessau, *Inscriptiones Latinae Selectae*, no. 6085.

18. A *praefectus vigilum*, a freedman, commanded the vigiles. Each vicus was led by a group of four *vicomagistri*, appointed annually by the emperor.

19. A *praefectus annonae*, an equestrian, supervised the grain supply. The *curatores aedium sacrarum et operum locorumque publicorum* were chosen from the senatorial order for extended terms, and were responsible for maintaining temples and public buildings, the traditional tasks of the aediles. Under their control were various *subcuratores* of the equestrian order, assigned to specific jobs, as well as ever more elaborate staff of technical, administrative, and custodial personnel. Special commissions also were established, such as the *quattuorviri viarum curandarum* to maintain the streets and roads, the *curatores* of the individual roads outside the city, and *curatores* to maintain the aqueducts, the sewers, and the bed and banks of the Tiber. Under Augustus there were three *curatores aquarum* as well as a board of *curatores alvei Tiberis et riparum*. Trajan later consolidated the responsibilities into the office of the *curator alvei Tiberis et riparum et cloacarum urbis*.

20. *CIL* 6.9711.

21. For a discussion of the size of the Senate and its quorum, the locations, arrangements, and procedures of Senate meetings, and a restored plan of the seating arrangements of the Curia Iulia, see L. R. Taylor and R. T. Scott, "Seating Space in the Roman Senate and the *Senatores Pedarii*," *TAPA* 100 (1969): 529–582. On special occasions the Senate met in other places, usually in a temple because of the requirement for an inaugurated space. See J. E. Stambaugh, "The Functions of Roman Temples," *ANRW* 2.16.1 (1978): 554–608, esp. 580–582; and D. L. Thompson, "The Meetings of the Roman Senate on the Palatine," *AJA* 85 (1981): 335–339.

22. The foundations of the single-spanned Arcus Tiberii lie between the Rostra and the Basilica Iulia. The arch does not appear in Figure 9, since its location would be out of sight behind the Temple of Saturnus.

23. The Porticus is shown in plan form at the bottom of Figure 9; the Arcus Septimii Serveri has been omitted. Recent general surveys of the

Forum are M. Grant, *The Roman Forum* (New York, 1970); and P. Zanker, *Forum Romanum: Die Neugestaltung durch Augustus* (Tübingen, 1972).

24. Vitruvius (3.3.2) tells us that the columns were arranged in the "pycnostyle" arrangement, which means they were placed closer together than normal. This would have created the illusion that the façade of the relatively small temple was bigger, and this narrow end of the Forum broader, than they really were. See Richardson, "Tribunals," pp. 228–229.

25. A single-spanned Arcus Augusti was built south of the Temple of the Deified Iulius in 29 B.C. to commemorate the victory over Antony. The triple-spanned arch erected in 19 B.C. contained *fasti,* lists of consuls and of generals who had celebrated triumphs. These inscriptions are published by A. Degrassi, *Inscriptiones Italiae,* vol. 13.1 (Rome, 1947), and summarized by P. MacKendrick, *The Mute Stones Speak* (New York, 1960), pp. 150–153. The Porticus Gai et Luci was located north of the Temple of the Deified Iulius, in some way joining it to the Basilica Aemilia. The location of the Arcus Augusti of 19 B.C. is disputed. According to a standard opinion (*PDAR* 1:92–101, 2:532), it stood to the south of the Temple of the Deified Iulius, and the earlier arch was destroyed to make room for it. More recently F. Coarelli, *Il Foro Romano,* vol. 2 (Rome, 1985), pp. 258–308, has argued that the later Arcus Augusti should be restored north of the temple, between it and the Porticus Gai et Luci.

26. J. C. Anderson, *Historical Topography of the Imperial Fora* (Brussels, 1984).

27. Other monuments celebrated the importance of the city—e.g., the Milliarium Aureum, a golden milestone placed by Augustus next to the Rostra to mark the distances along the roads that led to Rome; and the Umbilicus Romae, a Severan monument placed at the other end of the Rostra to mark the center or "navel" of the city.

Chapter 8. Services, Public and Private

1. The money to pay for these beneficences came from income from the sponsors' farms, both as rents and directly from the sale of produce; from booty won in wars; from the profits, ill-gotten or otherwise, of duty as governor in the provinces; and from the interest on loans made to cities and to other aspiring politicians.

2. C. Nicolet, *The World of the Citizen in Republican Rome* (Eng. tr. Berkeley, 1980), pp. 336–337.

3. These tribunals eventually covered treason, embezzlement of state property, electoral bribery, provincial extortion, murder by violence or poison, adultery, and (perhaps) tampering with the grain supply. See *Paulys Realencyclopädie der classischen Altertumswissenschaft,* vol. 24 (Stuttgart, 1963), s.v. "quaestio."

4. The praetor urbanus supervised the *triumviri capitales.* The aediles and trimuviri capitales had the dangerous job of controlling a crowd of disaffected women and war refugees in 213 B.C. (Livy 25.1.10), and were charged with investigating the charges and patrolling the streets during prosecution of the Bacchic cult in 186 B.C. (Livy 39.14.10). The triumviri guarded the city gates at night (Livy 39.17.5), and during the principate were charged with burning certain books forbidden by Domitian in A.D. 93 (Tacitus, *Agricola* 2.1). See W. Kunkel, *An Introduction to Roman Legal and Constitutional History* (Eng. tr., 2nd ed., Oxford, 1973), pp. 64–69; and E. Echols, "The Roman City Police," *Classical Journal* 53 (1958): 377–385. W. Nippel, "Policing Rome," *JRS* 74 (1984): 20–29, provides an excellent survey of police functions during the republic.

5. These *carnifices* were distinguished by the gruesomeness of their occupation, and they had to wear special red hats, live outside the city (Cicero, *Pro Rabirio Perduellionis* 16), and after their death be buried with those who had committed suicide (Festus, p. 56L). The Atrium Libertatis functioned as a kind of police station and detention center (Livy 25.7.12; Cicero, *Pro Milone* 59–60).

6. The praetorian cohort in a republican army was the special guard of the commanding officer. Under Augustus, there were nine cohorts, but only three were stationed in the vicinity of Rome. Tiberius built the Castra Praetoria and installed all nine cohorts, plus the three urban cohorts, there. The number of praetorian cohorts was increased to twelve under Caligula and Claudius, sixteen under Vitellius, reduced to nine under Vespasian, and raised to ten under Domitian. Each cohort had 1,000 infantry and 300 cavalry. See A. Passerini, *Le coorti pretorie* (Rome, 1939).

7. The immediate bodyguards of the emperor were the *Statores Augusti,* a special contingent billeted in the Castra Praetoria, and the mounted *Equites Singulares,* quartered in their own barracks on the Caelian (the *Castra Priora* and the *Castra Nova Severiana*).

8. The number of urban cohorts was increased to seven by Claudius, reduced to four under Vitellius, increased to five under Antoninus Pius (of which only four were actually stationed in the city of Rome), and reduced again to three under Caracalla. Each cohort, commanded by a tribune, contained 1,000 men, and each soldier served for twenty years.

9. Plautus, *Amphitryon* 153–164; Propertius 2.29, 3.16; Juvenal 3.278–315.

10. The sailors were quartered in the Castra Misenatium, just east of the Colosseum, and the Castra Ravennatium, near the Naumachia Augusti in the Trans-Tiber region.

11. P. K. Baillie-Reynolds, "The Castra Peregrinorum" and "The Troops Quartered in the Castra Peregrinorum," *JRS* 13 (1923): 152–167, 168–189.

12. K. Hopkins, *Death and Renewal* (Cambridge, 1983), pp. 1–3; T. P.

Wiseman, *Catullus and His World: A Reappraisal* (Cambridge, 1985), pp. 5–10; R. MacMullen, "Judicial Savagery in the Roman Empire," *Chiron* 16 (1986): 147–166.

13. An episode that T. R. S. Broughton, *Magistrates of the Roman Republic* (New York, 1951), 1:220, assigns to 241 B.C. suggests that a commission of three, perhaps identical with the triumviri capitales, had some responsibility for fire control (Valerius Maximus, *Memorabilia* 8.1, damn. 5). For lists of fires and floods mentioned by Livy and Tacitus, see R. F. Newbold, "The Reporting of Earthquakes, Fires, and Floods by Ancient Historians," *Proceedings of the African Classical Associations* 16 (1982): 28–36, esp. n. 3.

14. In 22 B.C., Augustus assigned 600 slaves to serve as the aediles' fire department, but in 7 B.C. he transferred them to the jurisdiction of the *curatores viarum* (Dio Cassius, *Roman History* 54.2.3–4, 55.8.6–7). The *vigiles* were created in A.D. 6, and placed under the command of a *praefectus vigilum* recruited from the equestrian order. Each of the seven cohorts had 1,000 men, under the command of a tribune (*CIL* 6.222).

15. Remains have been found of the stationes of the V Cohort on the Caelian and of the VII Cohort in the Trans-Tiber region. Cf. Nash, *PDAR* I: 264–267, s.v. "Cohortium Vigilum Stationes." *CIL* 6.222 records the redecoration of a shrine in the *statio* of the V Cohort. The barracks of the vigiles at Ostia (II.v.1), with a large central courtyard surrounded by two stories of dormitory rooms and, at one end of the court, a ceremonial space with statutes of the emperors, gives a good idea of the vigiles' living arrangements.

16. Here was kept the equipment needed for fighting fires—carts and carriages, pumps (*siphones*), sponges on poles, buckets, shovels, and axes, and other types of demolition equipment. Cf. P. K. Baillie-Reynolds, *The Vigiles of Imperial Rome* (Oxford, 1926), and L. Homo, *Rome impériale et l'urbanisme dans l'antiquité* (Paris, 1951), pp. 172–198.

17. E. B. Van Deman, *The Building of the Roman Aqueducts* (Washington, D.C., 1934), emphasizes techniques of construction. T. Ashby, *The Aqueducts of Ancient Rome* (Oxford, 1935), traces the routes of the aqueducts. J. G. Landels, *Engineering in the Roman World* (Berkeley, 1978), pp. 34–57, introduces technical aspects.

18. A. T. Hodge, "Vitruvius, Lead Pipes, and Lead Poisoning," *AJA* 85 (1981): 486–491.

19. A law in Justinian's *Digest* (9.3.5.12) refers to an amphora suspended above the street in a net. G. Hermansen, "The *Medianum* and the Roman Apartment," *Phoenix* 24 (1970): 342–347, draws a parallel to street vendors in Naples who strike a deal with a customer in a window above: the customer lets down a basket or net with the money, and the vendor puts the merchandise in it to be hauled up.

20. The administration of the aqueducts was under the control of the emperor, who appointed the *curator aquarum*, a man of consular rank who in turn was assisted by *adiutores*, technical advisors of high social standing; *procuratores* (instituted by Claudius), who held most of the day-to-day administrative authority and were generally imperial freedmen; and a permanent staff of *aquarii*, skilled slaves (originally Agrippa's 240, increased to 700 by Claudius).

21. Sewers of polygonal masonry appeared in the Etruscan towns of Spoletum and Veii in the fifth century B.C.—M. Blake, *Ancient Roman Construction in Italy* (Washington, D.C., 1947), pp. 73, 75. The brook that flowed through the Forum Romanum may well have been channeled during the Etruscan period in Rome.

22. Under the republic, the censors were responsible for sewer construction, the aediles for maintenance. Under the early principate, it is not clear whether the water commissioner (*curator aquarum*) or the river commissioner (*curator alvei Tiberis et riparum*) was in charge of the sewers. The ambiguity disappeared under Trajan, who clearly put them under the river commissioner, with the new title *curator alvei Tiberis et riparum et cloacarum urbis*.

23. Suetonius, *Augustus* 42.1–2, *Claudius* 18.2; Tacitus, *Annals* 12.43.1; A. R. Hands, *Charities and Social Aid in Greece and Rome* (Ithaca, 1968), pp. 100–108; Z. Yavetz, *Plebs and Princeps* (Oxford, 1969), pp. 86–91, 96, 107–109, 119–124; F. Millar, *The Emperor in the Roman World* (Ithaca, 1977), p. 372.

24. Pliny (*Panegyricus* 28) alludes to the alimenta, and two inscriptions give basic data from Ligures Baebiani, in the southern Italian hills (*CIL* 9.1455), and Veleia, in the Po Valley (*CIL* 11.1147). Modern discussions: Hands, *Charities and Social Aid,* pp. 108–115; R. Duncan-Jones, *The Economy of the Roman Empire* (Cambridge, 1974), pp. 288–319.

25. R. M. Grant, *Early Christianity and Society* (New York, 1977), pp. 124–145.

26. Evidence for the care of slaves comes from descriptions of farm life. Columella (*On Agriculture* 11.1.18; 12.1.6), for instance, insists that on an estate the *vilicus* ("steward") and his wife were to show special solicitation for sick slaves, and provide an infirmary (*valetudinarium*) where they could recuperate. Not all masters were willing to expend time, money, and attention on sick slaves, however, and some dumped them in the Temple of Aesculapius. Claudius tried to discourage this by decreeing that if such a slave recovered, he would be allowed to go free (Suetonius, *Claudius* 25.2). Even in the legions, soldiers were cared for chiefly by other soldiers, not by professional physicians. See J. Scarborough, *Roman Medicine* (Ithaca, 1969), p. 71.

27. Vitruvius 1.4.1–7 and 8.3.20–4.1; Celsus, *De Medicina* 1.1.1; Frontinus, *Aqueducts* 2.93.

28. Celsus, for example, in the *Prooemium* to his work, gives an account of the main tenets of the three Hellenistic "schools": the Dogmatists, who emphasized anatomy; the Empiricists, who preferred philosophical reasoning; and the Methodists, who emphasized treatment of the individual patient. See Scarborough, *Roman Medicine,* pp. 38–51.

29. V. Nutton, "*Archiatri* and the Medical Profession in Antiquity," *Papers of the British School at Rome* 45 (1977): 191–226.

30. Scarborough, *Roman Medicine,* pp. 18–19, 60, 111–112.

31. Like other tradesmen, medici organized themselves into collegia: *CIL* 6.9566, 29805 (from Rome); 9.1618 (from Beneventum).

32. *Medicinae* and *tonstrinae* are juxtaposed as popular hangouts in Plautus, *Amphitryon* 1013, *Epidicus* 198; Horace, *Satires* 1.7.3.

33. Testimonia: E. J. and L. Edelstein, *Asclepius* (Baltimore, 1945), 1:431–452.

34. Cf. the tombstones of *negotiatores artis cretariae*: *CIL* 3.5833; 13.1906, 8793. Pliny disapproves of medici in his time who no longer mix their own compounds but buy them ready-made from fraudulent dealers (*Natural History* 34.108).

35. For a list of diseases mentioned by just one author, see E. F. Cordell, "The Medicine and Doctors of Horace," *Bulletin of the Johns Hopkins Hospital* 12 (1901): 233–240.

36. R. Lattimore, *Themes in Greek and Roman Epitaphs* (Urbana, Ill., 1962), pp. 181–202; *CIL* 6.10096, 15346; Cicero, *Letters to His Friends* 4.5; Catullus 96; Propertius 4.11. Cf. Pliny, *Letters* 3.16.2; 4.21; 5.16.

37. For a description of the school day in the third century A.D., see H. I. Marrou, *A History of Education in Antiquity* (Eng. tr. New York, 1956), pp. 360–366; A. C. Dionisotti, "From Ausonius' Schooldays? A Schoolbook and Its Relatives," *JRS* 72 (1982): 83–125.

38. E. Rawson, *Intellectual Life in the Late Roman Republic* (Baltimore, 1985), pp. 66–99, 320–322.

39. Suetonius's *On Grammarians* is an interesting source for the social status and circumstances of several important *grammatici* in the late republic and early principate. Nearly all were freedmen, and some were very poor in spite of their fame and ability (9, 11, 20). Others managed to live very luxuriously (23). Suetonius also mentions where some of them conducted their lessons: Marcus Antonius Gnipho taught in Julius Caesar's home when Caesar was a boy, and later gave lessons in his own residence (7). Pompey's freedman Lenaeus taught "on the Carinae, near the temple of Tellus, in the region where Pompey's house was" (15). Marcus Verrius Flaccus taught in the atrium of Catulus's house on the Palatine (17). Lucius Crassicius taught in an upstairs shop (*pergula*) (18). Gaius Julius Hyginus

taught in the Palatine Library, of which he was in charge under Augustus (20); presumably Gaius Melissus, in charge of the libraries of the Porticus Octaviae, also gave lessons there (21).

40. C. A. Forbes, "The Education and Training of Slaves in Antiquity," *TAPA* 86 (1955): 321–360; A. D. Booth, "The Schooling of Slaves in First-Century Rome," *TAPA* 109 (1979): 11–19; R. A. Kaster, "Notes on 'Primary' and 'Secondary' Schools in Late Antiquity," *TAPA* 113 (1983): 323–346.

41. See S. B. Platner and T. Ashby, *Topographical Dictionary of Ancient Rome* (Oxford, 1929), s.v. "Bibliotheca Asini Pollionis," "Bibliotheca Apollinis Palatini," "Bibliotheca Porticus Octaviae," "Bibliotheca Templi Divi Augusti," "Pacis Templum," and "Forum Traiani." L. Richardson, "The Libraries of Pompeii," *Archaeology* 30 (1977): 394–402, suggests that the Shrine of the Lares on the east side of the forum at Pompeii may have been a public library (Pl. 16).

42. See S. Treggiari, *Roman Freedmen during the Late Republic* (Oxford, 1969), p. 255, on the slave and freed *tabellarii* used by Cicero to deliver letters.

43. The letters Marcus Caelius Rufus wrote to Cicero convey a good sense of the formal and informal means by which news made its way around the city—Cicero, *Letters to His Friends* 8.

44. D. Scagliarini Corlàita, "La situazione urbanistica degli archi onorari nella prima età imperiale," in *Studi sull'arco onorario romano*, Studia Archaeologica no. 21 (Rome, 1979), pp. 29–41; F. S. Kleiner, *The Arch of Nero in Rome* (Rome, 1985).

Chapter 9. The Commercial City

1. Even basic goods like pottery and lamps, which we know were distributed widely, were manufactured on a small scale. In the late first century B.C., a cluster of workshops at Arretium, for example, dominated a wide market, including that of Rome, but as far as can be determined only a few were large enough to have even 60 workmen—G. Pucci, "La produzione della ceramica aretina: Note sull'industria nella prima età imperiale," *Dialoghi di Archeologia* 7 (1973): 255–293. In the first century A.D., these workshops were supplanted by others in southern Gaul, and later these gave up the dominance to others farther north. The distribution patterns are interesting; they emply that there may have been family connections between the earlier factories in Arretium and some of the later ones in Gaul, and also that negotiatores were active in marketing the wares. A shipment of fine pottery, perhaps typical of a certain kind of high-quality merchandise, was found in its shipping crate in a house at Pompeii— D. Atkinson, "A Hoard of Samian Ware from Pompeii," *JRS* 4 (1914): 27–

64. In general, see H. J. Loane, *Industry and Commerce of the City of Rome (50 B.C.–200 A.D.)* (Baltimore, 1938), pp. 63–65; D. P. S. Peacock, *Pottery in the Roman World: An Ethnoarchaeological Approach* (London, 1982); and K. Greene, *The Archaeology of the Roman Economy* (Berkeley, 1986), pp. 156–167. On the importance of middlemen, operating on a small scale to manage apartment houses for wealthy owners, and the absence of any large-scale modern capitalism in the real estate industry, see B. W. Frier, *Landlords and Tenants in Imperial Rome* (Princeton, 1980), pp. 21–39.

2. L. Casson, "The Role of the State in Rome's Grain Trade," *MAAR* 36 (1980): 21–33; J. Rougé, *Ships and Fleets of the Ancient Mediterranean* (Middletown, Conn., 1981). The great-grandfather of the emperor Vespasian was said to have made his fortune as a contractor of agricultural labor (Suetonius, *Vespasian* 1.4). In a common pattern, large entrepreneurs sent slaves or freedmen as *institores* ("agents") to manage a shop or branch factory, sometimes at considerable distances from the original establishment. W. V. Harris, "Roman Terracotta Lamps: The Organization of an Industry," *JRS* 70 (1980): 126–145, uses this phenomenon to explain the widespread distribution of signed "Firmalampen" over vast distances, from Italy to Gaul. Cf. E. M. Staerman and M. K. Trofimova, *Schiavitù nell'Italia imperiale, I–III secolo* (Rome, 1975).

3. On the cities' contribution to the economy of the empire, see C. Goudineau, "Les villes de la paix romaine," *Histoire de la France urbaine,* ed. G. Duby (Paris, 1980), 1:365–381; P. Leveau, "La ville antique: 'Ville de consommation'? Parasitisme social et économie antique," *Etudes rurales* 89–91 (1983): 275–287; J. Andreau, "Les financiers romains entre la ville et la campagne," *L'origine des richesses dépensées dans la ville antique,* ed. P. Leveau (Aix-en-Provence, 1985), pp. 177–196. A classic argument for the city's contribution to the benefit of all society, including the country, is J. Jacobs, *The Economy of Cities* (New York, 1969).

4. K. Hopkins, "Economic Growth in Towns in Classical Antiquity," *Towns in Societies,* ed. P. Abrams and E. A. Wrigley (Cambridge, 1978), pp. 35–77; K. Hopkins, "Taxes and Trade in the Roman Empire (200 B.C.– A.D. 400), *JRS* 70 (1980): 101–125.

5. J. K. Evans, "Wheat Production and Its Social Consequences in the Roman World," *Classical Quarterly* 31 (1981): 428–442.

6. P. Garnsey, "Famine in Rome," *Trade and Famine in Classical Antiquity,* ed. P. Garnsey and C. R. Whittaker (Cambridge, 1983), pp. 56–65; Evans, "Wheat Production," p. 428 nn. 3–4, lists shortages in 75*, 66, 57*, 41, 40*, 39, 38, 36, and 22* B.C.; in A.D. 5, 6*, 7, 19, 32*, 42, 51*; and under Nero, Otho, Antoninus, Marcus Aurelius, and Commodus* (asterisks indicate years or reigns in which rioting was recorded). In addition, Domitian (Suetonius, *Domitian* 7.2) issued a decree that limited the

cultivation of vines, apparently to encourage farmers to grow more-essential grain.

7. D. R. Brothwell and P. Brothwell, *Food in Antiquity* (London, 1969); L. Moritz, *Grain-Mills and Flour in Classical Antiquity* (Oxford, 1958).

8. G. Rickman, *Roman Granaries and Store Buildings* (Cambridge, 1971); G. Rickman, *The Corn Supply of Ancient Rome* (Oxford, 1980).

9. In 58 B.C., Publius Clodius Pulcher as tribune passed a law that made the grain at the monthly distributions free of all charges to all citizens. Pompey in 56 B.C. tried to bring some order into the lists of citizens eligible for the free ration of grain. Julius Caesar tried to draw up a new and more accurate list, and he also established two *aediles Cereales* with special responsiblity for the grain supply.

10. Until this time, the distribution of grain (to between 100,000 and 200,000 citizens each month) was held at various warehouses throughout the city, but in the middle of the first century A.D. it was centralized at the Porticus Minucia in the Campus Martius. Seneca (*De Brevitate Vitae* 19.1) describes the duties of the praefectus annonae: "that the grain be poured into the horrea, unhurt by the dishonesty or neglect of those who transport it, that it not collect moisture and be spoiled or overheated, that it tally in weight and measure."

11. Trajan recognized the *collegium* of the bakers and granted its members special privileges; and he recognized the annona as a *munus*, which exempted the wealthy shippers and businessmen involved in the grain supply from the need to provide other public services. Aurelian substituted baked bread for grain. Diocletian required the sons of bakers to become bakers, and the private property of the bakers to become part of the assets of the collegium to which they belonged.

12. The Epagathus and Epapthroditus who owned one of the horrea at Ostia (I.viii.3) seem by their names to have been freedmen.

13. E. Tengström, *Bread for the People* (Stockholm, 1974); Rickman, *Corn Supply*, pp. 120–143, 202–206.

14. B. J. Mayeske, "Bakers, Bakeshops, and Bread: A Social and Economic Study," *Pompeii and the Vesuvian Landscape* (Washington, D.C., 1979), pp. 39–58. Bakeries are shown in plan in Figures 12 and 13.

15. The word *macellum* is derived from a Greek word meaning "latticework" and possibly referring to the screens in front of individual shops.

16. N. Nabers, "The Architectural Variations of the Macellum," *AJA* 72 (1968): 169.

17. Details of the oil and wine trade are known because of stamps on the handles of the amphorae in which these bulky liquids were shipped. Loane, *Industry and Commerce*, pp. 16–26; E. Rodriguez Almeida, *Il Monte Testaccio: Ambiente, storia, materiali* (Rome, 1984); D. P. S. Peacock and

D. F. Williams, *Amphorae and the Roman Economy* (London, 1986); and the articles on Cosa cited in Chapter 16, notes 4 and 5, of the present volume. For general surveys of the Roman agricultural economy, see K. D. White, *Country Life in Classical Times* (London, 1977); and Greene, *Archaeology of the Roman Economy*.

18. A series of Pliny's letters (3.19, 8.2, 9.37) illustrates the agricultural system in Etruria at the end of the first century A.D.; cf. the commentary on these passages in A. N. Sherwin-White, *The Letters of Pliny* (Oxford, 1966). See also R. MacMullen, "Market-Days in the Roman Empire," *Phoenix* 24 (1970): 333–341.

19. Varro (*On Agriculture* 3.16.10) tells of the Veianii, who got rich by raising bees on a single acre they had inherited. The importance of beekeeping is reflecting in the attention it receives in Columella, *On Agriculture* 9, and in Vergil, *Georgics* 4. The Romans preferred the honey of bees that fed on thyme.

20. Varro, *On Agriculture* 3.17.2–10; Seneca, *Naturales Quaestiones* 3.17–18, *Epistulae Morales* 95.42. On the fishery at Cosa, see Chapter 16 of the present volume.

21. I.xiii.8. This garum factory is discussed briefly in E. LaRocca and M. and A. deVos, *Guida archeologica di Pompei* (Rome, 1976), pp. 228–229, and W. F. Jashemski, *The Gardens of Pompeii* (New Rochelle, N.Y., 1979), pp. 195–196. Cf. T. H. Corcoran, "Roman Fish Sauces," *Classical Journal* 58 (1963): 204–210; R. L. Curtis, "The Fishing Industry of Pompeii," *AJA* 84 (1980): 202–203; and idem, "The Salted Fish Industry of Pompeii," *Archaeology* 37.6 (1984): 58–59, 74–75.

22. G. Duckworth, *The Nature of Roman Comedy* (Princeton, 1952), pp. 249–253, lists the examples of clever and faithful comic slaves. E. Segal, *Roman Laughter* (Cambridge, Mass., 1968), pp. 99–136, reminds us that these slaves are literary creations made to inhabit a world of fantasy; the passage from the *Digest* paraphrased in the text shows, however, that they had real-life prototypes, even though they were probably considerably more respectful than their comic counterparts.

23. According to P. A. Brunt, "The Roman Mob," *Past and Present* 35 (1966): 3–27, esp. 15, among the jewelers and goldsmiths in Rome whose tombstones survive, 58 percent were freedmen, 35 percent were slaves, and only 7 percent were freeborn. (This does not necessarily mean that only 7 percent of the goldsmiths were freeborn, but it does show that a large number of slaves and freedmen were active in that trade.) J. E. Skydsgaard, "The Disintegration of the Roman Labour Market and the Clientela Theory," in *Studia Romana in honorem P. Krarup,* ed. K. Ascani et al. (Odense, 1976), pp. 44–48, suggests that even without large networks, the rich controlled much of the commercial activity of cities because their clients operated the small shops: "Splitting up of production into many small

units gave the well-to-do financier an enormous social and political prestige, which for him was more precious than increased profit." Cf. M. Finley, *The Ancient Economy* (Berkeley, 1976), passim.

24. Appendix A in R. MacMullen, *Roman Social Relations* (New Haven, 1974), pp. 129–137, lists evidence for the neighborhoods of Rome and other cities. Among his examples of specific tradesmen (p. 134) are a *faber lecticarius ab cloaca maxima,* an *argentarius de Velabro,* an *argentarius Macelli Magni,* an *aurifex extra portam Flumentanam,* an *aurifex de Sacra Via,* a *tonsor de Vico Scauri,* and a *caelator de Sacra Via.* On these and other topics relating to the business life to Rome, the standard work is still Loane, *Industry and Commerce.*

25. We hear a lot, however, about fortunes being lost in long-distance trade and shipping; cf., for example, Cato, *On Agriculture,* praef., and Aulus Gellius 3.3.14. On the chatty, friendly atmosphere of the mercantile neighborhood and the trade associations that sprang up in it, see MacMullen, *Roman Social Relations,* pp. 72–87.

26. *CIL* 6.9346, 9545, 33872, 37804; 10.6492. See E. Van Deman, "The Neronian Sacra Via," *AJA* 27 (1923): 383–424; E. Van Deman, "The Sacra Via of Nero," *MAAR* 5 (1925): 115–126; Loane, *Industry and Commerce,* pp. 133–135; S. Panciera, "Tra epigrafia e topografia: 1. Negotiantes de Sacra Via," *Archeologia Classica* 22 (1970): 131–138.

27. Loane, *Industry and Commerce,* pp. 123–126.

28. Ibid., pp. 69–71; S. Treggiari, "Jobs in the Household of Livia," *Papers of the British School at Rome* 43 (1975): 48–77.

29. W. O. Moeller, *The Wool Trade of Ancient Pompeii* (Leiden, 1976), pp. 77–78, 102–103; cf., for an example, his discussion of the *textrina* of the Minuci at Pompeii (I.x.8), p. 19.

30. Loane, *Industry and Commerce,* pp. 33–35.

31. Moeller, *The Wool Trade,* p. 79.

32. On shoemaking and tanneries, see Loane, *Industry and Commerce,* pp. 77–79, and the citations of appropriate tomb inscriptions. The shoemakers of the capital may well have included three Jewish immigrant "leather workers" known from the New Testament: Priscilla, Aquila, and Paul—R. Hock, *The Social Context of Paul's Ministry: Tentmaking and Apostleship* (Philadelphia, 1980). Well-preserved vats and rooms from a tannery remain under the Church of Saint Cecilia; see *PDAR,* s.v. "Coraria Septimiana."

33. On the Horrea Agrippiana, see F. W. Shipley, *Agrippa's Building Activities in Rome* (St. Louis, 1933), pp. 81–83. The regulations governing such leases are preserved in a *lex* concerning the Horrea Nervae near the Porta San Sebastiano between the Via Appia and the Via Ardeatina (*CIL* 6.33747, 33860; cf. Loane, *Industry and Commerce,* p. 115).

34. Tomb inscriptions record *vestiarii* whose shops were in the Horrea

(*CIL* 6.9972, 10026; 14.3958) and on the Cermalus Minusculus just above (*CIL* 6.33920), which indicates the kind of grouping of similar traders noted earlier. Cf. *PDAR*, 1:475.

35. Domitian enforced the laws that kept the shopkeepers (*institores*) in their shops (Martial 7.61), and a law recorded by Papirianus, who died in A.D. 212, required merchants to keep the streets in front of their shops clear (Justinian, *Digest* 43.10.1).

36. Examples in Rome exist, but for the most part are not easily accessible. The shops built into the side of the Church of Saints John and Paul on the Caelian exemplify the row of tabernae facing the street. An insula under the Via Nazionale (P. Harsh, "The Origins of the Insulae at Ostia," *MAAR* 12 [1935]: 7–66, fig. 19) had rows of long, narrow shops fronting on several wide alleys. A large complex built in Hadrian's reign along the Via Lata, near the present Piazza Colonna, was criss-crossed by a grid of narrow streets lined with tabernae—G. Gatti, "Caratteristiche edilizie di un quartiere di Roma del II secolo d.C.," *Quaderni dell'Istituto di Storia dell'Architettura* 35–48 (1961): 49–66. The shops on the ground floor of the insula on Via Giulio Romano, next to the Victor Emmanuel Monument (cf. Fig. 18), seem to have been grouped around a courtyard, as were those in the Horrea Agrippiana (Pl. 2) and, next to them, in the complex under the Church of Saint Anastasia—P. B. Whitehead, "The Church of S. Anastasia in Rome," *AJA* 31 (1927): 405–420. For a general typology of these tabernae, see Loane, *Industry and Commerce*, pp. 62–63, and A. Boëthius, *The Golden House of Nero* (Ann Arbor, 1960), pp. 158–161.

37. W. L. MacDonald, *The Architecture of the Roman Empire*, vol. 1 (New Haven, 1965), pp. 75–93.

38. Cf. Horace's picture of the auctioneer (*praeco*) Volteius Mena (*Epistles* 1.7.56–69), who was known for hustling and for relaxing as appropriate, for making money and using it, for enjoying the company of his unassuming friends, his house, and the amusements of the Campus Martius.

39. J. Andreau, *Les affaires de Monsieur Jucundus* (Rome, 1974).

40. The values are those established under Augustus. In general, see M. Crawford, *Coinage and Money under the Roman Republic* (London, 1984); and Greene, *Archaeology of the Roman Economy*, pp. 45–66.

41. We know from the parable of the vineyard in the New Testament (Matthew 20:1–16), for example, that a denarius (four sesterces) was a good wage for a day's agricultural work; assuming that day laborers in the Palestinian countryside did not find work every day, we might figure about 200 denarii as an annual income. This accords with what we know of the salaries paid to Roman soldiers in the first century of the principate: legionary soliders were paid 225 denarii a year, auxiliary troops between 100 and 200. A basic slave's ration, according to Seneca, *Epistulae Morales* 80.7, was 5 denarii and 5 modii of grain; therefore, a slave's (subsistence?)

allowance would amount to 30–40 sesterces (7.5–10 denarii) a month. R. Duncan-Jones, *The Economy of the Roman Empire* (Cambridge, 1974), pp. 146–147, calculates the average value of a modius at 2–4 sesterces, and concludes that 5 modii a month would provide the equivalent of 3,000–3,500 calories a day, "close to modern ideals of 3,300 calories per day for male adults."

42. These figures come from Pompeii and are discussed by R. Etienne, *La vie quotidienne à Pompéi* (Paris, 1966), pp. 229–233, along with *CIL* 4.4000, 4227, 4428, 4888, and 5380 (an expense account for three persons, including a slave, which covers cheese, bread, oil and wine, and an occasional fish, onion, date, pear, incense, handkerchief, seal, and lamp— or an average of 2 sesterces per person per day). Duncan-Jones, *Economy of the Roman Empire,* pp. 140, 238–248, adds some prices mentioned in Petronius, *Satyricon* 44, 45, 57, 68, 71, 97. See also the innkeeper's inscription from Aesernia, *CIL* 9.2689 (translated in Chapter 10, page 182, of the present volume), and Rickman, *Corn Supply,* pp. 143–155.

43. Pliny (*Natural History* 13.92), for example, refers to an exotic table that sold for 1,300,000 sesterces, enough to buy a large farm. As an illustration of the great gulf between rich and poor, D. MacKenzie, "Pay Differentials in the Early Empire," *Classical World* 76 (1983): 267–273, shows the great gap between soldiers at the bottom and the top of the legionary pay scales.

44. Duncan-Jones, *Economy of the Roman Empire,* pp. 348–350.

45. B. W. Frier, "The Rental Market in Early Imperial Rome," *JRS* 67 (1977): 34–35.

46. This episode has been much discussed, and very different lessons have been derived from it. See M. I. Finley, *The Ancient Economy* (Berkeley, 1973), p. 75; L. Casson, "Unemployment, the Building Trade, and Suetonius, Vesp. 18," *Bulletin of the American Society of Papyrologists* 15 (1978): 43–51; and P. A. Brunt, "Free Labour and Public Works at Rome," *JRS* 70 (1980): 81–100.

47. When speed was necessary, as in the rebuilding of the city after Nero's fire, convicted criminals also were pressed into service (Suetonius, *Nero* 31.3).

48. R. Meiggs, *Trees and Timber in the Ancient Mediterranean World* (Oxford, 1982), pp. 325–370; J. Ward-Perkins, "The Marble Trade and Its Organization: Evidence from Nicomedia," *MAAR* 36 (1980): 325–338; J. C. Fant, "Four Unfinished Sarcophagus Lids at Docimium and the Roman Imperial Quarry System in Phrygia," *AJA* 89 (1985): 655–662.

49. When Verres as aedile needed to have the columns on the Temple of Castor repaired, he turned to a contractor with whom he set up a sweetheart deal (Cicero, *Verrines, Part Two,* 2.1.130–154).

50. *CIL* 6.1060, 9405, 10300; J.-P. Waltzing, *Etude historique sur les cor-*

porations professionnelles chez les Romains, vol. 2 (Louvain, 1896), pp. 117–121.

51. Justinian, *Digest* 45.1.137.3. Cf. Brunt, "Free Labour," p. 87, and D. E. Strong, "The Administration of Public Building in Rome during the Late Republic and Early Empire," *Bulletin of the Institute of Classical Studies* 15 (1968): 97–109.

52. See J. B. Ward-Perkins, *Roman Imperial Architecture* (Harmondsworth, 1981), p. 70, on the Colosseum. *CIL* 31603 shows that the building of the Via Caecilia was let out to a different contractor (*manceps*) for each short stretch; see Brunt, "Free Labour," p. 85.

53. New analyses of construction in *opus reticulatum* dates it to the last two decades of the second century B.C. rather than the middle of the first century, where the earlier scholarly consensus had placed it: this new technique, in which the irregular facing *opus incertum* was replaced by an arrangement of facing stones in a regular, net-like pattern, was less strong structurally (Vitruvius 2.8.17) but may have been more efficient and a reflection of large-scale construction operations with more specialized labor—F. Coarelli, "Public Building in Rome between the Second Punic War and Sulla," *Papers of the British School at Rome* 45 (1977): 1–23. It is estimated that the number of slaves doubled during the second century B.C.— P. Gros, *Architecture et société à Rome et en Italie centro-méridionale aux deux derniers siècles de la république* (Brussels, 1974), p. 12. For evidence of intense real estate speculation in the last century of the republic, see Plutarch, *Marius* 34.2: during the first half of that century the price of a certain villa at Baiae increased more than thirty times. The high price of Cicero's town house on the Palatine in 62 B.C. also is symptomatic, as is Strabo's hint (5.3.7) that speculators were very active in the second half of the century. On the technology of the Pantheon, see R. Mark and R. Hutchinson, "On the Structure of the Roman Pantheon," *Art Bulletin* 68 (1986): 24–34.

Chapter 10. Households and Housing

1. K. Hopkins, *Death and Renewal* (Cambridge, 1983), pp. 117–119; B. Rawson, "The Roman Family," *The Family in Ancient Rome: New Perspectives,* ed. B. Rawson (Ithaca, 1986), pp. 7–15; R. P. Saller and B. D. Shaw, "Tombstones and Roman Family Relations in the Principate: Civilians, Soldiers, and Slaves," *JRS* 74 (1984): 124–156.

2. S. Treggiari, "Jobs in the Household of Livia," *Papers of the British School at Rome* 43 (1975): 48–77. She lists (pp. 64–65) the important inscriptions of large urban *familiae* attested by grave inscriptions, and (pp. 72–77) the jobs that are attested in Livia's household, which we should probably envision in the House of Livia and House of Augustus on the

Palatine. See also G. Alföldy, *The Social History of Rome* (Eng. tr. Totowa, N.J., 1985), p. 137.

3. Treggiari, "Jobs in the Household of Livia"; W. V. Harris, "Towards a Study of the Roman Slave Trade," *MAAR* 36 (1980): 119.

4. Seneca (*De Tranquillitate* 8.6), for example, says that a poor man could consider himself wealthy if he had two lowly slaves and a room with a little more space than he was used to.

5. He had the right to reject it, and exposure and abandonment were facts of Roman life, even if we cannot be sure how common they were.

6. The details and sources for the wedding celebration are collected in J. Carcopino, *Daily Life in Ancient Rome* (Eng. tr. New Haven, 1940), pp. 80–84.

7. On funerary rites, see J. M. C. Toynbee, *Death and Burial in the Roman World* (Ithaca, 1971). The political and social implications are discussed in C. Nicolet, *The World of the Citizen in Republican Rome* (Eng. tr. Berkeley, 1980), pp. 346–352.

8. D. G. Orr, "Roman Domestic Religion: the Evidence of the Household Shrines," *ANRW* 2.16.2 (1978): 1557–1591; D. P. Harmon, "The Family Festivals of Rome," *ANRW* 2.16.2 (1978): 1592–1603.

9. H. H. Scullard, *Festivals and Ceremonies of the Roman Republic* (Ithaca, 1981), pp. 74–76, 87, 205–207. The Saturnalia market set up at the Porticus Neptuni recalls the modern Befana Market in the Piazza Navona in late December and early January, in observance of Epiphany.

10. E. Gjerstad, *Early Rome*, vol. 2 (Rome, 1956), p. 139; F. Coarelli, *Roma sepolta* (Rome, 1984), pp. 56–60.

11. The plan resembles the Bronze Age Greek *megaron*—A. G. McKay, *Houses, Villas, and Palaces in the Roman World* (Ithaca, 1975), p. 15; A. Boëthius, *Etruscan and Early Roman Architecture* (Harmondsworth, 1978), pp. 106–107, however, expresses doubts. The plan also resembles houses in certain Etruscan cities: J. B. Ward-Perkins, "Veii: The Historical Topography of the Ancient City," *Papers of the British School at Rome* 29 (1961): 32.

12. In fact the earliest known examples of an atrium are in Marzabotto, a fifth-century Etruscan city—G. Mansuelli, "La casa etrusca di Marzabotto," *MDAI(R)* 70 (1963): 44–62; McKay, *Houses, Villas, and Palaces*, pp. 19–22.

13. An additional type discussed by Vitruvius, the "testudinate," seems to be a simple hip roof, and is restored on some of the houses in the view of the early Forum Romanum (Fig. 7).

14. A. Laidlaw and J. Packer, "Excavations in the House of Sallust in Pompeii," *AJA* 75 (1971): 206–207. A similar plan is seen in the nearby House of the Surgeon (VI.i.10), which is earlier, however, having been built

in the fourth century B.C., when limestone was used for the exterior walls
—Boëthius, *Etruscan and Early Roman Architecture,* pp. 82–84, 88.

15. Livy 6.25.9; Suetonius, *Augustus* 45.4; Martial 1.70.13–14.

16. Vitruvius (6.3.1) distinguishes between the "tetrastyle" atrium,
which had four columns, one at each corner of the compluvium, and the
"Corinthian," which had a larger number of columns surrounding the im-
pluvium and made the atrium look like the peristyle of a Greek house. On
interior decoration, see E. J. Dwyer, "Sculpture and Its Display in Private
Houses of Pompeii," in *Pompeii and the Vesuvian Landscape* (Washington,
D.C., 1979), pp. 59–77; and D. L. Thompson, "Painted Portraiture at
Pompeii," ibid., pp. 78–92.

17. F. E. Brown, *Cosa: The Making of a Roman Town* (Ann Arbor, 1980),
pp. 64–69.

18. Z. Yavetz, "The Living Conditions of the Urban Plebs in Republican
Rome," *Latomus* 17 (1958): 500–517; P. A. Brunt, "The Roman Mob," *Past
and Present* 35 (1966): 3–27.

19. At the end of the first century A.D., Proculus still kept up the tradition of an open atrium in his house on the Palatine; cf. Martial 1.70. Pliny,
Letters 5.6.15, in describing his villa in Tifernum, mentions its "old-fashioned atrium" (*atrium ex modo veterum*). Vitruvius prescribes the atrium
house as the standard, but he is reflecting the program of the Augustan
period, which looked back at republican traditions as standards to be imitated, a program that was seldom carried out in the succeeding centuries,
whether in architecture, society, or politics.

20. W. F. Jashemski, *The Gardens of Pompeii* (New Rochelle, N.Y., 1979),
concentrates on Pompeii. P. Grimal, *Les Jardins Romains* (Paris, 1969), devotes more attention to the city of Rome. P. Zanker, "Die Villa als Vorbild
des späten pompeijanischen Wohngeschmacks," *Jahrbuch des Deutschen
Archäologischen Instituts* 94 (1979): 460–523, suggests that upwardly
mobile types, such as the successful businessman and the prosperous
freedman, used garden paintings in an attempt to imitate the traditional
Roman sense of the aristocrat as country gentleman.

21. The Regionary Catalogue of the fourth century A.D. (see Chapter 6,
notes 6 and 7) gives a total of 1,719 private houses (*domūs*) in the city, in
contrast to 46,602 *insulae*; it is not clear whether the *insula* here means an
entire tenement building or an individual apartment. The Catalogue also
lists several private homes of distinguished Romans: the House of Philip on
the Caelian; the House of Brittius Fraesens on the Oppian; the House of
Dio on the Palatine; the Houses of Cilo, Cornificia, and Hadrian on the
Little Aventine; and the House of Trajan on the Aventine.

22. Vitruvius (6.5.2) may have had some such room in mind when he
wrote that men of affairs need to have "basilicas," as well as libraries and
picture galleries, in their houses. Cf. Y. Thebert, "Private Life and Domestic

Architecture in Roman Africa," in *A History of Private Life: From Pagan Rome to Byzantium*, ed. P. Veyne (Eng. tr. Cambridge, Mass., 1987), p. 378.

23. The vocabulary and residential patterns of these apartments have been explained by G. Hermansen ("The Medianum and the Roman Apartment," *Phoenix* 24 [1970]: 342–347; and *Ostia: Aspects of Roman City Life* [Edmonton, 1982], pp. 17–53) and by B. W. Frier ("The Rental Market in Early Imperial Rome," *JRS* 67 [1977]: 27–34; and *Landlords and Tenants in Imperial Rome* [Princeton, 1980], esp. pp. 3–20, drawing on such legal passages as Justinian, *Digest* 9.3.5.1–2). Frier (*Landlords and Tenants*, pp. 39–47) emphasizes that many members of the upper classes, including even senators, rented apartments.

24. For a plan, see J. M. Packer, "The Insulae of Imperial Ostia," *MAAR* 31 (1971): 117, fig. 64.

25. A. Boëthius, *The Golden House of Nero* (Ann Arbor, 1960), pp. 159–161, uses the modern Italian expression "palazzo di tutti" to describe this type of insula. The other types in his scheme are a single row of tabernae; two such rows back to back; and three or four rows grouped around a courtyard. Packer, "Insulae of Imperial Ostia," pp. 6–15, suggests another typology of Roman mass housing, based on the functions of the ground floor of the insula: shops, apartments, factories, or workrooms grouped around courtyards in various combinations.

26. J. M. Packer, "La casa di Via Giulio Romano," *Bullettino della Commissione Archeologica comunale in Roma* 81 (1968–69): 127–148. The house under the Church of Saints John and Paul on the Caelian offers a sense of the insula neighborhood: a building with tabernae facing the street, later walled up and converted into a large private dwelling; a neighborhood public bath; and an enclosed courtyard with a nymphaeum.

27. Frier, "Rental Market," p. 28 n. 8, lists references to insularii working for the great families of the early principate; see also *CIL* 6.5857. An officinator of the Insula Vitaliana in Rome (*CIL* 6.33893), Critonia Philema, managed the popina in the Insula of Critonius Dassus (*CIL* 6.9824); both Philema and Dassus had been slaves of Quintus Critonius, and Dassus had apparently earned enough as a sculptor or engraver to buy the insula and give his friend Philema a job. A shrine at the Insula of Bolanus was dedicated to Hercules, perhaps as a patron of all the tenants (*CIL* 6.67).

28. The *Letters* of Cicero and Pliny document the comings and goings at the villas of the ruling class. See L. Casson, *Travel in the Roman World* (Toronto, 1974); J. P. V. D. Balsdon, *Life and Leisure in Ancient Rome* (New York, 1969), pp. 224–243.

29. Two other luxurious examples are the House of Octavius Quartio (Loreius Tiburtinus, II.ii.2) and the Estate of Julia Felix (II.iv.2), near the Amphitheater on the Via dell'Abbondanza. Both were upper-class houses

converted into rental facilities in the last years before the destruction of the city.

30. E. Gibert, "Hôtelleries et hôteliers de Pompéi," *Caesarodunum* 7 (1972): 325–334.

31. Jashemski, *Gardens of Pompeii*, pp. 171–172. We have what amounts to an adverisement for such an inn's garden, in the poem *Copa* of the *Appendix Vergiliana*, in which the proprietress entices the customer with promises of shade, refreshment, and entertainment.

32. H. T. Rowell, "Satyricon 95–96," *Classical Philology* 52 (1957): 217–221; Frier, "Rental Market," pp. 31–32.

Chapter 11. City and Suburbs

1. The Roman inclination to denigrate city life: R. MacMullen, *Roman Social Relations* (New Haven, 1974), pp. 28–31; Juvenal 3; Pliny, *Letters* 1.9. Praise of life in the country: Horace, *Epistles* 1.7, 14; Martial 1.55 and 12.57; Pliny, *Letters* 2.17 and 5.6 (among others).

2. Suetonius (*Vespasian* 5.4) tells how a stray dog once wandered into the emperor's breakfast room, carrying a severed human hand found at a crossroads.

3. In Rome teams of *iuvenes vici* are attested which seem to have been a kind of neighborhood boys' club; see S. Panciera, "Tra epigrafia e topografia: 3. Regiones, vici e iuventus," *Archeologia Classica* 22 (1970): 151–163, and MacMullen, *Roman Social Relations*, pp. 68–69. Political graffiti at Pompeii show that *vicini* banded together to support the candidacies of a favorite son (*CIL* 4.171); see, in general, M. Della Corte, *Case ed abitanti di Pompeii* (Rome, 1954).

4. F. Castagnoli, "Topografia e urbanistica di Roma nel IV secolo a.C.," *Studi Romani* 22 (1974): 429.

5. The sources are collected in G. Lugli, *Fontes ad topographiam veteris urbis Romae pertinentes,* vol. 8, pt. 1 (Rome, 1960), pp. 125–154. Cf. R. Witherstine, "Where the Romans Lived in the First Century B.C.," *Classical Journal* 21 (1926): 566–579; and R. G. Nisbet, *M. Tulli Ciceronis de domo sua ad pontifices oratio* (Oxford, 1939), pp. 166–170, 206–209.

6. The details of the plaster model are based on several fragments of the Forma Urbis that show the buildings on each side of the Clivus Suburanus as it climbs the Esquiline behind the Thermae Titi and the Thermae Traiani: tabernae, insulae, horrea, and the monumental Porticus Liviae group themselves around a warren of crooked streets.

7. G. Carettoni et al., *La pianta marmorea di Roma antica* (Rome, 1960), p. 148, frag. 543.

8. F. O. Copley, *Exclusus Amator: A Study in Latin Love Poetry* (Baltimore, 1956).

9. F. W. Harsh, " 'Angiportum,' 'Platea,' and 'Vicus,' " *Classical Philology* 32 (1937): 44–58.

10. F. Coarelli, *Guida archeologica di Roma* (Milan, 1974), p. 18, argues for a sixth-century date; E. Säflund, *Le mura di Roma repubblicana* (Lund, 1932), pp. 44–75, who proposed a fifth-century date, was followed by M. Todd, *The Walls of Rome* (Totowa, N.J., 1978), pp. 13–14.

11. The bucolic theme was a commonplace of Alexandrian literature in the Hellenistic Age, as represented chiefly by Theocritus. It became very popular in the Augustan Age, as interpreted by Vergil, Horace, and Tibullus (see Chapter 4 of this volume). Juvenal's Third Satire is a sardonic treatment of the same theme.

12. The stucco reliefs from this villa, now in the Museo Nazionale, are discussed by E. L. Wadsworth, "Stucco Reliefs of the First and Second Centuries Still Extant in Rome," *MAAR* 4 (1924): 23–34, and by B. Andreae, *The Art of Rome* (Eng. tr. New York, 1977), pp. 118–121, who also gives a plan. Tradition identifies this as the Villa of Clodia, the sister of Publius Clodius, who was (perhaps) the "Lesbia" of Catullus, and it is amusing for us to imagine the smart set that Clodia typifies enjoying a villa like this one, especially in view of Cicero's spicy description of such goings-on (*Pro Caelio* 36). More likely, the villa was built in 19 B.C. for Julia, the daughter of Augustus—H. G. Beyen, "Les *domini* de la Villa de la Farnesina," *Studia varia C. W. Vollgraff . . . oblata* (Amsterdam, 1948), pp. 3–31. Other important villas in Rome are the Horti Sallustiani and Horti Lucullani, the Villa of Livia at Prima Porta, the Villa of the Quintilii on the Via Appia, the Villa of Sette Bassi on the Via Latina, and the Domus Aurea of Nero.

13. Cf. Vitruvius's "basilica," mentioned in Chapter 10, note 22, above.

14. The paintings are interpreted as a representation of a Dionysiac initiation ceremony by M. I. Rostovtzeff, *Mystic Italy* (New York, 1927), pp. 42–55. E. LaRocca and M. and A. deVos, *Guida archeologica di Pompei* (Rome, 1976), pp. 342–346, interpret them as a satiric mime show.

15. The Villa of the Papyri in Herculaneum was the model for the John Paul Getty Museum in Malibu, California—N. Neuerburg, "The New J. Paul Getty Museum," *Archaeology* 27 (1974) 175–181.

16. The Scipios were apparently unusual among the republican aristocracy in using inhumation rather than cremation. On the restoration, see F. Coarelli, "Il sepolcro degli Scipioni," *Dialoghi di Archeologia* 6 (1972) 36–106.

17. Cf. the tombs of Lucius Minucius Plancus in Gaeta; Marcus Valerius Messala Corvinus at the sixth milepost of the Via Appia, known today as the Casal Rotondo; Marcus Lucilius Paetus on the Via Salaria north of Rome; and Caecilia Metella at the third milepost of the Via Appia.

18. *PDAR*, s.v. "Sepulcrum Eurysacis." The fictional freedman-entrepreneur Trimalchio (Petronius, *Satyricon* 71) also is shown planning

for a showy, somewhat vulgar tomb for himself and his wife.

19. LaRocca and deVos, *Guida archeologica di Pompei*, pp. 328–334; J. M. C. Toynbee, *Death and Burial in the Roman World* (Ithaca, 1971), pp. 118–126.

Chapter 12. Social Life in the City

1. To divide the day (and also the night) into twelve equal hours was natural for a people whose clocks were the movement of the sun across the sky and of its shadow across a sundial. When water clocks came into use, they had to be specially calibrated to account for the variable length of day.

2. J. P. V. D. Balsdon, *Life and Leisure in Ancient Rome* (New York, 1969), pp. 19–26, gives a detailed account, with references, of the way Romans spent the morning. For libraries, cf. Vitruvius 6.4.1. and an inscription from Athens stating that a library would be open from the first to the sixth hour: R. E. Wycherley, *The Athenian Agora*, vol. 3 (Princeton, 1957), p. 150.

3. The emphasis that the *Copa* (in the *Appendix Vergiliana*) places on the cool bowers of her garden makes it seem that she is addressing a midday clientele—W. F. Jashemski, *The Gardens of Pompeii* (New Rochelle, N.Y., 1979), pp. 167–181.

4. A. Colini et al., *La pianta marmorea di Roma antica* (Rome, 1960), frag. 21.

5. For a literary description of such a grand imperial bath, see Lucian, *Hippias* 4–8. For a reproduction of Palladio's plan of the Thermae Titi, see J. B. Ward-Perkins, *Roman Imperial Architecture* (Harmondsworth, 1981), p. 72, fig. 33. On sculptural decoration, see M. Marvin, "Freestanding Sculptures from the Baths of Caracalla," *AJA* 87 (1983): 347–384.

6. Balsdon, *Life and Leisure in Ancient Rome*, pp. 35–36, gives examples and references to various dinner parties; the guest list usually included between three and nine guests.

7. On menus, the ranking of guests, entertainment, and slaves' duties at dinner parties, see ibid., pp. 40–53.

8. See Y. Thébert, "Private Life and Domestic Architecture in Roman Africa," *A History of Private Life: From Pagan Rome to Byzantium*, ed. P. Veyne (Eng. tr. Cambridge, Mass., 1987), pp. 371–372: "Reading how Juvenal or Martial . . . inform their guests in writing of the sophisticated, falsely modest menu of the dinner they are about to eat, with promises of properly moral, intellectual conversation, we see that there is no real difference between them and Trimalchio. For all these hosts the dinner is an occasion to teach, to preach a philosophy derived ultimately from the master's personal history."

9. Jashemski, *Gardens of Pompeii*, pp. 179–180, discusses restaurants

as meeting places for workers and tradesmen.

10. The Greek word *thermopolium,* which is often used in modern books to describe these street-front snack bars, does not seem to have been used as part of the Romans' restaurant vocabulary—T. Kleberg, *Hôtels, restaurants et cabarets dans l'antiquité romaine* (Uppsala, 1957), pp. 5–31.

11. There are many unresolved questions about the significance of these laws, and we are not sure whether the different archaeological data at Pompeii and at Ostia reflect a chronological difference or simply a local one resulting from Pompeii's role as an agricultural market and Ostia's role as a commercial port. See Kleberg, *Hôtels, restaurants et caberets,* pp. 40–46, with the review by H. T. Rowell in *AJA* 62 (1958): 123–125; and G. Hermansen, "Roman Inns and the Law," *Polis and Imperium: Studies in Honour of E. T. Salmon,* ed. J. A. S. Evans (Toronto, 1974), pp. 167–181. R. Meiggs, *Roman Ostia* (Oxford, 1960), pp. 428–430, cites evidence that drinks and a few canapés of olives and fruit were the chief items consumed in the inns of Ostia.

12. J.-P. Waltzing, *Etude historique sur les corporations professionnelles chez les Romains* (Louvain, 1895–1900); F. M. DeRobertis, *Storia delle corporazioni e del regime associativo nel mondo romano* (Bari, 1972). On the professional activities of collegia, see R. MacMullen, "A Note on Roman Strikes," *Classical Journal* 58 (1963): 269–271, and his *Roman Social Relations* (New Haven, 1974), pp. 72–87. On collegia of immigrants and expatriates, see G. LaPiana, "Foreign Groups in Rome during the First Centuries of the Empire," *Harvard Theological Review* 20 (1927): 183–403. On *collegia iuvenum,* see Chapter 8, page 138, of the present volume. Inscriptions from Lambaesis (*CIL* 8.2551–2562, 2586, 2601, 2636, 2733, 2751, 18070) give some idea of the groups of soldiers and veterans that existed. A typical *collegium tenuiorum* was the Collegium Dianae et Antinoi at Lanuvium; *CIL* 14.2112 records its constitution and bylaws.

13. On the Ostian guilds and their scholae, see R. Meiggs, *Roman Ostia,* pp. 311–336; and G. Hermansen, "The *Stuppatores* and their Guild in Ostia," *AJA* 86 (1982): 121–126. On meeting places of collegia with religious purposes, see J. E. Stambaugh, "The Functions of Roman Temples," *ANRW* 2.16.1 (1978): 588–591.

14. E. Gabba, "The *Collegia* of Numa: Problems of Method and Political Ideas," *JRS* 74 (1984): 81–86, warns against a naïve use of this passage.

Chapter 13. The City and the Gods

1. For a general survey and bibliography, see J. E. Stambaugh, "The Functions of Roman Temples," *ANRW* 2.16.1 (1978): 554–608.

2. The building complex is described by K. M. Phillips, "Bryn Mawr College Excavations in Tuscany, 1971," *AJA* 76 (1972): 249–255. For sup-

plementary dating information, see E. O. Nielsen and K. M. Phillips, "Bryn Mawr College Excavations in Tuscany, 1973," *AJA* 78 (1974): 265–278.

3. F. E. Brown, *Roman Architecture* (New York, 1961), analyzes the ritual function of space as the most important element in Roman architecture.

4. Vitruvius (1.7.1–2) listed a set of principles for the rational siting of temples: civic gods like Jupiter on a high place overlooking the city; gods of merchants like Mercury in the forum or emporium; literary types like Apollo and Bacchus near the theater; athletes like Hercules at the amphitheater or circus; war gods like Mars on the drill grounds; service-oriented deities like Venus at the port. There is no clear evidence, however, that his precepts were ever followed.

5. Shortly after its construction, the cella of Temple B was enlarged, and a wall was built between the columns, making them appear to be engaged to the cella wall.

6. Pliny, *Letters* 9.39.3, points out that such colonnades are practical as well as beautiful, since they offer shelter from rain and sun.

7. See Chapter 3, page 39.

8. The Senate had to meet in an inaugurated *templum* so that the auspices could be taken, but it was not limited to the Curia in the Forum. It often met on the Capitoline in the Temple of Iuppiter, in the Forum in the Temple of Castor before 63 B.C., and in the Temple of Concordia thereafter. During the principate it met most often in the Temple of Apollo on the Palatine, the Temple of Concordia in the Forum, and the Temple of Mars Ultor in the Forum Augustum. Outside the pomerium, the Senate met in the Temple of Apollo or the Temple of Bellona to receive ambassadors or generals, to assign provinces to governors, and to declare war.

9. On the cult of Magna Mater in Rome, see M. J. Vermaseren, *Cybele and Attis: The Myth and the Cult* (London, 1977), pp. 38–63, 113–125.

10. Most of our information about these festivals comes from monuments and literature of the late republic and the Augustan period; from calendars inscribed at Rome, Antium, Praeneste, Caere, and elsewhere, published in *CIL* 1.205–282 and A. Degrassi, *Inscriptiones Italiae*, vol. 13.2 (Rome, 1963); and from poets like Tibullus and Ovid, who commemorate their revival.

11. Starting in 153 B.C., the official new year began on January 1. Before that the consuls assumed office on March 15, although according to A. K. Michels, *The Calendar of the Roman Republic* (Princeton, 1967), pp. 97–101, January 1 was made the start of the civil year as early as the middle of the fifth century B.C. See the reviews of Michels' book by R. M. Ogilvie, *Classical Review* 19 (1969): 330–332, and A. Drummond, *JRS* 61 (1971): 282–283.

12. For details see H. H. Scullard, *Festivals and Ceremonies of the Roman*

Republic (Ithaca, 1981), which replaces W. W. Fowler, *The Roman Festivals of the Period of the Republic* (London, 1899).

13. The banquets of the Salii were proverbially good meals. They were held in small hostels called *mansiones Saliorum* or in temples, as for instance in the Temple of Mars Ultor (Suetonius, *Claudius* 33).

14. J. P. V. D. Balsdon, *Life and Leisure in Ancient Rome* (New York, 1967), pp. 244–245, comments on the increase in the number of feriae, and emphasizes that life and business went on as usual on most of these days.

Chapter 14. Roman Holidays

1. L. Barzini, *The Italians* (New York, 1964), pp. 89–90, argues that the love of spectacle is the single most powerful force dominating social and political activity in modern Italian life: "In other parts of the world substance always takes precedence and its external aspect is considered useful but secondary. Here, on the other hand, the show is as important as, many times more important than, reality."

2. J. P. V. D. Balsdon, *Life and Leisure in Ancient Rome* (New York, 1969), pp. 267–270, refutes the notion that the whole population did nothing for vast periods of time, idly gaping at the games. Even accepting his figures, however, it is possible to emphasize the great amount of productive leisure the city enjoyed in the topsy-turvy time of the ludi. Balsdon, ibid., pp. 264–267, gives examples of political demonstrations in the theater, and Z. Yavetz, *Plebs and Princeps* (Oxford, 1969), pp. 8–37, analyzes the role of such demonstrations during the principate.

3. L. R. Taylor, "The Opportunities for Dramatic Performances in the Time of Plautus and Terence," *TAPA* 68 (1937): 284–304, discusses all the evidence for the number of days devoted to theatrical ludi during the republic, and also discusses (pp. 302–303) the social standing of the playwright and his troop of actors.

4. The effect must have been similar to a modern production of *Aida* at the Baths of Caracalla, complete with elephants. Pompey's games to celebrate the opening of his theater were probably held just before the Ludi Romani in 55 B.C., which (since the calendar was out of phase) was the hottest time of the year. In his *Letters to His Friends* 7.1, Cicero implies that the front seats where the senators sat were not very desirable, and that the smell of all those mules might have had something to do with it. Valerius Maximus, *Memorabilia* 2.4.6 tells us that to alleviate the heat, Pompey arranged for streams of water to flow through the theater. On the date of the performance, see R. G. M. Nisbet, *Cicero in Pisonem* (Oxford, 1961), pp. 199–200.

5. The ludi scaenici at the games of Flora (April 28–May 3) were always

raucous, sexy mimes (Valerius Maximus, *Memorabilia* 2.10.8; Ovid, *Fasti* 5.331–354; Pliny, *Natural History* 18.286).

6. J. A. Hanson, *Roman Theater Temples* (Princeton, 1959); T. P. Wiseman, "Clodius at the Theatre," *Cinna the Poet and Other Roman Essays* (Leicester, 1974), pp. 159–169.

7. See Pliny, *Natural History* 36.113–117, for a disapproving account of theaters built in 58 B.C. and 52 B.C.

8. M. Bieber, *The History of the Greek and Roman Theater*, 2nd ed. (Princeton, 1961), pp. 147–253; G. E. Duckworth, *The Nature of Roman Comedy* (Princeton, 1952), pp. 73–101; W. Beare, *The Roman Stage*, 3rd ed. (London, 1964); J. H. Butler, *The Theater and Drama of Greece and Rome* (New York, 1972), pp. 73–126; and Balsdon, *Life and Leisure in Ancient Rome*, pp. 267–288. E. Segal, *Roman Laughter* (Cambridge, Mass., 1968), analyzes Plautine comedy as a reflection of the reversal of roles and values during the ludi. L. R. Taylor, "The *Sellisternium* and the Theatrical *Pompa*," *Classical Philology* 30 (1935): 122–130, presents evidence for the exuviae and the procession to the theater.

9. Inscriptions of horse-racing personnel: *CIL* 6.10044–10052. The *stabulum* of the Green (*Prasina*) faction may have left its trace in the name of the Church of Saint Lawrence in Prasino (or Damaso), incorporated in the Renaissance Palace of the Cancelleria. Several inscriptions that mention the "Greens" were also found in the southern part of the Campus Martius, along the route of the present Corso Vittorio Emanuele (*CIL* 6.20044, at Saint Lucia near the west end of the Corso; *CIL* 6.10058, at the Cancelleria; *CIL* 6.10061, at the Piazza S. Marco at the east end of the Corso). This, in conjunction with the listing of *stabula IV factionum VI(II)* in the Regionary Catalogue as monuments of Region IX, "Circus Flaminius," implies that the four stables were situated in the southern end of the Campus Martius. Sources are cited in S. B. Platner and T. Ashby, *A Topographical Dictionary of Ancient Rome* (Oxford, 1929), pp. 494–495, and in J. Marquardt, *Römische Staatsverwaltung*, 2nd ed., vol. 3 (Leipzig, 1885), p. 521, n. 3.

10. Balsdon, *Life and Leisure in Ancient Rome*, pp. 314–324; H. A. Harris, *Sport in Greece and Rome* (London, 1972), pp. 184–237; H. A. Cameron, *Circus Factions: Blues and Greens at Rome and Byzantium* (Oxford, 1976); J. H. Humphrey, *Roman Circuses and Chariot Racing* (Berkeley, 1986).

11. Taylor, "*Sellisternium*," discusses the lectisternium, a republican phenomenon. Forms of solemn thanksgiving during the principate are described by G. Freyburger, "La supplication d'action de grâces sous le Haut-Empire," *ANRW* 2.16.2 (1978): 1418–1439.

12. L. R. Taylor, "New Light on the History of the Secular Games," *American Journal of Philology* 55 (1934): 101–120.

13. H. H. Scullard, *Roman Politics, 220–150 B.C.* (Oxford, 1951), pp. 24–25, 172, comments on the use of the games in electoral strategy and the passage of sumptuary laws in 196, 182, and 179 B.C. to impose some limits.

14. On the venationes see Balsdon, *Life and Leisure in Ancient Rome,* pp. 302–313, and G. Jennison, *Animals for Show and Pleasure in Ancient Rome* (Manchester, 1937).

15. *Pollice presso* ("with the thumb pushed [down?]") was the signal to spare; *pollice verso* ("with the thumb turned [extended, perhaps toward the chest?]") was the signal to kill. On the shows see Balsdon, *Life and Leisure in Ancient Rome,* pp. 288–302; M. Grant, *Gladiators* (London, 1967); and J. Pearson, *Arena: The Story of the Colosseum* (New York, 1973), pp. 93–143.

16. D. Dudley, *Urbs Roma* (Aberdeen, 1967), p. 144: "[The designers of the Colosseum] expended a good deal of technical ingenuity to enable some 50,000 people to glut by proxy their sadistic instincts, and to prevent them, while so engaged, from getting out of hand in a riot." Cf. K. Hopkins, *Death and Renewal* (Cambridge, 1983), p. 29: "Gladiatorial shows and their accompanying executions provided opportunities for the reaffirmation of the moral order through the sacrifice of criminal victims, of slave gladiators, of Christian outcasts and wild animals. The enthusiastic participation by spectators, rich and poor, raised and then released collective tensions, in a society which traditionally idealised impassivity (*gravitas*)."

17. The ancient sources are full of appreciative accounts of elaborate triumphal processions—for example, Livy 3.29.4–5, 10.7.9–12, 34.52; Plutarch, *Aemilius Paulus* 33–35; Josephus, *The Jewish War* 7.119–157. A recent discussion is H. S. Versnel, *Triumphus: An Inquiry into the Origin, Development, and Meaning of the Roman Triumph* (Leiden, 1970).

Chapter 15. The Theory and Practice of Building Towns

1. Examples are Megara Hyblaea in Sicily from the seventh century B.C., Selinus in Sicily and Poseidonia/Paestum on the west coast of Italy from the sixth century B.C., and Thurii at the southern end of Italy from the fourth century B.C.—J. B. Ward-Perkins, *Cities of Ancient Greece and Italy: Planning in Classical Antiquity* (New York, 1974).

2. No ancient text specifically states that these rituals were conducted at the founding of colonies, but it seems a safe inference, based on the allusions in ancient sources to the ritual at the foundation of Rome and the archaeological data from Cosa and elsewhere. J. Rykwert, *The Idea of a Town: The Anthropology of Urban Form in Rome, Italy, and the Ancient World* (London, 1976), pp. 44–48, 65–68, 117–135, interprets the orthogonal town plan as an expression of religious cosmogony, a projection of the four

quarters of the heavens, and a ritual re-creation of the universe. This approach is criticized by F. Castagnoli, *Orthogonal Town Planning in Antiquity* (Eng. tr. Cambridge, Mass., 1971), pp. 74–81. "The theory of the celestial *templum* has no relation whatsoever to city planning" (ibid., p. 130). It may, of course, have had a great deal to do with the design of temple precincts and the centuriation of farmlands. Cf. J. LeGall, "Rites de fondation," *Studi sulla città antica: Atti del Convegno di Studi sulla Città Etrusca e Italica Preromana*, ed. G. Mansuelli and R. Zangheri (Bologna, 1970), pp. 59–65; S. Finocchi, "Significato dei rapporti tra cinta fortificata e piano negli insidiamenti preromani," ibid., pp. 39–52; R. Bloch, "Urbanisme et religion chez les Etrusques," ibid., pp. 11–17; and R. Martin, "Quelques aspects des rapports entre l'urbanisme italique préromain et l'urbanisme grec," ibid., pp. 67–73.

3. As a result of modern scholarship, we are not as completely sure as the Romans were that these rituals all came from the Etruscans; they may well have roots beyond the Etruscans in the common Indo-European heritage of the Latins and other Italic peoples, as argued by G. Dumézil, *Archaic Roman Religion* (Eng. tr. Chicago, 1970), 2:660–672.

4. Castagnoli, *Orthogonal Town Planning*, pp. 96–121, discerns four categories of Roman orthogonal plans: (1) the "Hippodamean Type" with streets crossing at right angles, oblong blocks of houses, and no clearly indicated main streets, as at Cosa; (2) a type in which two axial main streets cross at the center of a rectangular enclosing wall, with square house blocks, as at the original settlement at Ostia; (3) a variation of this borrowed from military camps, in which two main streets are parallel, as at Aosta; and (4) a variation of the second type in which the blocks are rectangular.

5. Later tradition claimed that Ostia had been founded by Ancus Marcius, but the republican-period walls of tufa, which define a small fortified settlement, suggest a date between 350 and 338 B.C. See Chapter 18.

6. E. T. Salmon, *Roman Colonization under the Republic* (Ithaca, 1969).

7. In contrast to the predominant reliance Romans placed on strategic considerations, the Greeks paid equal attention to commercial factors and were sensitive to the geographic ecology of the site. The founding of Roman colonies seems to be one more example of the relentless Roman tendency to impose human factors on the natural landscape through force of will.

8. Caesar's colony at Urso (Osuna), in Spain, officially called Colonia Genetiva Julia Urbanorum, is informative because we have the text of its charter, which established a typical colony government. Urso had a council or *curia* composed of the *ordo decurionum*, the "decurions." Its executive consisted of two duumvirs and two aediles assisted by lictors, aides, musicians, soothsayers, and public slaves. Pontiffs and augurs tended to religious needs. The charter required the duumvirs and aediles to hold

gladiatorial, theatrical, and circus games regularly; guaranteed certain emoluments to temples; regulated burials, public roads, and aqueducts; and allowed the community to impose five days' public-service labor each year on all resident males, whether colonist or not. It also prohibited large-scale pottery and tile manufacture, possibly to protect some existing monopoly, but more likely to prevent the energies of the colony from being diverted from agriculture to manufacture. E. G. Hardy, *Three Spanish Charters* (Oxford, 1912), pp. 7–60, gives the text of the inscription, *CIL* 1².594.

9. O. A. W. Dilke, *The Roman Land Surveyors: An Introduction to the Agrimensores* (Newton Abbot, 1971). The text of Hyginus's work is published in F. Blume et al., eds., *Die Schriften der römischen Feldmesser,* vol. 1 (Berlin, 1848), no. 6.

10. F. E. Brown, *Cosa: The Making of a Roman Town* (Ann Arbor, 1980), pp. 15–18.

11. E. T. Salmon, *The Making of Roman Italy* (Ithaca, 1982), pp. 45, 137–139.

12. *CIL* 4.8863, from Pompeii, and 6.32505, from Allifae, are typical. They and other similar lists are collected in A. Degrassi, *Inscriptiones Italiae,* vol. 13.2 (Rome, 1963), pp. 300–306. They should be used in conjunction with a map of ancient Italy and the article by R. MacMullen, "Market-Days in the Roman Empire," *Phoenix* 24 (1970): 333–341, which includes this striking image (p. 337): "Urban fairs . . . were less necessary than rural ones. In a city, after all, a merchant could always find customers. They came in from the circumjacent farms and villages regularly. It was as if the city each morning drew in and exhaled a deep breath of country air." For the commercial relationships between the city and the country, see M. I. Rostovtzeff, *Social and Economic History of the Roman Empire,* 2nd ed. (Oxford, 1957), pp. 192–207; and R. MacMullen, *Roman Social Relations* (New Haven, 1974), pp. 28–56.

13. B. D. Shaw, "Rural Markets in North Africa and the Political Economy of the Roman Empire," *Antiquités Africaines* 17 (1981): 37–83, provides a good general discussion, with a clear distinction between periodic rural markets, which tended to be held twice a month in Africa, reflecting older Berber practice, and permanent markets, which were integrated into the structure of the ancient city. Shaw discusses the market at Casae (pp. 54–56), emphasizing both its strategic location in the territory of the Musulami, native tribes that could become restive, and the general political importance of markets in tribal social systems. Pliny (*Letters* 5.4) tells of a senator who attempted to set up such a market in Cisalpine Gaul, but who was prevented from doing so by local interests in nearby Vicetia (Vicenza).

14. The charter was originally published by G. Seure in "Voyage en Thrace: L'emporium romain de Pizos," *Bulletin de Corréspondance Hellé-*

nique 22 (1898): 472–491. A text is printed in W. Dittenberger, *Sylloge Inscriptionum Graecarum,* 3rd ed. (Leipzig, 1915–1924), no. 880. It is discussed in Rostovtzeff, *Roman Empire,* pp. 251–252, 426–427, 648 n. 93, 724 n. 51.

15. Polybius (6.27–32) describes the normal practice in his day: The *praetorium* (commander's quarters) was laid out first, flanked by the *quaestorium* (quartermaster's office) on one side and a market on the other; in back was a street 100 feet wide and, beyond it, space for auxiliary troops to camp. In front of the quaestorium-praetorium-forum line was the main street of the camp, the *via principalis,* 100 feet wide; in front of it tents of the legionary and allied troops were arranged along five streets 50 feet wide, perpendicular to the *via principalis;* another street, 50 feet wide, was called the *via quintana* because it lay just beyond the fifth rank of tents counting from the via principalis, to which it was parallel; between the tents and the defensive rampart at the perimeter of the camp lay an empty interval 200 feet wide for drills.

16. The standard Teubner text of [Hyginus], *De Munitionibus Castrorum,* was edited by A. von Domaszewski (Leipzig, 1887). For a collection of plans of military camps, see M. Morini, *Atlante di storia dell'urbanistica* (Milan, 1963), pp. 70–71, 97.

17. R. MacMullen, *Soldier and Civilian in the Later Roman Empire* (Cambridge, Mass., 1963), discusses the relationship between soldiers and the neighboring towns (chs. 2, 4), as well as the role of soldiers as the "middlemen of Roman culture" (p. 96). On Lambaesis see P. MacKendrick, *The North African Stones Speak* (Chapel Hill, 1980), pp. 221–227. For more detail see M. Janon, "Recherches à Lambèse," *Antiquités Africaines* 7 (1973): 193–254.

18. Salmon, *Roman Italy,* pp. 3–4, 13–14, 61, 136–137, 177–181.

19. In Gaul, the names of settlements indicate various original functions: a fort (*-dunum*), a market (*-magus*), a transportation center (*-briva,* "bridge," or *-ritus,* "ford"), a shrine (named for sacred groves or springs). See D. Van Berchem, "Réflexions sur la dynamique du développement des villes antiques," in *Thèmes de recherches sur les villes antiques d'occident,* ed. P.-M. Duval and E. Frézouls (Paris, 1977), pp. 21–28.

20. On the distribution patterns of Roman settlements, see R. Chevallier, *Roman Roads* (Eng. tr. Berkeley, 1976), esp. pp. 185–209; I. Hodder and M. Hansell, "The Non-Random Spacing of Romano-British Walled Towns," *Man* 6 (1971): 391–407; G. Charles Picard, "Observations sur la condition des populations rurales dans l'Empire Romain, en Gaule et en Afrique," *ANRW* 2.3 (1975): 98–111; P.-A. Fevrier, "The Origin and Growth of the Cities of Southern Gaul to the Third Century A.D.," *JRS* 63 (1973): 1–28; G. Fabre, "Le tissu urbain dans le nord-ouest de la Péninsule ibérique," *Latomus* 29 (1970): 314–339; R. G. Goodchild and J. B. Ward-

Perkins, "The *Limes Tripolitanus* in the Light of Recent Discoveries," *JRS* 39 (1949): 81–95; D. van Berchem, "Permanence et discontinuité de la ville dans le temps et dans l'espace," in *Thèmes de Recherches*, pp. 35–38; M. Le Lannou, "Le rôle des communications fluviales dans la genèse et le développment des villes antiques," ibid., pp. 29–34; A. L. F. Rivet, "The Origins of Cities in Roman Britain," ibid., pp. 161–172.

21. On towers and *burgi* (derived from the Greek word *pyrgos*, "tower"), see MacMullen, *Soldier and Civilian*, pp. 37–41.

Chapter 16. Cosa

1. F. E. Brown, "Cosa I: History and Topography," *MAAR* 20 (1951): 5–114; and idem, *Cosa: The Making of a Roman Town* (Ann Arbor, 1980).

2. S. L. Dyson, "Settlement Patterns in the Ager Cosanus," *Journal of Field Archaeology* 5 (1978): 251–268. A small farm of the early second century B.C. has been excavated at Giardino Vecchio, about 4 kilometers inland northeast of the town, cf. A. Carandini, ed., *La romanizzazione dell'Etruria: Il territorio di Vulci* (Milan, 1985), pp. 106–107. On the Villa of Settefinestre see A. Carandini and S. Settis, *Schiavi e padroni nell'Etruria romana: La villa di Settefinestre dallo scavo alla mostra* (Bari, 1979), and, briefly, K. Greene, *The Archaeology of the Roman Economy* (Berkeley, 1986), pp. 89–92, 106–108.

3. Cicero's *Letters to His Friends* 5.6.2 is addressed to Sestius, and in 13.8.3, Cicero refers to money he has borrowed from him. In 44 B.C., he mentions Sestius's villa at Cosa (*Letters to Atticus* 15.27.1). Cf. Cicero's *Letters to Atticus* 11.7.1; 13.2.2.

4. D. Manacorda, "The Ager Cosanus and the Production of the Amphorae of Sestius: New Evidence and a Reassessment," *JRS* 68 (1978): 122–131; E. L. Will, "The Sestius Amphoras: A Reappraisal," *Journal of Field Archaeology* 6 (1979): 339–350.

5. A. M. McCann and J. D. Lewis, "The Ancient Port of Cosa," *Archaeology* 23 (1970): 200–211; A. M. McCann et al., *The Roman Port and Fishery of Cosa* (Princeton, 1987), esp. pp. 137–159, 321–342.

6. At about the same time, a very similar temple was built at the port. F. E. Brown, "Cosa II: The Temples of the Arx," *MAAR* 26 (1960): 143–145, suggests it was dedicated to Portunus. See also McCann, *Roman Port*, pp. 129–136.

7. V. J. Bruno, "A Town House at Cosa," *Archaeology* 23 (1970): 232–241.

8. J. Collins-Clinton, *A Late Antique Shrine of Liber Pater at Cosa* (Leiden, 1977).

Chapter 17. Pompeii

1. L. Richardson, *Pompeii: An Architectural History* (Baltimore, 1988).

2. P. Castrén, *Ordo Populusque Pompeianus: Polity and Society in Roman Pompeii* (Rome, 1975).

3. The House of Sallust (Fig. 12), the House of Pansa (*CIL* 4.138; Fig. 13), and the Estate of Julia Felix (*CIL* 4.1136) are examples; see Chapter 12, pages 173, 179.

4. The popularity of Isis's cult was also indicated by the increased preference for Egyptian motifs that was expressed in the decoration of many Pompeiian houses during the first century A.D. In contrast, the Temple of Fortuna Augusta was not repaired at all; the reason for this may have been that the imperial cult would thenceforth focus on the new Temple of Vespasian in the Forum.

Chapter 18. Ostia

1. The indispensable modern work is R. Meiggs, *Roman Ostia* (Oxford, 1960; 2nd ed. 1973); the account in our text is derived from Meiggs's, where detailed references can be found. The mechanics of shipping and transloading are discussed by L. Casson, "Harbour and River Boats of Ancient Rome," *JRS* 55 (1965): 31–39. On topographical and social details of life in Ostia, see G. Hermansen, *Ostia: Aspects of Roman City Life* (Edmonton, 1982).

2. Christian travelers usually passed through Ostia on the way to Rome, although ships from the Greek East normally called at Puteoli and travelers found their way up to Rome along the Via Appia. Meiggs, *Roman Ostia*, p. 71, notes that in both these anecdotes we have to deal with upper-class conversations, as is also the case in the seaside dialogues in Suetonius, *De Rhetoribus* 1 and *Aulus Gellius* 17.1. The distance from Rome to Ostia was too far to walk, and only those rich enough to be able to travel by carriage came down from Rome to enjoy the sea air. On Jews and Christians at Ostia, see Meiggs, *Roman Ostia*, pp. 587–592 and bibliography.

Chapter 19. Arelate (Arles)

1. Brief accounts of Arelate in English are given by O. Brogan, *Roman Gaul* (Cambridge, Mass., 1953), pp. 89–92, and P. MacKendrick, *Roman France* (New York, 1972), pp. 61–64. For more detail see L.-A. Constans, *Arles* (Paris, 1928). A. Grenier, "La Gaule Romaine," in *An Economic Survey of Ancient Rome*, ed. Tenny Frank, vol. 3 (Baltimore, 1937), pp. 473–479, lists the evidence for the city's economy. The inscriptions from Arelate are collected in *CIL* 12.593–990, 5804–5824. The evidence for grain is the

close connection of citizens of Arelate with the annona in Rome; for oil, the *diffusores olearii* mentioned in the Amphitheater (*CIL* 12.714 and Justinian, *Digest* 14.3.13). For textiles the evidence is circumstantial: (1) they were certainly an item of wholesale trade at Trier, on the Moselle, as shown by relief carvings on monumental tombs there; (2) the mention of imperial weaving mills in the fourth century A.D. document *Notitia Dignitatum Occidentis* (11.54 and 12.27) implies the existence of a textile industry; and (3) perhaps the centonarii are to be thought of as weavers.

2. The father of Pompeius Paulinus may well have been the father-in-law of Seneca and prefect of the annona in Rome under Nero. If so, Seneca dedicated his essay *De Brevitate Vitae* (1, 18–19) to him. The cognomen of A. Annius Camars indicates his local origin, for the region south of Arles is still known today as the Camargue. The inscription commemorating Titus Iulius was published by F. Benoît in *Gallia* 11 (1953): 109–110 and is discussed by M. Clavel and P. Lévêque, *Villes et structures urbaines dans l'Occident Romain* (Paris, 1971), pp. 209, 211–212; he was the son of a citizen, also named Titus Iulius, apparently one of Caesar's veterans; his name implies that he was an auxiliary soldier who received citizenship from Caesar upon discharge from the army. Favorinus was a close friend of Aulus Gellius, whose *Attic Nights* are filled with anecdotes about the orator; Favorinus's biography appears in Philostratus, *Lives of the Sophists* 1.8.

3. The careers and connections of Euporus and Eleuther are put in social context by M. Christol, "Rémarques sur les naviculaires d'Arles," *Latomus* 30 (1971): 643–663.

4. On urbanistic developments in Arelate in late antiquity, see R. E. M. Wheeler, "The Roman Town-Walls of Arles," *JRS* 16 (1926): 174–193; and R. M. Butler, "Late Roman Town Walls of Gaul," *Archaeological Journal* 116 (1959): 25–50.

Chapter 20. Thamugadi (Timgad)

1. Primary documents on Thamugadi are the inscriptions collected in *CIL* 8.2340–2346, 17811–17939. For the bibliography on which this survey of Thamugadi is based, see R. Stillwell et al., eds., *Princeton Encyclopedia of Classical Sites* (Princeton, 1976), pp. 901–902.

2. J. Lassus, "Une opération immobilière à Timgad," in *Mélanges d'archéologie et d'histoire offerts à A. Piganiol*, ed. R. Chevallier (Paris, 1966), 3:1221–1231.

3. M. Leglay, "La vie intellectuelle d'une cité africaine des confins de l'Aurès," *Hommages à L. Hermann* (Brussels, 1960), pp. 485–491.

4. The Berbers may have left their mark in the Temple of Saturn north of town. In African cities, Saturn is the name generally applied to the Baal of the Phoenicians and Berbers, and the relief sculpture found in this sanc-

tuary retains the local native style. The upper-class names recorded on the inscriptions of the veteran colony of Thamugadi are all good Roman names, whereas in other African cities other demographic realities appear. At Leptis Magna, for instance, an old Punic-Berber town was granted the status of a colony by Trajan; its ruling class contined for most of its history to be of predominantly native stock. In the late first century A.D. we find a Roman citizen of equestrian status, Septimius Severus (Statius, *Silvae* 4.5), who was completely Italicized; although he had been born in Leptis, it is possible that his parents had migrated from Italy. In any event his grandson, who became the emperor Septimius Severus, spoke Latin with a heavy accent, which indicates that Punic continued to be spoken as the ordinary language all through the second century A.D. Scholars of the early twentieth century tended to see Romanization as a benign force embraced by the natives, and in urban centers like Leptis and elsewhere this seems to have been the case; recently, however, historians have emphasized that Romanization was limited to the upper classes in most of the African provinces, and that the lower classes tended to resist. T. R. S. Broughton, *The Romanization of Africa Proconsularis* (Baltimore, 1929); L. A. Thompson, "Settler and Native in the Urban Centers of Roman Africa," *Africa in Classical Antiquity* (Ibadan, 1969), pp. 132–181; A. Deman, "Matériaux et réflexions pour servir à une étude du développment et du sous-développment dans les provinces de l'empire romain," *ANRW* 2.3 (1975): 3–97.

Index

Index

Octavianus), 48–50; father of, 185.
See also Augustus
oecus (pl. oeci), 165, 170
officinator, 178, 361 n. 27
Oil, olive, 81, 145–148
Opimius, Lucius, 113
opus: caementicum, 168; craticium, 128,
168; incertum, 358 n. 53; quadratum,
163; reticulatum, 271, 358 n. 53;
sectile, 174
ordo decurionum, 282, 370 n. 8
Ostia
—Basilica (I.xi.5), 273
—baths: Forum (Terme del Foro,
I.xii.6), 272, 274; of Neptune
(Terme di Nettuno, II.iv.2), 272,
273; of the Seven Sages (Terme dei
Sette Sapienti, III.x.2), 178, 272, 321
—commerce, 153, 268–269
—fabri tignarii, 155
—Forum, 271, 273
—founding of, 246, 250, 268
—fullonica on Via degli Augustali
(V.vii.3), 152, 272, 316
—Horrea: Epagathiana (I.viii.3), 272,
274, 353 n. 12; Grandi (II.ix.7), 272,
273; of Hortensius (V.xii.1), 272,
273; republican (V.xii.2–3), 271,
272
—houses: of Amor and Psyche
(Domus di Amore e Psiche, I.xiv.5),
173, 272, 274; Casette-tipo (III.xii,
xiii), 175, 272; of Diana (Casa di
Diana, I.iii.3,4), 175–177, 272, 274;
of Fortuna Annonaria (V.ii.8),
171–172, 272, 274, 320; Garden
Houses (Case Giardino, III.ix),
172–173, 175, 272, 274, 319;
"Imperial Palace," 274; of
Nymphaeum (Domus del Ninfeo,
III.vi.1), 173, 272, 274; of the Round
Temple (Domus del Tempio
Rotondo, I.xi.1), 172, 272; on Via
dei Vigili (II.iii.3–4), 172, 272, 318
—Insula: of Charioteers (Casa degli
Aurighi, III.x.1), 178, 272, 321; of
Serapis (Casa di Serapide, III.x.3),
178, 272, 321
—markets: IV.v.2, 271–272;
Maggazzini Repubblicani, 271
—Piazzale delle Corporazioni (II.vii),
269, 271–272, 276
—population, 269–270, 274

—as port of Rome, 69, 75, 103
—restaurant ("Thermopolium," I.ii.5),
272, 315
—schola: of fabri (I.xii.1), 210; of
stuppatores (I.x.3), 210–211, 272,
317; of Trajan (IV.v.16), 272, 274
—stie, 268
—temples: of Cybele, Attis, and
Bellona (Campo della Magna
Mater), 270, 272; of Hercules,
271–272; of Jupiter (Capitolium),
272–273; of Mithras, 270;
republican (Quattro Tempietti,
II.viii.2), 217, 271–272; of Rome
and Augustus, 272–273; of Serapis
(III.xvii.4), 270, 272
—Theater (II.vii), 269, 271–273, 272
—Via dei Vigili, 189, 272, 318
—vigiles, barracks of (II.v.1), 272,
348 n. 15
—walls, 271
Otho, 72
Ovidius Naso, Publius (Ovid), 65

Paestum, 369 n. 1
Pageantry. See Spectacle
pagi, 252
Paintings
—in public places, 24, 110, 218,
333 n. 10
—wall, 165, 170; First Style, 164, 263;
Second Style, 42, 63, 66, 165–166,
192, 206, 230; Third Style, 71;
Fourth Style, 74, 206
Pantomimes, 207, 229
Parks, 42, 57, 72–73, 79, 121, 187
paterfamilias, 52, 55, 135, 158, 159,
161, 164, 194, 214
patria potestas, 342 n. 35
Patricians, 16, 17, 22, 338 n. 9
Patrons. See clientela; Clients
peculium, 96, 97
Peddlers, 184, 199
Peristyles: in baths, 204; in houses,
164, 165, 168, 170, 171, 192, 263,
360 n. 16. See also Parks
Petronius Arbiter, 93, 97, 182
Philippi, battle of, 48, 54
Philosophers, Greek, at Rome, 33–34
Pizus, 250
Planning, city, 20, 243–248, 256,
370 n. 7
platea (pl. plateae), 35, 188

383

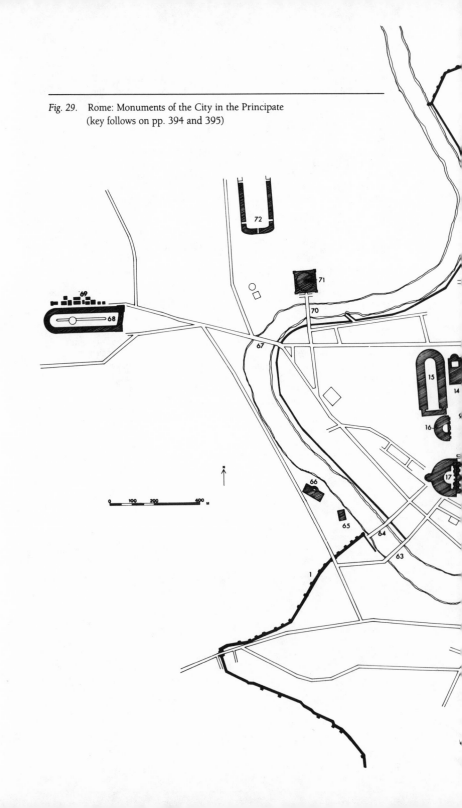

Fig. 29. Rome: Monuments of the City in the Principate
(key follows on pp. 394 and 395)

Key to Figure 29

1	Muri Aureliani	23	Divorum Templum
2	Ustrinum, Mausoleum Augusti	24	Temple of the Via delle Botteghe Oscure (Temple of Bellona; Porticus Minucia?)
3	Horti Luculliani		
4	Obeliscus Augusti, Solarium	25	Theatrum, Crypta Balbi
5	Ara Pacis Augustae	26	Circus Flaminius
6	Temple of Sol	27	Porticus Octavia (?)
7	Ustrinum Marci Aurelii	28	Temple of Hercules Musarum, Porticus Philippi
8	Columna Marci Aurelii Antonini		
9	Stagnum Agrippae	29	Temples of Iuno Regina, Iuppiter Stator, Porticus Octaviae
10	Temple of the Deified Hadrianus		
11	Temple of Matidia	30	Theatrum Marcelli
12	Ustrinum Antoninorum	31	Temple of Apollo
13	Pantheon	32	Forum Holitorium
14	Thermae Neronianae (Alexandrinae)	33	Republican Wall (Murus Servii Tullii)
15	Stadium Domitiani	34	Temple of Iuppiter Optimus Maximus
16	Odeum		
17	Theatrum Pompei	35	Temple of Iuno Moneta
18	Porticus Pompei	36	Forum Romanum
19	Area Sacra del Largo Argentina	37	Forum Iulium
20	Thermae Agrippae	38	Forum Augustum
21	Saepta Iulia, Diribitorium	39	Forum Pacis (Temple of Pax)
22	Temple of Isis (Iseum et Serapeum)